Self, Sex, and Gender in
Cross-Cultural Fieldwork

D0761271

Self, Sex, and Gender in Cross-Cultural Fieldwork

Edited by
Tony Larry Whitehead
and
Mary Ellen Conaway

With a Foreword by **Michael H. Agar**

University of Illinois Press   Urbana and Chicago

© 1986 by the Board of Trustees of the University of Illinois
Manufactured in the United States of America
1   2   3   4   5   C   P   5   4   3   2   1

This book is printed on acid-free paper.

Library of Congress Cataloging in Publication Data

Main entry under title:

Self, sex, and gender in cross-cultural fieldwork.

  Bibliography: p.
  Includes index.
    1. Ethnology—Fieldwork—Addresses, essays,
lectures. 2. Cross-cultural studies—Addresses,
essays, lectures. 3. Anthropologists, Women—Ad-
dresses, essays, lectures. I. Whitehead, Tony Larry.
II. Conaway, Mary Ellen.
GN346.S45   1986   306   85-8597
ISBN 0-252-01248-8 (cloth; alk. paper)
ISBN 0-252-01324-7 (paper; alk. paper)

*To our children and other future contributors
to improved cross-cultural communication.*

Contents

Foreword

Ethnography, as a general process, has proved notoriously difficult to talk about. Little wonder. On the one hand, it enjoys the status of a mystical experience within anthropology, and not without reason, for mysterious things happen on the way to understanding an alien way of living. In apparent contradiction to its mystique, ethnography is "just there," the taken-for-granted ocean in which anthropologists swim. Whether mundane or mysterious, however, it is a rich and complicated experience, less concerned with "scientific control" than with the learning of pattern in activities controlled by others. Ethnography mixes science and art, analysis and intuition, detachment and intimacy in ways that call into question the value of those distinctions for characterizing the experience.

On the other hand, there are several statements in anthropology, scattered throughout time, that struggle with the nature of ethnography in productive ways. Further, our parallel cousins in sociology, participating as they do in a discipline that rewards methodological reflection more than our own, also have worked to develop a language to talk about ethnography so that we can achieve an ability to articulate it. The works of Howard Becker, Aaron Cicourel, and Erving Goffman come to mind. Still, a chasm remains between the realities of ethnographic practice and the language available to discuss it.

In spite of the difficulty of this task—the impossibility, perhaps—I think it is important to continue to develop such a language. Many others would agree, as indicated by the recent cycle of discussions of ethnography, of which this volume is an example. A language of ethnography is a natural area for growth in our discipline in terms of method, theory, and epistemology. Ethnography has always been an integral part of the core of whatever it is we are. By turning our abilities at critical reflection and the quest for pattern back onto ourselves, we move forward by gaining an understanding of what was previously implicit and in turn set up new questions for our attention, a process Margaret Mead characterized as going "from intuition to analysis."

Consider, too, that the dominant rhetoric for the discussion of social research as a general process fits poorly with ethnographic work. The traditional linear model of hypothesis–operationalization–sampling design–data collection–analysis is a powerful one, relevant to many questions that might be asked by one human group of another, but at most it plays only a partial role in ethnographic work. Yet the norm is to translate ethnographic work into this rhetoric when discussions move to a general level. The results are a bit like talking about a computer in cubic yards—you can do it, but somehow it misses the point.

As anthropologists, we also encounter the problem of articulating ethnography for those who are not familiar with it. Many of the contributors to this volume share with other anthropologists a concern for the uses of their abilities "outside the family." Whether as researcher or administrator, consultant or employee, the effective presentation of knowledge presupposes an ability to discuss its assumptions, the concepts that give it form, and the procedures by which it came about. One need only scan issues of *Practicing Anthropology* and *Human Organization* to see the debate this growing interest has generated.

So where is this badly needed language to come from? As mentioned, in the past ethnographers have tackled parts of the problem in helpful ways, and there are as well a variety of discussions now ongoing, some of them looking to other disciplines for inspiration. But whatever the helpful outside sources, the problem belongs to anthropologists. The language is implicit in our practice; therefore, it is up to us to reflect on that practice and ferret it out. This volume gathers together some attempts to do just that, with particular attention to the issue of gender. In various ways the contributors reflect on their own fieldwork and examine how gender influenced their ethnography. In doing so, they each take a key issue and draw it out of the context of informal conversations and into the arena of critical analysis. While their accounts raise more issues than they resolve, that is as it should be at this point in our efforts to articulate ethnography.

Let me mention a few of the issues involved. The editors planned the volume in three sections that explore the presentation of self, data collection, and overall research orientation. Such a division is to some extent artificial; clearly, for most of the contributions, a discussion placed in one division has consequences for the other two (and for others still). However, there is a context, as yet poorly understood, within which the distinct problems can be seen as interrelated. If we think of ethnography in general as the outcome of an encounter among different traditions, and if we note the centrality of gender roles in organizing part of a tradition for a person, then it is not difficult to understand why the influence of gender on fieldwork is so pervasive. The strength of this volume is that it documents the variety of ways that gender enters into ethnographic work, a variety that the context must eventually account for.

A second issue lies in the proper style for conducting ethnographic discussion. The chapters reflect a variety of blends of authorial and informant presence. If we take seriously the idea that ethnography is in part a function of the traditions that go into the encounter, then the tradition of the ethnographer belongs in the discussion as well. But it is not clear how to work the blend. On the one hand, the anthropologist takes the central role and the people studied become occasions for commenting on "what it means to me." On the other hand, the people are described in the passive voice, as if their characteristics are just there, waiting to be noticed. Few would hold with either extreme, but the vast number of possibilities in between remain to be explored, as illustrated by the differences among the presentations included in this collection.

A third issue is whether the differences make a difference. Ethnography is emergent—the starting point is negotiable, correctable. More often than not, things look very different at the end of the process. (Much like a wooden sailboat on a two-year cruise—by the time it returns to its home port, so many things have been repaired and changed, bit by bit, that it is now a different boat.) Clearly, in some cases gender sets limits on what can happen, period. But in other cases it is interesting to wonder if gender sets up different initial situations that in the process of emergence during fieldwork somehow end up at, or lead to, similar end points. In fact, perhaps in some areas gender is less an influence than cultural background or theoretical predilections. Again, the answers are not presented in this volume, but there is material here to fuel the discussion.

In brief, what we have is a collection that takes seriously the influence of a core part of an ethnographer's tradition—gender—on the way the ethnography unfolds. These essays add some badly needed critical reflection to our ongoing task of making sense out of who we are and what it is we do. The next job for each of the authors, and for others who share their concerns, is to imagine the context—the "pattern that connects," in Bateson's words—that ties the various pieces together. When we have that, some of the syntax and semantics for our language of ethnography will be in place. Imagine the interesting problems, of a sort we can't now envision, that will lead to.

                                                                    Michael H. Agar

Acknowledgments

This book has been in the making for seven years. The topic is problematic; and for some, quite controversial. We are grateful to the University of Illinois Press for bringing forth the volume, to Elizabeth G. Dulany, managing editor, for her support, and to Theresa L. Sears, who copyedited the book manuscript. We are indebted to our contributors for their continued support and patience. We also would like to thank four people who at various times served as Whitehead's graduate research assistants and undertook the time-consuming tasks of photocopying, proofreading, and copyediting various drafts; correspondence and telephone calls; and generally keeping Whitehead and the project moving: Kathy Luchok (1981–82), Erma Wright (1982–83), Laurie Price (1983–84), and Anne Salter (1984–85). They also contributed a great deal to our discussions on the issues raised in the chapters.

Other graduate research assistants who contributed in some way to this volume include Jennifer Bass, Susan Bailey, Joseph Thomas, and Anthony Nathe. For the bulk of the typing of drafts we are extremely grateful to Angie Long, secretary in the Department of Health Education at the University of North Carolina, Chapel Hill. Other members of the secretarial staff of that department who provided typing assistance are Francis Rountree, Vera Bennett, Linda Cook, and Arlene Wiggins, as well as Bonita Samuels of the Institute for Research in the Social Sciences at the University of North Carolina, Chapel Hill. Conaway acknowledges a staff development grant from Oregon State University which facilitated her editorial responsibilities.

Finally, Whitehead acknowledges his wife, Dr. Karen Gentemann, for her useful discussions of some of the issues brought out in this volume and for tolerating, along with their children, Malcolm and Anna, his many late nights working on the manuscript.

Deerfield
(Chapt. 10)

Newfoundland
(Chapt. 14)

Pine Ridge
Indian Reservation
(Chapt. 8)

Jamaica (Chapt. 13)

Dominican Republic
(Chapt. 5)

Venezuela (Chapt. 3)

Bequia (Chapt. 10)

Trinidad (Chapt. 4)

Guatamala
(Chapt. 5)

equator

Central Northwest
Amazon
(Chapt. 15)

Map 1. Field sites are keyed to the chapters
in which they are discussed.

Bier

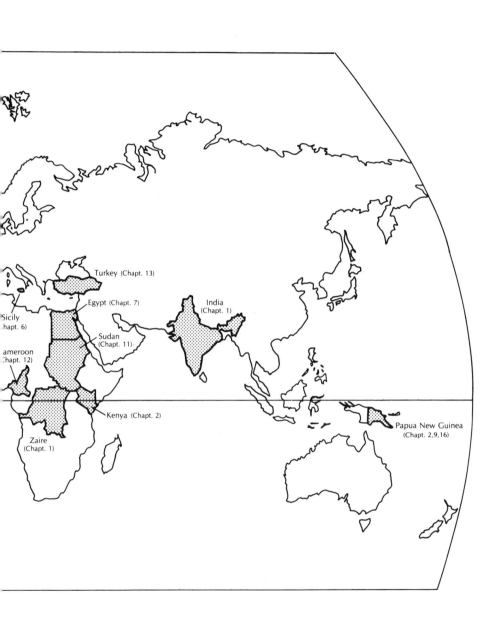

Turkey (Chapt. 13)

Egypt (Chapt. 7)

Sicily
(Chapt. 6)

Sudan
(Chapt. 11)

Cameroon
(Chapt. 12)

India
(Chapt. 1)

Kenya (Chapt. 2)

Zaire
(Chapt. 1)

Papua New Guinea
(Chapt. 2,9,16)

Introduction

TONY LARRY WHITEHEAD and MARY ELLEN CONAWAY

This book is about the systemic relationship between the experience of doing cross-cultural fieldwork and the fieldworker's sense of gender self. The term *systemic* is used because the accounts collected here address the feedback process involved in the relationship between the fieldworker and the field community; that is, the impact of the personality and actions of the fieldworker on the field community, which simultaneously has an impact on the personality and actions of the fieldworker.

Although each chapter was written by an anthropologist, this is not a book for anthropologists only. As Hymes (1969:4) noted: "The professional label of the anthropologist as one who studied alien cultures that was popular at the turn of the century is gone. Other professionals now also observe and live in cultural settings including sociologists, political scientists, social psychologists and economists." Members of various disciplines who are, or plan to become, engaged in cross-cultural fieldwork will find much to reflect on here, as will non-research-oriented professionals who work in unfamiliar cultural settings, including military, medical, and diplomatic personnel, missionaries, agronomists, and others involved in cross-cultural volunteer situations such as the Peace Corps.

When anthropologists undertake cross-cultural fieldwork it is called ethnographic research. But because this book is meant for a broader audience than anthropologists or researchers, the words "ethnography" and "research" are used sparingly. Instead, the more generic concepts of *fieldwork* and *fieldworkers*, employed by numerous disciplines, are used often and freely; and so are the concepts of *host community, host population,* and *field community* (the specific study site), rather than the more traditional research concepts of *research community* or *study population*. We trust that our readers will find this terminology neither alien nor difficult.

Interaction in any social setting, cross-cultural or otherwise, requires continual assessment of the setting in terms of patterns of interaction, as well as our status vis-à-vis others in that setting. If we are to be truly reflexive,[1] we also must assess the impact of these

1

patterns/roles and statuses on the self, and the self's response to these socioculturally based ascriptions. Such assessments are necessary to human communication; indeed, they are the foundation of culture and social interaction. Furthermore, sociocultural categories, including gender ascriptions (roles and statuses), are symbols of "units of meaning" which are used to interpret behavior. The methods of assessment in everyday interaction are participation and observation, which also happen to be the prevailing methods used by trained anthropologists. Those readers not trained in anthropology need not despair, however, since all humans are, in a sense, "amateur" anthropologists.

Although not intended solely for an anthropology audience, this volume contributes directly to two emerging areas of interest in that discipline: the inclusion of self in professional reports on fieldwork; and the impact of the fieldworker's sex and gender identity on fieldwork processes, and of fieldwork on the fieldworker's view of gender and gender self-identity. In the past, anthropologists have argued the importance of reporting on the systemic relationship between the fieldworker's sense of self and the fieldwork experience (see Nash and Wintrob 1972), although the endeavor has not been very popular. Like other social scientists, anthropologists traditionally have tried to achieve objectivity through scientific rigor. They frequently viewed (and some still do) personalized accounts of field experiences as unmitigated self-indulgence. Such confessional narratives were regarded as appropriate for travelogues but of no value to objective scientific writing (Dumont 1978:4; Swallow 1974:45–55). To be scientific, however, we must reveal our methods; and when such "confessional" anthropologists stated their methods, they acknowledged that their own field behavior and person were part of their data (Myerhoff and Ruby 1982:27). Rabinow (1977:10) summarized this professional contradiction: "As graduate students we are told that 'anthropology equals experience'; you are not an anthropologist until you have the experience of doing it. But when one returns from the field the opposite immediately applies: anthropology is not the experiences which made you an initiate, but only the objective data you have brought back."

With an increasing number of anthropologists still experiencing this contradiction, an earlier agrument is now being revived that anthropology is different from other social sciences insofar as it is shaped by the experiences of fieldwork. The discipline is becoming receptive to the idea that what happens to the fieldworker's sense of self is critical to the success of the fieldwork enterprise. The processes of field adjustment, data collection, and interpretation are influenced by both the self the fieldworker brings to the field and the self the fieldworker becomes. The concept of self is a consequence of social experiences; it emerges as the individual is able to take the view of others and act toward him-/herself as others act (Mead 1962:171). Because of this social process the self undergoes change as the individual becomes involved in new, "socially significant" experiences.[2] Indeed, cross-cultural fieldwork of some duration involves socially significant experiences of considerable impact. The fieldworker typically becomes immersed in another culture's realities and undergoes certain experiences as a result of which he or she will never be the same (Sanday 1979:527). Consequently, depersonalized reporting does not reflect either the methods or the experience of anthropology.

In addition to the influence of the fieldworker's sense of self on fieldwork, gender-related dynamics between the fieldworker and his or her host community also influence the fieldworker's adjustment to the field situation, his or her attitudes toward and relationship with the study population, the types and amounts of data collected, and the subsequent interpretation of that data. For example, adjustment to the field in Burma was difficult for Weidman (1970:242), who initially expected her fieldwork experiences to be "continuously gratifying" but instead found them to be a "struggle from beginning to end." Although she dressed in Burmese fashion and took a Burmese name, she found her search for a study village to be frustrating, in part because single women do not live alone in Burma; and given the crime-ridden political climate at the time, everyone believed she was in danger but no one took responsibility for her safety (1970:245). As her disillusionment increased, she began to make contact with other Westerners and "to enter more and more into the life of the community of technical advisors" (1970:247). Briggs (1970:21–25) solicited adoption by an Eskimo family but soon found that the docile and helpful behavior expected of a daughter conflicted with her role as conscientious anthropologist. When her anger at a visiting white fisherman led to an irate outburst, she was ostracized by her host population. During this period of isolation she reported feeling tired and irritable and unable to determine whether or not she was imagining the coldness of her host (1970:37). Bohannan (1960:381–82) told of being bullied by a Tiv headman and wondered if she would have received the same treatment had she been a man. Powdermaker (1966:114, 156) spoke of not having the opportunity to collect as rich data from men as from women in Lesu because of gender, and of having to avoid being alone with a black man in Mississippi because of gender and race (at the time, black men feared being accused of accosting white women).

Significantly, female fieldworkers have made more frequent contributions to understanding the role played by a fieldworker's sex
and gender than have males (see especially Bowen 1954; Golde
1970; Papanek 1964; Powdermaker 1966; Wax 1971). When males
have addressed sex and gender issues in fieldwork they have dealt
more with issues of sexual desire or sexual behavior (e.g., Malinowski 1967; Osgood 1953; Rabinow 1977) than with broader issues
of the gender self. More recent work by women (e.g., Cesara 1982;
Scheper-Hughes and Clark 1983; Weiner 1976) continues to concentrate only on the field experiences of women. Nonetheless, there are
a number of views regarding the role of fieldworker sex and gender
identity that are worthy of further exploration and debate. Such
views include:

1. Female fieldworkers receive greater pressure to conform to local
gender ascriptions than do male fieldworkers (Golde 1970:5–6).

2. Female fieldworkers receive greater pressure to have sexual relations than do male fieldworkers (Golde 1970:1–18).

3. Female fieldworkers are allowed greater freedom in crossing local gender boundaries than are male fieldworkers (Bovin 1966:24;
Golde 1970:67–96; Papanek 1964:160–62; Cesara 1982:15).

4. Females are more sensitive than males to the field situation and
are therefore more likely to attempt to understand the systemic relationship between the fieldwork process and the fieldworker's sense
of self (Golde 1970; Rohrlich-Leavitt, Sykes, and Weatherford 1973;
Cesara 1982).

5. Sharing the field site with a spouse, children, or a colleague can
be prohibitive to the fieldwork process and to the type of introspection necessary for the growth of self and objectivity, particularly for
women (Powdermaker 1966:14; Cesara 1982).

Clearly, without more contributions from male fieldworkers, such
views will remain little more than conjecture. We believe that these
issues probably cut across sex lines and are greatly influenced by
the nature of the field site, the gender self of the fieldworker *regardless of sex*, and the gender strategy adopted in the field. But a better
understanding of how sex and gender identity of the fieldworker
influence fieldwork will not be possible without more field reports
from both men and women. To gather such diverse reports, for the
reasons explained earlier, we solicited accounts from both male and
female contributors.

The theme of this book is the influence of self, sex, and gender on
the fieldworker's adjustment to the field setting, on information gathering, and on data interpretation. As a consequence, the book is or-

ganized into three sections: (1) Self, Sex, Gender, and Field Adjustment; (2) Sex, Gender, and Information Gathering; and (3) Self, Gender, and Interpretation. The volume concludes with a chapter by Whitehead and Price which interprets the contributions of the various essays to the five views of female writers cited above. It is hoped that the summary chapter will serve as a springboard to further dialogue.

A word about terminology is in order. When the contributors to this volume submitted their manuscripts, they mirrored a common pattern in discussions of the topic of gender: a lack of consistency in the use of the terms *sex* and *gender*, and of related concepts. We have attempted to achieve some consistency by editorially refining distinctions between the concepts of sex; gender, or gender ascriptions; sexuality, or sexual behavior; and gender identity, or gender self. *Sex* is used to refer simply to the biological categories of male and female. *Gender*, or *gender ascription*, is used to refer to the role and status categories that social groups ascribe according to differences in sex. *Sexuality* and *sexual behavior* are used interchangeably to refer to that sphere of interpersonal behavior "which is most directly associated with, leading up to, substituting for, or resulting from genital union" (*Webster's Third New International Dictionary*, 1981:2081–82). *Gender identity*, or *gender self*, emerges as a result of socially significant experiences in which the individual is categorically responded to on the basis of his or her sex and the gender ascriptions associated with it.

Self, Sex, Gender, and Field Adjustment

Two major concerns of any person planning to live and work in another culture are what should be done to facilitate personal adjustment and what should be done to facilitate the success of his or her work. The gender self that is brought to the field culture and the gender categorizations ascribed to the fieldworker by the host community affect both of these concerns.

Gender ascriptions are a major form of social categorization that facilitate human interaction by defining acceptable ranges of behavior, which differ cross-culturally. The chapters in Section I present the various strategies used by the authors to adjust to unfamiliar gender ascriptions which affected their interaction with their host population and, as a consequence, their adjustment to the field situation and their success in accomplishing their work.

Turnbull reports that he accepted the gender ascriptions assigned to him by his host population, the Mbuti Pgymy. He argues that only through "acting and reacting" to the gender ascriptions assigned to us by our host cultures can we hope to achieve an adequate understanding of what is happening within that culture. However, Oboler reports that it was very difficult to accept the gender ascriptions assigned to her and her husband, Leon, by the Nandi of Kenya. Although she was the anthropologist who received funding to carry out the research, Leon was treated by the Nandi as the leader of the Oboler team and she was relegated to a traditional "subordinate" female role. Conaway reports that she simply refused to accept the gender stereotype of American females held by criollo men of Venezuela, as exhibited by her temporary roommate, also an American. Field stress developed because the type of behavior expected was in sharp conflict with Conaway's sense of self. She discusses the strategy she adopted—the neutral gender approach—and its limited effectiveness.

Sometimes it is difficult to accept host-defined gender ascriptions because gender role expectations are situational or change over time. Angrosino found this to be the case in Trinidad. He developed a range of responses to the expected gender-defined behavior, while at the same time permitting members of the host community to maintain their own beliefs about whether he had appropriately conformed to gender expectations. However, continually adapting to varying field situations might cause an identity problem for the field novice. How does one maintain a sense of a "home self," for example, when new "field selves" continually must be adopted? Gonzales analyzes a series of field experiences to show how gender assumptions associated with the marital and family status of the fieldworker aggravate this problem. She concludes that a fieldworker should develop a certain flexibility through repeated field experiences to facilitate adaptation to a wide range of situations and, with time, merge the field self and the home self into one "flexible" self.

Sex, Gender, and Information Gathering

The roles and statuses associated with both the female and the male sex are culturally defined. Because one's sex (biology) and one's culturally defined sexual identity (gender) specify basic pervasive and persistent patterns of interaction, they are major features of a people's cognitive system. To understand that whole system, it logically follows that data must be collected from both sexes. Fieldworkers often find that some topics are sex-specific and can only be investigated by one sex or the other; or, one might study one sex group during one period of time and return to study the other sex group at a different time. Gender boundary flexibility is most evident when the researcher is able to gain access to either sex group, or both, in one field site at one time.

The major theme of the essays in Section II is the problem of boundaries created by gender categories which limit the kinds of people with whom the fieldworker can interact and, as a result, which limit the types of information he or she gains access to. The authors here analyze their own fieldwork experiences by exploring: (1) the types of gender boundaries that existed in their field settings; (2) the ways in which gender ascriptions blocked their access to certain groups and sources of data; (3) the strategies adopted to overcome such boundaries; and (4) the ways in which gender ascriptions allowed access to various social networks and informational sources.

Giovannini reports that her adoption of the local Sicilian gender ascription of the socially restricted single female resulted in her exclusion from an important political process carried out primarily in male settings. When she found a very competent male informant to tell her what was going on, other critical problems of male-female interaction arose and necessitated termination of the relationship. In contrast to these de facto boundaries, Krieger reports that she voluntarily confined herself to what she believed to be the local gender category of restricted and modest female, not only because of her sex, but also because of the topic of her research (reproduction and family planning). However, she discovered that there was more flexibility in the role ascribed to her than she had anticipated and realized that she was unnecessarily creating barriers to information gathering.

Fieldworkers occasionally find that gender ascriptions based on characteristics other than sex can facilitate the fieldwork process. For example, in Section I Oboler reports that once she became pregnant (parenthood) her status among the Nandi was elevated, and Conaway implies that being married might have helped her fieldwork process because the criollo expect young women in foreign situations to be accompanied by a husband or a father. In Section II Wax reports that her age as well as her sex were an advantage in doing fieldwork in a Sioux community. Sioux of all age and sex categories were more willing to talk candidly with her, as an older woman, than with other members of the fieldwork team who were younger or male.

Various strategies can be developed for overcoming gender-related boundaries in collecting information. Scaglion reports that he was not permitted to interact with Abelam (New Guinea) females during the long (six-month) yam growing season because of fears of pollution. Consequently, he collected data on males and females during different field trips. Johnson employs Van Gennep's rites of passage framework to argue that a fieldworker must be incorporated into the field community, whether into the same sex category or the opposite one. He uses his field experiences among a group of male boat builders on the West Indian island of Bequia and among a group of female schoolteachers in the American Midwest to demonstrate his point.

Finally, while crossing sex and gender boundaries may be quite difficult in a highly sex-segregated society, Fluehr-Lobban and Lobban report on their success as a husband and wife team. Although they had different research interests while carrying out fieldwork in the Sudan, they found their individual research efforts were strengthened because they could depend on each other to provide information about the respective sex and/or gender groups to which each was assigned, and to which the other was denied access.

Human service programs sometimes require that fieldwork be carried out rapidly so that the information gathered can be channeled into program planning. Whitehead and Brown argue that when such fieldwork is requested in a highly sex-segregated society, a team of male and female fieldworkers is absolutely necessary. The applied research team simply does not have the time that independent anthropologists usually have to master cultural rules that might allow for the crossing of sex and gender boundaries. In addition, as Whitehead and Brown indicate, such short-term fieldwork also does not allow for the deeper interpretations that may be achieved through years of immersion in the field culture. If they want baseline data at all, program planners typically want only the sort of descriptive data that will enhance program effectiveness. Since these planners do not find the "deep interpretations" made by social scientists helpful, they usually do not afford their fieldworkers the time necessary to collect sufficient data for such interpretations.

Self, Gender, and Interpretation

Although the fieldworker brings a sense of self to the field, he or she may not be fully conscious of who that self is. Indeed, most humans seldom go through life pondering why they behave as they do. The researcher's professional training may contribute to a separation of self from experience (Myerhoff and Ruby 1982:2) in the name of objectivity, but a funny thing happens during fieldwork: the fieldworker discovers the self while trying to understand others (Myerhoff and Ruby 1982:1). Or, as Rabinow (1977:5) put it, fieldworkers arrive at "the comprehension of self by the detour of the comprehension of the other." Through the inquiries made by fieldworkers, members of the field community are asked to "objectify" themselves, to see their lives and themselves in ways they had never before considered (Rabinow 1977:118). At the same time, the fieldworker's inquiries often generate a similar personal self-discovery process. Such introspection can contribute to the efficacy of the fieldwork process as well as provide the fieldworker with a more thorough understanding of the field culture. As Buechler (1969:42) stated:

> ... an assessment of his position in the field is of utmost importance for any anthropologist, both in measuring his effectiveness as a researcher and as a tool for interpreting social relations themselves. At some time or other, probably every anthropologist is compelled to analyze his place in the society he studies because his position determines to a large extent what channels of information are open to him; the channels of pattern and culture information in turn are a crucial factor in defining the information itself. (emphasis added)

Introspection does not run counter to the scientific process, as has been traditionally thought, but rather may be regarded as the beginning of this process, for it leads to further reflection, including reflection on the most important object of study—the field culture. Denzin (1978:71) encapsulated this process in the following statement:

> The movement from insights to propositions and ultimately to theory follows from the continual focus on a core problem or set of issues. Problems and questions, not theory, create new perspectives. At some point in the reflective process a series of tentative solutions, often expressed as propositions, begin to emerge. The examination of these leads to other predictions, new concepts, and renewed empirical activity. As observations in the empirical world confirm tentative predictions, additional scope is added, and the relationship with previous research is discovered. (emphasis added)

Anthropologists believe that an individual can better understand a cultural system by being as much a part of that system as possible. In the type of reflexive empiricism being described here, the fieldworker is indeed being placed in that system by the host population. This reflexive process can be seen in most of the essays in Sections I and II. Turnbull gained a better understanding of the role of the various life-cycle stages in Mbuti gender relations because he was treated as a male at different stages of the life cycle during his successive visits to the field. As a female head of household in the Dominican Republic, Gonzalez gained a better understanding of the status of the female-headed household in that society. Fluehr-Lobban and Lobban not only came to understand the dynamics of sexual segregation in the Sudan by carrying out local gender roles, but they also came to understand how values supporting such a structure were socialized as they observed the enculturation process their young daughter experienced. Giovannini's symbolic interactionist assessment of her experience in a Sicilian village helped her to better understand the role of masculine honor in courting patterns in that community. And Johnson's reflections on his own gender-related roles and situations in a Midwest school system helped him to understand the role of gender in the functioning of that system.

In Section III the contributors focus specifically on how they worked through their own gender-related conflicts in the field to achieve a better understanding of both self and the sociodynamics of the host cultures. In sharing his experiences in Jamaica, Whitehead refers to Agar's (1982; based on Gadamer 1975) breakdown-resolution-coherence process as an external one that may be accompanied by a similar internal process. External breakdown for Whitehead resulted from his observation that the gender attitudes and practices exhibited by the men in his field community seemed to contradict those in the literature, as well as contradicting each other. Internal breakdown resulted from the ethnic- and class-defined gender-related behavior expected of him that conflicted with the sense of gender self he had brought to the field. Particularly distressing was the subservient behavior that fellow lower-class Afro-Americans directed toward him and other big men. Through the slow processes of internal and external resolution of both gender and ethnic issues, however, Whitehead reports discovering new insights about both self and the study community, which facilitated his efforts to exhibit appropriate behavior in his Jamaican field setting and also to achieve internal adjustment of his gender and ethnic selves to the challenges posed by fieldwork.

Another example of internal and external breakdown leading to resolution and new insights about self (internal coherence) and the study community (external coherence) is Davis's contribution. Reflecting on her field experiences and difficulties in Newfoundland while studying menopausal women, Davis tells us that she achieved not only an enhanced understanding of self but also a better understanding of how her own gender socialization and professional enculturation resulted in certain misconceptions about her research topic. She states that both her adjustment to the field site and her understanding of how women in her study community reacted to menopause increased after she stopped viewing all middle-aged women as "walking menopauses."

The relationship between internal and external breakdown-resolution-coherence is also evident in Jackson's account of her fieldwork among the Tukanoan people of the Central Northwest Amazon region of South America. As a result of the anguish of both types of breakdown, Jackson came to understand that her selection of a field culture was a consequence of her own conflicts with regard to her status as a woman and her contradictory preconceptions as to the status of women in her host community. She eventually realized that her view of female subordination was based on the Western concepts of female-male interaction into which she had been socialized. When the women in her host community did not see themselves as subordinate to males—and in culturally relevant ways they were not as subordinate to males as are women in Western societies—Jackson was forced to reflect on these paradoxes and subsequently to call for new definitions of dominance and subordination in male-female relations that would have broader cross-cultural implications.

Faithorn reports that she, like Whitehead, experienced feelings of discomfort in the field due to initially thinking that a social group with which she identified (women) was acting in a subservient manner. Kafe females in her New Guinea field site disappointed Faithorn because they behaved in a seemingly submissive manner toward males. What she failed to realize, at first, was that subservience and submissiveness are cultural constructs, regardless of whether they are used to interpret class interactions (as in Whitehead's case) or relationships between the sexes (as in her own and Jackson's experiences). The fieldworker who applies his or her own native concepts of relationships between social groups or categories to the social dynamics existing in the field risks profound misinterpretations. Faithorn, like Jackson, reports that she eventually understood that these Kafe women do not define their social status primarily in terms of their relationships to men, as do many Western women. Hence, the concepts of subordination and submissiveness had little or no relevance in analyzing female-male relationships among the population she studied.

In analyzing the essays in Section III according to the processes of internal and external breakdown, we realize some readers may argue that external coherence is biased because it results from an emotional need for internal coherence on the part of fieldworkers who belong to lower-status social categories in their own cultures. We reiterate, therefore, that prefield biases are inevitable for all fieldworkers, due to their experiences as social beings. The contributors to this volume maintain that prefield biases and the effects of human subjectivity on fieldwork must be addressed before the struggle for objectivity can even begin.

For the authors of these fieldwork accounts, it is the experience of internal breakdown that forces fieldworkers to address their own biases and that ultimately stimulates a more objective external coherence. Both internal and external resolution result from the realization that cognitive categories brought to the field may differ significantly from those held by members of the field community. The resolution process may begin internally as the fieldworker tries to understand why members of the host community react to him or her as they do; it may begin externally as he or she searches for local categories that foster an understanding of the indigenous culture. By trying to comprehend these local categories the fieldworker comes to better understand how he or she is being viewed by the host population and why. Wherever it begins, resolution requires facing prefield biases, including interpretations of the self with which we are most comfortable. In our opinion, this process of resolution promotes a less biased perspective for understanding the host culture and, in the process, provides the fieldworker with a refined understanding of the self brought to the field and of the transformed self that results from the fieldwork experience.

The primary message we hope to convey to the readers of this book is that fieldworkers owe it to their host communities and to themselves to reflect on what is happening to them personally and to the field community. Only by taking steps to achieve internal coherence can fieldworkers hope to correct prefield biases that impact negatively on field adjustment, information gathering, and data interpretation processes associated with cross-cultural fieldwork.

Notes

1. Babcock (1980:3), quoting Rousseau, defines reflexivity as the process of regarding "oneself as an other and to be aware of oneself as his own instrument of observation."

2. By socially significant experiences we mean simply those sociocultural experiences that contribute to the development of self.

References

Agar, Michael
     1982   "Toward an Ethnographic Language." *American Anthropologist*
           84:779–95.

Babcock, Barbara
  1980 "Reflexivity: Definitions and Discriminations." *Semiotica* 30(1/2):
        1–14.
Bohannan, Laura
  1960 "The Frightened Witch." In: Joseph Casagrande (ed.), *In the Com-
        pany of Man*, pp. 377–96. New York: Harper and Row.
Bovin, Mette
  1966 "The Significance of the Sex of the Fieldworker for Insights into
        the Male and Female Worlds." *Ethnos* 31(supplement):24–27.
Bowen, Elenore
  1954 *Return to Laughter*. New York: Harper and Row.
Briggs, Jean
  1970 "Kapluna Daughter." In: Peggy Golde (ed.), *Women in the Field*, pp.
        19–46. Chicago: Aldine.
Beuchler, Hans C.
  1969 "The Social Position of an Ethnographer in the Field." In: Frances
        Henry and Satish Saberwal (eds.), *Stress and Response in Field-
        work*, pp. 7–17. New York: Holt, Rinehart and Winston.
Cesara, Manda
  1982 *Reflections of a Woman Anthropologist: No Hiding Place*. New
        York: Academic Press.
Denzin, Norman
  1978 *The Research Act*. New York: McGraw-Hill.
Dumont, Jean-Paul
  1978 *The Headman and I*. Austin: University of Texas Press.
Gadamer, H. G.
  1975 *Truth and Method*. New York: Continuum.
Golde, Peggy (ed.)
  1970 *Women in the Field*. Chicago: Aldine.
Hymes, Dell
  1969 "The Uses of Anthropology: Critical, Political, Personal." In: D.
        Hymes (ed.), *Reinventing Anthropology*, pp. 3–79. New York: Ran-
        dom House.
Malinowski, Bronislaw
  1967 *A Diary in the Strict Sense of the Term*. London: Routledge and
        Kegan Paul.
Mead, George H.
  1962 *Mind, Self, and Society*. Chicago: University of Chicago Press.
Myerhoff, Barbara, and Jay Ruby
  1982 "Introduction." In: Jay Ruby (ed.), *A Crack in the Mirror: Reflexive
        Perspectives in Anthropology*, pp. 1–35. Philadelphia: University
        of Pennsylvania Press.
Nash, Dennison, and Ronald Wintrob
  1972 "The Emergence of Self-Consciousness in Ethnography." *Current
        Anthropology* 13(b):527–42.
Osgood, Cornelius
  1953 *Winter*. New York: W. W. Norton and Co.

Papanek, Hanna
  1964 "The Woman Fieldworker in a Purdah Society." *Human Organization* 23(2):160–63.
Powdermaker, Hortense
  1966 *Stranger and Friend: The Way of an Anthropologist.* New York: W. W. Norton and Co.
Rabinow, Paul
  1977 *Reflections on Fieldwork in Morocco.* Berkeley: University of California Press.
Rohrlich-Leavitt, Ruby, Barbara Sykes, and Elizabeth Weatherford
  1973 "Aboriginal Woman: Male and Female Anthropological Perspectives." In: *Women Cross-Culturally: Change and Challenge,* pp. 567–80. The Hague: Mouton.
Sanday, Peggy Reeves
  1979 "The Ethnographic Paradigm." *Administrative Science Quarterly* 24:527–38.
Scheper-Hughes, Nancy, and Mari Clark (eds.)
  1983 Confronting Problems of Bias in Feminist Anthropology. Special issue of *Women's Studies* 10(2).
Smalley, William
  1963 "Culture Shock, Language Shock, and the Shock of Self-Discovery." *Practical Anthropology* 10(2).
Swallow, D. A.
  1974 "The Anthropologist as Subject." *Cambridge Anthropology* 1(3):51–60.
Wagley, Charles
  1960 "Champukwi of the Village of the Tapirs." In: Joseph Casagrande (ed.), *In the Company of Man,* pp. 398–415. New York: Harper and Row.
Wax, Rosalie H.
  1971 *Doing Fieldwork: Warnings and Advice.* Chicago: University of Chicago Press.
Weidman, Hazel
  1970 "On Ambivalence in the Field." In: Peggy Golde (ed.), *Women in the Field,* pp. 239–66. Chicago: Aldine.
Weiner, Annette B.
  1976 *Women of Value, Men of Renown: New Perspectives in Trobriand Exchange.* Austin: University of Texas Press.

Self, Sex, Gender, and Field Adjustment

1

Sex and Gender: The Role of Subjectivity in Field Research

COLIN M. TURNBULL

Two of the major problems that every anthropologist has to face in the field are ethnocentricism and egocentricism. These problems become particularly acute when it comes to issues of gender and sexuality, since our own beliefs and practices are deeply embedded and seldom coincide with those of the host culture. Our much-vaunted dedication to detachment and objectivity not only does little to help on its own but may be a positive hindrance. Here, as elsewhere, ultimate objectivity may arise most fully from an immediate subjectivity, conscious and controlled. Then the very limitations seemingly imposed by expectations and ascriptions become advantages, charged with positive potential.

It is in this area that ethical considerations can also be particularly problematic for any fieldworker except those who pretend amorality. Our concepts of gender and related sexual behavior are such an integral part of our self-definition that to attempt to be or behave in any other way is not only a denial of self but a gross dishonesty, an immorality. Here the anthropologist might do well to learn from the discipline, methods, and techniques of drama, a field of study equally concerned with human and social behavior. Actors face similar problems as they find themselves on stage (the equivalent of being "in the field") in a wide diversity of social contexts. The only way in which they, or the director, can arrive at a real understanding of that context and present it truthfully and accurately to an audience is to make a total sacrifice of self, to aspire to nothing short of transformation (Grotowski 1968). This alone will enable actors to overcome the barrier of egotism that otherwise must always stand between them and that which they wish to understand and portray.

This is at the opposite pole from the anthropologist's nominal total dedication to objectivity and the language. We would be likely to dismiss all too readily the use of words such as "sacrifice" and "transformation" as smacking of romanticism. Anyone who has

17

worked with actors trained in this school, however, would instantly know that its method and techniques demand a discipline every bit as rigorous and, in some ways, even more demanding than our own. I do not suggest that we adopt the theatrical technique in toto, merely that we learn from it and, by combining it with our own approach to the study of human society, adapt it to our needs. Much of contemporary experimental theater is recognizing the richness of adapting the more objective, analytic method of social science to its needs; and where this is made to work it becomes evident that the dramatic experience, the truth ultimately realized on the stage, is at one with the structural reality. I will try here to use my own field experience to illustrate this process, this dual (anthropological and dramatic) approach. Throughout, I am referring primarily to the unmarried male anthropologist.

Mobility Through Gender Role Ascription

Role mobility is one of the other keys to successful handling of both gender and sexuality in the field. This becomes self-evident as one grows older and the sexual self changes, to a lesser degree than gender ascriptions. But even in the full flood of youth, when gender identification and the sexual drive are most powerful, mobility is perfectly possible and, of course, a major means of overcoming the limitations imposed by the adoption or ascription of any one specific role. Those of us who have been lucky enough to make frequent trips to the field over many years experience a natural role mobility as we ourselves grow older and change in these respects. But mobility can be achieved even during one field trip. And it is best achieved not by mere engineering, such as relocating in different villages within the same study area, or by objectively assuming different roles in different villages within the same cultural context, but by utilizing the dramatic techniques previously referred to, changing not just the location but the self.

Some may question just how far this is possible, particularly when the different expectations of gender and sexuality they face create a very real form of culture shock. Perhaps I was lucky in that, having been brought up as a child in a strict Scottish Presbyterian manner, I was thrown into the English public school system while not yet thirteen years old. So deep was the culture shock at that crucial age that I have seldom experienced such shock since. It was also a good and early lesson in cultural relativity with reference to both gender and sexuality. So when, as a philosophy graduate student with no training at all in anthropology, I found myself in bed, in India, with a very attractive young Hindu girl, who, because she called me "brother," expected nothing more (as did her parents) but tickling contests, I was able to respond in kind with a minimum of difficulty. My classificatory position in this family, some of whom I had met in Britain, allowed me a gender role with which I was familiar, but not my sense of sexuality. It was the girl's orthodox Hindu parents who told me to sleep with my "sister" because it was the only bed available. They had already imposed on me the responsibilities of my classificatory position as their "son." I had assisted my "father" in the search for a suitable groom for my "sister," and although this anthropologically commonplace situation was totally unknown to me, the dramatic reality of the situation was such that I found myself, including my sexuality, transformed at least to the extent that I only wondered at it long afterward.

Similarly, having studied anthropology and on my way to the field for my first professional fieldwork, there was a natural "rightness" about the insistence of an extremely powerful Ndaka chief that I sleep with one of his daughters. But here I was in trouble, this time for medical rather than moral reasons, for I was simply not willing to take the risk; the old chief and his entire family were ridden with leprosy and yaws, as well as syphilis. That very first night three daughters came to my room in succession and I declined each without having to give a reason. The old man, in a desperate effort to please me and make an acceptable and very Maussian gift, then sent one of his sons, equally diseased. But while the son was intended as a potential bedmate for this foreigner who must, it seemed (the chief later told me), suffer from "the European Disease" (homosexuality), the smart old politician sent food with his son, which I accepted. The issue of my gender and sexuality were left to be determined later, under less hazardous conditions.

On our first field trip few of us are neither sophisticated nor convinced enough of the validity of all the theories with which our heads are filled to respond instantly to a knock on the door and such a series of offers by making an intellectual analysis of the situation. We have probably all faced similar situations and have reacted spontaneously from within rather than with any careful application of the rational process. While mistakes are made, it at first seems surprising that they are so few in number. But it should not be surprising, for we are responding as actors respond to a dramatic situation: the drama is real and immediate and, as I have suggested, is the very reality that gives birth to the structural theory with which we habitually busy ourselves. Just as our minds respond logically to a theoretical context, so as actors do our bodies, our inner and outer selves, respond correctly (consonant with the structure) to the dramatic (real) context. At a later stage in our fieldwork we might be able to reason our way in and out of a wide diversity of situations with some success, but if we train ourselves as the actor does to *improvise*, to react to the actions of others without violating the inherent drama of the situation, we are perhaps on even safer ground, for our intellectual understanding of the social structure is never anything but partial, most of all while still in the field. Indeed, it is rather obvious that it is through action and interaction, in other words, as actors, that we often discover the structure.

Incidents such as these are of particular significance precisely because they involve both gender and sexuality, for our personal concept of self is at least as much associated with those factors as it is with our intellect, and in our youth probably a good deal more so. If we can find our way through such situations by reacting to them, rather than by attempting to find our way out of them by intellectualizing, then we can achieve several useful results. A successful resolution of the problem is more likely to be arrived at providing us with valuable ethnographic data (even if the resolution is not so successful!), and we are likely to discover more about ourselves as well as about the host culture. Further, to the extent that we react, improvising directly in response to the reality of the situation, we are being ourselves even as we discover, perhaps, a new self of which we were unaware. The field situation demands honesty at all times, and for us to be ourselves is the greatest form of honesty; it is also (at least in all the field contexts I have known) the most *convincing* demonstration of honesty from the point of view of our hosts. The more perceptive the reasoning and theorizing, the more it is likely to have the appearance of dishonesty or deception.

Again, I was lucky in that my field experience quickly taught me that my self was a much richer and more diverse thing than my upbringing had led me to believe. The Mbuti of Zaire, in particular, taught me that even my gender was not quite what I had thought it was, and not only in their specific cultural context. Their context merely formalized it with extreme clarity through their system of generational terminology which does duty for kinship terminology. Among the Mbuti, forest hunter/gatherers, gender is a variable thing, and so indeed is the sexual act; and the relationship between the two is not quite as simple as it is with Westerners. Mbuti expectations of sexual behavior, while according to gender, vary with age. The concept of variable gender is made very clear by the terminology which, in distinguishing four age levels (child, youth, adult, and elder), only distinguishes gender at the adult, or parental, level. The other terms, used in both address and reference, make no distinction of gender. It is only in addressing a parent at the adult (i.e., child-producing) level that gender is differentiated. This *may* be done when an adult, say, addresses a parent at the elder level, but rarely so. And at all levels those of your own age level are addressed again without gender differentiation, simply using the term *apua'i*, which includes sibling, friend, and mate.

This system of classification is primarily a delineator of specific rights and obligations that influence, if not determine, both effective and affective relationships. Individual and social behavioral expectancy in all respects, including gender sexuality, is linked directly to the age level of each individual. To a very large extent the individual's position is a matter of personal choice, though the natural process of aging obviously determines the position at both extremes. There is no formal age-set system; each individual advances at will from childhood to youth, youth to adulthood, and adulthood to old age, given the ability to conform to the expectations proper to that age level. There are no formal options, as found in some other societies, by which a male may choose to live his life as a female, with all the respect due to that position; but by the simple act of not marrying any Mbuti can, and a few do, avoid the realities (social, structural, and even personal) of being either male or female. In fact, much Mbuti life is lived in a kind of gender limbo, for even the division of labor according to gender is by no means rigid and exclusive at any age level. Obviously, motherhood is the one supreme and absolute exception to gender-specific behavior, but I rather suspect the Mbuti would say that fatherhood is an exception as well.

This was all brought home to me as I moved from one generational level to the other, ultimately reaching an elderhood that seemed somewhat premature to me but which the Mbuti found proper in terms of both structure and function. They would have approved of Radcliffe-Brown, except that they would have put function before structure. Given my total ignorance and inability even to feed myself when I was first with the Mbuti, I was clearly a child. I was placed in a childless family in that my "father" only had one child, a son, by a previous marriage, and that son was seriously crippled and with another band at the time. I was my Mbuti mother's first child; her husband had been unable to give her any. As a child, I was without gender except in the strictly biological sense (male sex), and despite my actual youth I found myself under exactly the same behavioral norms as all my siblings or *apau'i*, regardless of this biological accident. The terminology is extended to *all* who are living in any particular hunting band at any particular time. So, in point of fact, my parents were not childless, but until my arrival my "mother" was not a true adult because she was not yet a mother. From that point onward she was a mother equally to all other children in the band.

Because of my actual age, my progress through childhood was accelerated, and discussions around the campfires at night made it clear that the concern was with my sexuality and my probable inability to restrict myself as children naturally do to harmless play. Harmless, in this context, meant unfruitful. For ordinary children this is ordained by the lack of adequate physical development, but for me this was not so, the Mbuti said. Significantly, they kept me, as much as possible, apart from the highly flirtatious youths, and it was during this time that I came most in contact with the equally genderless elders who, rather like children, seemed to have neither sexual interest nor ability.

The time lag between my first and second field trips was magnified, and on my return I was immediately incorporated into the same band as a youth. My relationship with my immediate parents was little changed, except perhaps with my father, who was slightly less affective the more the relationship became effective (through my helping him, rather inadequately, on the hunt). But, in fact, what had happened was that my relationship with *all* my parents had changed, for in Mbuti societies youths are not only the critics but also the judges of adults, and their relationship with the elders is one of greater equality and difference. Elders also criticize adults but do not judge. I was still genderless in function, except, to some extent, on the hunt, and I found myself expected to relate to all my *apua'i* equally, regardless of gender. At first I was apprehensive, for female Mbuti youths are every bit as flirtatious as the male youths, and extremely attractive; yet the affection that was expected to exist between all *apua'i* at this level was evidently meant to be equal in quality as well as in quantity. It was a situation in which one might have expected both male and female homosexuality, yet there was no evidence of either in terms of intercourse. In other terms, however, there was no denying the warmth of affection and physical attraction manifested equally between all, regardless of sex. And since Mbuti tend to leave childhood and enter youth at any time after the age of seven or eight, the issue of sexuality does not really arise until late youth.

This moment in their lives is marked by the *elima* festival, which celebrates the first menstrual period (and hence potential motherhood/adulthood) of a girl. Flirtations take on a more serious tone, intercourse takes place, youthful couples "go steady," yet still it is the norm for affection to be distributed equally among all of one's *apua'i*. It was then I learned that falling in love can be a terrible kind of infidelity. The Mbuti can love as deeply and dearly as any, and in adolescence they find that sexual intercourse is a unique way of manifesting that love. But sexual intercourse is limited. It cannot be (or for them *is* not) practiced with *apua'i* of the same sex, nor by the very nature of things can it be practiced equally with all the *apua'i* of the opposite sex, although Mbuti youths do indeed make a brave attempt to distribute their favors as widely as possible.

Their ambivalence at discovering the relationship between gender and sex was made very clear to me through the custom of male youths sleeping together in clusters either around the campfires or in the bachelor huts, while the girls tend to sleep always in their parental homes. While the joys of sex were extolled, so was the inevitable consequence of variable affectivity bemoaned. It was a very real conflict among youths, with the sexual urge, on the one hand, working to intensify their affective lives, and the social urge, on the other hand, developed through childhood and early youth, working to reject such individual preference and selectivity. I was aware that adults and elders alike were watching me to see how I would behave as I matured into an older youth, or adolescent. From what had been said to me by my elders, as a child, and from what I had overheard, it was clear that they hoped I would enter the flirtatious activities of the older youths since this would inevitably lead, for them, to marriage, and I had made it clear that I was only going to be there for a maximum of two years at a time. It became obvious that marriage, for the Mbuti, was the coming together of a couple for the express purpose of having children. It was easy, then, for me to say I had no intention of getting married and still remain within the cultural norms. Many Mbuti youths delay marriage in order to enjoy the fun of youth and to be more certain of ultimately making the right choice of a lifelong partner. Divorce virtually never takes place, except when, as in my Mbuti father's case, there are no children, and then the Mbuti say it is not divorce for there are no children and therefore no "marriage."

That, however, did not entirely solve the problem for me, since now it became known to me that the Mbuti differentiate between two kinds of sexual activity, that which is designed to produce children and that which is not. The former is the proper and expected behavior of adults, of males and females; the latter is the proper and expected behavior of genderless youths, of embryonic males and females. There was no exemption that I could see from the latter; celibacy does not exist among the Mbuti. Bestiality and homosex-

uality would be more "normal" by their standards, for at least the
potential of the human body would be used more fully, if oddly. It
was in this way, by action and reaction, that I found my way through
a complicated maze of gender and sexuality norms that probably the
Mbuti themselves could never have made explicit to me and that
were not accessible through any literature. And it was also in this
way that I was led to note yet another significant difference between
these nomadic hunters/gatherers and their sedentary farming neighbors. For the latter, celibacy is both possible and profitable if one
wishes to accumulate supernatural power, to become either a priest
working for the social good or a sorcerer working for harm. It is certainly considered preferable to either bestiality or homosexuality.
(Incidentally, they reverse the order of the two alternatives cited by
the Mbuti, similarly separating both but preferring homosexuality
over bestiality with little practice of the first and none I could discover of the second.)

Now my problem was compounded since Mbuti moved in both
circles, the forest and the village worlds. To be celibate would mark
me as odd, at worst, among the Mbuti, but as a sorcerer among the
villagers (since I did not have the other skills necessary for the
priesthood). Yet to engage in the nonreproductive sexual activity of
the Mbuti youths would be tantamount to saying that I was preparing for marriage and reproduction, which would have been a dishonesty from the Mbuti point of view but would have been perfectly
acceptable to the villagers, whose custom it is to continue with
youthful escapades until conception takes place and then to become
betrothed.

The Mbuti say that sexual activity alone does not beget children;
there has to be intent, so they can go on flirting fully until they are
ready for adulthood. A couple announcing their intention of having
children will build a house together and start living together, and
shortly after nine months have passed they are likely to have their
first child. If there are herbal contraceptives or abortions, I could not
discover them; I did discover one, and only one, restraint enjoined
on youthful sexuality, and that was in the manner of the physical
embrace, a dubious form of contraception but perhaps significant
when coupled with the mental and social attitude. The Mbuti, of
course, quickly found a way out for me, negotiating with the village
chief (not the one with so many diseases) whose daughter was sent
to me in the forest, under the pretext of only sending her and another
girl to trade for meat. But Amina disposed of that pretext the first
night. Our relationship did not incur any expectation of marriage
among the villagers. That question would only arise if the young

woman became pregnant, which would doubtless have pleased her father, who could then have demanded appropriate bridewealth and who would have gained political prestige, if not power. It satisfied the Mbuti as to the normality of my youthfulness and my ability to continue to live with them as a real youth, while it satisfied the villagers that I was not a sorcerer.

What a wealth of ethnographic data came from that experience, from acting and reacting, from discovering all the time that there were larger selves hidden within me to which I need be true. There was also the joy and fullness that comes from deep human relationships, for without Amina it would have been impossible for me to learn, as the Mbuti youth do, to fulfill my social obligations with respect to affection while fulfilling my personal life. I cannot say how it might have worked out in other contexts, but since our affection became both mutual and deep, Amina and I together decided that, since we could never get married, it would be wrong for her to become pregnant; and in our own way we managed that until it became too difficult. Then we parted ... Amina leaving when the camp moved.

The Mbuti made one more attempt to preserve me as a youth, but on my next return to the field they pronounced me an adult, a male, and cast me in the only role open to unmarried, childless males, that of buffoon or clown, of which there is usually one in every band, sometimes two. This allowed me to pursue a celibate life, and by now I was able to deal better with the consequent suspicions this aroused among the villagers. I found that the role of clown among the Mbuti, reserved almost exclusively for cripples or unmarried adults, is not at all unlike that of priest among the villagers. A curious attitude of respect goes with the mockery heaped on such individuals. The Mbuti clown adds other behavioral oddities to his celibacy to make himself even more clownish. Given my height, color, and clumsiness, I had no need to do much more than be myself, yet the respect was there, even awe, particularly during the sacred *molimo* festivals. It is not that the clown is in any way sacred— far from it—but rather, like the priest, he is evidently a vehicle for the sacred.

Alas, I was not very effective in the role, for on my next (fourth) trip I was bounced into elderhood. Once again I became genderless. The expectation was of no sexual behavior, so all problems of that nature were removed. By now the issue of gender had become for me as insignificant as it was for the Mbuti, unless associated with that vital adult task of reproduction. As a genderless, sexless elder, once again my social horizons were changed. It was at this age level that I had much greater freedom of access to and intimate discussion with what we would call women; until then I had only known females as mothers, youths, or children, and while I had always fretted at the restrictions placed on me by my own classification, together with the accompanying role expectations, and by entering into the role fully and subjectively, more had been gained than had been lost. That, surely, is always the case, for we delude ourselves if we think for a moment that we can, as fieldworkers, have equal access to all areas of the field.

Summary

By returning to the field on several occasions, I was able to work my way through the system, or rather to be worked through it, experiencing these different implications of gender and sexuality at each level. Such good fortune is rare. But even in any one field trip it was possible to obtain different perspectives such as those I gained when moving from forest to village and back. And given the fact that the terms of address and reference, by which one is placed within the system, are only valid in the hunting band where the individual resides, by systematically visiting other bands I was able to explore more than one age level at a time and make useful comparisons and cross-check my data. These techniques are well known and frequently used. They are successful to the extent that the fieldworker can train himself/herself, as the actor often does, to voluntarily and totally relinquish the former self and discover a new self. It may not be quite the self we expected or were aiming for, but it is more likely to be the self that is right for that particular context. Such mobility, voluntary or imposed, also offers the fieldworker the greatest opportunity for participating while observing, the one self observing the other while still being the self of the moment.

This should not be mistaken for adopting the technique of the chameleon, for however consciously the fieldworker may plan such mobility and role change, it becomes self-defeating by becoming self-fulfilling if pressed too far. Having put a new set of circumstances in motion, the anthropologist then must accept the consequences and be moved rather than continue as the mover. Only in this way is it really possible for anthropologists in the field to be both ethical and moral, while accomplishing our legitimate goal of understanding another way of life, thought, and belief. Even then we might question the morality of interposing our presence in the first place, particularly in societies that may not have mechanisms for incorporating strangers. But where such mechanisms do exist, which is probably in the majority of societies, ethical and moral considerations are best resolved not by insisting on one's own code or by consciously adopting another, but rather by reaching inside and relinquishing the old, narrow, limited self, discovering the new self that is right and proper in the new context.

This is the sacrifice that Polish dramatist Grotowski demands of the actor and the director, and it is the sacrifice that every anthropologist in the field should be prepared to make. It is a sacrifice that leads to discovery that is simultaneously subjective and objective. By discovering within us that which is female as well as that which is male, by using the field experience to know ourselves more deeply by conscious subjectivity, the ultimate goal of objectivity is much more likely to be reached and our understanding of other cultures that much more profound. Without such subjectivity the comparative method loses much of its credibility; and as long as we confuse the participant-observer technique with mere role playing, our field observations will be superficial and trite no matter how ardently we seek to disguise the essential triviality with high-sounding jargon. Anthropology is both a science and an art, and in applying scientific method to inadequate data we delude ourselves. The area of gender and sexuality illustrates this as well as any.

Reference

Grotowski, Jerzy
    1968   *Towards a Poor Theatre*. New York: Simon and Schuster.

2

For Better or Worse: Anthropologists and Husbands in the Field

REGINA SMITH OBOLER

My conversations with other anthropologists suggest the common view is that the role of "anthropologist's husband" is fraught with peril and bound to cause problems in a couple's relationship. By contrast, the role of "anthropologist's wife" raises no such concern. It is assumed that a woman in our culture should be able to give up two years of her own life to further her spouse's career goals without experiencing undue distress, but that such sacrifice is much more difficult, if not impossible, for a man. I have heard tales of colleagues' husbands who suffered extreme psychological stress due to combined culture shock and boredom, whose relationships with their wives were strained by resentment over giving up their own career advancement, who failed completely to adjust to the expectations of the host culture and either retreated into escapist novels or insisted on provoking the local population through inappropriate behavior as a form of entertainment.

My own experience contains no such horror stories. However, I believe it reflects another type of danger common to the situation in which a female anthropologist goes into the field accompanied by a nonanthropologist spouse. The danger is that such a wife/husband team may be unable to adjust their accustomed interaction to a conjugal role pattern that is acceptable to their host culture, or they may be able to do so only at intolerable personal psychological cost. To say that an egalitarian conjugal pattern is now normal among professionals in Euro-American culture is, I hope, not naively overoptimistic. Although there are undoubtedly non-Western cultures where this is an appropriate conjugal role pattern (Bacdayan 1977), there are far more in which it is expected and assumed that the husband

---

Lorraine Dusak Sexton authored several passages contained herein; I regret that her postdoctoral research in New Guinea prevented her coauthoring the entire essay.

is the dominant figure in the husband/wife relationship. The contrast between the expectations of the anthropologist and the spouse and those of the research community with regard to the behavior of the husband and wife can cause problems both for the conduct of the research and for the relationship of the couple. This is especially true where the female anthropologist's position as principal investigator precludes an easy assumption of the subordinate role.

This tension between the definition my husband and I held of our own conjugal relationship and my position as principal investigator versus the conjugal role behavior expected of us by our friends and informants was the central problem of our fieldwork experience among the semipastoral, patrilineal Nandi of western Kenya. We chose, in the main, to adapt to Nandi behavioral expectations. This was valuable to our rapport with the community, though, as I will relate, it made it difficult for me to maintain optimal control over the course of the work in my position as head of the research team. A quite different way of handling the same problem was adopted by our friends Lorraine Dusak Sexton and George Sexton, who at the same time were doing fieldwork in Highland Papua New Guinea.

Although Nandi women's status has in a number of ways been undermined by forces stemming from the colonial situation (Oboler 1985), the Nandi have always adhered to a public ideology of male superiority and the dominance of husbands over wives. Here I will discuss, in the Nandi context, how we defined our roles as members of a research team and how we presented our own gender and conjugal roles in the course of daily life. I will then describe, through excerpts from my field correspondence with Lorraine Sexton, how she and her husband coped with the same types of problems. I will also consider the impact on my fieldwork of a somewhat unusual sex-role-related situation: my six months of pregnancy in the field prior to the birth of our first child three months after we returned to the United States.

The Anthropologist's Husband

My husband, Leon Oboler, is a professional photographer and filmmaker. At the time of our departure for the field, he had just finished course work for an M.F.A. in film. It was a convenient point at which to interrupt his own career path; he was not leaving a job and promotion possibilities to accompany me. Leon viewed anthropological fieldwork as a personal growth experience, and he was almost as enthusiastic as I was about the prospect of research among the Nandi.

Leon has always been interested in anthropology and welcomed the opportunity to live in another culture. He took anthropology courses and was employed in social science research projects during graduate school. One of his major interests has been visual documentary and ethnography; and in addition to whatever contribution he would make to my research, he planned to use the field experience as an opportunity to gather material to further his own career goals. Certainly the psychological cost of accompanying a wife to the field must be greater for a man whose own career and interests are further removed from any connection with social science and who, left entirely to his own devices, would choose quite different sorts of personal growth experiences.

It was Leon's choice to participate in the research process as completely as possible. This was not our first time working together on a field project—we both had been part of a large team involved in a community study in Philadelphia (Oboler and Oboler 1977), and we also had worked together on Leon's ethnographic-documentary film on a small-town volunteer fire company (*Volunteers*, copyright 1973 by Leon Oboler and Temple University). Prior to our departure, Leon prepared himself by reading East African ethnography and taking a course in Kiswahili, the national language of Kenya. Since the central focus of the research was changing gender roles, I was very pleased to have a male co-worker who could learn about this subject from the male perspective, which would be largely inaccessible to me.

George Sexton is a professional criminal justice consultant with a B.A. in sociology and a graduate degree in social work. To accompany his wife to Papua New Guinea he left a position as a research associate with a consulting firm, specializing in prison evaluation studies. His background and training in the social sciences, and his experience in a type of fieldwork—analysis through observation of a particular type of social institution, the prison—may explain why he adjusted so well to the field situation. Unlike Leon, however, George did not intend to use the field experience to further his own professional career. In fact, he left a very good job with no guarantee of being able to return to it after two years in the field. This difference in intent to benefit professionally from the field experience related to our respective decisions regarding the degree of husbands' involvement in the research process. As will become clear in the excerpts from our correspondence, the Sextons' decision was for George to participate less directly in Lorraine's research than Leon would in mine.

Getting Started: Defining Roles as Researchers

Before our arrival in Kenya, Leon and I decided that he would be a participant in the research, not merely a companion. However, the questions of how fully he would participate and how we would present our collaboration had not been resolved. Were we to be seen as completely equal colleagues in a research team, or as principal investigator and research assistant? To an extent, this decision was taken out of our hands by Kenyan governmental bureaucracy. My research clearance ran into a snag, with the result that we were in the country for several months without official permission to conduct research. During this time we became friendly with the ethnographic curator of the National Museum of Kenya, who gave us official appointments as collectors for the museum. Armed with this status and documentation of it, we were able to move to Nandi and start work before the research clearance actually came through. Thus, we first approached the district commissioner as "Mr. and Mrs. Oboler, collectors for the National Museum." The commissioner invited us to speak at a meeting of location and sublocation chiefs to explain our purpose in Nandi. Although I was the one who did most of the talking at this meeting (I was more fluent in Kiswahili), and although I explained to the commissioner that I was awaiting permission to conduct other research, the egalitarian first impression not only stuck but it was reinforced by subsequent events.

After the research clearance came through, a problem developed with our visas. According to Kenya's immigration policy, no man can live in the country as the dependent of a woman: he must be the independent holder of resident status, which means that he must hold his own research or work permit. Thus, my research proposal had to be rewritten for a team of two researchers, and Leon and I were both appointed research associates of the Institute for Development Studies. Our equal status went down in writing on all the official documentation we were required to file with government officials, from provincial commissioner to district commissioner to location chiefs. Our categorization as equal partners thus became a fait accompli. Later, when we were settled into a research community, we made a point of trying to clarify our situation with those people with whom we associated closely. We informed them that I, not Leon, was conducting the research as part of my work toward a degree and that I had been awarded money to do so. Still, we did not retreat from the basic interpretation that we were a team of equals. Since Leon planned to work hard in the research, it really seemed to me unfair to present him in any other way, especially in a culture such as Nandi where male prestige is so important.

Before our clearance came through we moved to the district center in our role as collectors for the National Museum. The day after we moved in, the chief of the central location asked us to attend a public fund-raising event for an elementary school in his location. It was our first chance to attend any type of event in Nandi, so we quickly accepted. During the affair, the chief requested that Leon make a speech explaining to the gathering our purpose for being in Nandi. I can remember vividly the feeling of frustration: "I'm the one he should ask to give the speech! Isn't it my research?" This experience was repeated at several other events, even when such invitations were extended by people to whom we had attempted to explain the details of our situation. It was not only that Leon was viewed as the natural leader of our partnership, but also that oratory in Nandi is largely a male prerogative. It is assumed that almost every man can speak comfortably in public but that only exceptional women can do so. Leon shared my frustration. He disliked being asked to speak for me as principal investigator, and since he had learned very little Swahili at this point, it was also difficult and embarrassing for him to speak publicly. However, there seemed very little choice but to go along with all of it, especially as these things were usually sprung on us unexpectedly. We commiserated with each other in private.

After several weeks of visiting various parts of Nandi District, we moved to the small community where we lived for most of our field stay and which was the central focus of our research. We chose this particular community because it seemed representative of what we had seen in the district as a whole. It was neither the most "traditional" nor the most "modern" community; it was not too close to the district center; and the residents indicated that they would be genuinely pleased to have us there. Our research site was a sublocation of 286 homesteads, the population of each averaging eight people and nine adult cattle. The average homestead landholding was about twenty acres. Of ever-married male household heads, 16.8 percent were polygynists, and two-thirds of them professed to be Christians.

When we arrived in the community, the sublocation chief called a public meeting to introduce us. I did most of the talking at this meeting, explaining in Kiswahili that I had been given money to carry out my work and that as a result of it I would receive an advanced university degree. I also carefully explained that both Leon and I would be doing the work, that we would both be asking questions, and I told the people what kinds of things we would be asking them about. My attempt to explain the primacy of my role in the research went largely unheeded. In the weeks that followed, men more frequently than women came to visit us to find out what we were doing, and they always sought out Leon rather than me.

Even the two people closest to us, our field assistants, had trouble dealing with the idea that Leon was not in command. While we were still living in the district center we hired two people to help with the research. Their duties were to assist with gathering census and numerical data, to transcribe tape recordings of interviews and various public events, to teach us the language, and to act as interpreters in interview situations until we gained sufficient language skills. When we moved to our research site these assistants moved with us. I thought it best to employ one man and one woman to facilitate interviewing members of both sexes on topics inappropriate for discussion with members of the opposite sex. Kipruto and Jebet were in their early twenties, spoke English, and were the Kenyan equivalent of high school graduates. I had interviewed all the candidates for the position of assistant with Leon in the background, occasionally inserting a comment. Kipruto was hired first, and he had not been with us very long before it became apparent that he had difficulty accepting female authority. He was charming, and as long as an authority relationship was not immediately involved in the interaction at hand, we got on extraordinarily well. I liked him and felt that he liked me. However, when I asked him to do something, he might do it or he might not. Gradually and unconsciously I fell into the pattern of letting Leon give Kipruto his instructions, because under this arrangement they were more likely to be carried out. When Jebet joined us I usually directly supervised her work. I realized later that Kipruto's definition of the situation came to be that he worked for Leon and Jebet worked for me, and along with this was the implication that in a husband/wife partnership the husband is always the ultimate authority.

I didn't realize soon enough that all this was happening, and Kipruto was so good at his job in so many other ways that when I did realize it I was reluctant to risk creating tension with him by making it an issue. As it turned out I made a mistake, because later, when it was necessary for me to supervise Kipruto's work more directly, establishing my authority created greater conflict than probably would have occurred if the issue had been raised earlier. In fact, though Leon and I had been very close to Kipruto, we parted from him with strained relations: a few months before we left the field, he suddenly quit his job just when we were counting on him to assist in a crucial piece of work, shooting footage for a 16mm film. Although the difficulties he had working under my supervision were not among the reasons he gave for leaving, in retrospect I feel that several quarrels I had with him over what he should be doing in the weeks before he left were precipitating factors. Quarreling is frowned on in Nandi; and for a woman to speak harsh and angry words to a man is especially bad. Kipruto's definition of the situation—that he worked for Leon—also created a problem for Leon by making it impossible for him to escape the field situation even temporarily. If Leon decided to spend a day reading science fiction instead of working, Kipruto took his cue directly from Leon and didn't work either, particularly if his task for the day happened to be something like transcription, which he disliked doing. This attitude forced Leon further into the role of co-researcher.

Sometimes I became anxious over having less than optimal control of the research. I began to think that we had made a mistake in our presentation, that I should have been clearer from start to finish, strident if necessary, about my role as principal investigator. But would this have had a negative impact on our research? As it was, both of us were throwing ourselves into fieldwork. Leon was getting involved in the community, being accepted by the men, and his work with them was invaluable to the research. We were getting almost twice as much data as a team as I could have gathered alone. And in view of the Nandi negative evaluation of women who "try to be bigger than their husbands," Leon's stature in the community would have suffered if I were obviously in charge.

Living in Nandi: Defining Gender Roles

We had decided that we wanted our ultimate research site to be a family compound in a small community so that we could be intimately involved in the round of daily life. Some young men from one community with whom we had become friendly persuaded the head of a compound near the sublocation Centre (a group of shops, grain mills, beer clubs, etc., clustered at a central point in an otherwise scattered settlement pattern) to offer us a place in his compound. Our host, Solomon, was seven years older than Leon and a member of the same age set of which Leon was considered a member. He was a significant figure in the community, noted as a hardworking local entrepreneur. A leader of one of the Christian denominations in the community, he was also deeply aware of and interested in Nandi tradition. Both he and his wife, Esther, though not formally educated, were characterized by a keen intelligence and a curiosity about the novel and exotic. They were already known in the community for their willingness to befriend strangers, particularly members of other ethnic groups. Although they had heard much about *wazungu* (whites), they had known none intimately and were curious to see what kind of people we really were. They accepted us into their compound largely because of their own independent interest in cross-cultural experiences—they wanted to learn about us as much as we wanted to learn about them.

The metaphor that made the most cultural sense of our relationship with Solomon and his family was that he and Leon should act toward each other as elder and younger brothers, and that I and the rest of the family should fall into behaviors appropriate to relationships stemming from this central metaphor. We were never formally adopted into kinship statuses, nor was there ever a perfect fit between our behavior and behavior appropriate to kinship roles. It was merely a metaphor that worked in many situations.

The rest of the household included Solomon and Esther's three sons, who ranged in age from eight to thirteen, their six-year-old daughter, Solomon's widowed mother, and his sister, an independent woman separated from her husband. We really came to feel that these people were family to us, and we developed close and confidential relationships with them, especially Leon with Solomon and I with Esther. We often accompanied them in their daily rounds and participated with them in the household division of labor by sex. It was especially serendipitous for my interest in working with women that Esther was a prodigious collector of information about local events. Because of this, and also because her kitchen shed was near a major path to the point in the stream (and later the piped water system) where women went to get water, she was the node of a local neighborhood gossip network. I spent hours sitting in her smoky kitchen, which was a natural gathering place for women of our immediate vicinity. Solomon had an empty building in his compound when we arrived, and as our ménage also included Kipruto and Jebet, we built another one near it. We usually cooked and ate separately from Solomon and Esther, and Solomon's mother and sister each cooked separately for herself. Sharing a meal in one or another house in the compound was a frequent occurrence, though not the statistical norm. Solomon and Leon ate together particularly frequently, sometimes at Esther's house and sometimes at ours.

Once settled into a living situation, we began serious work. I tried to be cognizant from the beginning of possible feedback from gender roles into the process of gathering data. I had been told that a female researcher always has an advantage over a male researcher, particularly in the study of gender roles, because she stands a better chance of gaining access to both sexes. A male researcher is unambiguously coded as male; if he spends too much time with women, it can be perceived as a sexual threat by male members of many, if not most, societies. A female researcher is not sexually threatening in the same way, and because she has higher status than the average woman in a traditional community for other reasons (e.g., because she is a Westerner or highly educated), she is able to move to some extent toward the higher-status sex/gender role. It is said that a female researcher working alone can establish a somewhat androgynous gender identity and gain equal access to both sexes.

I was worried that having Leon participate fully in the research would limit the possibility of my attaining such androgyny and therefore limit my access to men; that is, I was afraid the men would be willing to talk only to him and not to me. Since I foresaw this problem, I took pains to avoid it. I always made sure to interview men and to establish my role as somebody who asked a lot of questions of everybody. I never had any trouble getting access to men for interviews or getting information from them on most topics. The information Leon could get from men on some topics (e.g., male initiation, sex, cattle lending, how to handle a wife) was undoubtedly richer than that which I could get. Because I was usually busy interviewing people, we decided that Leon should be the one to taperecord public meetings and local court cases. I'm still not sure this was a good decision; though it did mean that I could make more effective use of my time, his regular appearance at important gatherings reinforced his image as leader of the team and as our representative to the community at large.

Gradually Leon and I both became incorporated into same-sex peer groups. Within these groups we were both under pressure to conform to acceptable gender ascriptions, though this pressure probably fell more heavily on Leon than on me. I mainly had to refrain from grossly inappropriate behavior. The women, particularly the "progressive" ones, allowed me more latitude in my behavior because they were (sometimes consciously and sometimes not quite so) seeking a model for greater latitude in their own behavior. I wore knee-length skirts and shirts that covered my shoulders, as was appropriate for a married woman. It was considered risqué for a woman to wear trousers, though I would have liked to, especially on cold evenings. Esther and other women sometimes urged me to do so, looking for someone to set an example so that they could follow suit, but I was afraid to offend community norms. Occasionally I was asked by male acquaintances, when I told them that I was interested in learning about the roles of men and women, if I had come to "preach women's liberation" to their women. Hence, I didn't want to do anything to contribute to this impression. In my attempt to conform I mainly had only to practice the public reserve of a good Nandi wife.

Because of beliefs associated with the highly structured male age-set system—beliefs about masculinity in general and rules governing relations between members of different age sets—exactly what behavior Leon was supposed to conform to was somewhat clearer. He was always under pressure to behave properly as a man, even at unexpected times. For example, his first trip to the river to bathe was a crucial test. In a spirit of camaraderie, as same-sex communal bathing is customary, he was accompanied by a number of young men. Tagging along was an enormous group of curiosity-seeking children and younger adolescents. There were two questions of primary importance to which everyone wanted to know the answer. First: Was Leon circumcised? In Nandi, male initiation involving adolescent circumcision is the most crucial event in the male life cycle, without which adult identity, entry into the age-set system, and marriage are impossible. It is also viewed as an important ethnic boundary marker. (Female initiation with clitoridectomy is also practiced but is frequently rejected today by young, particularly educated women.) Fortunately Leon, a Jew by ancestry and rearing, passed the test. I believe that an uncircumcised husband would have made fieldwork in Nandi extremely difficult for me. Circumcision is such a powerful symbol that an uncircumcised male could probably not achieve a level of acceptance necessary for successful fieldwork.

The second important question was whether Leon would shiver. He passed this test as well. It seemed very curious that I was told repeatedly how good it was that he did not shiver in the cold water. When I began to inquire into cultural concepts of masculinity and femininity, one of my standard questions was: "Is there anything a man might do that could make you think that perhaps he is not fully a man?" An answer that always appeared along with responses that to me were more expected was, "Well, he might shiver in the cold." This was so strange that I was convinced it must have some deeper significance. Further inquiry revealed that shivering is considered symptomatic of a loss of manly qualities which might occur if a man is exposed to female/child pollution or is ensorcelled into weakness of will by his wife. Leon's passing the ordeal by not shivering in the cold water proved not only that he was manly but that I was not a sorceress. Thus our behavior, but especially Leon's, was constantly being monitored even in areas that seemed to us both trivial and meaningless. Much of our continued acceptance was probably due to plain good luck.

As time went on, Leon's efforts to conform to Nandi male behavior and to be accepted by the men became more conscious on his part. For example, there is a characteristic style of male oratory which involves standardized gestures with a walking stick. Leon studied the style and got a walking stick, which he carried around with him. And he practiced. Eventually there were occasions when he was called on to speak in meetings. Although his linguistic ability was halting, he used the stick brilliantly. The Nandi loved it.

Because the range of male solidarity was wider than that of female solidarity, community-wide rather than restricted to a local neighborhood, Leon's ties with men had a broader base than my ties with women. While I worked in the fields with female friends from our immediate vicinity or visited friends and acquaintances outside the vicinity on an individual and less frequent basis, Leon pitched in with all the men of the sublocation (or substantial numbers of them) in communal work projects such as dam building. Through such participation he also developed a personal friendship with the sublocation chief, which was very helpful to our research. The chief went out of his way to help us where he could—for example, by making a list of all the households in the community from which we could draw a random sample for a community census. Although I think the chief would have helped us anyway, his relationship with Leon made him even more willing to do so.

Leon's tremendous success in adjusting to Nandi male role expectations and in being accepted as a man within the community of men was an obvious source of pride and pleasure to him. He had been concerned that he would not be able to adjust to Nandi society. He had had difficulty with foreign languages in the classroom, and he feared that he would not be able to learn a language well enough to communicate with anyone, and would therefore be extremely isolated in the field. We were both adjusting well and enjoying the self-confidence that came with the realization that we could handle this situation. We were both building positive self-images out of our success in making the adjustment, and at the same time each of us felt growing admiration for the other's ability to cope. These positive feelings about ourselves and about each other had a concomitant positive impact on our relationship. In one sense we fell in love again in the field. Each of us discovered in the other a person who did not emerge under the normal conditions of our previous ordinary lives but did so only under the extraordinary conditions of the field—and each of us liked and admired the other's emerging persona. I had been told that couples who share field experiences either break up or become indissolubly committed to each other. Although this is undoubtedly an overstatement, I think there is some truth to it. Difficult conditions bring out the best—and the worst—in people.

As Leon and I chose to conform, in the main, to Nandi general sex role ascriptions, so we decided to conform publicly to Nandi expectations about the roles of husband and wife. In our marriage we have always divided domestic labor equally. However, cooking, washing dishes, housecleaning, laundry, and carrying water or firewood are tasks considered inappropriate for a man—particularly a married man—in Nandi. It would have damaged our image in the community if Leon had been seen doing these tasks publicly. We decided that I would do those chores that had to be done out of doors and publicly (e.g., carrying water, laundry) and Leon would reciprocate by doing an extra share of those chores done inside the house and thus concealed from the community at large (e.g., cooking, washing dishes, making the bed). Kipruto and Jebet also took turns with the cooking and dishwashing. Jebet and I carried the water, as Kipruto would have been embarrassed to be seen doing this, and later I hired a local woman to do laundry on a weekly basis, as the task was just too time-consuming.

The members of Solomon's household and some of our close associates knew the truth about our division of labor, which they felt was fair since we were all very busy with our work. However, we couldn't have "come out of the closet" about our household arrangement without creating more controversy than we felt it was worth. As an example, one night, about dusk, I wasn't feeling well, and we were almost out of water. (By this time there was a piped water system at the road not far from our house, and we had built a bathhouse.) Since Leon wanted to bathe, he decided to take a water container and try to get water for his bath while no one was looking. Unfortunately, an old woman came along the road while he was drawing the water and began to harangue him: "You can't do that! It's not proper behavior! Where is your wife?" Although she calmed down when Leon explained the circumstances, such incidents taught us that we could not deviate very far from the norm without creating a stir.

The temporary rearrangement of what we considered an equitable division of labor was not particularly stressful for us. What was difficult was accepting Nandi husband and wife role behavior in the area of maintaining proper relations of respect between husband and wife. I was not free to argue with Leon or to question his authority directly in anyone's presence, and there were few occasions when we were able to be alone inside our own house. This situation was very difficult for me, especially when he did something to make me angry. I tried to bite my tongue, but didn't always succeed, and I'm sure I earned a bad reputation in this regard.

Thus, we partly chose and partly were pressured into conforming to Nandi gender role expectations. This conformity often caused us to feel disgruntled and frustrated in view of our long-ingrained impulses, and it was sometimes difficult for us to achieve at all. For this reason we were interested to learn that some friends were approaching the same problem differently.

An Alternative Approach

While we were in Kenya, my friend Lorraine Dusak Sexton and her husband were in the field among the Yamiyufa, a Siane-speaking tribe in the Daulo Pass region of Papua New Guinea. Our situations were similar in many ways. Lorraine and I were both working in patrilineal, traditionally "tribal" societies now at similar levels of integration into a national cash economy; we were both concentrating our attention on sex/gender roles; and we were both accompanied in the field by our husbands. We decided to correspond both about our data and about the frustrations of fieldwork, hoping this would provide us with a comparative perspective to enrich our understanding of our own field situations, as well as help us to see the proverbial forest as well as the trees.

Early in our correspondence, I wrote to Lorraine: "We've made a tacit decision to present ourselves as a research team in which Leon and I have equal status, not as a team in which I am the principal investigator and he is the assistant. . . . This arrangement has its drawbacks. Presenting ourselves as 'equal' means, within the context of this culture, that Leon is automatically assumed to be the leading force in our partnership. Therefore, it is often to him rather than to me or even to both of us together, that people turn for decisions about what we will do or explanations of what we're about." Lorraine wrote back:

> George and I have presented ourselves to people differently than you and Leon. From the beginning, as we were visiting villages, I did most of the talking, because my command of tok pisin (pidgin) was better than George's, and because I knew what I was looking for in a place. I think I explained before how our preliminary visits tended to turn into public meetings—I'd ask most of the questions with George bringing up issues I'd forget or points that interested him. I always presented myself as the person who was doing the research—on the preliminary visits no one asked about George's and my respective roles and authority.
>
> When we selected Yamayo, we told people that George might be getting a job in Goroka, which is what we thought at the time. Gradually people began asking what George was doing, and we explained as

clearly as we could—my University has sent me here to learn about
their customs. We explained about George's previous work . . . in the
U.S. and that he was in P.N.G. because I was here. I'm not sure what
people think about this, but they seem to have accepted it easily. They
probably think it's a little odd, but they probably expect some differences anyway because we're Europeans. I don't think it's seriously affected George's stature in the community.

If anyone is looked on as the "leader" of the research project, it's me.
I'm the one who always has notebook in hand to write things down,
my tok pisin is still a little better, and I'm the only one who's been
talking about learning a little tok ples (local language). When something's happening, we're both invited, but by now I think that people
realize that I'm more likely to attend. George comes to most events, but
he usually leaves before I do. I'm amazed at his tolerance—some events
are all day affairs broken up by hours of waiting around. At these times,
I see my life slipping away before me as I cook in the equatorial sun.

George doesn't take notes or do interviews for me, although I think
he'll help me when I start my labor input studies and when I start mapping gardens. We've talked about his doing interviews with me when I
start to do open-ended interviews around next August or September.

As I became frustrated over not being clearly defined as the head of
the research team, I sometimes wished I could start over again and
stand firm on this issue as Lorraine had done. However, for reasons
I've explained already, I'm not sure it was even possible to do this in
the Nandi context. My unassuming behavior as team leader was not,
after all, damaging the data-gathering aspects of my research.

More difficult for me was always acting like a good, subordinate
Nandi wife.

. . .[acting like a Nandi wife] means that I have to act subordinate and
I'm not supposed to argue with Leon, or give him advice, or contradict
him in any way. At first, we carried out a public charade and laughed
about it when we were alone. But it's really getting wearing to me, especially since male friends of Leon may be around quite a lot of the
time. I thought it might be possible to let a few of our closest friends,
who are quite accepting of our quirks as Europeans, see what our relationship is actually like, with all its give-and-take. But the few times
I've attempted insubordination, even in the presence of Solomon, for
example, or Kipkemei, it's been clear that they disapprove. Even Kipruto, who lives with us all the time, gets visibly annoyed if I argue with
Leon. I try to tone down any annoyance with Leon that I may feel, but
it's really difficult.

Lorraine and George had a different experience from ours in conforming to local expectations about husband and wife behavior.

I'm curious to know what people think of our household division of labor. George does most of the maintenance work, freeing me to hang around with people and write up notes. I usually cook dinner. George also takes care of the car maintenance (we have a lemon) and goes to town for supplies by himself sometimes. We decided that we weren't going to apologize for our way of doing things—*pasin bilong mitupela tasol* (just our custom). One of the local leaders told us that he liked the way we talked to each other, asking each other to do things instead of commanding the wife to do something. Of course, he hasn't changed his behavior as a result of our example. N., our best friend, walked in one morning when we were screaming at each other, clearing up the misapprehension that we are the 'perfect' couple. . . .

. . . we've taken a conscious stance that we will continue to do certain things our own way, such as sharing our domestic chores according to our wishes. We respect their customs and want to learn about them; they, as our friends, will have to respect our customs and learn about us, too. I firmly believe that it's a two way street to a certain extent. I think our goal as anthropologists is to "know," not to "be."

I admired the Sextons' stance on this issue and felt that I agreed with it in principle, but still it did not seem to be one that we could adopt in Nandi. For one thing, there seemed to be more congruence between what can go on between an American husband and wife and a Yamiyufan husband and wife than between Nandi and American husband/wife behavior. It was acceptable, for example, for Lorraine to shout and argue back, as a Yamiyufan woman might do the same. Also, there is a difference between Yamiyufa and Nandi in their general attitudes toward deviance. As Lorraine described it: "Yamiyufans don't demand a great deal of conformity from us nor, I'm fairly sure, from each other. One of the frustrations of fieldwork, which is also indicative of the tenor of this society, is the pidgin phrase '*em laik bilong em, tasol.*' That's what s/he wanted to do, it's his/her business. A double-edged statement: people can do what they want to do; it's nobody else's business. Don't mean to imply that there aren't rules, but there is a good deal of latitude in how you go about complying with them." I responded: "In Nandi, being polite (*ketalait*) and being rude (*kingelel*) are two very important semantic categories. . . . It seems to me that the usual response of a Nandi to a violation of a norm depends very much on his/her general feeling towards the person involved. If it is negative, the explanation for the behavior is that 'that is a very rude person.' If it is positive, the behavior will be reinterpreted in such a way that it doesn't really constitute a violation of a norm. The response, in short, is either condemnation or rationalization—but *not* dismissal as 'none of my business.'"

Leon and I were required to conform to Nandi norms of behavior far more than Lorraine and George seemed to have been required to conform to Yamiyufa norms. Yet there was another factor involved in our decision to behave as Nandi—an attempt to disassociate ourselves from a well-established, negative image of Europeans.

> . . . acting like Nandis means . . . *not* acting like *wazungu* (whites). Remember that the only model people around here have for what white people are normally expected to act like is a colonial one. The racist aspects of colonialism were probably more clearcut here in Kenya than almost anywhere else, because it was a settler colony. . . . The oldest people here saw their land taken away and given to Europeans. People were forced to go to work in European-owned tea estates to pay taxes. All but the youngest people learned a set of rules for interaction with Europeans which required them to behave in the most demeaningly subservient way. . . . Because this is such a rich, fertile area, it was areas near to here that were set aside for European settlement. So the Nandi were on very familiar terms with the white settler brand of colonialism. We want specifically to dissociate ourselves from behaviors they associate with this type of European.

It pleased us when people would comment to us, with approval, that we acted just like Nandis because this implied that they viewed us as unlike the Europeans they had previously encountered.

Mostly, our attempts to conform to Nandi expectations about husband/wife behavior were an elaborate exercise in role playing, although we did internalize some norms: "I do really feel like I've internalized the rules for proxemic behavior between husband and wife. Remember that from a Nandi point of view, if Leon and I were to openly display affection by embracing, holding hands, or whatever in public, it would hardly be less scandalous than having sexual intercourse on the street in Philadelphia. Could you bring yourself, from whatever conscious motive, to have sexual intercourse in public? At this point, the idea of embracing Leon publicly is almost equally repugnant to me. . . ." Even after we returned to the United States, we found that it was difficult for us to touch each other in public situations. For a time after our return, this was a source of strain in our relationship, a problem we had to work consciously to correct.

Sometimes I felt we were being dishonest about the way we presented our relationship. Certainly, too, it would have been less stressful for us personally not to have to live a charade. At the time, these considerations seemed to be counterbalanced by my belief that our status as pseudo-Nandis in the eyes of our informants created a rapport which made it possible for us to enter situations and obtain information that might otherwise have been inaccessible to us. This belief now seems questionable in view of the fact that the Sextons made little or no attempt to conform to Yamiyufa stereotypes about appropriate husband/wife role behavior yet did not damage the richness and quality of Lorraine's ethnographic data or limit her access to the range of possible social situations. However, Nandi is not Yamiyufa. Appropriate behavior between husband and wife is the key to Nandi thinking about gender roles. Nonconformity to cultural norms is not simply dismissed and we were strangers in the community with no previous reputation to fall back on. Could we have defined our roles as husband and wife substantially differently? On final reflection I think not, though of course I can never know for sure. Different approaches are appropriate to different societies, and each ethnographer must grope her/his own way toward appropriate behavior in her/his own particular situation.

Changing Gender-related Roles

One of the personally most difficult things Leon and I both had to deal with in the field, independent of the fieldwork process itself, were the deaths of several people close to us. We were struck with a sudden realization of our own mortality and an impatience to get on with life, to stop delaying all the other things we had put off in favor of graduate study. I had a year of support from my grant after we returned to the United States, and then I would seek employment. We wanted children, but in our life plan there seemed to be no right time to start a family. The present seemed as good a time as any we could foresee, so six months before our scheduled departure from the field we took the biggest step of our lives together: we gave up the prevention of pregnancy, with immediate results. The potential danger of pregnancy in an isolated rural setting somehow did not occur to us. In retrospect, I think that my own ideas about this subject had taken on a Nandi (or generalized rural African) cast. Pregnancy and childbirth are such day-to-day occurrences in a traditional community that I had come to accept them very much as a matter of course. Pregnancy seemed to be the normal state for a young, healthy woman.

My pregnancy had a mixed impact on the course of the research. The first trimester was physically draining. The pace at which I could track down people and interview them necessarily slackened. I tried to channel most of my energy into my work, and as a result I sometimes dropped into bed in the evening without having eaten dinner. We were involved in an ongoing time-allocation study that involved observing the activities of the members of selected households at randomly selected times. Sometimes, in the case of the most distant of the study households, that meant getting up at 5:30 A.M., which was just too much for me to manage in those early months of pregnancy. Leon diligently took up the slack in this area of research, as well as taking over more of the household work. He was wonderfully considerate, so much so, in fact, that this was the only time he received outright approbation for participating in domestic work. Some of my female friends commented to me privately that it was good that he was now helping me and that they wished their husbands would do likewise. "To be pregnant is very hard work," I was told. "Men do not realize that."

Esther recognized my symptoms even before I did, and she was not one to be reticent about spreading good news. She had known I was using birth control, though most people probably thought I was barren. As news of my pregnancy made the rounds, a remarkable thing happened: my rapport with the women, which I already thought was quite good, took a sudden, dramatic turn for the better. In people's minds I had moved from the category "probably barren woman" to "childbearing woman," similar to a change of gender. Young married women of childbearing age, those who were most likely to be part of the group at Esther's kitchen, were suddenly much more at ease with me and began to treat me fully as one of them. Many more confidences and jokes were directed my way. They were not only willing but now were actually eager to talk with me about children, pregnancy, childbirth, motherhood. Everyone we knew was joyous—no other word can describe it—over our change in status. Men who had been urging Leon to take a second wife no longer did so. As my pregnancy became more visible, all the old people in our social network stopped by regularly to spit on their hands and rub them on my swelling abdomen as a blessing.

I heard through the academic grapevine that someone I knew had become pregnant before leaving for the field and that certain members of her department had commented that she could not possibly be pregnant and give birth in the field and still do reasonably good fieldwork. I wrote to Lorraine:

> All this leads me to wonder what people are saying about my pregnancy. After all, any of the same arguments could be applied to me. How can you be pregnant in the field and do decent fieldwork? And it's true that I did lose time from work due to illness in the early part of pregnancy, and I'd have got a lot more done if I hadn't been pregnant.

But I'm working extra hard now to make up for it. I think my fieldwork will be good, and better than that of many people who've had no such impediments as pregnancy. . . .

Undoubtedly, a kid is an impediment to whatever one might be doing professionally. On the other hand, when, really, is a *better* time in the life of an academic anthropologist? When you're trying to write your dissertation? When you're looking for a job? When you're working full-time with a possibly inflexible schedule? When you're established and have finally got the perfect situation and are forty years old?[1]

Departure

As my pregnancy advanced, the end of our time in the field drew closer. I planned to have the baby in Philadelphia, yet it was difficult for us to face the thought of leaving Nandi. Solomon's family had become like true kin to us, and we knew the relationship was permanent. For one thing, we had become cattle owners in Nandi. Solomon's family set up a small formal gathering in which they gave us one of their heifers, "to be a link between our two families forever," and we had bought another. I explained at the time:

We are going to buy a cow and leave it in Solomon's herd forever. One of the reasons for this is that people frequently tell Leon that he should own a cow—it is not good for a man to have not even one animal. It is common for men to spread their cattle around among relatives and friends. In the past, this was a form of protection against having your entire fortune disappear in one raid. But it was also, and still is, a way of cementing social bonds. Getting a cow and leaving it with Solomon will mean that we will have a permanent tie to the community, that there will be a permanent bond between Leon and Solomon, and, if our cow reproduces, we will have other cows to give as presents, for example, as contributions to bridewealth payments. . . .

Our last weeks in the field were seemingly a constant round of farewell gatherings, including one set up by the newly active local women's association. The women gave me a beautifully worked beaded hat of the type used by female initiates during the 1950s and 1960s, which they said was a "true symbol of Nandi womanhood"; Leon received a male authority stick from the men. Speeches were made to the effect that we would always have a home in the community because we had shown ourselves to be worthy of the status of Nandis.

We have not returned to Kenya yet, but we keep in constant contact by mail with our Nandi friends. We also have done some fundraising for a special project sponsored by the women's association.

We now have two daughters, and they both have Nandi names in addition to their English names; and the eldest has even learned a few simple Nandi phrases. There is no question that when we do return we will be welcomed as long-absent kin. I feel that the degree of rapport we had, and which we continue to maintain with our research community, is remarkable. Much of this was due to Leon's participation in the fieldwork process and to our decision to behave as good Nandis. On balance, though we made mistakes, I don't think these two basic decisions can be counted as such.

Spouses in the Field: General Considerations

What generalizations can be drawn from our experiences as an anthropologist and husband team in the field? Many of the benefits and problems of being in the field with a spouse are the same whether the spouse is male or female. A fieldworker accompanied by a spouse escapes the awful loneliness and total isolation that lone fieldworkers often experience. Although my field experience was at times difficult, because I had someone to share it with I did not feel the kind of acute suffering that I have often heard described as the almost inevitable fate of the fieldworker. Having someone to talk to about things that we observe and experience often results in more than an idiosyncratic perspective on these events. In a sense, however, the researcher accompanied by a spouse may learn less than a lone researcher because there is a temptation to use the relationship to isolate oneself from total immersion in the field culture. This can be a major drawback, particularly in the area of language. If the researcher has someone with whom to speak his/her native language, fluency in the local language may not come as quickly as it might if the researcher were required to converse in the local language or not at all.

It seems to me that there are several broad questions relevant to the issue of being in the field with a spouse, particularly a husband. First, what should be the role of the anthropologist's spouse in the field situation? The answer, of course, depends on personal interest. Is the spouse mainly there to keep the researcher company, or does he/she have an independent interest in the cross-cultural experience? Would he/she want to do something similar if not married to an anthropologist? There is no reason why a spouse cannot be a formal participant in the data-gathering process if he/she is so inclined. The additional data thus gained can be extremely valuable, especially if the spouse has some social science training and experience. Having a fieldworker of each sex creates automatic access to both sexes in situations where it is often difficult for a male researcher to speak (or speak intimately) with women, and vice versa. I am certain that because of Leon's participation in the research I ended up with much more material than I could have obtained had I worked alone. However, I also think that Leon, because of personal inclination, did better as a co-researcher than would those spouses who are not themselves social scientists.

Second, does it make a difference if the spouse is male or female? In the broadest sense, no. There is no intrinsic reason why the value to a male researcher of his wife's participation and the value to a female researcher of her husband's participation should not be equal. Since, as noted above, a male researcher can be sexually threatening and thus have more restricted access to female informants than a female researcher has to male informants, a woman— whether researcher or spouse—is a particular asset in the field. There is a long tradition in our discipline of wives functioning as unacknowledged research assistants. Yet, because many cultures lean ideologically toward male dominance, some special care must be taken in the case in which the nonanthropologist spouse is male. As I have noted, the female anthropologist must guard against the loss of potential to define her gender identity somewhat androgynously. I believe that I successfully avoided this pitfall, though not entirely, mainly because I was continually conscious of it. It was certainly there in the Nandi field setting, waiting to trap the unwary.

Third, how should the spouse's role in the research project be presented? This question probably creates much less difficulty in the case in which the spouse is female. The ubiquitousness of male dominance[2] creates a problem around the issue of "who's in charge," especially for an anthropologist and husband team. While the researcher understandably wants people to know clearly who the principal investigator is, if the spouse is working equally hard on the research, is it fair not to present him/her as an equal colleague? In a male-dominated culture this can create a problem for the female anthropologist, whose role as principal investigator may be overlooked even though attempts are made to make that role clear. This was a continual problem in our case, one that not only arose in personal interactions in the field but was exacerbated by the requirements of the host government. A presentation in which the husband, while participating in the research, was clearly the subordinate member of the team would have been untenable in Nandi, as I am sure it would be in a great many cultures.

Fourth, how should the couple's roles and relationship as husband and wife be presented? In general, there are two competing imperatives of fieldwork that enter into the resolution of this question: (1) be honest about yourselves with your informants; and (2) avoid radical deviation from community norms that might seriously impair rapport and interfere with the conduct of the research. These imperatives can sometimes become contradictory if the fieldworker senses that what he/she perceives as an honest self-presentation would bring a response of shocked disapproval from the community. One must feel one's way, attempting to be sensitive to the values of the particular culture, negotiating a path between these two imperatives which incorporates each to the greatest degree possible. Some of the questions that enter into this negotiation include: Are husband and wife roles relatively rigid in this culture or not? Is this an area of great salience and concern to people? How tolerant is the culture of deviance in general? And, on a somewhat different note, how will you feel and how much tension will be generated between you and your spouse if you try to behave in accordance with the culture's norms rather than your own? Even where conformity would clearly benefit the course of the research, the personal psychological costs may be too great. In Nandi, Leon and I faced a situation where wives who are too assertive relative to their husbands, or those who exercise too obvious domestic power, are suspected of having ensorcelled their husbands to make them weak-willed. Both parties in such a relationship suffer a social stigma. Further, unlike the situation the Sextons found in their field site, the general Nandi response to deviance is not to dismiss it as "none of my business." People acquire cumulative reputations which are extremely important for their social standing. Thus, we did not feel free to be too open about the egalitarian nature of our relationship. This did create a lot of strain for us personally, particularly for me, and I frequently wondered if the cost was too high or if there were some way we could go about defining our relationship differently without sacrificing our reputations.

While the fieldworker must be careful not to deviate too far from community norms, there are also problems with too much conformity. Golde (1970:9) summed up this consideration: ". . . the greater the extent to which the anthropologist can remain outside the existing system of roles and expectations, the freer she will be to pursue her own goals; to the extent that she attempts to conform to a structural role . . . she becomes more constrained." It is necessary to balance the benefits for efficient conduct of the research, of being able to do what needs to be done without worrying about the constraint of acting like a good wife as defined by the culture, against the benefits derived from improved rapport if informants perceive you as essentially the same as themselves.

The contrast between our experiences and those of the Sextons shows clearly that there is more than one set of workable answers to the questions posed above. Whichever path is chosen, however, our experiences do show that the situation of being an anthropologist in the field with a nonanthropologist husband can work—and not only that, but make an irreplaceable contribution to the success of the research as well. Viewing anthropological fieldwork as merely another job often helps the fieldworker keep things in perspective and get on with the work at hand. It is undeniable, however, that successful fieldwork is also a peak life experience, a time of sensual bombardment with new stimuli, of incredible intellectual excitement, of self-discovery. It is an adventure which is a joy to share with a loved and respected partner.

Notes

Most of this article is based on fieldwork in Nandi District, Kenya, during 1976 and 1977. My special thanks to Lorraine Dusak Sexton for allowing me to use her correspondence. I wish to express thanks also to the National Institute for Mental Health, the National Science Foundation, and the Woodrow Wilson National Fellowship Foundation, for financing the research with predoctoral training grants and fellowships. I am grateful to Denise O'Brien, Cathy Small, Diane Freedman, and Debbie Kane, who read and commented on an earlier draft of this paper. All personal names of Nandi friends and associates have been fictionalized to ensure their anonymity.

1. After reading the preceding section, several friends and colleagues commented to me that it reflects my own unjustified feeling that I had to rationalize my decision to become pregnant. This feeling stems from the basically antifeminist notion that bearing and rearing children are necessarily antithetical to career interests, that one can be a mother or a career scholar but not both. I accept this criticism as valid; it is an issue over which I still feel conflict, especially now, eight years and two children later, as I struggle to prove pragmatically in my own life that it can be otherwise.

2. This is not the appropriate forum to address how nearly universal the phenomenon of male dominance is (but see, e.g., Bacdayan 1977; Begler 1978; Parker and Parker 1979; Poewe 1980; Sanday 1981). Suffice it to say that I believe, at least, that a strong case can be made for the proposition that the large majority of world societies are characterized by some type or degree of male dominance.

References

Bacdayan, Albert S.
  1977 "Mechanistic Cooperation and Sexual Equality among the Western

Bontoc." In: Alice Schlegel (ed.), *Sexual Stratification: A Cross-Cultural View*, pp. 270–91. New York: Columbia University Press.

Begler, Elsie B.
    1978   "Sex, Status and Authority in Egalitarian Society." *American Anthropologist* 80:571–88.

Golde, Peggy
    1970   "Introduction." In: Peggy Golde (ed.), *Women in the Field: Anthropological Experiences*, pp. 1–18. Chicago: Aldine.

Oboler, Regina Smith
    1985   *Women, Power and Economic Change: The Nandi of Kenya*. Stanford: Stanford University Press.

———, and Leon Oboler.
    1977   "Mothers and Daughters in a Blue Collar Neighborhood in Urban America." In: Jack R. Censer and N. Steven Steinert (eds.), *South Atlantic Urban Studies*, vol. 1, pp. 170–97. Greenville: University of South Carolina Press.

Parker, Seymour, and Hilda Parker
    1979   "The Myth of Male Superiority: Rise and Demise." *American Anthropologist* 81:289–309.

Poewe, Karla
    1980   "Universal Male Dominance: An Ethnological Illusion." *Dialectical Anthropology* 5:111–25.

Sanday, Peggy Reeves
    1981   *Female Power and Male Dominance: On the Origins of Sexual Inequality*. Cambridge: Cambridge University Press.

3

The Pretense of the Neutral Researcher

MARY ELLEN CONAWAY

Indifferent about gender, without judgment on cultural content, free of prejudice, the ideal, the neutral researcher—there used to be such a person in our mind's eye, in our ethnographies and our seminars. As an undergraduate in the early 1960s, I was fascinated with the prospect of study in another culture. Both women and men studied for and practiced fieldwork, and these exercises seemed to carry them outside the common categories of gender- and sex-defined behavior. Whereas men became doctors, dentists, and lawyers, and women were nurses, hygienists, and legal secretaries, anyone could be, potentially, an anthropologist. Well-known women, Margaret Mead in particular, had done field research just as men had. To travel to a far-off, "exotic" place, live with the "natives," endure local housing and food customs, and collect data were but a test of the power of knowledge and scientific method over cultural norms, over personal preference or prejudice. Social scientists were above or outside the usual cultural constraints when they did research. The image of the neutral researcher included the nuclear scientists and engineers who argued their right to create, develop, and go in any research direction without moralizing about the probable result of their work. They were also outside the bounds of the usual cultural conventions. Just because they created something like a nuclear bomb was no reason to make them morally responsible for how politicians might use it.

Anthropologists were no different. Courses in field methods focused on unbiased data collection, on neutrality in the cultural laboratory, as field sites were often called. Two means anthropologists have used for establishing an image of neutralization—or more precisely, a nonthreatening role—are adoption into an indigenous kin unit and pretending to have no gender, or at least no gender constraints. How many dozens of ethnographies tell us of the life cycle—birth to death—of a certain people? And from how many of these can we determine, for certain, that the ethnographer saw a birth, observed rites of passage, mourned with a widow? We've all pretended that the influences of our sex and our gender can be substituted for by talking to the right informant.

Thus entranced by anthropology, and desirous of being a good student, I had no felt need to reconcile the ideal image of the neutral researcher with personal experience and logical deductions. When I began graduate studies in the late 1960s, I read dozens of books and articles on field methods, ethics, and general field experiences. Some women anthropologists indicated that gender boundaries have directed aspects of their work, but how they handled these restrictions was given only the slightest description (Wax 1971; Powdermaker 1966). Older women on college faculties who had done field research in anthropology continued to tell me that being female makes no difference when doing fieldwork. In seminars, faculty men sometimes mentioned peripherally the presence of their spouses at their research sites or boastfully, or with nervous laughter, a sexual interaction or confrontation. Yet I never heard in any course, in any seminar, an acknowledgment that who we are sexually and what our gender norms are have definite impacts on data collection. That I should reconcile the "scientific" approach—the pretense of the neutral researcher—with my own data-collection experiences was a postponed exercise.

By the time of my departure for a year in Venezuela, I felt prepared for difficult field conditions, research orientation, note taking in an alien language, and all the other realities that graduate studies are said to prepare one for. Still uneasy that something was missing in my training, I asked several advisors on the university staff about interpersonal relations with local people. "Don't marry one" and "take birth control pills" were their responses. We were to maintain the pretense.

Field Site

Prior to arriving in Venezuela, I established contact with a Venezuelan anthropologist who extended herself in a collegial manner beyond my expectations. With her guidance I was able to meet government requirements for fieldwork and establish field site living quarters within two weeks of my arrival.

The field site, Puerto Ayacucho, capital of the Federal Amazon Territory, has the environmental characteristics of both a savannah and a tropical forest. The surrounding region is geographically marginal because it is on the lower edges of the *llanos* and the upper edges of the tropical forest in an economically unproductive and sparsely populated area. The term *marginality* also describes the sociocultural system with limited integration of groups, individuals, and places into the national scene. Puerto Ayacucho is peripheral to national events, a genuine frontier town that depends on the sustaining influx of government monies rather than on local production and export; on indigenous-produced foods rather than factory-prepared ones; and on the lure of frontier challenges. Its residents, nearly all recent migrants (all but the very young and the native Americans), experience the limitations and languidness, the excitement and opportunities that life on a frontier evinces. The town population was around 10,000 in 1974, composed of native American groups, criollos,[1] Lebanese, Syrians, Brazilians, Colombians, North Americans, and others. The major language is Spanish.

I lived in a brick house with internal plumbing in the older, main section of town. The indigenous group I chose to work with, the Guahibo, were recent circular migrants (Conaway 1984) living on the outskirts of the town. Only three of the more than eighty indigenous settlements had water spigots in or near their dwellings; two of those also had outhouses, and one had a concrete floor. Thus, my daily activities found me interacting in the cultural environments of both a town criollo setting and a peripheral indigenous one.

Criollo and Indigenous Gender Roles

The criollo view of gender roles is tempered by the frontier circumstances, including a standard of living that requires women to contribute substantially to the household income. A double standard for women and men is the accepted ideal, however. Criollo women are appropriately escorted at night or travel in twosomes. Young women and men should not be familiar in public, but men may shout obscene comments at women and make invitations. Men pay for entertainment and food. To be appropriately feminine, women wear a lot of makeup, very tight pants and blouses, and protect themselves from the sun. Associations between nonrelated adults are discussed as possible sexual liaisons. Town gossip usually includes the latest tryst, the participants' eventual (and appropriate) repentance, and reconciliation with a spouse. Both women and men drink publicly, though more men than women are found in sidewalk taverns during daylight hours. Women maintain the household by cleaning, cooking, taking care of the children, and engaging in small-scale economic activities such as making meat-vegetable pies for sale at the market and during holidays, or taking in laundry. When men are not employed, which is rather frequently, they sit around town in front of the shops and in the plazas, talking and resting.

The indigenous view of gender roles shares some similarities with the criollo view—that is, economic circumstances dictate cooperation between women and men. The Guahibo, who number over 4,000 on the Venezuelan side of the Orinoco River, practice some hunting, gathering, and fishing. They are also horticulturalists, and some of them have recently adopted Western agricultural methods and crops. Both women and men travel freely. The families I knew best held discussions and reached a consensus about their economic and social plans. Women have the primary responsibility for child care and food preparation, but I saw men care for children by seeing to their toilet needs and by feeding them and playing with them. Men have primary responsibility for constructing shelters and for heavy garden work. Guahibo enjoy hearing about sexual liaisons, especially among young people, as long as particular kinship and religious beliefs are respected. Above all, they feel that a person should not be alone and that a variety of male and female relationships are to be expected.

The Guahibo have a delightful sense of humor which extends to gender roles and more than once saved me from awkward situations. In one such instance, early in my field research, I was mapping and identifying house types and had discovered specific areas of indigenous concentration. In the course of this work I met a Guahibo man, around sixty years of age, who delighted in sharing with me his life story and the history of the region. His wife had died a year earlier and he had resolved to live in town permanently. He offered to introduce me to "all the Guahibo" in town. I departed ebullient—my first informant! After our third session, when I rose to depart, he extended his slight, four-foot-ten-inch frame and, quick as lightning, rubbed his nose across my clavical. I left disturbed. Future quick movement on my part prevented repetition of his affectionate behavior, but he tried other tactics. My distress was alleviated by the Guahibo who were entertained by the man's behavior. They laughed, teased, and joked about him, and thought me tolerant, if not overly so, of his hopes for a new wife.

I found gender role expectations among the criollo more confining because they take them more seriously than the Guahibo do. Refusing to accept a ride from a male criollo would be taken both as an affront to maleness, to his perceived male power and control, and a denial of female weakness, namely, the need for protection from the sun and from undue stress. Some of these criollo boundaries of appropriate behavior impinged on my definition of self as an independent person willing to work to support my goals. For example, during the entire year of my town residence I was asked repeatedly where my male guardian was. Since I was unmarried and my father and brothers were in the United States, the criollo wondered who was looking after me. How could I survive without being cared for? As a result, I received sympathetic marriage proposals from men who desired to "look after me."

After a few weeks of coping with this situation, I found such inquiries and expectations routine. With criollo and indigenous gender roles and my own cultural baggage in tow, I developed a behavior pattern I thought was ambiguously feminine, almost like a mythological-style powerful person, a testimony to neutrality. I looked like a female but did not behave like local females. Since my research design did not require me to become an *integral* part of either the criollo or Guahibo social structures, I developed and maintained my fieldwork self-image. This behavior, however, evolved and became pronounced not only in the context of the townspeople and surrounding inhabitants, but also because of the living arrangements I had made.

The Glitch

Prior to selecting a living site in their research area, anthropologists have been advised to consider political circumstances, including kinship ties and power structure, location and condition. Yet the overriding influence is often the availability of housing. According to Wax (1971:7), "the scarcity of housing is one of the most difficult (and least discussed) practical problems in participant observation," and once living quarters are established, attempts to change them require delicate handling. She argued that "most field experiences that involve living with or close to the host people fall into three stages." The first is one of "initiation or resocialization, when the fieldworker tries to involve himself in the kinds of relationships which will enable him to do his fieldwork—the period during which he and his hosts work out or develop the kinds and varieties of roles which he and they will play" (1971:16).

Such cautions rang in my head as I agreed to share a house with a woman in the Peace Corps who had been in Puerto Ayacucho for a month. She assured me that she had rented the last vacant house, and indeed she had. She also had obtained a small table and three plastic chairs, a refrigerator, a small wash basin, and a window screen; and she even had the shower nozzle moved from over the toilet to over the floor, a costly project. The house had two small rooms, two larger rooms, and small bath and kitchen areas—big enough, I thought to myself. My roommate, whom I shall call Virginia, had requested to work with indigenous people as her Peace Corps assignment. A Venezuelan anthropologist welcomed the possibility of research assistance and assigned a series of readings to Virginia during the first few months of her service in Caracas.

The impact of my living arrangements with Virginia permeated my personal life and my work. I had never before known anyone like her and was temporarily blind to her character. The acquaintance lasted two and a half months before I admitted to myself that her relationship with the community was unusual and disruptive. I was uncertain about what to do and so continued to share the house for another month.

In truth, I couldn't walk on the street with Virginia without hearing poetic or lewd remarks in reference to her blond hair or braless-ness. Groups of men serenaded at our window at 3:00 A.M. and afterward entered our house to drink beer and talk with Virginia. On other days, from 8:00 A.M. on one man or another would come to the house—Samuel to study English, Antonio to talk about anthropology, José to discuss a plane trip. Often, too, these visitors remained from late evening until early morning. Antonio liked to stay all night and use my toothbrush before bedtime. Often and publicly, Virginia had broken through the boundaries of locally accepted gender and sexual behavior. Her clothing and actions ceased to be seen as cute and appropriate for a young, attractive woman when married men called on her, or when single men brought household goods with the expectation of marrying her, or when she openly slept with a man in a hammock at a local recreational water hole which families frequented.

Although I functioned well within local gender boundaries, doubts about my intentions were evident in the criollo community. After all, I lived with Virginia, many men had entered and left our house at all hours of the day and night, and for the first six weeks of my stay we were frequently seen together. I had to work at establishing an identity distinct from Virginia's. Fortunately, the Guahibo saw little of her, so I worked among them with ease. But when I walked through town on a mapping project or to reach a peripheral town location, some criollo man or another would occasionally shout an obscenity or make a derisive remark. The younger men who sought Virginia's company frequently stopped me in the street to inquire about her.

Since Virginia told everyone she was an anthropologist on a research assignment, I expressed to my Venezuelan colleague, my graduate advisor, and two of the government employees who contributed substantially to my data collection, my concern about the effects of this deception on future anthropological research and also my concern about the image being presented of foreign researchers and American women abroad. United States citizens had not only just lost the war in Vietnam but were increasingly being told that they were not welcome in other countries to conduct research. The two Venezuelan men responded that people in the community did not equate Virginia's behavior with mine, but not all community behavior verified their judgment. My female Venezuelan colleague opined that the young men's behavior with Virginia was unusual for Venezuelan men, atypical in her experience. My graduate advisor (male), said, in essence, "Latin boys will be boys."

My data collection was influenced by the situation in that I delayed interviewing the leading criollo male entrepreneurs who were also the richest and highest-status people in town. I didn't know if I could face them, if they would say "no interview" or else assume that I had come for other than research purposes. However, since they hired more native Americans than other employers in town, information about their enterprises—the number of persons they employed, when they employed indigenous people, what they paid them, and their attitudes toward them—were very pertinent to my study. After several months' delay, I memorized the twelve questions on my two-page interview form and made appointments with these men. I got very specific information but no more; the men's posture, gestures, and tones of voice indicated a nervousness, even an irritation at my presence. I asked the questions as fast as I could before being ushered out, for they were all "busy." The final interview (thank heaven it was the final one or I would have lost my nerve and not continued) was cut short, never to be completed because the informant was "too busy." Although I also needed government statistics and information on development plans and political attitudes, since the territorial government was in a state of flux, my contacts with male government employees were often treated as invitations to a rendezvous, or else my inquiries were considered "cute." More than once I was sent on a wild goose chase for departmental heads or field representatives of some agency who had "just the information" I wanted.

Because of my precarious situation I never collected data at night. Instead I used that time to write up notes, correspond, read, and prepare for the next day's work—anything but face the body grabbing and the belittling comments that flowed from some people's mouths as heavily as the liquor was poured and with meanings as shallow as the Orinoco River waters. The afternoons before holidays and Friday afternoons found criollo and indigenous men alike stumbling the streets, grabbing at me to "sit and listen," to "understand," through the drivel, belches, and farts. Personally I churned inside. I demanded that Virginia put a stop to the early morning serenading, but the stream of male visitors continued. Attempts were made by Virginia and her male friends to "find a man" for me, under the false assumption that I would prefer daily "diversions" to field research.

After three and a half months Virginia was transferred back to Caracas. Over the next couple of months fewer and fewer of her male coterie dropped by the house or stopped me on the street to inquire if she had returned. My work picked up substantially, and the number of remarks by strangers on the street about my appearance or gender decreased. The effects of Virginia's behavior were long-term, however, as I would soon discover.

Nearly every Saturday morning I went to the market areas where government trucks brought in indigenous people and their products. About 6:30 one morning, after nine months in the field, an assistant to the territorial governor staggered toward me after an all-night drunk. How much did I want, he asked. I replied quietly, so as not to embarrass him, that I was not interested, and then I eased into the crowd. The market activities gained momentum and made it relatively easy for me to duck into groups to avoid repeated attempts by the assistant to approach me. Twice I got cornered, however, and the price he was willing to pay for my services went from twenty to forty dollars. Around 9:00 A.M., out in the open market area, the man lurched at me yet again, his reflexes slowed by the liquor he had drunk. I pulled back, protecting my camera from the sticky ice cream he was holding. Loudly he asked, "How much do you want? Eighty dollars?" This time I replied in a regular tone of voice, "I'm not interested. Leave me alone." "You don't understand," he responded. "Virginia understood." I responded in anger, "I'm not Virginia!" Those criollo who heard the exchange smiled. I had made my point well, and publicly. Emotionally drained, I went home and slept for two hours. The event, though most unpleasant, marked a change in community perceptions of me. Communications thereafter seemed to be easier.

Resolution

My response to this entire situation was slow in coming. I feared my research goals might be in jeopardy and that I might be unable to collect sufficient and satisfactory data to complete my project. These fears indicated the tensions and frustration I was experiencing, common in fieldwork but exacerbated in my case. With no real role model and no ready advice on the gender and sex aspects of my field situation from faculty advisors, colleagues, or peers, my strategy became twofold: to appear less feminine by local standards—and therefore less "available"—and to work endlessly on my research.

Hindsight has made me realize that my less feminine, supposedly more neutral image served as a mask, one that had some, but little, effect. To the populace in the town I was still a female and much too young to be genderless, as old women are considered. I wore odd-looking, loose-fitting clothing, no makeup, and flat-soled shoes. I approached social interaction among criollos with caution, accepting invitations to "diversions" only when they involved several people, but not female-male pairing. I paid for supplies and services rather than accept them as signs of friendship, as invitations, or as exchanges requiring reciprocity. I walked two to five miles a day visiting informants, mapping the town barrios, and observing indigenous behavior rather than accept transportation with men who had known Virginia. I refrained from the pleasure of a late afternoon beer in a tavern and did not permit my indigenous informants to visit me at my house, although several asked repeatedly to see how I lived.

With such a contrived image I felt better, as if I had stemmed the tide of public discussion about my motives and had begun to establish a semblance of professional research activity. Actually, my persistent work pattern, businesslike relationships, and affiliation with the Organization of American States[2] as a grant recipient served well to separate my behavior from Virginia's. The mask of genderlessness probably was unnecessary, but I only realized that after months of trying to pretend I was beyond gender classification.

Carrying out research in an ethical and scientific manner was of great importance to me. As the living arrangements with Virginia impinged more and more on my daily activities, I had begun to work harder and longer. I mapped the whole town, including house construction types, economic enterprises, and public service areas. I created a file on businesses and used that information to establish rapport and hold informal discussions regarding the employment of indigenous people. I avoided unpleasant encounters with Virginia's acquaintances by knowing every street and walkway, and by observing peoples' behavior so closely that I could predict it and hence maneuver into positions favorable to me.

The kinds of interruptions brought about by Virginia's actions created in me a need to confirm my research progress. I wrote quarterly evaluations stating what I had accomplished and what I intended to do in the next quarter. I developed systematic recordkeeping on each informant and every aspect of the research problem. As a result, I saw my own progress and knew that I was achieving my research goals. My inability to acquire certain kinds of information or to participate in specific activities due to my early association with Virginia was nearly inconsequential in view of the intensity of effort and level of organization the situation led me to develop. I had overcompensated, but I learned something in the process.

Conclusions

My intense experience in Venezuela, and the analysis undertaken for this account, helped me to understand and interpret my undergraduate and master's level fieldwork situations in North America as well as in Venezuela. The facade of a gender-neutral researcher role, and the concomitant assumption of a separate status outside the usual cultural parameters, helped me to comprehend a wider range of neutral pretenses assumed by researchers, including apolitical and amoral stances. The agricultural specialist, the computer salesperson, or the physicist are no more immune to culturally defined gender roles than the anthropologist.

In spite of efforts in the late 1960s by Berreman (1969), Hymes (1969), Gough (1967), and others, the concept of acting neutrally is still presented as a viable option, implicitly and explicitly, to graduate students in anthropology (and in other fields). Berreman (1969:89) wrote that, "as students of man, we have made a value choice for mankind, and it is inconsistent to their claim of sterile scientism which precludes the realization of the humanistic heritage of social science. As a corollary to this, we believe that neutrality on human issues is simply not an option open to anthropologists." Hymes (1969:48) concurred: "Anthropology is unavoidably a political and ethical discipline, not merely an empirical speciality. It is founded in a personal commitment that has inescapably a reflective philosophical dimension."

Gender neutralization has been but one facet of the overall concept of personal neutrality. It is not a possible, nor even a necessary or desirable, mode for field research, any more than theoretical or ethical neutrality is possible or desirable. Because most of us grow up with specific gender and sex patterns, we tend to consider them as biological-universal givens, which they are not. Sex and gender—sex in particular—have always been major cultural determinants of what we are allowed to do. Past attitudes about the "appropriateness" of discussing these topics prior to cross-cultural work and current laws related to equal rights in the United States should not deter our efforts to understand and clarify the functions of self and cultural definitions on our research and occupational activities.

The study and teaching of cross-cultural sex and gender characteristics should be approached with the same thoroughness and respect for cultural diversity that we are familiar with in other aspects of anthropological studies. The interaction and symbolic interaction studies of Edward T. Hall and Erving Goffman are used widely to introduce business personnel and diplomats to new cultural milieus. If anthropology is to be truly the science of humanity, then the thoroughness that has been devoted to studies of social organization should now be applied to understanding self, sex, and gender in cross-cultural experiences.

Notes

My sincerest thanks to Roberta Hall and Nelly Arvelo-Jimenez for critical readings of my paper.

1. In Venezuela, *criollo* originally referred to the descendants of European settlers, but it since has come to signify all that is original, typical, or folk, as opposed to that coming from abroad.

2. The Organization of American States is highly respected in Venezuela, and to my surprise it is known in Puerto Ayacucho, too. I received a monthly stipend from the Caracas office of OAS and was required to wire them to indicate receipt prior to depositing the check in the local bank. These transactions were not kept private by those who performed them.

References

Berreman, Gerald D.
    1969   "Bringing It All Back Home: Malaise in Anthropology." In: Dell Hymes (ed.), *Reinventing Anthropology*, pp. 83–98. New York: Vintage Books.
Conaway, Mary Ellen
    1984   *Still Guahibo, Still Moving: A Study of Circular Migration and Marginality in Venezuela*. Relaciones Antropologicas (Occasional Publications on South American Anthropology), parts 1–2, nos. 1–2. Greeley: University of Northern Colorado.
Gough, Kathleen
    1967   "New Proposals for Anthropologists." *Economic and Political Weekly* (Bombay), Sept. 9.
Hymes, Dell
    1969   "The Uses of Anthropology: Critical, Political, Personal." In: Dell Hymes (ed.), *Reinventing Anthropology*, pp. 3–79. New York: Vintage Books.

Powdermaker, Hortense
  1966   *Stranger and Friend: The Way of an Anthropologist*. New York: W. W. Norton and Co.
Wax, Rosalie H.
  1971   *Doing Fieldwork: Warnings and Advice*. Chicago: University of Chicago Press.

4

Son and Lover: The Anthropologist as Nonthreatening Male

MICHAEL V. ANGROSINO

Preliminary Remarks

The volume of which this essay is a part addresses the question of how the definition of gender roles in different cultures affects the lives and research enterprises of anthropological fieldworkers. No good anthropologist carries the presuppositions of his or her religious background, political creed, or moral value system into the field and expects them to blend automatically with the lifeways of people of other cultures. Yet we rarely give serious consideration to our assumptions about gender identity, almost as if we are somehow convinced that such an identity is a universal characteristic that could not possibly cause any misunderstandings. This idea is a cruel delusion. If we consider the vagaries of the terms *man* and *woman* even in the social landscape of our own society, we should be able to appreciate that the fact that we are physically one or the other gives us no firm clues as to what that physical symbol will mean in another culture. This conclusion is something we are rarely trained to be sensitive to, despite the years of preparation that go into the first field experience. Since our biological sex is one aspect of our persona about which we can do relatively little in the course of a field experience, we should pay more attention to the cues related to the biological marker we project and to the implications that such cues have for the kinds of behavior that will and will not be tolerated by our hosts in the field.

I want to make two basic points in this article, illustrating them with examples from my own field experience.

1. The fieldworker is obliged to adapt to the most nearly comfortable version of the appropriate gender identity permissible in the host culture. This point ought to be studied critically *before* going to the field, with the expected degree of comfort of fit playing as important a role as theoretical or methodological interests in the selection of a suitable field site.

2. The fieldworker must make every effort to ensure that this comfortable identity is the least threatening one possible in the eyes of the host society.

My concern with "comfort" as opposed to "threat" derives from the work of Wilson (1974), who addresses the problem of "dual socialization" in colonial societies. Members of such societies are typically taught to revere the behaviors and standards of the metropolitan power; this external value system is termed a system of respectability. By contrast, unless colonial peoples are totally consumed with an ambition (often unrealizable) to escape their homelands, they must still function in the local social networks; the system of indigenous values that orient a person's life is termed a system of reputation. The two systems are complementary rather than contradictory, but their simultaneous influence has a decidedly tension-inducing effect on the development of the colonial personality. Actions, vocabulary, gestures, associations, styles of dress, of eating, of housing, types of personal relationships, and so forth, are all clearly demarcated as to their respectable or reputable character; and the individual's social persona is evaluated in terms of which system's character predominates.

In the West Indian society in which I conducted the fieldwork described here, there was a great deal of concern—covert but still very strong—about what Erving Goffman calls "the presentation of self." People were careful (if not always conscious) of the kind of social persona they were projecting, and they took pains to project a desirable image. This desire was particularly acute because my fieldwork was with an ethnic group (Indians in a society politically dominated by blacks and whites) that, while proud of its own traditions and by no means inclined to abandon them, was still mindful of the need to "get along" in the wider world outside the traditional village. The most threatening people in such a society are not those who are aggressively at one extreme or the other of the respectability/reputation continuum. Rather, they are the people who exhibit a social ambivalence, probably because one never knows how to "take" them, in the local phrase. The outsider, the fieldworker, is unfortunately not really free to choose to be an extremist; he or she cannot be either definitely "respectable" or explicitly "reputable" for fear of alienating a large portion of the potential informant pool. For example, a white male North American who acted in a clearly "respectable" fashion (wearing expensive clothes, espousing monogamous principles, advocating moderation in drink and dance, and so on) would miss out on the richness and diversity of men's social life in the rumshops, a considerable segment of the local culture. By the same token, should he adopt a "reputable" image and hang out exclusively in the rumshops, "cat around" openly with loose women, and in general become a "street-corner idler," he would be accused of having "lowered himself" and would not be taken seriously.

The challenge, then, is to land somewhere in the middle *without* being so ambiguous in the social clues given out that one does not fit into any meaningful social categories. The problem is that no culture has explicit rules about what symbols are and are not considered threatening. The process of building up an acceptable local persona is thus a trial-and-error affair. For this reason, a corollary to this essay's two main points is that the process of adaptation does not make fieldworkers hypocrites, sneaking around and concealing their own personality; rather, adaptation is a mark of respect for the people whose lives they have come to share. If the compromise means that all sources of data are not equally open—if, for example, a man in a given culture is not permitted free discourse with women—then so be it. If anyone still believes the myth of the fieldworker being like a sponge soaking up "everything," then that person will find no solace in the field. We are, after all, not sponges without personalities—we are individuals with social characters, part of which we consciously choose for ourselves, part of which is imposed on us by the people we live among. This is no less true in the field than it is at home.

The title of this essay includes the two major components of my social persona during the course of my fieldwork.[1] Hence, I will discuss the process whereby I made use of that dual role of son and lover, a persona that was comfortable (eventually) to me and non-threatening to my hosts.

Ethnographic Background

My fieldwork took place, with unintended irony, in the romantic West Indies and focused on the overseas Indian population of the region—that is, descendants of people brought to the Caribbean on indenture contracts to replace the emancipated slaves on the sugar plantations. The two large mainland territories of Guyana (British Guiana) and Surinam (Dutch Guiana) and the formerly British island of Trinidad were the major recipients of this Indian migration; today their populations have Indian segments that range from approximately 35 percent in Trinidad to approximately 55 percent in Guyana. The Indians have remained a rural population for the most part, and until World War II their traditional culture was not noticeably changed. But in the past generation the Indians have become quite visible both politically and economically, and currently they are reaching toward some semblance of modernity as they compete with their Creole neighbors. The Indians remain a highly distinctive group with a strong sense of ethnic identity (see Angrosino 1974 for a more detailed analysis).

My research dealt with the mental health implications of acculturation and focused on alcoholism as a social pathology—how it was conditioned and how it was treated in a community that was in a state of social and cultural flux. Trinidad was the main field site, as its Indian community was the most socially liberated of the three areas. To this end I spent a great deal of time with members and families of the Alcoholics Anonymous groups on the island, which were overwhelmingly Indian in composition. As a result, I was able, as a researcher, to see virtually all of the island, since at the time there were some forty active groups in all parts of Trinidad and on its sister island, Tobago. During my stay I boarded with a family in a largely Indian village, a circumstance that proved critical in influencing what I learned during that year—not only about Indians in the Caribbean, but about myself, as a person and a researcher.

Finding a Place

Before I began to consider the implications of my social persona in the fashion described earlier, I blithely went about making decisions on the basis of rational, graduate-school-digested criteria. The first question was where to live. As a single person and an impecunious graduate student, I had learned to fend for myself as cook and housekeeper, but in the interests of saving time and energy, I was not willing to do all that in the field. In effect, I decided to become someone's dependent; however, I was quite open as to the kind of living arrangements I would make.

When I arrived in Trinidad I sought the counsel of a distinguished doctor, an acquaintance of one of my professors. Unlike most Creoles (the Trinidad Indian term for "blacks"), he had a deep interest in Indian culture, and he and his English wife had many friends in the Indian community. Some months later they bought a house and moved to a rural Indian village. The doctor and his wife enthusiastically agreed that the best place for me would be with a family—as they so rightly pointed out, the Indian community is built on the bedrock of the family. I was soon to learn the soundness of this advice, just as I learned that even "sociopathic" Indians such as alcoholics continue to live enmeshed in family concerns, even in the depths of their illness.

The couple first took me to the house of a locally revered *pandit*

(Hindu priest) whose daughter was the doctor's nurse. The *pandit* and his wife were ready to welcome me as a boarder, as a favor to the doctor, but they pointed out the obvious—their tiny house was filled with many children and seemed to be a poor place to work or study. The doctor's wife suggested that if I bought a secondhand desk to put in a corner of the crowded house, then I would at least have a private space for myself. Through a friend she heard of an Indian family not too far away who was selling some furniture, and so we went to see what they had to offer. The eldest son had just gone to Canada to work, and another son had just been married. As a result, the family was selling the large desk and the clothes cupboard the sons had used as schoolboys. This family had a large house with a now-empty room, and, even more importantly, we got along very well together. We spent a delightful afternoon chatting, and by the end of the day agreed that I would move in as soon as possible. Certain details, such as the monthly amount I would pay for food, laundry, and other services, were settled, and that seemed to be that. I could now get on with the work of "doing ethnography" in the village.

My complacency evaporated quickly, however. On the first morning there I took a village tour down the road with one of the family's younger sons; I wanted to make a sketch map of the environs. As far as I was concerned, I felt I could explain what I was doing in the village. But the friendly, almost joshing question, "Buh who you is, man?" that I must have heard at least a dozen times that morning took on a special meaning and urgency in the Indian context. It wasn't long before I began to ask myself, "Buh who you is, man?"

The problem was not, of course, that I was an American, for the island had seen plenty of them. Nor was it that I was a student planning to write a book—Indians seem to have an innate sense of the importance of their culture and rather take it for granted that foreigners should come to learn about their religion, philosophy, arts, and so forth. No, the problem was that I was an unattached man, and that was a category of social creature that could not be explained by the catchall "student," and certainly not by the even more exotic "anthropologist." It was too ambivalent a category in local terms, and so I was something of a threat to the local expectations of decent behavior.

The Male Image in Trinidad Indian Culture

The single person is a rarity in most societies where anthropologists have done fieldwork, but in the West Indies the single state is neither unknown nor condemned. However, it does have connotations quite different from its North American counterpart. There is a vast literature on the intricacies of the domestic cycle in the West Indies, in which marriage or other permanent unions form only a part (see, e.g., M. G. Smith 1962, 1973; Horowitz 1971; R. T. Smith 1971; Slater 1977). Among West Indians of low socioeconomic status, people may go through the better part of their adult lives engaging in a series of consensual unions before getting married. This is not the case among the Indians of the West Indies, for in their community marriage is still the norm, and it is accomplished at a fairly early age. But these Indians have come to share the lower-class Creole attitude that marriage does not necessarily mean fidelity for the man. Indian women still have nothing remotely approaching the freedom of their Creole sisters, and an unfaithful wife is still the object of scorn and revulsion. Yet a married man is expected only to fulfill a family obligation by propagating his line; he is not expected to love his wife or even to enjoy his sexual encounters with her, even in the basest "animal" sense. Because a wife is by definition a "good woman," she is not supposed to be practiced in the sexual arts. A man might well be suspicious of and angry with a wife who turned out to be exciting in bed. Thus, to get the "good" sex denied him at home, the Indian man, like his Creole counterpart, is expected to live up to the old calypso image of the man being like a bee, carrying his pollen from flower to flower. Married men are expected to seek their "extra ginger" with an "outside woman" at one or more points in their lives, and some well-fixed Indian men may maintain a mistress for years in her own house in another village.

The essence of the Indian male game, however, is discretion. A Creole man might brag of his sexual conquests and other manly adventures; such bragging is, in fact, one of the great themes of the indigenous musical art form, the calypso, and is a key feature of the local reputation system. The Indian man is expected to practice the same behavior, but he is not to talk about it, except in the most private circumstances. Whatever their feelings toward their wives and children may be, Indian men still believe in the sanctity of marriage and the family, and they would almost rather give up their "extra ginger" than have their affairs become common knowledge in their own villages. Some Indian men are thus prodigious travelers, with girlfriends stashed away in villages beyond the circle of gossip which includes their own families. The flashy dress and flamboyant public demeanor of the Creole man on the prowl are kept in the closet of the Indian man. He may well become a dashing bon vivant in the company of his girlfriend, but he does so only rarely in his hometown. The most flagrant example of this double life in my circle of informants was one man who didn't even drive a car at home, preferring humbly to walk or use the proletarian bus; this same man owned a motorcycle which he kept at his girlfriend's house in a distant village, and the two would go roaring around with great abandon, often drunk, through the quiet back lanes of a sugar plantation.

The reputation of the Indian man is based not on proof of what he does but on common assumptions about what he must be doing. A married man who isn't unbearably ugly, dirt poor, or a *saddhu* (Hindu ascetic) is expected to seek "extra ginger"; and therefore, even if no one has any evidence that he is doing so, it will become "common knowledge" that he is. In a sense, the man is assumed, approvingly, to be guilty of infidelity until proven innocent. And his wife, not incidentally, will join in the tacit approval, since this means he will not "bother" her so much. She will only be roused to righteous indignation if the boundaries of discretion are breached and too many of the sordid details become known to her and to people she knows.

And what of the unmarried man, particularly one of clearly eligible age? Quite simply, he is not to be trusted in and of himself, for he is, even more markedly than a married man, "on the prowl" and is probably all the more desperate. He is thus a potential threat to the virtuous wife, the fallen mistress, and the nubile daughter alike. I suppose I knew all of this, as the literature cited above and many other writings clearly describe these male attitudes in West Indian societies. But I fell prey to what may well be a more common error than many of us would like to admit: I assumed that the people I was studying would recognize that I was no more than an interested outsider, someone who respected their life-style, of course, and wanted to learn about it, but not one who could be expected to conform to it in all its particulars or be judged by its standards. I assumed, in short, that these people had mastered their ethnocentrism, a vain hope in light of the difficulty most professional anthropologists have in living up to that ideal. It is certainly possible that "my" people were, on the conscious level, aware that people from the United States did things differently and that I was there for serious purposes, not for hanky-panky. But most of us, even professional anthropologists, also operate on a level of subconscious evaluation of the way things are. As far as my new friends were concerned, I might well be a student and a white person from the United States and an anthropologist—but I was still a man, an unattached man, and deep down they all knew that that could mean only one thing.

There was a further aspect of this imposed gender that I was less intellectually prepared for, because to my knowledge it had not been reported in the social science literature. In the works of the fine Trinidad Indian novelist V. S. Naipaul, I had read about the fixation of the Trinidadians with "the Yanks," American troops stationed on the island during the lend-lease days of World War II. His stories "Until the Soldiers Came" (1958) and "A Flag on the Island" (1966) are vivid and poignant illustrations of the image that this small band of Americans, "fighting" in one of the most obscure corners of the war, created in the minds of the people of Trinidad. Even though I had read these stories before going to the field, I accepted them only as the witty exaggerations of a creative artist. I found, however, that the legend of the Yanks did indeed persist some thirty years after their departure. The Americans not only built the first real highways and airports on the island, and thus helped it along the road toward modernization, but they also opened up a large number of well-paying service jobs at their bases. With this newfound affluence came the model of how to use the wealth: the soldiers, not particularly preoccupied with the terrors of war, had relatively little to do on their island hideaway, and as the legend now goes, they invented rum-and-Coca-Cola and the modern version of the Trinidad "bacchanal" that is still celebrated in song and story. They rode their jeeps through the streets of the town picking up girls and singing "the blacker the berry, the sweeter the juice." They dashed out to Manzanilla, which even today remains a kind of romantic cliché, a remote, tropic-paradise, palm-fringed beach. There it was "all day, all night Marianne"—and, needless to say, it was not seashells she was playing with, as in the laundered American version of the calypso.

By a quirk of the Pentagon draw, a large number of the American men stationed on the island were from Texas, and whatever they were actually like, they seemed to have impressed themselves on the islanders as being uniformly blond, of gigantic stature, and always chewing gum. "Saga boys" from the island quickly imitated the casual dress of the Americans and also appropriated the soldiers' loping gait and twanging drawl. Until the recent surge of Black Pride made such WASP models unacceptable, these traits remained the very image of the "real man." The islanders' subsequent interaction with Americans have often been in the form of cruise-ship tourists, less prepossessing in the physical sense but just as randy and even more free-spending than the soldiers. Thus, it is no surprise that the islanders' image of Americans was one derived from sensational melodrama rather than real life. Since I am dark complected, I was often asked whether I was "pure American," the general consensus being that although my grandparents had been immigrants, I was enough of a "real American" now to live up to the expectations of the image, regardless of my physiognomy.

Becoming a Son

In the minds of many of the villagers, then, the question "Buh who you is, man?" was already answered: I was an American "cowboy." Since I was going to be living on the island for a long time, they assumed that I would not be satisfied with a casual fling with a town prostitute but would require a more permanent bit of "ginger" in a set-up household. As it happened, however, the family with whom I boarded (I shall call them the Jawabs) had three eligible daughters, the eldest of whom was approaching the dangerous Indian cut-off age of spinsterhood. She had been "sickly" as a child and hence was not married. Moreover, her father, who was especially protective of his daughters, could not bear the thought of marrying any of them off at the first opportunity. Therefore, the village gossip quickly developed that I was on hand as the intended husband of the eldest Jawab daughter. The story was given credence because of the father's well-known feeling that none of the local boys was good enough for his "darlin'."

There were some who could not believe that Mr. Jawab would be so innovative as to send all the way to America for a suitable son-in-law, and so they embroidered the tale, saying that because of my complexion I was not an American at all but an Indian from India— probably a Brahman, they added approvingly. I was told all this by the Jawabs themselves, who professed to be amused at the "wickedness" of their neighbors. Yet it was quite clear that they were not amused at all. Because of their Canadian connections, and because of Mr. Jawab's stint as a mechanic in England during World War II, they were somewhat sophisticated in the ways of the outside world. Although they understood what I was doing, it bothered them that others had made a match between one of their daughters and me. I later understood that their concern was a result of the fact that as long as people thought they had brought me in with marriage in mind, I could be considered a sexual threat to all of their daughters, and that made for a certain amount of discomfort all around.

These insights came to me over the course of several months of living with the Jawabs in their village, and of hanging around with men from Alcoholics Anonymous groups on various parts of the island. For a while I tried to shrug off the troubling implications of my position, pretending that I didn't need to do anything about it, just waiting for everybody to realize that I had no intention of turning myself into a Brahman cowboy. But they didn't.

The problem solved itself three months later in a most touching way. I had lived quite happily with the Jawabs all the while and had come to like and respect them all. But a turning point in our relationship came during the family's annual house-*puja*, or "prayers." Devout Hindus are expected to renew the spiritual bonds within the household on at least an annual basis. This is done by calling in a *pandit* who picks an astrologically opportune time for conducting a three-day prayer service during which the house and its occupants are purified. On occasion, these prayers may become very elaborate affairs, with hundreds of invited guests, but for the ordinary family they are small-scale and private in nature. At the time of the Jawabs' *puja*, I indicated that I would like to go into full preparation with them—that is, I wanted to be ritually pure—and hence I began a strict fast with them. Since the younger children were going to school and the father was going to work, they could not maintain ritual purity all day long. So, as is often the case, it was the mother who represented the household and sat with the *pandit* during the services. Although I was not a Hindu, I was the only other member of the household able to remain ritually pure for the three-day period, and so I was asked, with great timidity, if I would be more than just an observer of the *puja*. It had been the family's practice to have the eldest son sit with his mother and the *pandit* during the *puja*. But he was now in Canada, and the next oldest son, married and living down the road, had converted to Catholicism. The next two sons, also adults and available, were indifferent Hindus and declined to participate. So I was elected, feeling as elated, no doubt, as Malinowski did on first learning the magical secrets of the Trobriand gardens.

Having attended other *pujas* during my earlier studies, I knew the formal sequence of ritual actions and was able to ring a bell on cue without making any gross mistakes that would have upset the sanctity of the event. Yet there was more to this experience than simply being able to see an "exotic" ritual from the inside. We sat on canvas sacks covering the wooden floor of the house, on three sides of a mud-and-cow-dung altar, enveloped in the camphor smoke and the aroma of burning flowers. We lived across the road from another *pandit*, and his dawn devotions, signaled by the blowing of a conch shell and the ringing of a bell, had become my alarm clock, the plangent notes having become familiar to me as they cut through the heavy tropical morning, putting an official end to the nighttime susurration of the insect chorus. The ineradicable perfume of burning pitch pine and camphor which permeates an Indian village had, for three months, been the background of my life. Now I was at the center of it, and I shortly realized that my eager immersion into the emotion of the *puja,* as well as my reasonably correct enactment of the service, worked a kind of magic on the other participants. From that time on the old *pandit* jokingly called me his "assistant," and Mrs. Jawab told me to call her "Mama."[2]

I was a new son of the family. The tacit recognition of this emergent identity subtly but clearly solved part of my earlier gender dilemma, although it inevitably opened up some new areas of uncertainty. My ambiguous status within the village was resolved, for as an informally adopted member of the Jawab family, by extension I was related to most people in the village, inasmuch as the modern Indian village retains its character as an extended kin group. In one fell swoop I was transformed from a potential threat against the decency of the village females to the brother or cousin (hence, protector/chaperone) of those my own age and the nephew of the older ones. There was never a formal adoption ceremony, and many people in the village never explicitly acknowledged the family tie. Undoubtedly, there were some who never cared a fig about my activities one way or the other. But my new status definitely made a difference with the people with whom I was working most directly. I was, quite simply, no longer an outsider of threatening sexuality—I had become a member of the family.

Becoming a Lover

This neutralization of my sexual presence worked wonders, especially for my own mental comfort. I had grown uneasy with the suspicions surrounding my actions and motives and was glad that I could now be explained in a way that enabled me to do my work, and one that was also, in many ways, quite flattering to my fieldworker's vanity. But there was a problem inherent in my transformation into a nonthreatening male within the village kin group: if I were no longer interested in the village belles, then which girls would I prowl after? As always, there had to be *someone.* As it turned out, this problem was exacerbated by my increasing involvement with the Alcoholics Anonymous groups.

In Trinidad the A.A. is almost exclusively a male society. Wilson (1971) has described the classic West Indian male peer group (which he calls the "crew," but which in Trinidad is called a "lime") and has made it clear that this group is the locus of a man's reputation. It is in the "crew," or "lime," that the man is freest to brag about his sexual exploits; and in the West Indian context the bragging is usually based on some fact. Since Trinidad Creole women, especially of the working class, are not expected to marry immediately, and since no particular stigma attaches itself to bearing illegitimate children, there is a ready availability of "ginger" for the men. The A.A. groups are not standard Trinidadian male "limes," of course, since their overt object is sobriety and a modification of the life-style. Yet they still make certain assumptions about a man's behavior, even if there is relatively less blatancy in discussing that behavior than there would be in a regular "drinking lime."

How could I transform my status as son of a particular village, and hence a single man available for sexual adventures in far-flung locales, into the least threatening role possible? I inadvertently played into the hands of those who sought to explain the mystery of my life-style by agreeing to travel to another village, about ten miles distant, to visit the main (female) informant of a graduate school colleague who had worked on the island the year before me. Usually when I needed to go somewhere, I could rely on one of the A.A. men to drive me. But I knew that they had very little patience for social calls that did not involve other A.A. members. The party I wanted to visit was Creole, and while individual relations between Indians and Creoles can be cordial despite the expressed hostility on the group level, I thought it best not to include any of my Indian friends in this venture. I took the bus into the nearby large town of San Fernando and then caught a taxi out to the village of the Creole family. I found the lady to be a charming and vivacious grandmother, and I eventually became quite fond of her and her family, visiting them from time to time as my schedule permitted. I always went there by myself in a taxi, and although I knew a few Indian A.A. members in that village, I never ran into them in the course of my visits.

It was with an old-fashioned, comedic double-take sense of surprise that I learned that my visits to that village had become the topic of A.A. banter. It happened at a group anniversary, a big celebration marking the foundation of one of the groups. As usual, the members were joking with one another in their congratulatory speeches—very much like a T.V. "celebrity roast" in which the guests of honor (in this case, the members of the group celebrating the anniversary) are held up to gently affectionate ridicule. Since the group in question was one with which I had done a great deal of special work, I was considered something of a member and so was included in the "roasting." I was reveling in a glow of rapport as a result of this inclusion when their joshing turned to my "secret" trips to the village of Penal. As it happened, I was not going to Penal at all but to a village close by, on the same taxi route. Clearly, I had been observed at the taxi stand in San Fernando, and it was assumed that I was going to Penal. Why? Most likely because one of my friends—the man with the motorcycle mentioned earlier—had his well-known "ginger" in that village, and although he never (as far as I could tell) told anyone else that I had ever accompanied him, it was widely assumed that I had done so and had become attached to another of that village's fair flowers. Discretion being the rule in such matters among Indians, we were all mercifully spared further inquiry into the details. Although I told people that I was not going to Penal, for "ginger" or anything else, but was going to the next village to visit an old Creole lady who had befriended a fellow anthropologist, I knew they didn't believe me. And I never did figure out the full extent of the network by which my clandestine taxi rides were observed and reported.

The common assumptions about my activities, false though they were, got me off the hook. Once I was believed to be attached to a specific woman in an ongoing relationship, I was no longer considered "on the prowl" and could be safely admitted as a guest in everyone's home. Wives and daughters no longer had to be hidden away.

Another inadvertently compromising incident served to seal my fate. One day I was traveling up to the capital city, Port of Spain, to buy film and other camera supplies. Not expecting to stay very long, I went there in a taxi instead of with an A.A. driver. At the taxi stand in San Fernando, a Canadian tourist lady got into the cab, obviously quite frazzled. She had taken a jaunt down to the more exotic southern part of the island, had become upset at the lack of tourist facilities, and was anxious to get back to her Port of Spain hotel and her husband. Hence, she paid the taximan for the remainder of the cab so there would be no other passengers and off we went. She was obviously relieved to see a face from home, and when we got to the hotel she invited me in for a drink with her and her husband. Needless to say, the taxi driver—a man I knew slightly and who was related by marriage to one of my A.A. informants—saw the "cozy" conversation in the back seat of the cab and then observed our decampment into the hotel, but not our totally innocent chat in the public lounge with the lady's husband. Thus I chalked up another way of coping—I picked up stray tourist ladies! The situation made for a nonthreatening set of behaviors because no A.A. man would dream of picking up a white tourist lady. I could thus indulge my "lust" without being a rival to any of my friends.

In many other field situations, this business about my sneaking around would have been a disastrous blow to my credibility, but in Trinidad it was all to the good. Once I got over my initial surprise and annoyance at the spread of false gossip, I found I was able to play along with the game, occasionally popping off to Port of Spain to go to the library, serene in the certain knowledge that my latest sexual adventure would, within a day, be discussed approvingly by my friends in A.A.

Implications of Assimilating to the Local Male Image

One of my non-A.A. friends was more directly solicitous of my needs and took steps to meet them. He was a young man, about my own age, who lived in the Jawabs' village and was a distant relation to the family. He set no store by the traditionalists' need to identify me with the family, however; we were simply friends. This young man, whom I shall call Terry, was an excellent examplar of the dichotomous life-style of the Indian man. In the village he was a model husband and father, a bit too attentive to his pretty wife, some of the older men said, but not to the point of folly. Yet in town he had a reputation as a "badjohn." The gossipmongers' details were vague, but I soon learned from Terry himself that he was up to more than just casual fooling around. He was, in fact, one of the most highly regarded pimps in the district, justly applauded by his clients for his strict standards of quality. He was, I'm afraid, a terrible racist; and as he served a strictly Indian clientele, he would permit no ladies in his employ but Indians. "But why would you let good Indian girls be corrupted like that?" I asked him with calculated provocation in mind. "Oh," he answered mildly in his urbane way, "it is far better for them to be corrupted in the service of Indian men than it would be for me to stand back and profit from miscegenation." He was the only nonofficial Indian who ever used that word with me, although the concept itself never failed to evoke cries of horror from Indians of all stations.

Indeed, Terry's boasts were justified. His girls were extremely beautiful and refined. He claimed that after they had earned all the money they wanted, he helped them go to the United States or Canada to finish their education, so that when they returned, their new status as high-class American ladies would wipe out the shame of their earlier "fall." I never ascertained whether he lived up to this promise, but it was typical of his style that he articulated it sincerely as a goal. Terry would not tolerate the village boys pestering him for his girls' favors; he aimed only at the best-placed business, political, and professional men, and I felt a curious thrill of mingled Graham Greene-ish intrigue and warm anthropological rapport when he condescended to introduce me into his business. By contrast, I had once accompanied a group of village boys on a jaunt to a "pleasure house" of indescribable squalor in San Fernando; I prudently—but also, I fear, prudishly—escaped and went to a movie instead. Terry, for all the implausibility of his racial purification theories, at least provided a safe haven. My commerce with him, as another adventure outside the realm of possibility for my A.A. friends, was highly desirable. It was further proof that I did, in fact, conform to the role expectations, yet in a way that threatened no one's "ginger."

I have saved for last an anecdote whose character I have only begun to fathom. I think that the request to write this essay on the implications and consequences of sexuality in the field moved me to think about it in new ways and helped me to understand it in a way that was not possible before. The story concerns an A.A. friend, whom I shall call Freddie. Freddie could have been invented by Naipaul himself, so archetypal was his obsession with being an American "cowboy." He had been raised by an uncle who was a bartender at a club frequented by the American soldiers, and he grew up savoring the delicious, incomprehensibly rich smell of Scotch. After he became an alcoholic, he drank rum like most Trinidadians, for to him it would have been a desecration to descend into the gutter carrying the hallowed Scotch. When I first met him, he had been a model of sobriety for several years, but he had not lost his impish cut-up's character. He was genuinely fond of his wife, a strong, striking, warm-hearted, long-suffering woman. (I recently noticed, in looking over some photographs, that Freddie was the only Indian ever to pose for me with his arm around his wife, an apparently casual gesture that seems to symbolize his easy-going way of life.)

But for all that, Freddie too had his "extra ginger"—quite a lot of it, in fact. I assumed that he was not rich enough to support a permanent "outside woman," although he had a number of obvious girlfriends who would wave seductively to us as we drove through San Fernando. As I've said, the important facet of a man's reputation is that his friends know that such extra activity is going on; the details are not necessarily important. Freddie had a charming way of dealing with his life—he was quite a storyteller, and it mattered little that his stories seemed not always to be based on hard truth. Neither did I think it odd that I was never introduced to these girls; his dealing in innuendo was, in fact, the proper way to play the game.

One night toward the end of my study, however, we were on our way to a remote village where a new A.A. group had just been set up and was holding one of its first organizational meetings. Freddie arrived early to pick me up, an unheard-of occurrence. Usually Freddie's "I'll pick you up at 6:00" meant anywhere from 8 P.M. until midnight. We drove down the highway, past the turn-off to the village where the meeting was to be held, and skidded off onto a rutted, dusty trace (an old canefield road). Freddie apologetically explained that he wanted to visit someone before the meeting and hoped I wouldn't mind. I didn't. He pulled the car up in front of a ramshackle *ajoupa* (thatch-roofed shack) with a sagging porch attached to it in very tenuous fashion.

Nighttime always seems to fall suddenly in the tropics; in the countryside, where there are no electric lights to cushion the impact, the onset of darkness can be a particularly startling thing. The afternoon had been rainy and the sky was still full of clouds, so that the moon and stars gave only the dimmest possible light. The little *ajoupa*, barely holding its own against some huge, lowering old mango trees, was bathed in a gloom so thick it could almost be tasted. We entered the shack without knocking and found the interior weakly illuminated by a small, spluttering kerosene lamp. The umbrageous little room was crammed with household detritus—a spindly table piled with dishes, a clothes wardrobe with no door, a smoky pitch-oil stove—and was itself partitioned with a faded piece of drapery hung on a frayed rope, its bluish color seeming to disappear into the dim haze.

While I was still trying to get my bearings I heard a woman's soft voice say, "So you come after all." I did not know whether she had been there all along, hidden in the murk, or whether she had quietly entered from somewhere else. Freddie turned in her general direction and said, in a voice of unusual gentleness, "How he doin'?" "You could see for yourself," the woman (whom I could not yet see clearly) replied. So Freddie pushed aside the blue curtain and there on a large, lumpy mattress lay an old, old man, so fragile that his bony body almost seemed to glow transparently in the dark. Freddie knelt down next to the bed and shouted in the old man's ear, "You lookin' good, Mamu. See I bring some bread and sweets. I also bring my friend Mikey."

The old man gave not the slightest indication that he had heard any of this, or even that he was aware of Freddie's presence, but Freddie seemed to feel that he had gotten through. While he was still talking the woman had noiselessly cleared a washtub off a chair and bade me sit down. She brought me a glass of "green," a locally manufactured soft drink of indeterminate flavor, notorious for its electric, poisonous-looking color. The room was stifling—the afternoon storm had only made the air more heavy than before—and the little house was full of gnats. I suppose I was, for the moment, too preoccupied with the strangeness of the situation to notice the wordless byplay between Freddie and the woman, but when I looked up, he was pointing at the wardrobe with his chin, a sparkle in his eyes that was discernible even in the shadows. The woman nodded and went to the closet, then pulled out a frock and disappeared behind the drape. Freddie glanced at me knowingly and winked. Soon the woman reappeared, wearing a bright red dress cut in a Chinese-dragon-lady pattern, slashed up the thigh. It did not suit her at all, this handsome but very stolid country woman with her worn features and coarse skin. She made no effort to model the dress, but stood there in the uncertain halo of the kerosene lamp with her arms hanging loosely at her side, as if waiting to bend over a cook-pot. Freddie stared at her with unabashed adoration in his eyes. "I go see you again soon," he said to her. She nodded heavily and sighed, "He not goin' to last the week."

I hastily swallowed my "green" just to be polite, although the pair were as oblivious to me as was old Mamu in the back room. We left the ajoupa with the woman still standing stiffly in her mandarin finery, and although the air outside was just as oppressive and gnat-laden as that inside, it seemed a relief. The absolute darkness of the canefields was preferable to the equivocal half-light of the shack. We drove off in unaccustomed silence, until Freddie turned to me and in his normally hearty, cheerful voice said, "They's nice people. I help them out sometimes." When I didn't immediately respond, he added, "The old man was a friend of my uncle. He not goin' to last the week, I hear."

So that was it, a kind of family obligation. But what of the woman? It crossed my mind that she might have been Freddie's girlfriend, yet it seemed too absurd. Freddie, the sparkling high-stepper with at least a half-dozen of San Fernando's liveliest girls—not to mention a truly extraordinary wife—having a special arrangement with that poor, sad creature? But of course it was true. Freddie had been seeing this woman for years, and the little ajoupa in the remote village was the best he could afford for her upkeep. He helped with her aged father's medical bills and, in addition to bringing groceries, indulged his private fantasies by bringing the woman dresses, usually of the most incredibly inappropriate sort. She had no pretensions of being a magazine glamor girl; she wore them out of gratitude.

Why had I been taken there? It was strange enough to be drawn in so close to a man's outside life, but stranger still when that life was so obviously out of tune with the entertaining romance about Freddie woven into our group's gossip. I realize now that Freddie was trying to bridge the remaining gap between us in the best way he knew how. I had been vouchsafed a confidence as deep as having been permitted to play a role in a Hindu ceremonial. I was not the white visitor to be feasted and flaunted, nor was I just another man brought around to share in the titillation of the sexual encounter. I was there because I could be expected to understand; I now knew both of Freddie's lives and could take them as they were, unadorned with the conventional mendacities, stripped of the clichés that make for a man's reputation. Just as I had gained an emotional insight into Hinduism by my participation in the *puja*, I had been granted an emotional perception of the reality of an Indian man's life in Trinidad, which is a matter of the need to satisfy one's urges and the desperate attempt to make a "bacchanal" out of the plain repast that is the lot of the average man, there as in our own society.

It is difficult to admit, but it is nonetheless true, that my ability to enter into these moments of epiphany was due not to my conscious, intellectual training as an anthropologist, nor even as a result of having taken pains to divest myself of ethnocentrism and do the "right" things to build rapport. Rather, it was simply the result of what I was—the single man, the devoted "son" with family obligations, and the reputed lover of outside women—that let me fit in. As a nonthreatening outsider I could be expected to understand. In a very special way, it was my final willingness to be the person I was thought to be, and to stop fretting over peoples' misconceptions about me, that made it possible for them to think that I would understand. I was, while I lived there, what they saw me to be. I had stopped fighting for a temporarily irrelevant "real" identity.

Notes

1. I am in no small way pleased that the title rings in a literary allusion to an author in so many ways the spiritual godfather to the topic of this volume.

2. Mr. Jawab was a reflective Hindu who loved to engage in learned discussions about philosophy and theology, but his wife was a "Hindu of the heart," to use the local phrase. She knew nothing about the sacred texts and had only the haziest idea of the vast antiquity of Indian religious thought; her faith was a living thing, however, integral to her way of life. Certainly, I had an affinity for Hinduism, and like so many others coming of age in the 1960s, I had dabbled in Eastern mysticism. But in Trinidad I learned that one cannot be a Hindu simply by professing beliefs or learning yoga. Hinduism there is a system of life that is fully meaningful only in the context of a community organization—in fact, it is an elaborated justification for community organization.

While I lived in Trinidad in the Jawab home, I felt myself taking emotional root in the Hindu context. This may well have been another of those factors of my personal character over which I had little conscious control but which bears some parenthetical notice here. I was reared in an ethnic Catholic neighborhood but had long felt alienated from its sense of a shared, communal understanding of a proper way of life, an uncritical faith that underscored every aspect of life and had a ready answer for any possible crisis arising in that small world. Such a life-style was not one that I would consciously have sought out at that stage of my life, but it was one that I felt enormously comfortable with, having slipped into it almost by accident. Although I had several good friends and excellent informants among the Muslims (some 15 to 20 percent of the Trinidad Indian population), I never felt as personally involved with Islam as I did with Hinduism. This was not an intellectual decision, and it really had nothing to do with my anthropological research on alcoholism. It was simply a subconscious tropism: I, too, while living in the village, was a "Hindu of the heart." The point is that there are many unexamined factors in our personal makeups which must be examined before we make a final decision as to a satisfactory field site.

References

Angrosino, Michael V.
  1974 Outside Is Death: Community Organization, Ideology and Alcoholism among the East Indians of Trinidad. Medical Behavioral Science Monograph Series. Winston-Salem, N.C.: Overseas Research Center, Wake Forest University.
Horowitz, Michael M.
  1971 "A Decision Model of Conjugal Patterns in Martinique." In: M. M. Horowitz (ed.), Peoples and Cultures of the Caribbean, pp. 476–88. Garden City, N.Y.: Natural History Press.
Naipaul, V. S.
  1958 Miguel Street. London: Andre Deutsch.
  1966 A Flag on the Island. Harmondsworth, U.K.: Penguin Press.
Slater, Mariam K.
  1977 The Caribbean Family. New York: St. Martin's Press.
Smith, M. G.
  1962 West Indian Family Structure. Seattle: University of Washington Press.
  1973 "A Survey of West Indian Family Studies." In: L. Comitas and D. Lowenthal (eds.), Work and Family Life: West Indian Perspectives, pp. 365–408. Garden City, N.Y.: Anchor Books (Doubleday).
Smith, Raymond T.
  1971 "Culture and Social Structure in the Caribbean: Some Recent Work on Family and Kinship Studies." In: M. M. Horowitz (ed.), Peoples and Cultures of the Caribbean, pp. 448–75. Garden City, N.Y.: Natural History Press.

Wilson, Peter J.
   1971   "Caribbean Crews: Peer Groups and Male Society." *Caribbean Studies* 10:18–34.
   1974   *Crab Antics: The Social Anthropology of English-speaking Negro Societies in the New World.* New Haven, Conn.: Yale University Press.

5

The Anthropologist as Female Head of Household

NANCIE L. GONZALEZ

"What will you be like when you go back to being your 'real self'"?
asked one informant.

In our quest to achieve greater understanding of a culture, by necessity we must continually strive for what we too blithely call "rapport." As with interpersonal relationships in our own society,
"becoming acquainted" may lead to varying levels of intensity and
degrees of intimacy. What is possible, acceptable, or proper in any
given case depends on a careful balancing of the nature of our anthropological goals, the willingness of our hosts to reveal their
thoughts, actions, and culture to outsiders, our skills in overcoming
their hesitations, and finally our own personal needs and limitations
which in turn are influenced by our age, sex and gender, ethnicity,
and individual psychological makeup.

Some argue that to become "too close" alters our objectivity and
may endanger our lives or psyches if we become entangled in local
disputes, involved in love affairs, or converted to local religious or
other ideological doctrines. Still, a few have done these things, with
varying results.[1] Most of us, whether because we have realized the
danger or because we have never actually wanted, attempted, or
achieved this level of closeness, have been satisfied with something
different—I will not say "less."

How do we become anthropologists? How do we become adults,
spouses, parents, and eventually elders? Clearly, our first ventures
as anthropologists into cultures different from our own occur, for the
most part, when we are still very young adults. As time goes on and
we continue in our chosen careers, we visit the "field" again and
again—but each time our "home identity" is a bit different. So too is

Reprinted from *Feminist Studies* 10 (1, 1984):97–114, by permission of the
publisher, Feminist Studies, Inc., c/o Women's Studies Program, University
of Maryland, College Park, Md., 20742.

our "field identity," for as we mature and take on different statuses in our own culture, this change is bound to influence our behavior in and reaction to what we find in other societies. Not only will we define our problems differently, but we will be perceived differently and accepted into different segments of the host society with more or less ease than before. And it matters not whether we visit the same or different cultures and communities over time. A young, unmarried woman who has never given birth is not likely to achieve field rapport in the same way as a grandmother aged fifty-five.[2] It will be a major thesis of this chapter that fieldwork itself contributes to the formation of our personalities, and thus of our "home identities."

My first field stint, ten weeks among highland Indians in Guatemala, was undertaken as an experiment, to see whether I really *liked* being an anthropologist. At the age of twenty-five, I had already given up one career because I was bored and generally dissatisfied with the everyday reality of the life it presented. Although I had been married briefly I had no children, and I presented myself to the community as an unmarried "schoolteacher" who wished to learn more about Guatemalans in order to describe their way of life to my students—who were only vaguely defined, of course, because at that time I had not yet begun to teach anthropology. Because Catholicism was the predominant religion of the country, I had thought it better not to mention my divorced status, and in retrospect I believe this was the best strategy. I had never really settled into the married state anyway, and many of my colleagues at the University of Michigan were unaware of my marital status, so this was consistent with my home identity at that time.

My spoken Spanish was quite deficient, even more so than that of the Indians, for whom it was also a second language. However, I had considerable facility in reading and writing and was able to provide services to the people in this sphere, which enhanced my image as a learned schoolteacher. When it came to matters of child rearing and especially childbirth, I met with what seemed at the time to be an inexplicable failure of communication. One time, for example, an obviously pregnant young woman feigned not to understand my questions about the forthcoming birth and denied that a baby was within her swollen body. She delivered two days later. Only much later did I discover that discussion of such topics with unmarried women or with primaparas was considered rude and embarrassing (see Paul 1974).

Diet in general, however, was an easy topic, especially because I had entered the community under the auspices of the Institute of Nutrition of Central America and Panama (INCAP) and because I was knowledgeable about the subject, this being the career I had just abandoned. INCAP was interested in beliefs and practices which might affect the nutritional and general health status of children, especially as these might explain the variable incidence of kwashiorkor (protein deficiency) in the population. I spent most of the summer investigating child-feeding practices (Gonzalez 1957; Gonzalez and Scrimshaw 1957).

A year later I returned to Guatemala to stay fourteen months, this time among the Garifuna (Black Caribs) on the north coast. As I have described in considerable detail elsewhere (Gonzalez 1969, 1970), I came to know the Garifuna far better than I had the Indians. Because I had visited the village briefly during my earlier field trip, I was seen as a returnee and was soon ensconced in a domestic establishment which was to color the way I viewed the Garifuna culture, the larger world, and ultimately my own place in both.

My field household consisted of a matriarchical elder in her fifties; her oldest daughter, then thirty-five, married, childless, and living apart from her husband; a younger daughter of thirty with three sons ranging in age from one to six years, each with a different father; and eighteen-year-old twin sons who were in and out of the house for varying periods in what seemed then a totally unpredictable fashion. Four other households were joined to ours by bonds of kinship and location, all facing a common yard. Two of these contained responsible and permanently resident adult males; the other two, like ours, were essentially female-headed households—a term with which I had not yet become familiar and which, in 1956, was not yet a common research topic for social scientists.

A census during the year revealed that about 45 percent of the Garifuna households contained no regularly present husband/father, even though adult males consanguineously related to the women often co-resided with them. Still, whether or not there were men present, women tended to be strong, independent, assertive, and competent. One male informant once told me, "There is nothing a man can do that a woman can't do as well or better." I watched and learned from these women, for whom I grew to have tremendous respect and admiration.

Although the only child of a divorced woman, I had not previously lived in a female-headed household in that my mother never maintained a domestic establishment during my youth. Rather, I was variously interned at boarding schools and in a series of "rent-a-family" situations, most of which did include a male, though I do not recall having regarded any of these men as a father figure. Thus, I experienced nuclear family life as a participant observer, in a sense, both at home and among my friends. Indeed, at that time, and among the people I knew, divorce was rare and households headed by women were nonexistent. Furthermore, not one of my close high school or college friends had a career woman as a mother. My own situation seemed at once unusual to others yet wholly natural to me because my maternal grandmother and her mother as well had both had independent careers, the latter having been widowed at an early age during the Civil War.

By the time I graduated from college, I was a singularly independent and unusually resourceful person, but at the same time I clung to the American middle-class feminine dream of marriage and a family as the only way for a woman to achieve adult fulfillment. At the same time, it did not occur to me that I could not combine these with a career. Although my own mother had not been able to do that, nor had she even been able to keep me with her during my childhood, I believed that I would be able to manage it if I just "tried harder."

In this chapter I suggest that my anthropological field experiences, combined with my own particular background, shaped my life so that I was not only able to come to terms with various of my own problems, but to understand better the very cultures I was studying. In addition, I show how, as a single female parent, I have been able to cope with raising two children in our contemporary American society while developing a full-time professional career. The particular strategies I employed were not all adopted from the Garifuna, but the main principles turn out to be very similar to theirs, as I will elaborate below. Although gender is clearly an important variable, as will be abundantly demonstrated throughout, I have chosen to focus more on the problems associated with definition of self as the anthropologist moves from role to role in both his or her own and other cultures (see Golde 1970).

The bulk of this chapter describes a fourteen-month field session in the Dominican Republic during which I lived as an unmarried head of a household which included my two sons, a dog, two cats, a servant/informant who later returned to the United States with us, and for varying periods three anthropology graduate students and the young son of one of them.

Fieldwork and Motherhood: Guatemala

Having married a (non-Garifuna) Guatemalan toward the end of my second fieldwork stint, I returned to Central America to write my dissertation after an additional semester of library work in Ann Arbor. My eldest son was born about five weeks after I defended that dissertation and just a year after I had left the field. Two years later my second son was born, and at about the same time a proposal to do fieldwork with both infants on a *finca* in Guatemala was declined. Although I was never given any official reasons for the decline, a friend and former professor from whom I had sought advice suggested that my new status as a wife and mother might well have given reviewers pause as to whether I could actually carry out the project. I was stunned, especially since I had never previously suffered either overt gender discrimination[3] or declination of a proposal. His explanation was more upsetting to me than the thought that I had simply not written convincingly and competitively. After all, the latter could be overcome. I was determined to work even harder than before.

A position at INCAP during the next four years allowed me the luxury of nearly continual fieldwork. As a young mother, now with a Spanish surname and a Guatemalan husband and residency, new doors were opened to me. Once in a great while I took a child with me to the villages, both Indian and Ladino, where I worked, but my husband and his family were so opposed to this practice, and the children usually so bored, that it was easier to leave them home with the servants and their playmates. During those years it was my own experiences in childbearing and breast-feeding which formed the backdrop for my research, most of which concentrated on just these subjects. In effect, my mostly female informants and I compared notes, exchanged complaints and remedies, and shared reminiscences and folk knowledge from our different cultures. They never saw my husband, as I rarely saw theirs, who were off to the fields long before I arrived. But we understood that our common interests in health, diet, and children were basically women's affairs. Whenever I wandered off into other subjects such as religion or politics, I was usually referred to the absent men, and it was always clear that these women were, as was I while married to a Guatemalan, subordinate to menfolk when it came to decision making at either the household or community level.

Because of my own family needs and expectations, I worked only half-time at INCAP, though I put in at least as much time at home analyzing and writing up data. My field excursions varied—sometimes I spent two or three long, eight-to-ten-hour days in a row in a village; other times I went out each day for two or three hours. As I have described elsewhere (Gonzalez 1970), this kind of timing most definitely limited the problems which could be studied, but it is also crucial to note that my home identity could be envisioned, if not understood completely, by these women. Unlike the reception I had received in 1955, I was now their peer as a married woman and mother.

They could and did discuss intimate subjects with me, including aspects of their sex lives, their fears for their children's well-being, and their reluctance to conceive so often. Yet we were never really friends and equals. That would not have been possible, I believe, even if I had been able to reside in their villages for longer periods of time, because of the fact that my husband was an educated upper-middle-class Ladino from Guatemala City. He never used anything but the familiar *tu* in addressing Indians and expected and received their deference. Class and ethnic differences were imposed on me and my informants by our common membership in the larger Guatemalan society. For better or worse I was "Doña Nancie," and so long as I behaved within their notions of how a matron of my class should, I could and did achieve their confidence, especially in women's affairs. So I accepted the godmother role when asked, received their small offerings of fruits and vegetables, and distributed simple medicines from the clinic—which fit the centuries-old patron-client relationship expected between Indians and Ladinos. I never actually learned very much about the rest of the culture aside from what I read or observed in passing. In part this was due to the fact that I did not live in the village and my visits were somewhat sporadic and infrequent. Also, I was simply not around when many things happened, so the sense of "wholeness" of the culture never came across. This is inevitable under such circumstances, I believe, though not necessarily detrimental in applied work.

Fieldwork and Matrifocality: The Dominican Republic

After seven years of marriage and three children, my husband and I decided we had irreconcilable differences, and my two sons and I left Guatemala permanently, leaving my year-old daughter in her father's custody. After teaching for three years at the University of New Mexico and carrying out research on the Hispanic population of the state, I secured a grant from the National Science Foundation to do a study of rural-to-urban migration in the Dominican Republic. By this time I had settled, more or less comfortably, into a new existence as head of a household. I had purchased a house and furniture; my sons were cared for by a live-in servant from Guatemala; my mother had moved her residence to Albuquerque, living in an apartment on the other side of town; and we had even acquired a dog. As an associate professor I had economic security; I purchased a life insurance policy and made a will. Distant cousins living in Albuquerque were frequent visitors to the household, as were several different male friends from the academic and business worlds.

In a way, my grant obliterated my earlier disappointment in not being funded, and I was confident that fieldwork with children aged seven and nine would be no problem. I rented the house, and my mother agreed to keep Bingo, our dog. Friends who had been in the Dominican Republic with the Peace Corps recommended hotels, valued friends, and even a housekeeper. I had been in touch with several professionals in the country, and on a reconnaissance trip the year before had looked into documentary resources, local institutions, housing, and even schools for the boys. I was ready. The boys were excited. My mother was reconciled to the thought of dog-sitting. We left in high spirits.

I have already described some of the practical problems we encountered (Gonzalez 1974), but never have I tried to analyze the situation as a whole in relation to anthropological theory and methodology, nor in relation to my own self-identity. As I look back on it now, I understand why a female head of household was far easier to "sell" among the urban poor and in some villages than it was among the power elite with whom I had also tried to establish myself. (The research plan had called for me to study the urban end of the continuum, while a husband/wife graduate student team lived in a nearby rural area which was undergoing out-migration. In the long run I ended up spending at least a quarter of my time in rural areas as well.)

I had assumed I would be living in or on the fringes of a lower-income barrio in the city, though in a "modern" house, and that somehow everyone would understand that this was natural and necessary for an anthropologist and that I would still be welcomed into "classier" circles. My previous experience in Guatemala suggested that I might even be lionized and my knowledge and opinions sought after, for I was aware that virtually no social scientific information based on ethnographic study existed for the country.

Alas! I grossly miscalculated. First of all, my efforts to find what I termed a "suitable" house were interpreted (in part correctly) as a signal that I had severely limited funding. Indeed, prices had escalated sharply over the previous year as more and more Americans arrived to help rebuild a country whose economy had been seriously imperiled by the events following the assassination of Trujillo and culminating in the arrival of United Nations "peacekeeping" forces in 1965.[4] My house in Albuquerque had been rented for $150 per month; anything comparable in Santiago cost $300 or more. But in fact, regardless of cost, I was not seeking something comparable—I merely sought minimal conveniences, three or four bedrooms so that I could accommodate my students when they came to town, and a location where I might find, as neighbors, recent arrivals from the countryside. I nearly despaired of success.

Living conditions in the city were difficult at that time, especially in relation to utilities, which I felt I needed to accomplish my research ends *and* provide a safe and comfortable home life for my children. Electric outages occurred at least once a day, and it was common to go for several days at a time with no running water. The more affluent houses had built-in storage tanks; the less well-off kept bathtubs and barrels filled, and those without such luxuries went without or stood in line with five-gallon kerosene tins when trucks sent out by the municipality came to their neighborhoods. Purified drinking water could also be purchased in ten-gallon bottles from local stores, although this added considerably to the grocery cost. Finally, existing telephone lines in the city were saturated and it was impossible to have a new line installed anywhere.[5] The custom was to rent the phone *with* the house or do without. Needless to say, the existence of a phone increased the rent considerably.

In weighing all the factors involved, it seemed clear that I would have difficulty finding a house which satisfied all my domestic and professional needs. In addition to the considerations mentioned above, I had to find a place in a district served by the bus from the private school to which I planned to send my sons. Although I had a car, I could not afford the time to transport them each day. Neither did I choose to jeopardize their education by sending them to other than a highly rated school. Actually, there were few choices, and I deliberately eschewed both the English-language school favored by most Americans and the poorly equipped and taught public schools in favor of the excellent (though rigid) boys' school run by the Christian Brothers. After settling briefly in a less than adequate place, I was fortunate enough to find a large, though very old and decrepit, house with a water tank and a phone very near the center of town, where we lived fairly comfortably the rest of the time.

Other matters related to the question of my financial standing included my clothes, which I had selected with the urban poor in mind and which were sturdy, mostly well-worn, and certainly not of the high fashion favored by Dominican first ladies; my failure to join one of the swim and tennis clubs (which I really could not afford); my lack of household furnishings; and the fact that I hired only one servant. (One USAID family had five—a cook, a laundress, a gardener, a nursemaid, and a general-purpose maid). Again, my living standards proclaimed my social status—I kept up with neither the Joneses nor the Garcías!

Compounding the problem was the fact that no one had ever heard of the University of New Mexico, and after the newspaper printed a short piece about me saying I came from Mexico, people were even more confused. "Associate professor" was taken to mean something like "assistant to . . . ," and few could understand why I should undertake to do all this if I were not writing a "thesis." Student status they understood, with all its concomitant poverty, but a mature woman, *head of a household* . . . !

The last straw really had to do with my being divorced. Through a special arrangement between Trujillo and the Vatican, divorce was simply not recognized in the Dominican Republic if the union had been blessed by the Church, and of course the "best" families always had church weddings. Thus, divorce was virtually nonexistent. Among the lower classes there were many common-law unions and subsequent separations, resulting in numerous female-headed households, but these were not expected to occur among "decent" people—and especially not among whites (Brown 1973). My divorced status seemed to embarrass the high-status people. They didn't quite know how to cope with it, so they often merely avoided me socially.[6] Had I to do it again, I would invent widowhood with appropriate rings and photographs.

As head of household, my sons' welfare was entirely in my hands, of course, and there were several matters in which their presence made a difference to my fieldwork. Boys of seven and nine get sick and have minor accidents from time to time, and finding a suitable physician for whom I did not have to wait in turn in a crowded anteroom was an accomplishment. One of the boys had a drawn-out bout with asthma, and in the course of treating him I learned all manner of folk medicine from concerned neighbors and friends, and eventually took him to a highly recommended *curandero*. He subsequently was sent back to the United States to spend six months with my mother before returning for the final summer with his brother and me.

Because I wanted the boys to be content and to enter fully into friendships with their peers, I spent considerable time throughout the year taking them to birthday parties and various school events where I dutifully mixed with the other parents. Actually, this kind of activity opened a number of doors and introduced me to several persons with whom I established good ongoing relationships, including the mayor and his wife. Friendships with their teachers and with the religious men who ran the school also served as springboards to other situations which proved exceedingly useful in the long run. For example, since some of the Christian Brothers were Cuban exiles, they introduced me to efforts being made by various other Roman Catholic Cubans in both urban and rural development.

One of my sons formed a close friendship with the son of a man who owned a local rice mill, and through this connection I secured entrée to the Chamber of Commerce and introductions to several small and large farmers whose farms I later visited. The other son soon made friends within our somewhat rundown neighborhood, and through him I came to know the local mothers and much about their lives which perhaps even their mothers did not know.

Two months after we arrived I received word from my mother that Bingo was arriving by freight the following week. The boys' joy in being reunited with him turned to sorrow when he was killed by a car in front of our house later in the year. His place was never really taken by the various kittens my younger son kept bringing home. People in the neighborhood soon caught on that he was a soft touch, and we might have been overrun with cats had I not set the limit at two (at a time). But his love for animals made him a lovable curiosity, and our house became a magnet for neighborhood children. We also had rabbits, though we must have been the only caretakers in history to have failed to get them to reproduce! I kept buying new ones to replace those that escaped while being cuddled by the various children who came to visit.

Gradually our lives took on the special patina which comes with feeling "at home," and my data collection flourished. Some of my original goals were altered as I discovered that rural and urban were not polar opposites, at least not in the Dominican Republic, and that the process of urbanization had to be understood in the broader context of agricultural and rural development on the one hand, and of international politics and trade relations on the other.

On balance, had I been alone during that field trip I *might* have been able to live a bit more elegantly, but given my age, New Mexican provenience, and divorced status, I doubt I could have achieved any greater rapport with the upper classes than I did. The children's presence probably tempered the notion that I was a fallen woman, and certainly their lives and experiences increased my opportunities and gave me insights through their eyes which I would not otherwise have had.

Last, but not least, I must also point out that fieldwork in a strange land always presents difficult moments and tensions when things go wrong. The presence of loved ones, and perhaps especially children, brings one back to peace and sanity. I will always remember the Dominican fieldwork as being the most difficult and distasteful I have ever undertaken, for reasons to which I have alluded here and have described elsewhere (Gonzalez 1974), but the fact that my children shared it with me has created a special bond between us. I doubt they knew at the time how unhappy I was, and unless they read this they may still be oblivious to how important they really were in getting me through the year.

A Single Parent in Academia: The United States

Whatever else I may have learned while in the Dominican Republic, I confirmed my confidence in myself as a female head of household. Although I had only been such for three years, I was finding that some of the Garifuna women's psychological strength was in me, too. I refused three serious marriage proposals during that year, any one of which would have offered greater financial security, social prestige, and an emotional refuge. But by now I was sure I could manage the first, I had abandoned the notion that the married state was the only respectable one for a woman, and I was developing a small network of close friends, both male and female, to whom I could turn for psychological and material support and assistance. My mother was an especially important source of help—providing small loans, various household furnishings, and childcare as needed until her death in 1977. Undoubtedly, the example from earlier generations of my own family was also important, but the Garifuna matrifocal household was the only one I had actually experienced, and it taught me that it could work *if* one fostered, nurtured, and used a diversified set of people and institutions in managing one's affairs. Unlike the nuclear family, which tends to turn inward, tries to be affectively and economically self-sufficient, and draws its strength from a strong bond between husband and wife, the female-headed household can only survive if the woman maximizes her extended kin, neighborhood, and friendship relations. In a sense, the Dominican Republic was my testing ground as an independent head of household, and I was even stronger on our return.

To put things in perspective, let me summarize the major coping mechanisms I have used since the birth of my first child and then go on to describe the years as head of household. To begin with, I was employed continuously throughout the twenty-three-year period and was the sole provider for seventeen of those years. At no time would it have been financially possible for me to have stopped working entirely, although there were three five-month gaps in employment following the births of each of my children. At no time was I without some kind of help with the household and the children. For a total of eleven of the twenty-three years I had live-in, nonkin help, five years of which were in Latin America. For nine years I had a close relative—either a husband or my mother—living under the same roof, and for thirteen years I had relatives or in-laws in the same city on whom I could call in emergencies and who offered moral support. My children started school early, in both cases at the age of three, and both spent some summers at camp or visiting my mother in another state. On one occasion I left both boys with their father in Guatemala while I attended a scientific conference and did a survey of Caribbean sites in preparation for the Dominican fieldwork.

By the time of my divorce, the basic patterns or coping strategies I needed were already familiar, and my new status merely required me to change the intensity and/or the relative amount of emphasis I gave them. Thus, I needed job security and a better income, since I was now solely dependent on my own resources. With considerable sadness I made the decision to leave Guatemala, where the employment opportunities were few. As a woman, I also ran the risk of losing custody of my sons, and in any case, had I stayed there, I would never have been permitted to take them out of the country without their father's written permission. This seemed too much of a limitation for a woman whose career depended on travel to such a large extent. Furthermore, as a noncitizen I worried about other limitations on my freedom of action and the security of property I might acquire. I did briefly consider becoming a Guatemalan, but on reflection that seemed unwise. Instead, I took a position at the University of New Mexico, having both good fortune and an excellent publication record due to my years at INCAP. My starting salary was nearly three times what I had earned in Guatemala and the cost of living was less.

Over the next seventeen years I moved frequently, always to accept a considerably higher salary, with consequent higher living standards and better opportunities for the boys. Often I needed to borrow money, and quite early I learned the value of establishing credit in my own name. Garifuna women had an advantage over me in that in their culture the fathers of their children could be called on for assistance, and in their absence the fathers' kin might be approached. Banks, credit unions, and charge accounts were my counterpart to the broader circle of kin from whom Garifuna women borrowed, although my third husband and his parents have remained solid supporters to the present time.

Kin, especially maternal relatives of the mother, are also important among the Garifuna in sharing responsibility for children. Although I had fewer maternal relatives, I did call on them, especially my mother. But my major source of help in this sphere were three individuals I brought sequentially from Guatemala, the Dominican Republic, and Mexico. The first two were young women, both of whom had worked for us in their own countries. When the boys became older I brought in a sixteen-year-old Mexican boy who was an ideal companion for them and of considerable help about the house and yard. Two years later he graduated from high school and went off on his own. After that the boys were old enough not to need special tending, and I relied on hourly help for household chores.

Although having these three people live with us was primarily a coping mechanism for me, I also learned a great deal about the migratory process and its meaning for these different people. My later interest in studying migrants in New York derived in part from observing their aspirations and problems. They became members of the household whose status was more like cousin than servant. I still receive Mother's Day cards from one of them, who now lives with her two children in New York.

I noted earlier that during my own childhood I had no friends whose parents were divorced. My sons, on the other hand, found many friends in this situation, more so as the years went by. Interestingly, however, they did not find any whose mothers were content and comfortable with the divorced, female-head-of-household status. Many were actively seeking new husbands or expressed increasingly bitter attitudes about men in general. In some cases the fathers were still the dominant figures, even in absentia. In most, the mother or father or both soon remarried and the children then had the new experience of dual family or alternate family living. In our case my sons more than once asked me to remarry, and in one case even picked the man! When I did try it again, it was all wrong, for all of us, and we quickly untied the knot, though remaining close friends. By this time I had achieved full financial security and the status of the Garifuna older women who once told me they didn't need the men—they could manage better on their own.

Discussion

It was during the Dominican fieldwork that an informant—an upper-class man—asked the question with which I introduced this chapter. It set me to thinking then and has haunted me ever since. In a way it implies that we are play acting, if not dissembling, while in the field. To the extent that we must adapt ourselves to the immediate situation in the field, we may indeed be living in a different style, doing different things, and even thinking some different thoughts. As such, fieldwork periods, like vacations, may be thought of as discontinuities in an otherwise fixed pattern of behavior. If one only goes to the field once or twice in a lifetime, this may be the best way to describe those periods.

But for most anthropologists, fieldwork is the very stuff of life. It not only provides the raw data on which we build theories to explain culture and society, but I believe it also becomes necessary to our mental health and to the maintenance of our professional and personal identities. Margaret Mead once asked me when and where I planned my next fieldwork. In my early forties, with the unpleasantness of the Dominican Republic still in my mind, I replied that perhaps I was getting too old for the field. "Nonsense," she snapped back. "Last summer I went up the Sepik with a pack on my back. You're never too old for fieldwork."

Obviously, she not only put me, nearly thirty years her junior, in my place, but she spoke a truth which I have only gradually come to understand: one is never too old for fieldwork so long as there are indigenous people of the same age out there. Since then I have returned to the Garifuna in Guatemala and Belize, studied their settlement strategies in the Bronx and in Brooklyn, and spent six weeks in a totally new kind of fieldwork in the People's Republic of China. It is now clear to me that my real self is an ever-changing entity, one which incorporates what I experience into the totality of my being. We do not have home identities and field identities, we merely have different presentations of self in accordance with the circumstances. Just as we behave one way at a neighborhood or departmental picnic and another way at the president's wife's tea, we try to fit into our surroundings; and the more experiences we have, the easier this process becomes. We usually refer to it as "sophistication."

Still, this does not address the question of how much intensity and intimacy is possible and desirable in field relationships. Short field stints, such as are required in certain types of applied work, can hardly be expected to lead to anything but cordial and casual, or superficial, interactions. It is enough if we can get the people to talk with us at all, and we must depend on their good faith and their desire to please the agencies we represent, as well as on our intuition and common sense and whatever internal confirming evidence we can muster, to ensure reliability. We cannot and do not get to know the people, nor they us. My first experience in Guatemala was like this. If short visits are repeated over a long period of time, however, as was the case when I worked for INCAP, more meaningful relationships may result. Still, only a portion of the total culture is likely to be revealed to us, just as only certain aspects of our own personalities become known to the people with whom we interact.

It is only with long-term, full immersion that deep intimacies may develop, and then only if the anthropologist is willing to "let go" and become involved. One close friend confided to me that he had declined to go through an initiation rite for young men because he feared psychological trauma would result—he knew he was already becoming "too close," and that was far enough for his purposes. Such aloofness may be easier if one is accustomed to living as a loner in one's own culture, or when one's family members are also part of the field experience.

The point I wish to make here is that one's real self is, or should be, present all the time if one is to do good fieldwork and remain sane. I further suggest that in time our home and field identities merge into a single self which is the product of our total life experiences. It may be that at any given time only certain parts of this self become visible and understandable to our informants. Some of them probably have a deeper desire to know us well than do others, yet they too may have to remain forever just outside whatever bounded circle of intimacy we allow ourselves. In other words, even when they can tolerate greater closeness, we may not be so inclined, and vice versa. The definition of "field rapport," then, is necessarily complex and a bit fuzzy on the edges.

The informant who asked about my real self was trying to know me better, I believe, but at the same time he was expressing his disbelief in (and disapproval of) professional women as heads of households. This, of course, reflects the general view of Dominican males of his class and also explains why I never again considered marrying a Latin American. He seemed not to understand how I could possibly like living this way, and that I therefore must be hiding myself and some other existence from him and other Dominicans. Such is still too often the view we encounter even at home—both in our personal lives and in the literature.

Fieldwork does present different opportunities and problems for women than for men, and many of the other contributions in this volume address that fact. Here I have tried to present still another kind of situation, which for social and cultural reasons has not often been experienced by anthropologists of either sex (see Frisbie 1975). Men as single parents are still a rarity in our society in general, and I am not aware of any male anthropologists who fall into this category. Women, by contrast, may well have cringed at the very thought of being alone with children in the field, for the burden of keeping even one's own self in good working order while accomplishing meaningful work can be awesome.

I have tried to show how being a single head of household may work and how it may actually benefit the research through providing emotional and practical support, as well as extra eyes and ears which observe better than ours at certain levels and in some arenas. Finally, I would argue that since fieldwork is the source of our data and a necessary activity for continuing professionalism, anthropologists should continue it periodically throughout their lifetimes, recognizing that each time will be different (even when we visit the same society) because *we* are different. Perceptive accounts which take this variable into consideration will enrich not only anthropology but our understanding of self.

Notes

1. It is not for me to recount here the stories passed down by word of mouth that play such an important role in the informal training of anthropologists. Most veterans in the field are aware that some of our colleagues have not returned from the field or have abandoned anthropology as a result of their field experiences; a very few may have achieved a satisfactory adaptation or adjustment of sorts. The subject demands separate treatment, but due to its sensitive nature it may never be handled adequately in print.

2. This is not to suggest that rapport necessarily becomes easier with aging—the opposite could be the case, depending on the type of culture involved, the flexibility of the anthropologist, and the nature of the problem. As I look back, I often think that my status as a "student" in the field was the best. Little was expected of me, and because I was presumably without power, influence, or money—and therefore harmless—I was often privy to situations I had to struggle to observe in later years.

3. Like most women of my generation, I realized only much later that I had various built-in defense mechanisms which prevented me from recognizing discrimination when it did occur. I now can look back and ferret out some instances, but the process is both painful and unproductive. For the most part I still tend to blame myself rather than my gender, except in the most glaring occurrences. I am far better at spotting injustices done to others and in analyzing policies for their possible discriminatory effects.

4. The USAID mission in 1967–68 was the largest in the world, next to that in Saigon.

5. I had heard stories about people buying new lines directly from the company "for a price." I even let it be known that I needed one and would be willing to pay for it, but since I had neither well-placed friends at that time nor appropriate affluence, I got no nibbles.

6. Just once I tried to have a dinner party to entice people to come to my home. I invited about ten couples, all from the upper social strata, along

with several Americans, but only one Dominican couple appeared. Some of the couples sent regrets the next day; others never responded.

References

Brown, Susan E.
   1973 *Women and Their Mates: Coping with Poverty in the Dominican Republic.* MS.
Frisbie, Charlotte
   1975 "Field Work as a 'Single Parent': To Be or Not to Be Accompanied by a Child." In: Theodore R. Frisbie (ed.), *Collected Papers in Honor of Florence Hawley Ellis*, pp. 98–119. Papers of the Archaeological Society of New Mexico, vol. 2. Albuquerque, N.M.: Hooper Publishing Co.
Golde, Peggy (ed.)
   1970 *Women in the Field: Anthropological Experiences.* Chicago: Aldine.
Gonzalez, Nancie L. (same as N. L. Solien)
   1957 "Cultural Change in a Guatemalan Community." *Papers of the Michigan Academy of Arts and Letters* 41:239–47.
   1969 *Black Carib Household Structure: A Study of Migration and Modernization.* Seattle: University of Washington Press (for the American Ethnological Society).
   1970 "Cakchiqueles and Caribs: The Social Context of Fieldwork." In: Morris Freilich (ed.), *Marginal Natives: Anthropologists in Cross-Cultural Research*, pp. 153–84. New York: Harper and Row.
   1974 "The City of Gentlemen: Santiago de los Caballeros." In: George Foster and R. V. Kemper (eds.), *Anthropologists in Cities*, pp. 19–40. Boston: Little, Brown and Co.
   ———, and Nevin S. Scrimshaw
   1957 "Public Health Significance of Infant Tropical Feeding Practices Observed in a Guatemalan Village." *Journal of Tropical Pediatrics* 3(3):99–104.
Paul, Lois
   1974 "The Mastery of Work and the Mystery of Sex in a Guatemalan Village." In: Michelle Z. Rosaldo and Louise Lamphere (eds.), *Women, Culture and Society*, pp. 281–300. Stanford, Calif.: Stanford University Press.

SECTION II

Sex, Gender, and Information Gathering

6

Female Anthropologist and Male Informant: Gender Conflict in a Sicilian Town

MAUREEN GIOVANNINI

During my fieldwork in the Sicilian town of Garre, my role as a female researcher placed the social honor of a male informant in jeopardy. In keeping with the objectives of the present volume, I draw on this case study to address a key aspect of the researcher-informant relationship—the part played by gender identity in establishing communication, structuring expectations, and generating difficulties for participants in the research context.

I begin with a brief overview of the setting, focusing on the sociocultural institutions most relevant to gender definitions in Garre. This is followed by a description of the events leading up to my informant's predicament. In the next section these events are analyzed according to a symbolic interactionist model of social behavior. This conceptual framework views all social interaction as an ongoing process in which participants, through their verbal and nonverbal behavior, construct the meanings and interpretations that define their relationship. By adopting a symbolic interactionist approach I seek to clarify the nature of participant observation as a creative process of communicative exchange while elucidating the impact of gender identity on that process.

The Research Setting

The town of Garre, with its 4,700 inhabitants, is situated in northeastern Sicily's mountainous interior. Until the construction of a small clothing factory in 1964, Garre was predominantly an agricultural community characterized by endemic underemployment and an economy that was below subsistence level. Economic relations were structured by an exploitative land tenure system in which a handful of aristocratic landlords possessed up to 70 percent of the landholdings. Here, as in other parts of rural Sicily, large estates called *latifondi* were divided into small plots for short-term rent or lease to individuals who were obliged to provide their own equipment, seed, and fertilizer.

The nuclear family has emerged as the dominant kinship unit in Garre. The family's importance, acknowledged by all Garrese, is related to the fact that this unit has provided the Garrese with the only long-term economic and emotional security available in an otherwise hostile social environment (Giovannini 1978). Thus, family members cooperate to ensure their mutual survival, while the family itself is pitted against other family units for access to necessary but scarce resources.

Similar to other Mediterranean societies, the contributions of Garrese women and men to the well-being of their respective families are carried out in separate but complementary spheres. In general, a man's responsibility is to provide for the material needs of his family and to protect the family patrimony from hostile outsiders. Correspondingly, a woman's role centers around domestic activities including childbearing and child-rearing. This gender-based division of labor, coupled with the endemic conflict over scarce resources in the public sphere, has structured Garrese conceptions of the nature of women and men and influenced their definitions of ideal female and male comportment.

In the public sphere of economic and political activities, "might makes right" as male actors attempt to maximize their interests, usually at the expense of others. This survival strategy is reflected in the Garrese view of men as innately predatory and self-serving. Women, by contrast, are largely excluded from activities in the public sphere; instead, they remain at home, performing important domestic tasks necessary to maintain the family. The fact that women's roles are restricted to the home, the spatial locus of family life, has contributed to a conceptual identification between women and the family. Like the family, whose economic and political boundaries are vulnerable, women are viewed as being inherently weak, vulnerable, and in need of male protection. This imagery is reinforced by certain female anatomical features imbued with cultural meaning—for example, the ability of women to be physically penetrated from the outside.[1] Based on these concepts of male and female nature, the Garrese reason that unprotected women will, sooner or later, fall victim to "naturally predatory" men. Their belief is aptly expressed in the proverb: "The lame goat [a female] will go to the mountain [go unprotected] just so many times before it is eaten [seduced] by the wolf [a predatory male]."

These views also find expression in the normative definitions of female and male behavior, both within the home and in the outer world. Since women are "weak and vulnerable" by nature, their male relatives must assume responsibility for protecting them. Indeed, for the Garrese the ability to protect one's women is an important indication of a man's social worth in comparison to other men. Failure to meet this duty renders a man a cuckold, and he becomes a laughingstock. As the Garrese say, "If a man cannot keep his house in order [i.e., protect his women], he is not much good for anything else." For her part, a woman must cooperate and avoid being alone with an unmarried man, since it would be in the nature of any "real man" to take advantage of the situation. Like their counterparts in other South Italian communities, Garrese women are admonished to exhibit chaste and modest behavior at all times—comportment that not only reflects positively on them but also signifies the social worth of their male kin.

The Case Study

As a graduate student focusing on South Italian society, I had become familiar with relevant studies on that area. Hence, I was aware of the pattern of beliefs, values, and practices that structure female-male relationships in the southern regions. At the same time, field accounts written by women working in similar areas had led me to believe that my status as an outsider would give me some immunity from indigenous gender-based norms (Papanek 1964). As it turned out, this assumption was disproven on many occasions, beginning with my first encounter in Garre.

When I arrived in town I proceeded to the town hall and introduced myself to four local officials, all of whom were male. After these officials had examined my numerous letters of recommendation, I broached the topic of lodging and inquired about the possibility of renting a small apartment. Immediately their faces froze as one of them, the vice-mayor, asked in a cold and suspicious voice, "And what would a young girl like you want with her own apartment?" Fortunately, I perceived the cause of their alarm and was able to redress my blunder by quickly replying, "Well, of course I don't *want* to live alone, but I didn't think that any other arrangement was possible. If I had a choice I would certainly prefer to live with a family where I could feel safe and secure." When they heard this, the taut expressions on the faces of all four officials gave way to relieved smiles. Then one of them, Signore Leone, explained that he and his wife had an empty room which they would be willing to rent out. I realized then that as a woman I could not live alone and

hope to gain the confidence of the Garrese. To facilitate my acceptance I gratefully accepted Signore Leone's offer.

During my first few weeks in Garre the Leone family introduced
me to their relatives and friends, as well as to other individuals they
regarded as refined townspeople. As time went on I was able to extend my contacts beyond this somewhat select group so that eventually I was interacting with people from virtually every age and
socioeconomic category in the town. There was, however, one major
limiting factor with which I had to contend. Because of my identity
as a woman and its implications in Garre, my informants were, by
and large, other women. Spending most of my waking hours with
women was valuable since it allowed me to develop a "female perspective" on those aspects of South Italian society that had usually
been described according to male viewpoints. On the negative side,
however, having to restrict myself to female informants also meant
that I was denied access to information about male-dominated domains such as political activities. This limitation became particularly problematic during the nationwide referendum on divorce
which took place while I was in Garre. Among the Garrese the de-
bates surrounding the referendum called into play a wide range of
local-level alliances and hostilities. At that time I was attempting to
map out the town's power structure—real as well as ideal—and
referendum-related events constituted a fortuitous opportunity to
observe political groups in action. Unfortunately, the most important
public encounters between town factions took place in the evening
when "respectable" women were safely at home. On these prerefer-
endum evenings, being a safe-at-home female anthropologist proved
highly frustrating.

Soon after the divorce referendum I unexpectedly encountered
Franco, a young Garrese man, who was willing and able to provide
me with the in-depth political data I was seeking. I met him at a
party I attended with the Leone family. Since such town parties included numerous chaperones, normal restrictions on female-male
interaction were temporarily lifted so that young people could converse and even dance together (albeit several inches apart). When
Franco and I began to talk I learned that he was a university student
majoring in engineering at his family's insistence. His father was an
unskilled laborer who, along with other family members, was sacrificing to provide his only son with an education that would benefit
Franco and raise the family's social status in the town. To conserve
scarce family funds, Franco lived and studied in Garre, traveling to
the University of Catania only to sit for his examinations, a common
practice among the students in Franco's generation, most of whom
came from families with modest economic means.

As we talked Franco told me that even though his parents believed engineering would provide him with a secure and prestigious future, he was more attracted to the political and social sciences. With that comment we launched into a discussion of the recent divorce referendum, and he described the various power factions as well as the behind-the-scenes strategies employed by political leaders to attract and maintain a following. I explained that I was very interested in this kind of information but that, as a woman, I had limited contact with men and male-dominated activities such as politics. Franco then expressed his belief that these restrictions on female behavior were discriminatory and served to reinforce the prevailing male domination over women. As a member of the Italian Communist party, he opposed all forms of repression, gender-based as well as class-based. At the end of our conversation Franco volunteered to provide me with any information I needed about local-level power relations, and I eagerly accepted his offer.

Our first meeting after the party took place in the Leone's living room, with Signore and Signora Leone present. The meeting was not very fruitful since both Franco and I were reluctant to discuss candidly the political factionalism in which Signore Leone himself was involved. After about one hour of superficial conversation, Franco got up to leave. As I walked him to the door, we decided to continue our discussion the following week in Catania. Both of us had business at the university, so we agreed to make the trip on the same day and meet over lunch in the university cafeteria.

The day in Catania proved to be very rewarding. Away from the curious eyes of the townspeople, we felt free to discuss not only my research but also other topics of mutual interest. That afternoon Franco stated that he wished to change his major from engineering to sociology. He explained that his objective was to understand better and eventually to help reform the socioeconomic and political institutions of Sicily. I was encouraging and gave him the names of several university professors in sociology and political science with whom he could discuss his plans.

In the next three weeks Franco and I met once more in Catania. During this meeting I constructed a chart of the local-level power structure while Franco explained the historical circumstances which had led up to the present situation. At the end of the afternoon our work was not quite completed, so Franco suggested that we stay in Catania one additional day. He said that we could both stay at his friend's apartment and finish our discussion there. I declined, since it would be difficult to explain my absence to the Leone family, and so we departed for Garre on the evening bus. Back in the town Franco and I managed to circumvent the local norms and meet briefly on two occasions, when we talked about my research as well as his planned shift to sociology. One meeting took place in a local cafe where Franco was seated and I "just happened" to walk in to purchase some postcards. His offer to buy me an expresso aroused no suspicion since it was something the Garrese often did to make l'Americana feel at home. The second meeting was held at the home of Franco's young cousin Concetta, whom I was visiting when Franco "just happened" to stop by.

During this period I was elated over the wealth of information that Franco, a knowledgeable and perceptive key informant, was providing. In addition, like a "true anthropologist" who learns by doing, through my meetings with Franco I was discovering how Garrese women could, and did, get around restrictive gender norms—for example, young women managed to spend time with their boyfriends without arousing suspicion by visiting the latters' female relatives (who usually gave their tacit approval). I had come to regard Franco as a trusted friend, someone with whom I could share ideas and opinions I was reluctant to discuss with other townspeople. In terms of my impact on him, I assumed that the presence of an anthropologist in Garre had provided the impetus for Franco to reevaluate his own career orientation. While regarding this as a positive outcome, I never contemplated the negative repercussions our relationship might have for him. Thus, I was totally unprepared for what happened.

Shortly after our last meeting in Catania, another party took place in the company of Signore and Signora Leone. Franco was present that evening and informed me that our relationship would have to end. The reason he gave was that several of his friends had become aware of our meetings and that despite his attempts to clarify the nature of our relationship, they assumed that Franco, being male, must have other intentions. These friends kept asking how things were progressing with l'Americana and goaded him by saying that if he did not manage to go to bed with l'Americana, then he was not really a man. As Franco described it, he felt trapped between two equally untenable alternatives. He could lie about our relationship and thus reaffirm his social worth as a "predatory man," while ruining my reputation as well as my research; or, he could continue to give an honest account, which would safeguard me but place his social worth in jeopardy. In an attempt to remove himself from this situation, Franco decided to end our relationship. As he spoke I recalled our last meeting in Catania, and his suggestion to remain an additional day now took on new significance. On hearing the entire story, I was confused and upset but agreed that he had found the only viable solution. Then, when the initial shock wore off, I began to ponder the events of the previous four weeks to better understand how my informant-friend's predicament had come about.

Participant Observation as Symbolic Interaction

To understand Franco's situation two related issues must be addressed. First, what were the sociocultural and interpersonal factors responsible for his situation? Second, how did I, as a researcher, a woman, and a friend, contribute to his dilemma? This, in turn, necessitates a conceptual approach which analyzes participant observation as a process of interaction involving the actions, perceptions, and cultural values of both researcher and informant. The theoretical perspective referred to as *symbolic interactionism* offers this kind of interpretive framework. To begin with, symbolic interactionism rejects traditional views of social behavior as structured by rigid, preexisting norms. Instead, social interaction is defined as a communication process where individuals symbolically convey messages about themselves, the other actors, and the social setting; at the same time they are perceiving and interpreting signals conveyed by others in the setting and adjusting their behavior accordingly (Goffman 1959).[2]

A key factor in this process is the human ability to "take the role of the other" in social situations (Blumer 1969; Turner 1968). This implies grasping the intentions of other social actors in the setting to facilitate communication and mutual agreement about a situation. Taking the role of the other is also involved in the creation and reaffirmation of the individual's sense of self, for viewing others as objects to whom meaning is assigned requires being able to perceive oneself as a separate entity for others. Thus, a sense of personal identity is formed largely through contacts with significant others whose attitudes and expectations help to shape the individual's self-image (Blumer 1969). In any social setting people bring with them this general sense of self—the "core self" (Kuhn 1964)—along with preexisting values and beliefs that influence their definition of the situation. Yet, since social interaction is an ongoing, formative process, these old meanings may be altered and new ones created through the reciprocal activities of participants (Blumer 1969; Denzin 1970; Turner 1962). As we shall see, this final point is of particular relevance to Franco's situation.

Viewing participant observation as symbolic interaction helps us to comprehend the dynamics between the fieldworker and the people he/she studies. The participant observer is continually taking the role of the other in order to discover culturally based attitudes, values, and role expectations. Anthropologists commonly refer to this as "getting inside the heads of one's informants." Less recognized among anthropologists is the fact that the participant observer role also involves sending cues about oneself and one's intentions to informants, as well as interpreting and acting on informant's responses. In this reciprocal feedback process researchers often attempt to attach meaning to themselves, their informants, and the situation to facilitate communication and cooperation.

Such a reciprocal feedback process is evident in my first encounter with the four Garrese officials. At that time I managed to create a more acceptable impression of myself based on their negative reactions to my initial "presentation of self" (Goffman 1959). Through that interaction and similar ones, an image of l'Americana emerged which the Garrese and I accepted. While both my roles as a woman and a researcher were incorporated into the image, my femaleness was the crucial defining feature on which expectations and evaluations of my behavior were based. As a woman I was believed to be weak and vulnerable, in need of protection against predatory males. Moreover, as a woman alone I constituted a threat to the existing social order where autonomous females were a dangerous anomaly. In the eyes of the Garrese, living with una famigghia onesta ("a respectable family") provided me with some protection and minimized my anomalous status in the town.[3]

As a researcher I was seen as someone who must gather information by observing community events and interviewing community members. These activities required more mobility than would normally be granted to a woman in Garre. Fortunately, however, the Garrese seemed willing to define such behavior as respectable so long as it could be interpreted as research-related and so long as my informants were female. In retrospect, I realize that I continually used verbal and nonverbal cues to stress the researcher aspect and play down the female aspect of my persona. My "impression management" (Goffman 1959) included dressing conservatively and carrying a large notebook whenever I left the house. It also involved explaining any trips outside of Garre in terms of my research rather than citing other reasons such as shopping or recreation.

Since most Garrese shared a basic set of assumptions about the nature of women, their expectations of me as a woman and even as a woman researcher were remarkably uniform. The one exception was Franco, who in some respects appeared to be a marginal member of his society. During our first meeting he singled himself out from other townspeople by criticizing the subordination of women in Garre and by stating that he was a member of the Italian Communist party. Although very popular in other parts of Italy, communism was condemned by most Garrese who belonged to either the Christian Democrat party or the Socialist party.

Perhaps at that point I should have remembered the advice of my mentors, who had cautioned against too close an association with deviant members of the society one is studying. As it turned out, I did not heed their warning because the prospect of access to important political data heretofore denied me proved too tempting. Also, looking back, I believe that my decision to see Franco again was influenced by another set of factors, personal rather than professional. While Franco's opinions deviated from the Garrese perspective, they largely conformed to my own worldview which, by Garrese standards, would have been considered deviant as well. For example, even though I agreed that my female status was an important characteristic, I strongly rejected the portrayal of all women, including myself, as innately weak and vulnerable. Such views notwithstanding, as a "marginal native" (Freilich 1970) living among the Garrese I was obliged to respect their attitudes and conform to their expected gender roles. Conformity proved difficult, emotionally as well as intellectually, and I often wished for the opportunity to speak my mind to someone whose opinions concurred with my own. In an important sense, Franco provided me with that opportunity.

As Franco and I continued to meet, a set of meanings and definitions of the situation began to emerge which were very different from those characterizing his and my other relationships with the Garrese. Contrary to most townspeople, Franco was an astute observer of his society and, at the outset, openly conveyed his dissatisfaction with many aspects of life in Garre. Reacting to his cues, I also expressed my opinions frankly and even discussed my research hypotheses as well as my preliminary findings with him. This positive feedback and my related expectations for Franco reinforced his original dissenting and critical stance toward Garrese society. Thus, through our mutual interactions, new reciprocal roles and related self-images emerged for both of us. Franco's marginality and dissatisfaction crystallized into a more clearly defined view of himself as a social critic and future social scientist. Both his initial behavior and my subsequent encouragement contributed to the process that culminated in his decision to major in sociology rather than engineering. At the same time my self-image as an anthropologist able to collect information even in the most difficult circumstances was progressively taking shape.

During that period Franco and I were forging another set of reciprocal roles as well, defined in terms of friendship rather than mere
research collaboration. Our friendship emerged out of symbolic
manifestations of trust and confidence in addition to our shared
ideas and beliefs. When Franco and I expressed opinions that most
Garrese might condemn, each was demonstrating a belief in the other's ability to understand and in the other's good faith. Trust was also
symbolically conveyed by my decision to meet Franco in Catania, a
potentially incriminating act, while Franco displayed his confidence
in me by a willingness to discuss many of his personal thoughts and
conflicts. In sum, our agreed-upon definition of the situation included not only common research interests but incorporated mutual
expectations that the other was a friend and confidant.

This definition of the situation soon broke down, however. According to symbolic interactionism, when individuals are together,
each brings meanings and definitions to the new situation. These
include self-images linked to role relationships with others who
may not be present at that particular time (Kuhn 1964). In Franco's
case, the self-identity and related meanings he brought to our relationship had been formed largely through his lifelong associations
with other Garrese. As discussed earlier, political-economic factors
in Garre have influenced greatly the female-male role relationships
as well as beliefs about the nature of men and women. According to
the Garrese, a man's aggressive and cunning nature has an adaptive
advantage because it allows him to compete successfully for scarce
resources needed for his family's well-being. At the same time these
traits make it possible for him to protect the family's patrimony, including its female members, from other men. Hence, in Garre great
importance is placed on a man's aggressive "male" nature because
this nature is related to normative behavior necessary to ensure family survival in a hostile world. It was within such a context that
Franco's primary sense of self, or core self, was formed through interpersonal relations with significant others who constantly stressed
his maleness. Of course, this sense of self incorporated a number of
role-specific self-images—son, brother, student, friend, Garrese, Sicilian—but it had as its defining and integrating feature Franco's
male status.

When Franco and I met, two new role-related self-images began to
take shape for him, those of research colleague and platonic friend.
While the three roles—male, colleague, and platonic friend—are
not intrinsically conflicting, in Garre they proved incompatible because the other partner in the latter two role relationships was a
woman. In the eyes of most Garrese, including Franco's friends, sex-

ual aggressiveness was an integral part of a man's predatory nature. Therefore, for them no veru omu ("real man") could base a relationship with a woman on mutual interests or friendship alone. Rather, given their beliefs about the nature of manhood, they assumed that a man's underlying motive in such a relationship would have to be seduction. Correspondingly, based on their views about the nature of womanhood, it seemed natural that a woman alone (as I was in Catania) would succumb to the advances of a "real man." If such a sequence of events did not occur, then the manliness of the man involved was placed in serious doubt.

Intellectually, Franco did not believe in these gender stereotypes, and more contact with men and women who defined themselves and him in other terms might have resulted in the emergence of a different core self. But at that time Franco's primary reference group was still formed by his male friends, and the sense of self they continued to reinforce in him was intimately linked to his maleness. When those friends discovered our relationship, they placed expectations on Franco that corresponded to their definition of maleness but that also totally contradicted my expectations of him as a research colleague and friend. Thus, within these sociocultural and interpersonal contexts it proved impossible for Franco to integrate the roles of male, research colleague, and platonic friend within a coherent and internally consistent sense of self.

Reflecting on the events in Garre, I can point to the ways in which I unknowingly contributed to Franco's predicament. Throughout our relationship I was an active participant in creating the meanings and definitions that emerged. These symbolic constructs stressed both our mutual research interests and our friendship and were significant to me personally as well as professionally. However, in my enthusiasm I failed to see that my behavior and expectations were helping to shape roles for Franco that would conflict with those he already held as a member of Garrese society. In part this was due to my incomplete understanding about the dynamics of participant observation where informants may be cast into roles to which they feel obligated to conform.

My limited perspective on our relationship and its negative consequences for Franco were linked to the gender-related values, beliefs, and self-image that I brought with me to Garre. When interacting with the Garrese I managed to put aside those constructs in order to meet their expectations of me as a woman. But unlike other aspects of life in Garre that were easily adjusted to, conforming to indigenous gender expectations often proved stressful. Indeed, the townspeople's assumptions about women and their alleged vulnerability were in complete opposition to my own self-image as an independent and resourceful woman. During my meetings with Franco this valued self-image was constantly reinforced, as was my culturally based belief that women and men are capable of being colleagues and platonic friends. These were important factors that influenced my definition of the situation and related expectations. Moreover, they also contributed to an unquestioning acceptance of our relationship, an acceptance that remained constant even when Franco suggested we spend the night at his friend's apartment in Catania. Instead of correctly perceiving his cues, I overlooked them and continued to respond to those aspects of his behavior that corresponded to the meanings I valued.

Perhaps if I had reflected on the importance of gender identity before going to the field and had assessed the implications of being a woman researcher in Garre, I could have anticipated Franco's predicament and thus acted with more caution. As it turned out, my own implicit cultural values, beliefs, and related self-image blinded me to the fact that our relationship, however positive from my perspective, would generate serious problems for Franco.

Conclusion

The preceding discussion of Franco's predicament leads to some important conclusions about the nature of participant observation and the relevance of gender identity therein. The analysis demonstrates that participant observation is best viewed as a symbolic interaction process where researchers play an active role in defining the situation and creating meaning. This perspective challenges the traditional image of the field researcher as a benign and impartial observer and recorder of sociocultural events. Instead, researchers are more realistically depicted as social actors whose very presence and ongoing activities significantly affect the lives of those being studied. In accepting this dynamic interpretation of participant observation, researchers are ethically obligated to assume responsibility for any negative consequences that result from their relations in the field. One hopes, of course, that researchers will be better able to safeguard the well-being of their informants once they gain greater insight into the participant observation process.

As the case study illustrates, such insight includes understanding the implications of gender identity for participant observation. To develop a comfortable balance between one's own gender identity and the host community's general expectations, researchers should become thoroughly familiar with gender-related indigenous beliefs and practices. Ignorance of local norms could result in culturally inappropriate behavior and thus cause serious misunderstandings between researcher and informant. Furthermore, since participant observation is a reciprocal process, researchers must also examine their own assumptions about gender identity and related behavior. Of all the beliefs that anthropologists bring to the field, those dealing with gender identity may be the most difficult to put aside, as they relate to one's underlying sense of self which, while ever present, often operates on an unconscious level. Realizing this, researchers can begin to assess their implicit views of gender identity and determine how these beliefs might influence their interactions with informants. Armed with such knowledge, they should be able to foresee and avert the kind of dilemma that evolved in Garre.

Notes

I would like to thank Sandra Joshel, Elizabeth Leeds, Tony Leeds, and Dennis Tedlock for their helpful comments on earlier drafts of this paper. Field research was conducted in Garre (a pseudonym) from December 1973 to December 1974 under the auspices of a Fulbright-Hays Fellowship.

1. Technically speaking, of course, men can also be penetrated. However, within the Garrese worldview such an act is regarded as unnatural and therefore a highly unlikely occurrence. See Giovannini (1981) for a full explication of the symbolic meanings conveyed by female anatomy in the Garrese cultural system.

2. Indeed, drawing from the works of Cooley (1922), Dewey (1922), and Mead (1934), modern proponents of symbolic interactionism emphasize the human ability to create, use, and interpret symbols as the basis for all social interactions which make society itself possible.

3. There were important qualifications associated with the Leone family's role in protecting me. It is true that living with them prevented me from being alone and thus minimized my vulnerability. However, since I was not a blood relative, their social reputation was not affected by my behavior. They were neither obliged to defend me against outsiders nor to take retaliatory action if a Garrese male made improper advances toward me.

References

Blumer, Herbert
  1969   *Symbolic Interactionism: Perspective and Method.* Englewood Cliffs, N.J.: Prentice-Hall.
Cooley, Charles H.
  1922   *Human Nature and the Social Order.* New York: Charles Scribner and Sons.

Denzin, Norman
   1970   *The Research Act: A Theoretical Introduction to Sociological Methods.* Chicago: Aldine.
Dewey, John
   1922   *Human Nature and Human Conduct.* New York: Henry Holt.
Freilich, Morris (ed.)
   1970   *Marginal Natives.* New York: Harper and Row.
Giovannini, Maureen
   1978   "A Structural Analysis of Proverbs in a Sicilian Village." *American Ethnologist* 5:322–33.
   1981   "Woman: A Dominant Symbol Within the Cultural System of a Sicilian Town." *Man* (n.s.) 16:408–26.
Goffman, Erving
   1959   *The Presentation of Self in Everyday Life.* New York: Doubleday and Co.
Kuhn, Manfred
   1964   "The Reference Group Reconsidered." *Sociological Quarterly* 5:6–21.
Mead, George Herbert
   1934   *Mind, Self and Society.* Chicago: University of Chicago Press.
Papanek, Hanna
   1964   "The Woman Field Worker in a Purdah Society." *Human Organization* 23:160–63.
Turner, Ralph
   1962   "Role Taking: Process versus Conformity." In: A. Rose (ed.), *Human Behavior and Social Process,* pp. 10–40. Boston: Houghton-Mifflin.
   1968   "Social Roles: Sociological Aspects." In: *International Encyclopedia of the Social Sciences,* vol. 13, pp. 552–56. New York: MacMillan.

7

Negotiating Gender Role Expectations in Cairo

LAURIE KRIEGER

From 1978 to 1980, I spent twenty months in a poor district in the Greater Cairo area of the Arab Republic of Egypt. I went to Egypt specifically to study traditional urban women: their notions about their anatomy and physiology; their social interactions; and how these factors affected their attitudes toward and acceptance of family planning methods. My emphasis on women derived primarily from my interest in family planning. There was, however, another reason for the feminine focus. As a young, single American woman I felt that I could not expect to interview men extensively without calling into question my "reputation."[1]

Even with my concentration on women, I expected to encounter many problems. I modified my behavior accordingly, to minimize irritation to my informants and to maximize their acceptance of me. Some of the anticipated problems indeed became real ones; many others never materialized. Notwithstanding, I predicated my behavior on the belief that various problems could arise unexpectedly if I did not follow the prescribed gender role as closely as I could. I also felt that if any of these problems did arise, my fieldwork might be permanently damaged.

This self-restriction sometimes limited the kinds of data I felt I could collect. For example, early in fieldwork I felt that the male point of view on an issue I had discussed with women would have been helpful, but I assumed that it would be unwise to attempt to interview men. By the latter part of my fieldwork I had discarded many of my self-imposed fetters and found myself collecting data from both husbands and wives on such topics as sexual practices, attitudes toward marriage and spouse, and attitudes toward and practice of family planning. Still, even when nearing the end of my fieldwork, I sensed that I could have done more to loosen my self-imposed bonds.

In this essay I will discuss some of the problems that began when I discerned something of the gender roles in the culture I was studying and then tried to determine how much of the female role I was expected to play. Associated with these problems is the matter of what a female anthropologist expects of herself and how she may alter her own preconceived gender role expectations before entering the field, or alter gender role expectations communicated to her by her informants once she is in the field. The essential question, then, is whether anthropologists need to internalize and express in their own behavior all information conveyed to them about gender roles in the cultures they study. In the beginning of my fieldwork, awed by tales of American anthropologists who broke Middle Eastern gender role expectations and consequently were subjected to terrible hardships, including physical and psychological harassment, I would certainly have said "yes." My answer now is "not necessarily." The anthropologist, with the assistance of her informants, may fashion a gender role for herself that accommodates the culture, the fieldwork endeavor, and the personalities of the individuals involved.

Component Problems

Gender role expectations in fieldwork consist of at least four parts: (1) distinguishing between what informants are actually communicating about how they expect the anthropologist to behave and what preconceived ideas the anthropologist brings with her or him; (2) distinguishing between what informants expect of each other and what they expect of the anthropologist; (3) distinguishing between aspects of gender role that are crucial and cannot be broken, even by an educated foreigner, and those parts that are less central; and (4) determining how to break or bend gender expectations to gain the freedom necessary to collect data.

Communication versus Preconception

Anthropologists enter the field with some knowledge of the culture they will study and some idea of what sort of behavior will be appropriate. Before going to Egypt, I of course knew that "unmarried girl" and "virgin" were (or should be) synonymous there. Hence, I conducted myself with what I thought was appropriate virginal modesty. I realized that my research on contraception would be greatly enhanced by data on sexual practices and frequency, but I assumed that Egyptian women would not discuss sexual behavior with a never-married female. Thus, I appeared slightly embarrassed when, every now and then, a sexual joke or a bit of sexual lore was repeated in my presence. Greeting any piece of sexual information with naive surprise (as well as a tactful question to elicit more such information), I felt that I was truly establishing my reputation as a "good girl." After several months, however, I became aware that my informants thought of me as a dim-witted prude on the matter of sex. Modesty was modesty, but surely even an unmarried girl didn't reach my age without some knowledge of sexual practices![2] In time I realized that virginity is, after all, a cultural as well as a physiological status. Because my behavior, while appropriate for a Victorian maiden, would not do for a virgin in Egypt, I was needlessly depriving myself of information. My informants had begun to explain to women I was only slightly acquainted with that their usual sexual joking and grabbing of each other's vaginas and breasts should not be done around me as I found such behavior unacceptable. Once I began to laugh at the jokes I had always found side-splittingly funny—it was with great difficulty that I had controlled my mirth during my "Victorian phase"—my informants relaxed perceptibly. They gradually included me in their explicit joking, although it still took much deliberate effort on my part to get them to agree to protracted interviews on sexual matters.

Our preconceptions of the culture we study come, in large measure, from publications of previous studies. Much of the recent literature on women in the Middle East (e.g., Nelson 1974; el Messiri 1978; Auerbach 1980; Wikan 1980) concentrates on what behavior actually occurs between males and females; earlier literature (e.g., Vielle 1967) tends to emphasize male ideal norms. When I first went to Egypt in 1978, much of the current literature had not yet been published or was generally unavailable. Although part of my hypothesis was that women might have a great deal of power and control over their lives through clever manipulations in interpersonal politics, I nonetheless had read the earlier literature on gender role in the Middle East. I also brought my American feminist perspective with me.

Thus, when I began questioning people on wife beating, I first asked them whether it was sinful (haram), shameful or socially disapproved ('ayb), illegal (mamnu'), or wrong (ghalat). I knew that a husband's physical chastisement of his wife is not sinful in Islam if he has first tried other methods of punishment and if she continues to be an offender. Given my hypothesis of women's power, however, I was shocked to discover that only one person I interviewed (a young, unmarried, academic high school–educated man) asserted that wife beating was wrong.

In the typical crowded alleyways (harahs) of Middle Eastern cities, many people live in a small space within low apartment buildings crammed next to each other. One's neighbors' business becomes one's own. Hence, I had no difficulty discovering which of the neighborhood wives had been or were being beaten on a given day. I reacted to the beatings with such an abundance of sympathy and concern that it often did not quite mask my horror at the physical violence to women. The other women of the *harah* gossiped about each beating, its severity, and its causes and results, shaking their heads and clucking their tongues. Yet they were dumbfounded, and even slightly amused, by my own overly empathic concern. Finally, one of the women asked, "Just what exactly do you think goes on? He [the husband] usually just smacks her [the wife] across the face a few times or maybe hits her with a slipper and that's it (*khalas*). Only sometimes, the husband is a very bad man" (i.e., only *some* husbands are bad men). I learned that many women considered beatings an almost inevitable, albeit very disagreeable, part of life.

Much later in my research, after I had witnessed many different kinds of physical punishment, I realized that corporal punishment was not restricted to wife beating and that my reaction was part of my own cultural baggage. In Egypt, physical measures for disobedience were generally sanctioned as a way of enforcing the rules by a person with protective authority over another person. The same woman whose husband had a right to strike her for disobeying him had the right, as a mother, to hit her children or, as an older sibling, to beat her errant teenage sister. I also saw several women pummel their adult unmarried sons. Still, controlling my reaction to this form of punishment was not easy. Fortunately, neither was it completely necessary. I discovered much about women's relations with their husbands and their feelings (while under a peculiar kind of stress) toward men as a class by visiting the recently chastened wife and displaying all the empathy I really felt but which was not forthcoming in such quantity from the woman's neighbors. The recently beaten woman gladly poured out her woes into the sympathetic ear of a foreign female who would not disseminate the information and who had no permanent stake in her social network. I found that the biased outlook of an American woman and trained anthropologist was not always disadvantageous, as long as I was aware of and able to control the expression of my biases.

Differences in Expectations

My initial question asks how to distinguish between what informants communicate about gender role and what preconceived ideas the anthropologist carries with her or him. The second question involves differentiating gender expectations informants have for themselves from those they have for the anthropologist. This question, too, involves preconceived notions. I will examine the effect on my fieldwork of informants' conceptions of Western women. Although many other personal qualities of the anthropologist intrude here, such as age, marital status, and the role of an educated social scientist, I will focus on the American or European female anthropologist as a Western woman.[3]

Increased economic ties between countries of Western Europe, Japan, North America, and the Third World have resulted in, among other consequences, importation by Third World countries of films and television programs produced in industrialized nations. There appears to be no thought given to the content and appropriateness of what is communicated by the industrialized countries in the exported media. Egypt obtains many movies and television series from the United States. For example, I have sat in a mud house, along with about thirty adults and children, and watched "Charlie's Angels" or "The Bionic Woman" on a television placed atop its own mud pedestal. In addition, during the last few years the great influx of Western tourists clad in shorts and bathing suits has contributed to the formation of Egyptian images of Western women. In my traditional urban field setting, everyone in my sample had seen American television programs and all had heard stories of Western female tourists—"loose" women who expose their bodies and associate intimately with men to whom they are not married. On the whole, this was the image my informants had of *all* Western women. They also voiced the belief that all American women were tall, svelte, and blonde. When I appeared on the scene—distinctly on the medium, plump, and dark side—I resembled the image my informants held of Egyptians rather than their ideal of Americans. I also took great care to dress modestly and thereby hoped to avoid offending my informants, to counteract their stereotype of American women, and to avoid being offended by the men on the street.

I remember feeling that my modest dress, accompanied by my physical features, may have made it easier to establish rapport, but it may also have raised the expectation that I would be more like my informants in other ways. My clothing was meant to convey adherence to the norm of modesty and was never intended to mimic exactly what my informants wore. As mentioned earlier, I tried to modify my behavior to accommodate a standard of what I conceived to be Egyptian correct behavior for an unmarried female, and may have gone too far in this endeavor. However, my adherence to Egyptian norms was rewarded, for my informants never once questioned my gender role behavior in terms of the two great categories of Egyptian womanhood: good woman/girl or prostitute. In fact, almost all of my informants commented on my *unexpected* modesty. I went home early in the evenings (generally before nightfall) unless I spent the night with a family in one of the *harahs*. Although my informants occasionally encountered me in other parts of Cairo, they never saw me with a male companion—I was scrupulous about avoiding situations that would indicate I was alone with any man, save an "adopted" relative. Gradually, I acquired a reputation as a *ragil* ("man"), that is, I could guard my own reputation and didn't require supervision. In general, to obtain data on sensitive issues I felt I had to obey Egyptian gender role norms almost more than Egyptians did, in order to counteract Imbabans' image of immoral Western females.

My informants did not communicate to me their expectation that I fit their gender code of modesty. On the contrary, they informed me in subtle and not so subtle ways that they expected me to drink, stay out late, and associate with men. "After all," they would say, "isn't Jamie Summers [The Bionic Woman] from your country?" Some of the more playful of my informants seemed to delight in trying to trap me into saying or doing something that would be considered shameful by their traditional urban values but which they assumed I did when in my own country. I consequently became adept at detecting the hidden motive behind the innocently phrased question or learning when I should not take a permitted behavior seriously because the real message was: "You may behave in this way, but if you do, you will live up to our ideas of Western girls." Although I had no intention of actually "going native," by observing many of the local rules I acquired the freedom to ask about dubious topics such as sex. I did not, however, follow a norm if I felt that adhering to it would unduly restrict my freedom to collect data, as I will discuss later in the chapter.

The Crucial and the Not So Crucial

In distinguishing between gender norms that must be followed and those that are less important, it is necessary to begin by ascertaining what the norms for gender are. At first, ferreting out all the minutiae of male and female roles was very difficult and anxiety producing. I was told by a helpful American friend that among traditional urbanites it was not appropriate for an unmarried girl to drink Egyptian coffee at a restaurant or at someone's home. A female who broke this norm would be considered "loose." This prohibition against "strong" drink was understandable to me, but the prohibition itself was not intuitively obvious. And there were many, it seemed innumerable, such rules. I lived in a constant state of fear, early in my fieldwork, that an unknowing breach of a gender role prescription would irrevocably cast me into the category of prostitute. Every bit of information about women's roles was treated as an inviolable law. I eventually became familiar with what the norms were and learned how they were followed, bent, or ignored, opting more and more for the dispensation given to a foreign female as I learned which norms would not seriously affect me if I disregarded or stretched them.

A critical technique for differentiating between what I should do to preserve my reputation and what I might do and still not endanger it was watching what people did, as well as listening to what they said they did, because the oral report often differed from the actual behavior. Another important means of distinguishing between critical and less important norms was to concentrate on what happened to a person who did not fulfill a gender role expectation. The mere fact that a woman disobeyed a rule did not mean that I was free to do so or that the rule was not extremely important. I witnessed occasional breaking of even some of the most crucial norms, such as the prohibition on dating for all females. The discovery of any such indiscretion was always followed by severe measures taken against the girl and perhaps her boyfriend. The general and somewhat obvious rule was that the more severe the punishment, the more crucial the norm, always taking into account who knew of the matter. A lesser crime might be more severely punished if, for example, it came to the attention of the neighbors or the girl's father. Misdemeanors might also be severely punished if they were repeated or if the person meting out justice was in a foul mood.

Lapses in approved behavior provided me with a guide to how far I could go in my own behavior. If my behavior or dress were found wanting and the only repercussion seemed to be teasing, I often ignored the pressure to conform. For example, during my first trip to Egypt I often wore a long skirt that had been made in Iran. It seemed very popular with the women I visited, so I had it copied in three different fabrics when I returned to the United States. During my second visit to Egypt I was ridiculed for wearing skirts with a zipper and snap in front. Two of the women I visited literally rolled on the floor with laughter, saying, "Everyone will think you dress that way so you can be undressed more quickly!" I determined that their concern was not focused on any similarity between my front zipper and a male fly (at least not admittedly so), and I therefore decided to continue to wear the skirts. I had never seen a traditional urban woman wearing a skirt that closed in the front, but I knew of nothing in Islam that prohibited it and told the women so. I opted for being a female from America where many women wear skirts that close in front.

Getting Around Gender Role Expectations

After exploring these three aspects of gender role expectations, I was in a better position to negotiate my own gender role with my informants and to find ways around gender role expectations. Two of the situations alluded to above formed a major component of my strategy for circumventing norms that interfered with my work: the interplay of behavior and ideal values, and my identity as a Western woman, albeit an atypical one.

Part of my education in circumventing norms dealing with gender-appropriate behavior came from my informants themselves. A favorite ploy practiced by these women in a conflict situation was the pitting of real behavior against the ideal. For example, a woman might have lied to another person and when confronted with that lie would yell, "Are you calling me a liar!?" (To call someone a liar in Egypt is a serious business.) Unless the person confronting the woman wished to escalate the hostilities, she (or he) would cease pressing short of openly declaring the woman in question to be a liar.

During the course of my fieldwork I searched for an image for myself that would be comfortable for me and my informants and that would still allow me the freedom to collect sensitive data. The general themes of my self-presentation were "good" Egyptian girl, student, and Western woman. Through conscious and unconscious interplay, many problematic aspects of my gender role became apparent.

Many women, for example, told me that it was shameful to fall in love (or, rather, to admit to being in love) before marriage; they grew to love their husbands only *after* marriage. Holding hands or kissing were considered very shameful until after marriage.[4] These people all knew from TV and from tourists that Western females engage in such behavior before marriage. When I told my informants at the beginning of my second field trip that I was engaged, as this was the term that would have been most understandable to my informants for the kind of relationship I had at the time, quite a few of those who had been extremely reluctant to talk to me about sexual matters were more willing to discuss these matters with me. Some of this change may have been related to a preconceived notion about affianced Westerners' sexual behavior. It is also possible that these informants simply stretched an existing norm to tell me the same things they would tell their daughters at a later stage in the marriage process.

Some men and women justified their revelations to me by saying that it was all right to speak about these matters since I was engaged and it would not be long before I was a wife (i.e., sexually active). I was uncertain that this justification expressed a cultural norm for engaged females. Rather, it probably represented an ingenious rationalization on the part of my informants to justify disclosure of intimate personal details to an unmarried foreign female student without compromising my reputation or their sense of what was correct. My closer rapport with them may have been a more important underlying reason for their increased garrulousness than my engaged status. Nevertheless, it is of interest to note the gender status terms in which they, too, manipulated gender categories.

The prostitute/good woman dichotomy is, as I indicated above, extremely important in Egyptian gender role ideology and encompasses many aspects of behavior which, to Americans, are unrelated to gender roles. Occasionally these discrepancies could be used by my informants and me to place me in a better position to collect the kinds of data I needed. Had I followed the Egyptian gender ideal exactly and told my Egyptian friends that I was not in love with the man I was engaged to, or that the engagement was arranged by our families, or that he and I had never kissed, my credibility would have been severely damaged. My informants were well aware that Western women do not follow this pattern, just as they were aware that many Egyptian women do not follow it either—although they were usually not willing to admit to such an exception to their values. The gap between the gender role ideology and what I observed between engaged couples, as well as the ways in which real and ideal values were managed, gave me a clue as to how I should behave. Whenever I felt it appropriate, I emphasized the difference between my culture and my informants' traditional urban culture. "In America we must fall in love *before* we marry," I would say; and I also admitted to having kissed my fiance, although I told my friends that traditionally this was about all that was permitted. I knew of several women's anguish at having been married by their fathers to men they did not care for, while they were not allowed to marry men they loved. The phrase "my father sold me for the money" was uttered by several women as an explanation for why they married their husbands.

To make my position and that of Western women more understandable to these Egyptian women, I explained our distinction between prostitutes and "good" women—that a prostitute in the West is a woman who takes money for sexual favors, and if a woman made an advantageous match without loving the man, people might say she was like a prostitute. This apparently hit a nerve, for many women expressed the belief that their marriages had been based solely on their fathers' greed. While the women may have felt that I had done more than just kiss my fiance (given Middle Eastern notions of women's uncontrollable sexuality), they could not say so; after all, I was not a prostitute by my own culture's standards. Like the situation of the liar discussed earlier, I had presented them with an ideal norm, and their expression of doubt at my statement would have been tantamount to calling me a liar and a prostitute. In effect, I fought ideal norms with ideal norms.

I believe that this contrast of real and ideal, traditional urban and Western, enabled both my informants and me to arrive at gender role expectations for me with which both they and I were comfortable and which could be stretched, or could stress different aspects, to accommodate a variety of situations unique to anthropological fieldwork.

Summary

In this essay I have discussed some of the difficulties involved in determining how much of the study culture's female role the anthropologist may play while still establishing rapport and guaranteeing the freedom needed to collect data. For me the issue can be divided into four component problems: (1) distinguishing between what informants communicate to the anthropologist about their behavioral expectations and the expectations brought to the field; (2) differentiating what informants expect of themselves from what they expect of the anthropologist; (3) distinguishing between crucial, unbreakable gender norms and less central norms; and (4) determining how to break or bend gender expectations to gain the freedom necessary for fieldwork. For each component problem I have presented the ways in which I became aware of the problem and the solutions I arrived at during the course of fieldwork. While each anthropologist must arrive at her or his own solution to these problems, structuring gender role presentation in the field into these four components may aid in thinking through the matter with greater ease.

Notes

During this period of research I was funded by grants from the Anthropology Department, University of North Carolina at Chapel Hill, Dissertation Re-

search Grants; the National Institute of Child Health and Human Development; and the American Research Center in Egypt, with funds provided by
the International Communication Agency.

1. A female's reputation is all-important in the Middle East, the circum-
Mediterranean area, and probably elsewhere as well (see, e.g., Herzfeld
1980; Peristiany 1966; Campbell 1964; Bailey 1971). *Reputation* is the concept of an individual held by people who know or have heard of her/him.
The group judges the individual's behavior and attributes traits to her/him.

2. When discussing informants' perceptions in this essay, I refer to females in the categories of traditional urban culture: an unmarried female,
whatever her age, is called a "girl"; a married woman is referred to as a
"woman."

3. Perhaps in other fieldwork situations, social class or ethnicity might
assume a similar importance.

4. The marriage process involves three steps which may be merged into
one or two, as long as the correct order obtains: *ishabka*, formal engagement
(often emphasized by a large celebration); *katb il-kitab* (the registration of
the marriage with religious officials); and *il dukhl*, consummation (literally,
"the entrance"). Any sexual relations are prohibited until after the *katb il-
kitab*. If pregnancy occurs after this ritual, but before the official consummation, the child is still acknowledged as legitimate because the couple is
officially married.

References

Auerbach, Liesa Stamm
 1980   Women's Domestic Power: A Study of Women's Roles in a Tunisian
        Town. Ph.D. dissertation, University of Illinois at Urbana-
        Champaign.
Bailey, F. G.
 1971   "Gifts and Poison." In: F. G. Bailey (ed.), *Gifts and Poison: The Pol-
        itics of Reputation*, pp. 1–25. Oxford: Blackwell.
Campbell, J. K.
 1964   *Honour, Family and Patronage: A Study of Institutions and Moral
        Values in a Greek Mountain Community*. Oxford: Clarendon Press.
Herzfeld, Michael
 1980   "Honour and Shame: Problems in the Comparative Analysis of
        Moral Systems." *Man* (n.s.) 15:339–51.
el-Messiri, Sawsan
 1978   "Self-Images of Traditional Urban Women in Cairo." In: Lois Beck
        and Nikki Keddie (eds.), *Women in the Muslim World*, pp. 522–40.
        Cambridge, Mass.: Harvard University Press.
Nelson, Cynthia
 1974   "Public and Private Politics: Women in the Middle Eastern World."
        American Ethnologist 1:551–63.

Peristiany, Jean G.
   1966 *Honor and Shame: The Values of Mediterranean Society.* Chicago:
          University of Chicago Press.
Vielle, Paul
   1967 "Birth and Death in an Islamic Society." *Diogenes* 57:101–27.
Wikan, Unni
   1980 *Life among the Poor in Cairo.* trans. Ann Henning. London:
          Tavistock.

8

Gender and Age in Fieldwork and Fieldwork Education: "Not Any Good Thing Is Done by One Man Alone"

ROSALIE H. WAX

During the decade 1969–79 there was an explosion in the number of textbooks on how to do fieldwork: some direct attention to the entire research process; some to exotic intercultural situations; some to illicit and countercultural activities; and others to exposing the intricacies of seemingly conventional American life. Some refer to "qualitative methods" or "participant observation," others to "ethnographic investigation." All have the salutary orientation of encouraging students to move beyond campus and the boundaries of their conventional living—to observe, inquire, and mingle with others, to record their observations, and then to analyze the resultant data.

My examination of these texts has revealed a common limitation or failing, one making the process of learning fieldwork hard for the persons attempting it and tending to make them feel unnecessarily inadequate, even when performing brilliantly. In formal and quantitative methods, the peculiarities of the individual tend to go unnoticed. Electronic data processing pays no heed to the age, gender, or ethnicity of the research director or programmer. But in fieldwork these basic aspects of personal identity become salient; they drastically affect the process of field research.[1] Nowhere is essential humanity more exposed than in the process of fieldwork.

The American system of education and commerce tends to treat persons as if they were interchangeable parts in mass-production activities. Federal regulations and bureaucratic principles tend to minimize and disregard differences among individuals by age, gen-

---

This is a slightly altered version of an article that appeared in *Social Problems* 26(5):509–23. It is reprinted here with permission of the Society for the Study of Social Problems and the author. The quotation in the title is from Black Elk, an Oglala Sioux priest.

der, or ethnicity. So when students reach field situations, they expect to be able to subordinate those aspects of themselves to the exigencies of performing research. Yet, paradoxically, in the field one's basic humanity is emphasized, and such essential traits as age, gender, temperament, and ethnicity become, if anything, magnified in the process of developing interactions with strangers.

Pine Ridge

When Murray Wax and I undertook our study of education on the Pine Ridge Indian Reservation, we were mature scholars and researchers. We had directed three workshops on American Indian affairs, had come to know many Indian college students well, and so thought we knew a good deal about Indians. We planned to study the schools, not only by attending class sessions and interviewing teachers, but by living in the Sioux community, attending community social events, and by talking informally with and interviewing parents, teenagers, and children. We hired two Indian college students as research assistants. One reason was that we had contracted to interview a hundred Indians of high school age and thought that young people could probably do this more easily than middle-aged college professors. Another reason was that "we thought that if a couple of young and educated Indians were given a fair notion of how to go about studying a community—if they actually saw it done before their eyes—they might, in the long run, help their people more than would any number of reports written by outsiders" (Wax 1971:181). Our research proposal was formulated on the assumption that each of us would be able to talk to and interview Indian parents of both sexes about their children, though we took it for granted that Murray would concentrate on the men and I on the women. We also assumed that each of us would be able to administer some interviews to young folk of high school age, though we expected that the young people would talk more freely to our Indian research associates.

Once we set foot on the reservation and began our fieldwork we found that most of our assumptions were inaccurate. Sioux men, we learned, tended to talk, work, and "go around with" men. Sioux women tended to talk, work, and "go around with" women. Married couples did not publicly socialize with each other. Indeed, I cannot recall that I ever saw a Sioux husband and wife engage in what I would call a genuine conversation. When movies were shown in the small local "hall," men sat on one side and women on the other. This meant that Murray and I were not able to use one of the most easy and natural ways of getting acquainted—visiting and talking with married couples like ourselves. (We were able to socialize with some of the Indian couples who live in Pine Ridge town and were accustomed to "White People's" ways. But this was not much help because our research was primarily directed at finding out how the folk who lived "way out on the reservation" felt about their children and the schools.)

We also found that when either of us approached an older man and asked, for example, "Is there anything that your children particularly like about the schools?" he invariably ignored our question and proceeded to deliver an oration on the general value of education. Although eloquent, these speeches did not tell us what we wanted to know. When we approached younger married men and asked similar questions they looked away bashfully and changed the subject. We soon discovered that only ignorant white people would put such questions to men. For among the traditional Sioux, all matters involving children or child-rearing—at home or in the school— were culturally defined as women's business. Young men simply did not talk about children.[2] Old men were expected to take only a general benevolent interest in the welfare of the young. This meant, of course, that if we hoped to continue with this crucial part of our research, we would have to alter our plan. We could not interview parents; we could interview only mothers and grandmothers.

At this point in our exploration I began to have a premonition that I was going to have to do more than half of my wifely share of this job. I was right, for we were told by Indians and by an experienced missionary that it would be most unseemly for Murray to interview any of the Indian women: if he called alone, there would be gossip; if he called with a female interpreter, there would be gossip about him and the interpreter. Since Murray was a man, he was, to the conservative or traditional Indian woman, either a sex object or a respect object. If the former, a polite female respondent would be obliged to joke and flirt with him; if the latter, she would have to turn her head away shyly and say nothing. Neither situation, in my wifely opinion, was likely to produce the kind of interview we needed for our study.

So, like it or not, I was the only member of our field research group who could do the job that had to be done. (I should add that in addition to being a woman I had the advantage of being fifty years old. Had I been a young, childless, married woman, the mothers would not have felt comfortable talking to me.)

Our next task was to find an Indian matron willing to be my guide and interpreter. This proved very difficult. The Indian woman on whose property we were living had several times refused Murray's request that she accompany me on visits to other ladies, saying, "The people are not yet ready to receive you." I did not know whether to believe her, but our experiences with her and her family had made me so anxious and ambivalent that I had lost my usual spunk and initiative (Wax 1971:213–47). But Murray was determined to proceed, and he sensibly decided to seek the advice of a respected Indian elder. By good fortune he called on Harry JumpingBull, an older man with whom he had exchanged a few words at the Sun Dance. Murray explained our research and laid particular stress on our plan to go about the reservation and talk to the Indian parents. "That," said Mr. JumpingBull loudly and decisively, "is a good idea!" Murray asked for advice on how to proceed, but Mr. JumpingBull merely sat erect and delivered a lecture on the problems of Indian schoolchildren as he saw them. Just as Murray was about to leave, Mrs. Cecelia JumpingBull, who had silently listened to the conversation with her face turned away to show respect, turned to Murray and said: "Your wife's name is Rosalie, isn't it? I have a daughter who has the same name like your wife. I'll ask her if she would care to go with your wife to talk to people."

Harry and Cecelia's daughter, Roselyn HolyRock, proved to be a sensible, intelligent woman who worked me to the point of exhaustion. Day after day we visited families with children of school age: the poor, the very poor, and the incredibly poor; married mothers, unmarried mothers, grandmothers and grandfathers; people whose children were studious and people whose children "fooled around and played hooky all the time." Sometimes we visited homes where even Roselyn's sharp eye could spy "no groceries anywhere," and sometimes we saw things so dreadful that I would just as soon not speak of them. All of the Indian women were willing to answer my questions (in English or Lakota), and once the short questionnaire was finished we would visit and gossip. It was from these gossip sessions that I began to understand what was really going on in the local community.

After our work was well under way, I asked Mrs. HolyRock whether she would find some other Indian women who would be willing to administer the interview, but she could recruit no one. I now suspect that had I been able to take the time to repeat the teaching-learning process I had followed with Mrs. HolyRock—that is, carefully explain the purpose of the interview to my potential research assistant, visit mothers with her, and with her assistance administer the interview in her presence—in brief, give her the opportunity to observe what an interviewer was supposed to do—

some of the Indian women might have been willing to undertake the job. American Indians are marvelously adept at learning by observing (Wax and Thomas 1961).

Although Murray was not able to interview mothers, it is only fair to note that he did far more than his share of the other research tasks. He interviewed school administrators and teachers, observed in classrooms, did all the quantitative research, and performed all of the tedious administrative chores.

Trying to Interview Indians of High School Age

For weeks Murray and I instructed our two young Indian research assistants in the art of interviewing, urging them to keep field diaries, to attend and observe what went on in the high school classrooms, and to talk to some of the young people of high school age. One of our assistants, Robert V. Dumont, Jr., listened carefully, followed or improved on our suggestions, and week by week proceeded to turn himself into a splendid fieldworker. The other proved to be a genial goof-off who was no help at all. But even the able and industrious Robert was, as yet, not having much success in talking to young people. Consequently, when one of the middle-aged Indian men with whom Murray was on good terms responded to his perplexities by offering to bring a couple of youths to our home-office, Murray was elated.

I was out on the reservation with Mrs. HolyRock and did not witness what happened. But on my return, Murray, looking unhappy and exasperated, told me that the young men had proven reticent to the point where they had perplexed even their sponsor, and he could not understand it. I reassured him and volunteered to try my hand at interviewing the adolescent girls. (After all, I thought to myself, I had interviewed fanatics in Tule Lake and recluses in New England. I could most certainly interview Sioux girls.) But the fact is that I fared no better than Murray. Accompanied by Mrs. HolyRock I went to the local school and tried for hours, gently putting well-chosen and unthreatening questions to teenage girls. I got nothing but timid glances, whispered monosyllables, and a few I-don't-know's. Mrs. HolyRock then asked the questions in Lakota. Although she had known some of the girls all their lives, she had no more success than I. On the drive home she kept shaking her head and saying, "I don't know what's the matter with those girls."

Eventually Murray and I learned that most Indian adolescents talk freely only to members of their own peer group (their pals), or if they have problems and need help, to an uncle, aunt, or grandparent. (We also learned that our troubles had been augmented by our former hostess—the woman who had insisted that "the people were not ready to accept us"—who had been spreading a rumor that Mrs. HolyRock and I were trying to recruit Indian girls for the Armed Forces.) Thus, in time, Robert Dumont, our young Indian research assistant, obtained some marvelously illuminating interviews, but only after he had spent many months making friends with some of the young men. Equally fine interviews were obtained by Mrs. HolyRock (once people had begun to laugh at the rumor), for she was able to talk to any person who, according to Sioux kinship, was classified as her niece or nephew. We also found that most people were willing to answer a written questionnaire administered in the classroom. Apparently, writing on a piece of paper did not put them under the strain of social interaction with a stranger. These written questionnaires, however, were not as instructive as the oral interviews, and we would have been unable to interpret them correctly without the background and understanding furnished by the oral interviews and the observations of the interviewers.

It should be noted that while gender, age, and status restricted certain areas of our research to particular individuals, there were many essential research tasks that could be performed by all or any of us. Murray and I were able to interview school administrators or teachers of either sex, though Robert Dumont had trouble with some of the white administrators because he was a young Indian. All of us were able to observe and record what was going on in the classrooms or playgrounds, though Mrs. HolyRock excelled in this work because she saw things that escaped us, knew the native language, and also understood the sign language the children used to outwit the teachers.

Fieldwork as Teamwork

Mead (1970:326) remarked that in fieldwork, "a husband-and-wife team, or a team in which there is a great discrepancy of age, whether of the same or opposite sex, works better than a team of two men or two women of the same age. Each piece of knowledge that either member of the team acquires speeds up the learning of the other or others. If this is accepted enthusiastically, without rivalry, then any team of whatever composition, but especially one contrasted in sex or age, will be able to do, not twice, but four or five times as much work as one person working alone." In our fieldwork on Pine Ridge, Murray, Mrs. HolyRock, Robert Dumont, and I represented an almost ideal example of such a team. We were human beings with diverse skills, specialties, advantages, and disadvantages, and we joined forces and worked together to do what we considered a worthwhile piece of field research. We met almost daily, shared what we knew or had found out, asked each other for advice, helped each other, and stood by each other. In some ways we resembled the *Bremer Stadtmusikanten* of Grimms's tales: the ancient donkey, hunting dog, cat, and rooster who joined forces and, by doing what came naturally to each of them, drove the thieving rascals from their home. Be that as it may, the virtues of our Sioux monograph are, in considerable part, due to the fact that the fieldwork was conducted by the unfaltering cooperative industry of a diverse group of people: old, young, male, female, American Indian, and white. (Readers may wish to compare this conclusion with that of Fujisaka and Grayzel [1978], who make an excellent case for multiresearcher project design which is coordinated but separate.)

All Things Excellent Are as Difficult as They Are Rare

I have encountered no fellow fieldworkers who have had experiences quite like those I have described. Indeed, though we made the attempt, we ourselves were unable to duplicate them later when, a few years after our Pine Ridge study, Murray and I again undertook a study in American Indian education, this time on a much larger scale. Since we had good reason to respect the power and efficiency of a fieldwork team composed of people of different gender, age, and cultural background, we hired a young white female assistant professor to live and study the school in a rural community, a male Indian to interview Indian high school students and observe classrooms in a small town, and a middle-aged Indian man who we hoped would advise us and introduce us to the traditional men. We also had planned to hire a mature Indian woman to interview matrons and a young Indian woman to interview high school girls. But "almost everything went wrong: the institutions that funded and sponsored us made errors; the local power groups that feared our project and tried to eject us made errors; our research assistants made errors; and we made errors. Worst of all, none of these errors turned out to be 'lucky mistakes' in the sense that they forwarded or improved the nature of the research. After seven or eight months the situation was so messy and looked so hopeless that Murray and I were ready to drop the whole business and move our research project to another location. The major reason we stayed and stuck it out to the end was that we were asked to do so by two of our Indian assistants (Wax 1971:279).

What we had not realized was that we were entering an explosive and oppressive political situation where the local power groups would regard any well-funded research group directed by outsiders as a threat. Had we entered the field with strong political clout, such as an endorsement from the Commissioner of Indian Affairs, or had we allied ourselves with the local "Establishment" from the beginning, we would not have had so much trouble and we might have been able to develop into and function as a work team. Had we understood the situation and structured our research so that each of us could have concentrated on getting the data as rapidly as possible—before the storm broke—we would have accomplished more.

Murray and I now perceive that we handicapped ourselves by becoming the directors of a large research project rather than simply being the principal fieldworkers. At Pine Ridge, with our more modest contract, we not only did a great deal of our own fieldwork but we spent a great deal of time consciously and unconsciously teaching our assistants how to do fieldwork. At our second and more ambitious project, Murray spent much of his time on administrative duties and I concentrated on visiting the mothers of schoolchildren. Had either of us spent more time actively participating in the field experiences of our assistants, had we taken them with us on visits, interviews, and classroom observations, we might have been able to develop a fairly good fieldwork team. We also would have perceived, early in our investigation, that one of our assistants was genuinely incapable of doing fieldwork and that another had no interest whatever in the hard work involved in studying schools.

Advantages and Disadvantages of Gender and Age

It is obvious that a fieldworker's gender, age, prestige, expertise, or ethnic identity may limit or determine what he or she can accomplish. Or, to put it more positively, in fieldwork each gender and each age level has its own particular and peculiar advantages. Women can sometimes accomplish what men cannot, and vice versa; young people can sometimes accomplish what older people cannot, and vice versa. On the whole, however, the most advantageous and rewarding situation is probably that of a mature woman. Indeed, as Mead (1970:322) remarked, "women field workers have an easier time the older they look or are willing to look." Fischer (1970:272, 278) notes that when she and her husband were studying a New England community, she had a less difficult time than he did because she was able to join and participate in various organized women's groups. There was no comparable group for her husband other than the volunteer fire department, for most of the men in the community commuted to work. Fischer also believes that in most communities mature women will help a strange woman more easily than they will help a strange man.

Mead appears to have gotten along well with women in all of her field situations. In her fieldwork on an Omaha reservation, at age twenty-eight, she noted how much easier it was for a woman to talk to the women than for a man to talk to the men (Mead 1932:133). She also knew how to get along with men in the field: at age 36, on her first walk through a village in New Guinea, she pointedly identified herself as a knowledgeable and discreet woman by remarking loudly, "No, I won't go into the House Tambaran, that's the men's house. I am a woman"—which pleased the old men so much that "they shouted it up and down" (Mead 1978:192). (It would be my guess that Mead's announcement also pleased the women.) And among the Manus, "endowed by the people with fewer years but greater seniority than [her] actual age of fifty-three," Mead (1970:321) was given the privilege of accompanying a group of men on a fishing expedition.

Among the Sioux I found that postmenopausal women were not only respected but feared. They gave long moralistic talks at certain ceremonies, and they might, as a group, visit people who were behaving improperly and "talk to them." Yolanda and Robert F. Murphy (1974:105–6) note a similar experience among the Mundurucu: "An old woman may sit where she pleases, and men will actually defer by making room for her. She may talk on whatever subject interests her, and if this requires that she interrupt the men, then so be it. Her opinions are freely given—and listened to—on matters of community concern, and they are shown marked respect." During her work among the Houma (a mixed French-Indian community of southern Louisiana), Fischer (1970:272) tells us, "My being a woman lessened their suspicions. It was difficult even for the Houma to imagine that a woman would be acting as a spy to gather information and use it to prosecute would-be medical practitioners or to get control of signatures to dupe the people to their little remaining title to land." And Powdermaker (1966:113–14) remarks that "a woman alone in the field has certain advantages. Social separation between the sexes is strict in all tribal societies. Male anthropologists say it is difficult for them to be alone with the native women, because the men (and the women, too) suspect their intentions. . . . My relations with the women were more chummy than with the men, and data from the former were more intimate." The men, however, understood Powdermaker's work, assisted her, and invited her to their feasts.

When David Riesman was conducting a study of political apathy he suggested that I try my hand at administering his long and highly structured questionnaire to some working-class people. His research assistants (all men) had been unable to get virtually any response. Then thirty-six, I did try my hand, and the first woman I interviewed gave me responses that ran to forty typewritten pages. At the time I attributed my success to the fact that I had spent a good deal of my life with working-class people and knew how to approach them (Wax 1971:8–9). I still see this as an important factor, but I now recall that all of these phenomenally successful interviews were with middle-aged or elderly women. On the one occasion when I tried to interview a young man, I did not do so well.

From personal experience I would judge that a mature woman— or a woman who is able and willing to assume a mature and responsible appearance—will almost always have a marked advantage in doing that very demanding variety of fieldwork known as door-to-door interviewing. Not only does she appear less threatening than a man or a young person, but most respondents are likely to assume that she will be more knowledgeable and understanding. When my husband and I were studying Indian education in a small town in Oklahoma, I was obliged to go from door to door looking for Indian parents to interview. I introduced myself by saying: "My husband is doing a study of Indian education and he has asked me to help him."

Mature women have exercised this advantage in fieldwork from the very beginning of anthropological and ethnological studies. It is no accident that of the nine portraits appearing on the book cover page of *Pioneers of Anthropology*, six are of women. As early as 1884, two of these, Erminnie Smith and Alice Fletcher, had done fieldwork among American Indians on their own. These pioneers were followed by Matilda Stevenson, Elsie Clews Parsons, and Frances Densmore. All of these women entered their fieldwork careers rather late in life, and most of them were relatively well-to-do. They could afford to pay Indian assistants and were not dependent on any foundation or university. To the Indians they must have appeared to be rich, powerful, and formidable beings. Lurie (1966:81) has given us so illuminating and insightful a description of the lives and careers of these women that I need add no more than that they seem to have been extraordinarily able, self-reliant, and courageous individuals with "an exceptional amount of drive and a sense of adventure."

I know of only one field situation in which mature women found themselves at a disadvantage. Cassell (1978:23–24) reports that in an ethnographic study of schools, male and young female researchers were able to develop good relationships with school principals: male researchers developed a relationship with "an element of camaraderie"; young female researchers found that principals "went out of their way to show and explain things to them." But older female researchers found that the principals were uncomfortable "with women they could not pigeonhole in a secretarial or teaching capacity."

The Territorial Disadvantage of the Male Fieldworker

In tribal or traditional communities the married and mature women do the essential chores, prepare and often provide the food, rear the children, and make sure that the basic obligations and rituals of kinship are maintained. They see that their young kin are properly married and, by all manner of subtle pressures, see that their relatives behave themselves. In some communities women are the moving force behind the maintenance of hard feelings or feuds between families or kin groups. By contrast, the men sit in council, make laws, go hunting, fight enemies, perform public rituals, and engage in public displays of singing, dancing, and athletic prowess. Also, the men, or at least some of the men, remember and recite the traditional stories involving sacred or wonderful events and ceremonies. Women also tell stories to each other, but these are usually concerned with current events: marital misconduct, accidents, assaults, illnesses, births, quarrels, relatives having good or bad luck— in short, all manner of notable, deplorable, scandalous, tragic, or comic happenings (Wax 1971:239; Murphy and Murphy 1974:8–9, 116–18, 133–36). Indeed, with some reservations, one might say that in tribal or traditional communities, be they the Old Icelanders, the BaMbuti of the Ituri forest, an urban community of Italian immigrants, or a congregation of Orthodox Jews, the role of women is basic, fundamental, central, and social; the role of men, for all its excitement, public authority, or solemnity, is ornamental, peripheral, and cultural.

For fieldworkers, this means that a mature woman usually has no difficulty in becoming a participant in the women's group or groups. She also may have only slight difficulty in talking with certain men, and in time, and with modest difficulty, may even be permitted to observe and study some of the men's activities. A male fieldworker, however, can under no circumstances associate with the women or learn much about them; that he should attempt to do so is unthinkable. Consequently, a male fieldworker who accepts the responsibility of studying a whole culture or a whole community without the active cooperation of a woman fieldworker finds that he has committed himself to performing an impossible task. Some male fieldworkers, like William Foote Whyte, have sensibly chosen to limit their research to those areas open to men. Whyte (1943) was able to associate and talk with the street-corner boys and subsequently with the male politicians of an Italian-American neighborhood and his descriptions of these organizations are now considered classic. But he made no attempt to perform a comparable study of the Italian-American women, nor did he claim to have done so.

Other male fieldworkers, proceeding on the assumption that the aim of fieldworkers "is to encompass a whole, and as many parts of that whole in as much detail as possible," have not fared so well. Some of them, to my mind, seem to ignore or repress the fact that they attempted the impossible, for when they give us descriptions of how they did their fieldwork they simply do not tell us anything about what happened when they approached women. Others seem to imply that women's affairs are not a significant part of the whole. For example, Spencer (1965) in his book on the Samburu, devotes one chapter to discussion of the status of women. His description of how the women appeared to him and of how he obtained his data do not inspire confidence in his understanding of the whole:

> Throughout much of day, women sit together in the shade of a tree inside or close to the settlement, gossiping and often doing some handiwork. The (male) leaders sit or lie in the shade of another tree rather far from the settlement and gossip and hold their discussions. The two groups remain separate and usually out of sight of one another, and each is engrossed in its own view of the world. The elders' gossip group has a certain atmosphere of dignity and authority, for it is there that all important decisions are made during discussion and only elders may join it. The women's gossip group has no atmosphere of dignity and authority; small children play around it and it is joined by girls of all ages and a myriad of flies. Elders do not care to associate with it and the *moran* [initiated young men who are not yet married] avoid it altogether. *It was not possible to collect first hand material on the gossiping of women during my field work,* but my impression and that of the elders was that it was confined to domestic affairs and long detailed accounts of recent conversations and happenings. *It would not proceed to discussing serious matters of importance as the gossiping of elders frequently did.* (italics mine)
>
> On the whole I found women were quite ignorant of many aspects of the total society and usually unhelpful as informants. Outside the affairs of their own family circle they often showed a certain indifference. They were less inquisitive than males and less quick to grasp situations. They found it harder to comprehend my remarks and questions.

I had the impression that they had never been encouraged to show much initiative of their own, and this was a quality which they simply had not developed. . . . Their demeanor was sometimes listless and frequently sour. They often lacked the general conviviality and warmth that typified the adult males, and it was only with the ameliorating circumstances of middle-age that they tended to acquire it—and many never did. (1965:230–31)

Were I to comment on Spencer's approach from the point of view of a traditional matron, I might say that this is precisely the kind of explanation one might expect from a young, anxious, and somewhat imperceptive *moran* who naively accepted the elders' impressions of women as gospel truth. But since I am a fieldworker and a professor I will say only that I find Yengoyan's (1970:412–13) account of his rapport with Mandaya women of the Philippines a much more comprehensive and unbiased depiction of what a male fieldworker is likely to encounter:

With Mandaya women, rapport was very poor. Female *ballyan* (part-time medical practitioners and mediums) either limited their conversations with me or totally avoided me. Even in questioning about "neutral" subjects such as the time spent in planting, husking rice, and so forth, their replies were short and uninformative. Furthermore, females systematically kept me from observing the rituals surrounding the planting and harvesting of rice. In most cases these rituals were held in areas inaccessible to me, or I was told about them after they were over. This secretiveness among the females was most effective in excluding me from these areas of Mandaya culture.

During no time in the field did I so much as consider obtaining a female field assistant. Since I was unmarried at the time, hiring a female assistant would have implied that I wanted her services for purposes beyond my basic field interests. To avoid gossip on such matters, I seldom dealt directly with females and interviewed them only in the presence of their husbands, male siblings, or fathers.

Forge (1972:266) implicitly makes the same point when he remarks that during his fieldwork with the Abelam of New Guinea he had only two really successful interviews with women.

One is moved to suggest that in this kind of field situation a single man would fare better if he dismissed the mythical notion of studying the whole and concentrated his energies on studying the men. Alternately, as Tylor (1885:93) suggested a century ago, he ought to obtain the assistance of a woman and do a cooperative study: "And one thing I particularly noticed was this, that to get at the confidence of the tribe, the man of the house, though he can do a great deal, cannot do it all. If his wife sympathizes with his work, and is able to do it, really half the work of investigation seems to fall to her, so much is to be learned through the women of the tribe which the men will not readily disclose. The experience seemed to me a lesson to anthropologists not to sound the bull-roarer, and ward the ladies off from their proceedings, but rather to avail themselves thankfully of their help.

Young People

For most young people a first field experience is an educational adventure, but it is usually difficult and it can be painful, discouraging, depressing, and sometimes even agonizing. Some of these discomforts might be avoided if young fieldworkers and their research supervisors were made more aware of the fact that young persons in the field have certain inescapable disadvantages. There are some things that they simply cannot be expected to do. On the other hand, as was demonstrated in our study of Pine Ridge, young people have certain distinct advantages and they can do certain kinds of research which are out of bounds for older persons.

In many societies being young and inexperienced can be an advantage because many people regard a young stranger as ignorant, helpless, and as standing in need of guidance. Like a child,[4] the young person is relatively harmless and threatens no one. If the young persons are courteous, intelligent, and genuinely want to learn, they will usually be assisted, protected, instructed, and eventually enlightened by some older person or persons.

Many young fieldworkers have been helped by establishing (or, sometimes, being gently pushed into) a dyadic relationship with an older person who is willing to be their mentor. Thus, Lurie (1972), on her first field trip among the Winnebago, was referred by Indian neighbors to John C. Decora, a respected, elderly blind man, who as Lurie puts it, became "my self-appointed instructor in field technique." She had been told by her professor, J. Sydney Slotkin, that she should take no fieldnotes in the presence of informants. But when Decora, though blind, sensed that she was taking no notes, he said sternly, "When I tell you something, it's important and I expect you to write it down so you get it right." He also told her, "It's a good thing to have 'honest writing'" (1972:6). One of Murray's and my graduate students was able to develop a similar relationship with an elderly Hopi woman who, as it turned out, had also assisted Malinowski and other distinguished ethnographers. This lady instructed him in proper behavior and in the Hopi language so that he was, in time, able to initiate and complete an excellent study of the Hopi

schools. (He was also able to fulfill his doctoral language require-
ment, for his instructress wrote a letter informing the Department of
Anthropology that he had achieved the linguistic competence of a
six-year-old Hopi child.) A young female student of ours developed
a somewhat different but equally fortunate relationship with the
members of a middle-aged women's bowling club. The ladies took a
personal interest in her research and went out of their way to be
helpful.

As demonstrated by our experiences at Pine Ridge, young men,
like Robert Dumont, are often able to develop a good fieldworking
relationship with their male age peers. The classic example, of
course, is Whyte's *Street Corner Society*. A more recent example is
Freilich's (1970) study of Mohawk structural steel workers. These
researches could not have been carried out by an older man or by a
woman. And, significantly, none of these young men tried to study
the whole community. Had they attempted to approach women, they
might have found themselves in serious trouble.

Young Women

Young female fieldworkers—and by young I mean women in their
twenties—appear to have the most difficult time in the field. This is
particularly so if they enter the field alone. Almost all of the younger
female students in our fieldwork courses seem to have more trouble
initiating and carrying out their projects than do the young men. If,
for example, they attempt door-to-door interviewing, they find that
some older men are likely to respond to their questions in a joking,
condescending, or flirtatious manner. As their instructor I can do
little to help them except to explain that these older men think this
is the proper way for an elder to treat a pretty young woman. It is no
reflection on their interviewing skills or on their status as a student
or fieldworker. In my experience the best procedure is to relax and
get what information one can. Sometimes the older men will shape
up and begin to take the interview seriously. If not, one can always
talk to the women.

One of our graduate students, a young married woman in her early
thirties, set out to study urban American Indian mother-child relationships. She found that the Indian mothers, whether young or old,
would not accept her into their groups because she herself was not
a mother. However, during the period that she was trying to establish
rapport with Indian mothers, she made a few close friends among
her female age-mates. These friends welcomed her presence and assistance in an Indian protest movement. In consequence, she was

able to conduct the first field study of an American Indian demonstration at a meeting of the Society for Applied Anthropology.

One of the singular disadvantages of the young female fieldworker trying to study a traditional group is that, unlike young men, she may find it impossible to participate in the ongoing activities of her female age-mates or to develop a satisfactory relationship with them. In such societies young unmarried girls or women do not organize themselves into peer groups corresponding to those organized by the young men. Indeed, our studies of Sioux girls of high school age indicated that most had only one or two close girlfriends. Sometimes their most significant social relationship was with one older girl or with a female teacher. Many pictured themselves and the other girls as engaged in a passionate and ruthless competition for the attention of handsome and virile young men. They desperately wanted to be popular, and they enjoyed being envied by the other girls. In such a situation a young attractive female fieldworker would, almost inevitably, be defined as a formidable competitor. If she were a college graduate or had considerable status, however, she might be regarded as someone to whom one could talk, in whom one could confide, and from whom one might get valuable information about grooming, deportment, and the arts of sociability.

Lurie (1972:155), who undertook her first fieldwork among the Winnebago when she was an undergraduate, reports: "It was my age peers . . . who gave me serious field anxieties with their scornful teasing. I often found them incomprehensible in their seemingly aimless, hedonistic outlook and total lack of middle-class career expectations." And Golde (1970:80), who went into the field alone at age twenty-nine, tells us that in Guerrero, the villagers insisted on defining her as a young unmarried girl: "Being an unmarried girl meant that I should not drink, smoke, go about alone at night, visit during the day without a real errand, speak of such topics as sex and pregnancy, entertain boys or men in my house except in the presence of older people, or ask too many questions of any kind." She was propositioned by boys, men, and even by married men, and astutely comments: "The perception of me as a target of attention must have affected my ability to become friends with the unmarried girls, who, with some exceptions, were withdrawn and unreachable. As in the case of my landlord's niece, they may have been afraid that I would somehow taint them; in other cases they were actually hostile, perhaps seeing me as a potential competitor. . . . The villagers could not conceive that a man and woman could be platonic friends or have repeated conversations that were not preliminary to sex" (1970:87).

Despite the disadvantages of being young and female, it is encouraging to remember that a considerable number of young women have managed to do outstanding fieldwork and produce outstanding field reports. Mead (1978:19) was only twenty-three when "with the courage of complete ignorance" she did her fieldwork in Samoa. Her letters from the field indicate that she was a person of notable common sense, good judgment, determination, tact, fearlessness, and diplomatic skills. As she herself remarked, she had the sense of "being invulnerable as long as I was moving in the right direction" (1975:143). The accounts of their first field trips written by Peggy Golde and Laura Nader are equally impressive and, as fieldworkers, they display many of the same characteristics as Mead. One can only conclude that a person with sufficient intelligence, guts, persistence, and flexibility can do a fine piece of fieldwork even though she may also be a young woman.

On the comforting side, one may suggest to young women that since older women have less trouble doing fieldwork than older men, the disadvantages of youth will inevitably develop into the marked advantages of maturity. On the humorous side, it might be well to recall how Lurie (1972:157) was unexpectedly and vehemently given professional status by a young Indian man. When, at an Indian gathering, a drunken young man from another camp made unwelcome advances, a large, ferocious Indian youth from her camp took the offender by the collar and with one hand "lifted him off the ground and shook him, wagging a reproving finger in his face with the other hand. 'Lishen you, she's no girl. She's an anthropologisht!'"

Fieldwork as Education

Most of the literature on fieldwork makes no mention of the very important fact that fieldwork provides a unique educational experience whatever the person's age or gender. I first became consciously aware of this fact on the Pine Ridge Reservation when Murray and I attended a teachers' meeting at which the participants spent most of their time restating their conviction that the life of the Sioux children outside of school was "meager" and "lacking in experience." One teacher even assured us that the Sioux have no music. The superintendent of schools told Murray: "The school got this child from a conservative home, brought up speaking the Indian language, and all he knows is Grandma. His home has no books, no magazines, radio, television, newspapers; it's empty! He comes into the school and we have to teach him everything" (Wax, Wax, and Dumont

1964:67). Since Murray and I had been living with and visiting Sioux families for some time and had become familiar with the variety of exciting experiences in which the children engaged when they were not in school, we were at first bewildered by the ignorance displayed by the teachers. But when we learned that almost none of the teachers or administrators had ever visited a Sioux family or had attended any Sioux get-together or ceremony, we began to understand. Their (to us) almost incredible ignorance rested on the fact that they had scrupulously avoided doing anything that resembled fieldwork.

Some ten years later I was asked to participate in a study of fieldwork, and other educators and I decided to interview people who had done fieldwork about the impact that the experience had had on them. I was astonished by the enthusiasm of the respondents (see Wax 1976). Many said that it was in the field that they developed self-reliance and self-confidence, and many emphasized that their field experience had made them aware of the complexities of social or cultural situations about which they had previously been ignorant or about which they had had an inadequate or incorrect view. About 90 percent of the respondents asserted that *both* classroom and field learning are essential to education. In the field, they said, learning is personal and humanizing because "it deals with people."

Gender Is Not Always Important

It is probable that a fieldworker's age almost always limits, to some degree, the kind of situation he or she is able to study. I doubt that persons past their mid-twenties can ever become genuine participant observers in an adolescent or teenage group. Teenagers may sometimes permit a young adult to hang around with them, and they may come to regard the fieldworker as an understanding friend, but nevertheless he or she is always "different." In most other fieldwork situations a person who can claim to be thirty or more years old is likely to have an advantage over a younger or an unmarried person.

A fieldworker's gender, on the other hand, may in certain situations be a relatively unimportant factor. The members of voluntary associations such as churches, clubs, or community improvement associations usually do not care whether a researcher is male or female. Indeed, many people will permit a fieldworker to assume the role of a journalist, reporter, scholar, or professional person. When they do this, they usually do not care whether the person who is listening to them is a man or a woman.

At the Tule Lake Center where, during World War II, those Japanese Americans who had refused to pledge written allegiance to the

United States were confined, I was able to conduct repeated interviews with some of the organizers of an underground pressure group—the Resegregationists—who hoped to force the administration to conduct yet another segregation. They defined themselves as the leaders of those people who were "truly loyal to Japan" and "wished to return to Japan immediately." Some claimed to head groups of young men "who would obey their every command"; some were fanatics; and some were self-proclaimed terrorists. But whatever they might be, they talked to me voluntarily, not because I was a woman or a particularly skillful interviewer, but because they placed me in the role of a sympathetic scholarly reporter who had assumed the task of recording their worthy and public-spirited sentiments for posterity. All of them enjoyed making speeches and some of them, on occasion, made pronouncements which they hoped I would relay to the administration. I did not call on any of these leaders or would-be leaders except by appointment. They usually sent for me, although on a few occasions I did write, asking for permission to visit. It is noteworthy that whenever I called on any one of these men, I rarely spoke to him alone. If he was married, his wife was present and she usually took an active and even an aggressive part in the conversation. If unmarried, the respondent invariably arranged that the interview take place in the presence of an elderly man or woman. These men, I suspect, were taking precautions against the possibility that I might accuse them of behaving improperly.

In the relocation centers, my most helpful respondents were married couples of my own age (early thirties). They permitted me to visit at regular and relatively frequent intervals, and we engaged in genuine, lively, and often very frank conversation about past, present, and future happenings. Sometimes I would ask for their views on current events and sometimes they would volunteer opinions or information. Not infrequently they asked me questions. We came to regard each other as friends, helped each other, and exchanged gifts. I correspond with several of these couples to this day. All but one of these couples were *Kibei*, that is, they had been born in the United States but had been sent to Japan for a part of their education. The director of the Evacuation and Resettlement Study repeatedly instructed me to make contacts with young Nisei, most of whom were in their teens or early twenties, but I was unable to do so. But with Nisei my age or older I got along very well. Indeed, these older Nisei went out of their way to protect me during tense and dangerous periods. On one occasion a Nisei friend told me that "if all hell should break loose" I should come and stay with his family in the center. There, he assured me, I would be safe (Wax 1971:132). On another occasion an older Nisei friend wrote me a letter advising me to stay out of the center for a while. (A Japanese American accused of being an informer had been murdered.) Subsequently my friend explained that immediately after the murder some fanatics were announcing that "a Caucasian would be next" (Wax 1971:138).

I do not believe that my rapport with political activists and terrorists, with my helpful and concerned friends, or with the scores of other respondents who talked to me only occasionally was significantly influenced by the fact that I was a woman. What was important was that I was a Caucasian of some status who listened to them. I surmise that any man who had the tenacity, sensitivity, industriousness, plain guts, and the manic sense of mission that I had in my early thirties could have done as well (or as poorly) as I did. And perhaps the fact that I was a strapping five feet ten and weighed (then) about 180 pounds helped a bit.

Now, more than forty years later, as I review my fieldwork in the Japanese relocation centers, I perceive that I consistently overlooked an important area of research. While I talked to many women in the course of my visits, I did not make any attempt to join any of the various women's groups or organizations. I am sure I would have been welcome to attend certain of the night-school classes or cultural study groups, and I was on excellent terms with a number of Japanese women who would have spoken for me. I think if any of my female friends had invited me to attend a class or group I would have done so. On the other hand, the fact that the idea of participation in a woman's group never occurred to me suggests that at that time I was not yet prepared to define myself as a woman. I was a university student and a researcher. I was not yet ready to accept myself as a total person, and this limited my perspective and my understanding. Those of us who instruct future fieldworkers should direct them away from this diminution of self. We should encourage them to understand and value their full range of being, because only then can they cope intelligently with the range of human experience they will encounter in the field.

Notes

1. *Women in the Field* (1970), an illuminating collection of essays by female anthropologists, edited by Peggy Golde, is, as far as I know, the only work that focuses on the specific problems of women in the field.

2. Male schoolteachers or dormitory workers were an exception to this rule. They talked about the schoolchildren freely and often with great insight.

3. I was once told that a young male anthropologist trying to do fieldwork in India began to get his work under way only when he approached people and said, "My father has asked me to do this."

4. Some older Sioux told us that all white people they encountered were "like bright or clever children" because, on one hand, they possessed remarkable technical knowledge but, on the other, they did not know how to behave properly toward other people.

References

Casell, Joan
  1978   A Fieldwork Manual for Studying Desegregated Schools. (Prepared for the National Institute of Education under NIE G 78 0046.) Washington, D.C.: Government Printing Office.
Fischer, Ann
  1970   "Field Work in Five Cultures." In: Peggy Golde (ed.), Women in the Field: Anthropological Experiences, pp. 267–89. Chicago: Aldine.
Forge, Anthony
  1972   "Tswamung: A Failed Big-Man." In: Solon T. Kimball and James B. Watson (eds.), Crossing Cultural Boundaries: The Anthropological Experience, pp. 257–73. San Francisco: Chandler.
Freilich, Morris
  1970   "Mohawk Heroes and Trinidadian Peasants." In: Morris Freilich (ed.), Marginal Natives: Anthropologists at Work, pp. 185–250. New York: Harper and Row.
Fujisaka, Sam, and John Grayzel
  1978   "Partnership Research: A Case of Divergent Ethnographic Styles in Prison Fieldwork." Human Organization 37(2):172–79.
Golde, Peggy
  1970   "Odyssey of Encounter." In: Peggy Golde (ed.), Women in the Field: Anthropological Experiences, pp. 67–93. Chicago: Aldine.
Lurie, Nancy Oestrich
  1966   "Women in Early Anthropology." In: June Helm (ed.), Pioneers of American Anthropology, pp. 29–82. Seattle: University of Washington Press.
  1972   "Two Dollars." In: Solon T. Kimball and James B. Watson (eds.), Crossing Cultural Boundaries: The Anthropological Experience, pp. 151–63. San Francisco: Chandler.
Mead, Margaret
  1932   The Changing Culture of an Indian Tribe. New York: Columbia University Press.
  1970   "Field Work in the Pacific Islands." In: Peggy Golde (ed.), Women in the Field: Anthropological Experiences, pp. 293–331. Chicago: Aldine.
  1975   My Earlier Years. New York: Pocket Books.
  1978   Letters from the Field. New York: Harper and Row.

Murphy, Yolanda, and Robert F. Murphy
    1974   *Women of the Forest.* New York: Columbia University Press.
Powdermaker, Hortense
    1966   *Stranger and Friend: The Way of an Anthropologist.* New York: W. W. Norton and Co.
Spencer, Paul
    1965   *The Samburu: A Study of Gerontocracy in a Nomadic Tribe.* Berkeley: University of California Press.
Tylor, Edward B.
    1885   "How the Problems of American Anthropology Present Themselves to the English Mind." *Transactions* 3:81–95 (Anthropological Society of Washington).
Wax, Murray L., Rosalie H. Wax, and Robert V. Dumont, Jr.
    1964   "Formal Education in an American Indian Community." *Social Problems* 11(4), Supplement.
Wax, Rosalie
    1971   *Doing Fieldwork.* Chicago: University of Chicago Press.
    1976   "Fieldwork as Education." In: E. Rose (ed.), *Forms and Formulations of Education,* pp. 120–48. Study Commission on Undergraduate Education and the Education of Teachers. Lincoln: University of Nebraska.
————, and Robert K. Thomas
    1961   "American Indians and White People." *Phylon* 22(4):305–17.
Whyte, William Foote
    1943   *Street Corner Society.* Chicago: University of Chicago Press.
Yengoyan, Aram A.
    1970   "Open Networks and Native Formalism: The Mandaya and Pitjandjara Case." In: Morris Freilich (ed.), *Marginal Natives: Anthropologists at Work,* pp. 403–39. New York: Harper and Row.

9

Sexual Segregation and Ritual Pollution in Abelam Society

RICHARD SCAGLION

The Abelam are a group of approximately 50,000 swidden horticulturalists living in the foothills of the Prince Alexander mountains in
the East Sepik Province of Papua New Guinea. Abelam grows yams,
taro, and sweet potatoes as staples; sago and breadfruit are other
popular foodstuffs, and the hunting of wild pigs, various birds, and
small animals (wallaby, bandicoot, opossum) is also common. My
research has been with Samukundi dialect speakers in the most
northerly region of Abelam territory, and during each of my field
trips I have lived in Neligum village.

Kaberry (1941, 1941–42, 1965–66) was the first researcher to describe the Abelam. She worked with the Central or Mamukundi dialect group. The first extensive investigations of the other Abelam
subgroups were by men: Eastern and Southern Abelam, by Forge
(1962, 1966, 1970a, 1970b) and Lea (1964, 1965, 1973); Western Abelam by Scaglion (1976, 1978, 1981, 1983). Another female researcher, Losche (1982), has recently worked with the Western
Abelam.

Sex Roles

Division of labor by sex is an organizing principle in Abelam society, where women's and men's roles are clearly defined. Generally
speaking, relationships between the sexes are relaxed and informal,
and men and women often interact in both economic and social contexts. Women collect firewood and water and do the everyday cooking. Occasionally they may be assisted by males in food preparation,
such as in scraping coconuts, but the major responsibility belongs to
women. Women are also responsible for taking care of children, although they may be assisted by men. Women sew and make string
bags, used for carrying almost everything, and pottery, now largely
replaced by metal pots. They also look after the pigs, which are
butchered and cooked by men. Generally speaking, men do the

hunting, build the fences and the houses, weave mats, and cut timber. They also do the majority of craft work, including carving ritual wooden objects, painting with clays and ochres, shaving and sharpening spears, and decorating utilitarian objects.

In many common economic activities men and women can be seen sitting together, each working on their own tasks. This is evident in gardening, where women and men often cooperate. Men clear the heavy bush and cut down large trees while women cut smaller or secondary undergrowth. Women frequently burn off the brush and do the weeding later on. Women plant and harvest taro and, generally, greens, bananas, and sugarcane. Men are solely responsible for the cultivation of ceremonial long yams (waapi) and, generally, for planting shorter yams (njambi). Taro gardening and taros themselves are particularly rich in female symbolism and imagery, while the long yams personify maleness.

Abelam feel that it is inappropriate for one sex to perform tasks generally allocated to the other. They usually feel sorry for a single adult forced to take on those tasks ordinarily belonging to a spouse; they make disparaging remarks about the laziness of siblings or close relatives of the opposite sex who allow this to occur. Once, before I fully realized the "femaleness" of taro, I mentioned publicly that I might plant some in my garden the next day. Several of my adopted female relatives immediately offered to do it for me to spare me (and themselves) the embarrassment of my doing it by myself.

Husbands and wives, and less frequently sisters and brothers, often sit together in the mornings, discussing the day's forthcoming activities as they eat breakfast. During the day sexes are often separated as women garden and men either hunt or tend ceremonial yams, although at times a wife and husband may garden together. People generally return to the village in the evening, with the women usually gathering around cook houses to prepare food, and the men gathering around rest houses or yam houses to gossip, smoke, and chew betel nut. When in small groups, men and women will often eat together and chat during the evenings, but larger gatherings are usually segregated by sex. Wife and husband occasionally sleep together, although the more common pattern is for the women to sleep in a cook house with the small children and for the men to sleep in yam houses or rest houses.

Thus, men's work and women's work are distinct and clearly defined among the Abelam. Each sex may perform certain duties belonging to the other, although the general feeling is that this should not be necessary. The tone of intersexual relations is friendly and relaxed, except regarding yam and initiation affairs as described below.

Many of the accounts in this collection underscore the difficulties experienced by a researcher of one sex in gathering information about the attitudes and beliefs of the other sex, particularly information concerning sex roles and status. In describing the "nature" of males and females and their gender "identity," researchers obviously have sex biases, and it is important to note that my own perceptions about what Abelam women and men should be are largely a result of what Abelam men themselves think they should be. With this bias in mind, and with the above description of what Abelam men and women actually do as background, I now proceed to an examination of what Abelam women and men ideally should "be."

The main responsibility of a man is to provide certain "extras" for both his family of orientation and procreation. Samukundi Abelam land is fertile, and it is generally recognized that with modest effort a woman can plant and harvest enough staple crops to feed her family. Life is enhanced, however, by "quality" food, or kwaami, a category consisting largely of meat (especially pig) and more recently of canned fish, corned beef, and rice. Men are responsible for providing this type of food, for both consumption and exchange. Large well-made houses, status and prestige, interpersonal networks, and so on, also enhance life measurably, and again, these are largely the man's domain. A "good" man is hardworking, kind, good-humored, and generous to his relatives, yet he cannot allow others to take advantage of him, particularly in political matters. He should be capable of obtaining prestige items either through traditional exchange or cash labor, and he should distribute these items both to his family and to others so as to further enhance his prestige.

Women are expected to provide basic foodstuffs, to bear and raise children, and in general to run the household. "Good" women are hardworking and are not argumentative. Female sterility is grounds for divorce, and both males and females feel sorry for barren women. (Traditionally it is not thought possible for a man to be infertile as long as he is capable of sperm production and sexual intercourse.) A good woman will cheerfully carry out her domestic tasks, cooking "complex" meals such as yam or banana soup rather than simply cooking yams over a fire. In general, she should efficiently manage day-to-day household affairs, freeing her husband and/or male relatives to engage in hunting, yam growing, and political affairs.

Sexual Antagonism

Despite the obvious bifurcation of sex roles, there is a central structural equality of Abelam women and men in both labor and role expectations as well as in mythology. Before Losche's (1982) work became available, I spoke of the relationship between the sexes in Abelam as one of "duality" and "balanced opposition." Here I adopt her term "complementary opposition," since it is more parsimonious and more accurately represents the overall situation in Abelam as I found it.

"Sexual antagonism" has been a common analytic device for the examination of sex roles in Highland New Guinea (see, e.g., Read 1952; Meggitt 1964; Langness 1967; Lindenbaum 1972; Strathern 1972; Brown and Buchbinder 1976), although this approach has been criticized recently (e.g., Weiner 1976; Feil 1978). While I do not wish to renew the debate here, I do feel that Highland societies seem more "sexually antagonistic" than Abelam society. Both Abelam women and men freely admit the importance and complementarity of the opposite sex, although there is a certain amount of antagonism, which I describe below largely from a male point of view.

Abelam men, when speaking to one another, tend to describe women as being rather childlike and not really competent to take care of things themselves, particularly in sexual matters. The expression "Taakwa bakna, ndu rate, rakwa jok" provides interesting insights into male perceptions of females. The phrase translates very loosely as "Women are just women—when their man is around, they stay and behave," the implication being that when left on their own women are likely to get into trouble. This is consistent with the male perception of women as childlike, but it also reflects male insecurity about sexual matters. Because the Abelam are polygynous, male extramarital relationships, while not really condoned, are considered less serious than female extramarital relationships. If a married man has a relationship with an unmarried female, she can be viewed as a potential spouse; however, a married woman's affair challenges her husband's exclusive sexual rights and often precipitates rather serious conflicts (Scaglion 1976, 1979, 1981). Women are not really thought to be able to control their sexuality: it is assumed that young, unmarried girls will be somewhat wayward; hence, older brothers tend to assume some responsibility for controlling them. By contrast, young men are thought to be able to assume responsibility for themselves in sexual matters.

Ortner (1974) has suggested the existence of a universal devaluation of women and their activities relative to men. Certainly, Abelam men do assume an air of sexual superiority, which women overtly accept. However, when one peels away this layer of superficial male sexual superiority, one finds an underlying respect for women on the part of men and an obvious sense of self-worth on the part of women.

In Abelam society children (the domain of women) are considered just as important as ritual (the domain of men). Women have secrets relative to birth whereas men have ritual secrets; each is excluded from the other's domain and neither seems to feel unworthy because of this exclusion. Both sexes recognize their vital part in structuring the other's domain: semen is necessary for conception, just as ample garden produce and pigs are necessary for ritual life.

Joking about sex status is permissible in Abelam society, at least between age peers, but is rarely undertaken in an antagonistic spirit. To gauge the reactions of different women, I sometimes have made disparaging comments about the worth of females, as Abelam men might do. Statements such as *"Taakwa bakna jok"* ("Women are rather inconsequential"), usually are answered with something like, "Oh, so you men can have children by yourselves," or simply by turning the phrase to indicate that men are the inconsequential ones. It is my impression that while women overtly accept certain things Westerners might view as sexual inequality (the sexual double-standard, occasional beatings, exclusion from male yam and initiation activities, etc.), they tend to view males as somewhat "big-headed"—filled with self-importance and rather childlike—in these matters, and thus perceive a complementarity of the sexes.

I found Abelam sexual division of labor quite satisfying personally. I generally enjoyed the men's tasks and the Abelam male role and took readily to them. Given my substantial wealth (by Abelam standards), it was not difficult to provide my Abelam family with luxury and prestige goods and thus fulfill expectations of a "good" man. Tasks such as house building, at which I was not particularly adept, were easily and traditionally accomplished: I "hired" men to help me. When I had to clear a garden, reroof my house, and so on, I let it be known that I needed help. Friends and male relatives came to my aid, and I later rewarded these people with presents and help in return. Thus, I traded their expertise for my wealth, learning and practicing male tasks in the process.

Given my previous statements about Abelam male perceptions of females, I hesitate to admit that in the field I too was most comfortable with these perceptions of sex roles. I have little interest in domestic tasks such as cooking and cleaning, performing them only grudgingly in the United States, so I was euphoric to be freed of them in the field. While my own perceptions of females are certainly different from Abelam males' perceptions, I had no moral or ethical problems in assuming an air of sexual superiority consonant with that of the Abelam male. In fact, I am less comfortable with what are for me the redefined sex roles of men and women in the United

States, for here I find myself trying to "watch" my sexism. (For example, in this essay I have taken pains to intersperse the phrase "women and men" with "men and women," which I personally find more "natural.")

As a consequence, when in the field I do not attempt to make personal adjustments or to redefine myself in any way to the Abelam. I have not experienced any of the personal difficulties or adjustment problems to everyday sex roles and status described by other contributors to this volume. In truth, I felt from the beginning that I could be myself in day-to-day interactions. However, during the yam-growing season it did become necessary to curtail my interaction with women, even though I found this to be awkward, "unnatural," and problematic for data collection, a difficulty I will now explore.

Ritual Segregation

For six months of the year, Abelam men grow certain varieties of ceremonial yams (*Dioscorea alata*) in special yam gardens. Menstrual blood and contact with female genitalia, however indirect, are thought to be detrimental to yam growth. Consequently, men observe sex taboos and generally avoid women throughout the growing season.

Yam planting begins at the end of the dry season, usually in late August or September. A formal ceremony marks the beginning of the planting season and the end of the period of relative sexual freedom. However, limited sexual relations continue for a time until men actually begin planting yams. Once the yams have been planted, a variety of taboos are observed to encourage yam growth. Yams are viewed as sentient beings who are aware of both events and surroundings. They are upset by social conflict and particularly by menstrual blood and aroused female genitalia. Should they become aware of such things they will not grow well. Consequently, there are taboos against social conflict, fighting, and any sort of discord, as well as against sexual contact, sexual joking, and any sort of activity likely to physically arouse women. Since any sexual activity at all is likely to endanger yam growth, homosexuality among men is not substituted for heterosexual relationships during this time. Because yams prefer tranquility, and because meat is thought to be a "strong" or "hot" food associated with aggression, taboos against *kwaami*, a category of food consisting mainly of meat, are also in effect during the yam-growing period.

The end of the growing season is marked by formal yam displays, usually commencing in February, which signal the cessation of the taboos. In fact, men often resume sexual activity somewhat earlier when they personally have harvested their own yams. Thus the yam-growing period extends from late August or early September through February or March, with transitional periods at the beginning and end of the season.

Abelam men are serious about their yam beliefs. The taboo against sex results in a birth season during which nearly all children are conceived after the yams have been harvested (Scaglion 1978). Seasonality in social conflict (Scaglion 1979) and in other areas of behavior (Scaglion and Condon 1979) are also evident. Yam growers avoid contact with menstruating women and, in fact, with anyone at all suspected of having engaged in sexual activities. Young people are particularly distrusted, since they are generally considered unable to control themselves. Older men are often heard cautioning their daughters or whatever young men will listen about the dangers of sexual encounters during the growing season. Concern over ritual pollution also results in a significant decrease in social visiting and communal eating during this period. Men generally will eat only food cooked by their own wives or a small number of trusted others, and in extreme cases some men will even cook for themselves. As a general pattern, any unnecessary contact with women is to be avoided.

Once the yams have been harvested, a ceremonial period begins in which yam displays, accompanied by singing and dancing, are common. Relationships between the sexes again become relaxed. After the yam displays, male initiation ceremonies are held, and again there is some ritual segregation of the sexes, although not as pronounced or prolonged as segregation during yam growing.

Male initiation consists of four stages: *Kutaakwa, Wulketaakwa, Lutaapu,* and *Putilago*.[1] Boys and young men pass through one stage, wait several years, and then pass through the next. The village is divided into two ceremonial moieties (*ara*), with each *ara* initiating members of the opposing *ara* in different years. At each stage boys and young men are segregated for a month or more while they undergo purification. During this time, men involved in the initiation activities are expected to avoid unnecessary contact with women to prevent ritual pollution. Women are rigidly excluded from observing preparations for the ceremony and from the ceremonies themselves. Initiation ceremonies do not take place every year, however, but rather every third or fourth year; hence, they do not have as great an impact on relationships between the sexes as does the ceremonial yam complex.

In contrast to the male initiation complex, female rites of passage surrounding puberty are individual affairs. The newly menstruating female (*naramtaakwa*, or "decorated woman") is first secluded in a menstrual hut. After cessation of the blood flow, a modest public ceremony is held during which the young woman is washed, decorated, and presented to the community. Male relatives take an active part in the actual ceremony.

Ritual Pollution

My first trip to Neligum village began during the yam-growing season. However, by the time I had adjusted to village life and become reasonably conversant in Tok Pisin, the lingua franca of the area, the ritual season had begun. Consequently, I observed free and easy relationships between the sexes, though my informants indicated that six months hence sexual relationships would cease completely. I was skeptical, assuming that this was ideal rather than real behavior. It seemed "unnatural" to me that virtually an entire population would refrain from sex for six months, particularly one that had clearly shown its sexuality during the ritual season. I guessed that people would reduce sexual contacts but continue to have occasional sexual relations with preferred partners in private.

I was thus unprepared for the seriousness of yam taboos and the changed relationships between the sexes. The free and easygoing associations between females and males to which I had grown accustomed were no longer permitted. Men could no longer flirt with unmarried women (a personal favorite activity during my early fieldwork), engage in any kind of sexual joking, or even chat with women. Even very indirect contact was viewed as polluting in ways I could barely imagine, and I quickly ran foul of these taboos. For example, when I carry something that isn't heavy and then need to use both hands to do something, I have a habit of tucking the object between my legs, rather than setting it down, to free my hands. While in the field I am accustomed to carrying a shoulder bag in which I keep betel nut and tobacco (for gifts) and my notebook, pens, and so on (Abelam men also carry such bags). I remember once, early in the yam-growing season, when my bag slipped off my shoulder while I was leaning over attempting to cut a vine. I tucked the bag between my legs, severed the vine, and looked up to find my male companions viewing my actions with horror. It seems that if I had previously had a sexual encounter, the "pollution" would quickly have gotten into my bag and affected the tobacco and betel nut. If I then gave these polluted materials to a yam grower and he ingested them, his yams surely would not grow well and he himself would probably be sick.

I soon learned the complex and indirect ways in which pollution could be transmitted: through material objects, in food, through fire, and so on. As I have indicated, older men are always suspicious that younger men cannot contain themselves and may be having sexual contact; consequently, they tend to avoid them or at least to fear possible pollution from them. I learned, through my own mistakes, that young men shouldn't even bathe in pools frequented by older yam growers, since water can also transmit pollution.

While I attempted to avoid what I considered unnecessary contact with women, I continued to talk to them, to frequent different households, and to eat food cooked by a variety of women. Several older men, apparently disturbed by what they viewed as my dangerous contact with the opposite sex, began to avoid me and prohibited me from entering their yam gardens. I soon realized that under such circumstances it would be impossible to continue gathering data on women's activities, to closely observe cooking techniques, taro gardening, and so on. This was particularly unfortunate since there are certain female gardening activities which only take place during that time of year. I thus began to avoid virtually all contact with women and attempted to avoid any activities that might indirectly pollute yam growers. Had I chosen to continue interacting with women, I would have been excluded from all subsequent yam activities and male initiation rites. Since these male ritual complexes were more directly important to my work in legal and political affairs, I decided to forego observations of women's work and concentrate on understanding the male ceremonials.

In later years, on shorter trips to the village, I have been able to fill in some of the gaps in my data by ignoring yam-related activities and interacting mainly with women. It should be understood that men are not strictly forbidden to interact with women during the yam-growing period; but if they choose to do so, they will be shunned by yam growers. Since I had already gathered data on yam growing, and since I was often absent from the village during the day observing conflict management elsewhere, I found it possible to forego male companionship in the village for these short periods. I am sure that some of the more traditional yam growers will forever view me with suspicion because of this behavior; others will forgive me provided that I follow the taboos in the future.

Implications for Data Collection

Abelam ritual is quite colorful and spectacular, and yam displays and initiation activities are of great importance to the social and spiritual fabric of life in the village. However, because of the ritual separation of sexes, anyone having undue contact with women would likely be excluded from male ceremonial activities. Kaberry, a European woman, was able to have herself defined in a different category from Mamukundi Abelam women, and as such she was permitted to observe male ritual activities. Losche (1982) also reports on yam and male initiation activities, apparently from firsthand observation. Samukundi Abelam generally follow yam taboos quite rigidly, and, at least in Neligum village, I think that any resident woman would be denied access to most yam gardens and yam magic. Even if a resident European woman were "redefined," I imagine that she would not be permitted to interact frequently with Abelam women and also observe yam-related activities because of the possibility of indirect pollution.

Because of this ritual separation of the sexes, any researcher, whether male or "redefined" female, would have difficult choices to make regarding data collection. If a researcher were interested in a theoretical topic necessitating knowledge of male ritual activities (religion or politics, for example), certain female activities simply could not be extensively observed. While I have managed to interact with females during yam-growing periods while on short trips to the village, there are certain activities I could never observe without becoming permanently polluted. For example, females retire to somewhat isolated menstrual huts for several days a month, where they are prohibited from cooking, doing craft work, and so on. Because of the danger with which Abelam males associate menstruation at any time, I certainly could not enter a menstrual hut and observe activities, and it would be inappropriate and unwise to even ask extensive questions about menstruation.

Some of this prohibition of my free action with women may derive from my own close identification with the Abelam male sex role. I sought to be perceived as a "normal" Abelam male, and for these reasons it may be that Abelam find it easy to pigeonhole me, expecting that I will follow appropriate male patterns in all things. Perhaps another researcher, female or male, who has associated less closely with a traditional sex role could more freely interact with both sexes. The best data collection strategy, however, would probably be a female and male researcher working together. Naturally, during the yam-growing season this team would have to split up, sleeping in separate houses and avoiding situations in which people might suspect them of sexual activity. By each sex adopting appropriate gender identification and role behavior, complete data could be collected.

The foregoing discussion has broader implications for one of the main topics of this volume: that boundaries created by culturally imposed sex categories limit the persons with whom a researcher can interact and can consequently limit the type of information collected. For a researcher working alone, choices about what to collect must be made. Furthermore, a certain schedule for data collection may be imposed: if one chooses to observe male ritual behavior, female activities such as child-rearing, cooking, water gathering, and so on, would be best observed during the ritual season.

On the basis of the Samukundi Abelam case, it is obvious that culturally imposed sex categories can define interaction style, intensity, and timing of relationships between the sexes, again determining the nature of information access. Abelam cross-sex friendships are quite easily developed during the ritual season, and I count certain Abelam females among my friends. I tend to be loose, informal, and joking in my interpersonal relationships, an interactional style quite in keeping with cross-sex ritual season Abelam patterns. Such an interactional style is impossible during the yam-growing season, and opposite-sex friendships must suffer as a result. People must depend on same-sex friends for intense personal interaction during this time; consequently, these types of friendships tend to be the closest. I found it annoying to have to curtail my female friendships during yam growing, particularly since I did not share most Abelam beliefs about ritual pollution, and I know many young Abelam men who shared my impatience with the yam taboos. As education and knowledge of alternative lifeways increase, problems concerning perceived ritual pollution will also increase as young people redefine sex roles. Perhaps this will ultimately result in a relaxation of yam taboos without the concomitant abandonment of ceremonial yam growing. For the present, however, problems of complete data collection by a lone researcher remain.

Notes

I have worked with the Abelam on and off for some ten years, my most sustained period of investigation being a span of some fifteen months between November 1974 and January 1976. I returned about six times for several months in 1979–81 while working elsewhere in Papua New Guinea, and again for several months in 1983. Research for this paper has been supported at various times by the National Institute of Mental Health; Faculty Research Grants Committee, University of Pittsburgh; and the Law Reform Commission of Papua New Guinea. All support is gratefully acknowledged. I also wish to express special thanks to Moll Apulala, Malemole Urukwaapi,

Narasimbi Urukwaapwi, and Kulukwombe for information about ritual matters, and to Donna Jambiuwi for information concerning women's roles and activities. P. J. Teer provided helpful comments on the manuscript, although it will be obvious that I did not always follow her advice.

1. Forge (1970a:270) and Losche (1982:300) both report an eight-part initiation sequence. While my informants indicated that each of the four parts I have described was subdivided, they claimed that the subdivisions were performed at the same time. This could reflect either a later elaboration of the initiation cycle in the areas studied by Forge and Losche or an earlier breakdown in the traditional system in my area. Undoubtedly, in Neligum, extreme emphasis on the ceremonial yam complex has resulted in a concomitant deemphasis on the initiation complex, when compared with other Abelam villages described in the literature.

References

Brown, P., and G. Buchbinder
   1976   *Man and Woman in the New Guinea Highlands.* Washington, D.C.: American Anthropological Association.
Feil, D. K.
   1978   "Enga Women in the Te Exchange." *Mankind* 11:3.
Forge, J. A. W.
   1962   "Paint—A Magical Substance." *Palette* 9:9–16.
   1966   "Art and Environment in the Sepik." *Proceedings of the Royal Anthropological Institute* 1965:23–31. London.
   1970a   "Learning to See in New Guinea." In: P. Mayer (ed.), *Socialization: The Approach from Social Anthropology,* pp. 269–91. New York: Tavistock.
   1970b   "Prestige, Influence and Sorcery: A New Guinea Example." In: *Witchcraft Confessions and Accusations,* ASA monograph no. 9, pp. 257–75. London: Tavistock.
Kaberry, P. M.
   1941   "The Abelam Tribe, Sepik District, New Guinea: A Preliminary Report." *Oceania* 12:233–58, 345–67.
   1941–42   "Law and Political Organization in the Abelam Tribe, New Guinea." *Oceania* 12:79–95, 209–25, 331–63.
   1965–66   "Political Organization among the Northern Abelam." *Anthropological Forum* 1:334–72.
Langness, L. L.
   1967   "Sexual Antagonism in the New Guinea Highlands: A Bena-Bena Example." *Oceania* 37:161–77.
Lea, D. A. M.
   1964   *Abelam Land and Sustenance.* Unpublished Ph.D. dissertation, Australian National University, Canberra.
   1965   "The Abelam: A Study in Local Differentiation." *Pacific Viewpoint* 6:191–214.

1973   "Stress and Adaptation to Change: An Example from the East Se-
       pik District, New Guinea." In: N. C. Brookfield (ed.), *The Pacific in
       Transition*, pp. 55–74. London: Edward Arnold.
Lindenbaum, S.
1972   "Sorcerers, Ghosts and Polluting Women." *Ethnology* 11:241–53.
Losche, D.
1982   *Male and Female in Abelam Society: Opposition and Complemen-
       tarity.* Unpublished Ph.D. dissertation, Columbia University.
Meggitt, M.
1964   "Male-Female Relationships in the Highlands of New Guinea."
       American Anthropologist 66(pt. 2):202–24.
Ortner, S. B.
1974   "Is Female to Male as Nature Is to Culture?" In: M. Z. Rosaldo and
       L. Lamphere (eds.), *Women, Culture and Society*, pp. 67–87. Stan-
       ford, Calif.: Stanford University Press.
Read, K. E.
1952   "Nama Cult of the Central Highlands, New Guinea." *Oceania* 23:1–
       25.
Scaglion, R.
1976   *Seasonal Patterns in Western Abelam Conflict Management Prac-
       tices.* Unpublished Ph.D. dissertation, University of Pittsburgh.
1978   "Seasonal Births in a Western Abelam Village, Papua New
       Guinea." *Human Biology* 50:313–23.
1979   "Formal and Informal Operations of a Village Court in Maprik."
       Melanesian Law Journal 7:116–29.
1981   "Samukundi Abelam Conflict Management: Implications for Legal
       Planning in Papua New Guinea." *Oceania* 52:28–38.
1983   "The 'Coming' of Independence in Papua New Guinea: An Abelam
       View." *Journal of the Polynesian Society* 92:463–86.
———, and R. G. Condon
1979   "Abelam Yam Beliefs and Sociorhythmicity: A Study in Chronoan-
       thropology." *Journal of Biosocial Science* 11:17–25.
Strathern, M.
1972   *Women in Between: Female Roles in a Male World.* London: Sem-
       inar Press.
Weiner, A.
1976   *Women of Value, Men of Renown: New Perspectives in Trobriand
       Exchange.* Brisbane: University of Queensland Press.

10

Ethnographic Research and Rites of Incorporation: A Sex- and Gender-based Comparison

NORRIS BROCK JOHNSON

The amount and kind of access fieldworkers have to another culture is often associated with their degree of incorporation into the group or subgroup under study. The process of incorporation is defined by van Gennep (1960) as a series of transitions deriving clarity and meaning through their expression in ritual ceremony and events collectively termed *rites de passage*. Until being granted exposure to appropriate rites-of-passage experiences, the field researcher may remain in the terrible liminal "stranger" state with which we are all familiar (Agar 1980).

In this chapter I shall discuss the impact of sex and gender role expectations on rites of transition and rites of incorporation by contrasting two instances of my own ethnographic research: among a primarily female host group in a rural village in the midwestern United States, and among a primarily male host group on an island in the British West Indies. Employing van Gennep's *rites de passage* scheme and his concept of the stranger, I will focus on similarities and differences in the events and activities leading to varying degrees of incorporation into these groups. By way of conclusion, I will suggest some methodological strategies I have found useful for reducing the time spent, in each case, in the liminal stranger phase of fieldwork.

Schoolteaching, Women, and Rites of Incorporation in Deerfield

Deerfield is a rural village in the midwestern United States, comprising 166 square kilometers. With a population of only 2,793, you

An expanded version of this essay appeared under the title "Sex, Color, and Rites of Passage in Ethnographic Research" in *Human Organization* 43 (2, 1984):108–20. Portions are reprinted here by permission of the Society for Applied Anthropology.

can easily pass through the village in less than five minutes on the state highway that bisects it. When I carried out ethnographic field-work there during 1974–75, I was interested in researching the institutions linking small, local communities like Deerfield to the supralocal social and cultural networks of large-scale industrial state-level societies. In Deerfield, the school system is that major institution. Thus, to better understand the manner in which education functioned as an agent for sociocultural transmission and national integration clearly meant gaining access to the school in general and to its classrooms in particular.

Stopping

Van Gennep tells us that the stranger initially will be stopped, and I found this to be true in Deerfield. If you have ever tried to visit a public school unannounced, you know that they are shrouded in isolation, especially the elementary schools; you are literally stopped at the door. The rituals by which strangers are permitted to enter, if they are permitted, are both obvious and stringent. You must first state your business to the authorities and then wait while your reasons for being in the school and your credentials as parent, re-searcher, salesperson, or whatever are verified. Both male and female strangers are subjected to this entry ritual.

Public schools, especially the elementary level on which I fo-cused, have been shown to be a predominantly female setting (Dree-ben 1968; Mayer 1961:3–4, 24–25). I found this to be true in one sense but not true in another. Of the eighteen elementary school-teachers in Deerfield, only three are males and they teach at the fifth- and sixth-grade levels. At these so-called upper grades, the most prestigious "advanced" courses are taught, thus reinforcing the dif-ferential status of male teachers. Although in the majority, female teachers all teach the lower-status courses. In trying to gain initial entry to the classrooms, however, I was struck by the fact that males controlled access to the building: first I had to present my case to the all-male school board, then to the white male superintendent and the two black male building principals. This stopping period lasted several days, and each time I entered or left the school I had to stop at the principal's office, near the outside doors, to report my movements.

Waiting

The waiting phase of my relationship with the Deerfield teachers proved variable. For brevity I will focus here on my relationships with the female teachers, since they were in the majority. The process of researching classrooms controlled by females was marked by subtle cross-sex tensions and feelings of distance I did not notice with the male teachers. The female teachers initially were more reserved toward me; there was little of the free banter I exchanged with the males. For quite some time, in most cases, there were no moves by the female teachers to "pass" me on to more involved levels of relationship. For what I remember as a considerable amount of time, months in some instances, I was kept in a liminal state. My feeling was that the female teachers were reacting to me as a *male* stranger. The problem was not one of physical incorporation into the classrooms but of the significant degree to which they kept me at an interactive distance. And I did not feel that all of the problem was simply due to sexual difference. I began to notice the effects of gender expectations in the school itself.

My first clue to the structure of sex and gender relationships within the school was the fact that male administrators not only controlled access to the building but to the classrooms as well. Initially, I asked the building principals (not the teachers) if I might observe in each of the classrooms; then, before entering each classroom, I made the same formal request of the teacher. Two teachers withheld their permission and remained unconvinced of my purely academic motives. They may have felt I was going to spy on them for the administration or for some state evaluation agency. Before I was allowed into a classroom, the teacher asked me where I was from, why I was there, and what I was going to do with the data I collected. Their suspicion, not so much of me but of my role, was obvious. Once inside the classroom, my pattern was to sit for the entire day in the back of the room taking notes on the events and activities I observed. After class there would be a brief exchange with the teacher prior to her departure. This went on for some time. I was "in" the classrooms yet "out" of more involved contact with the teachers. I was not developing the depth of relationship I needed for purposes of interviewing.

I began to notice that the defensiveness of the female teachers toward me was attributable in part to their structural position in a sometimes not so subtly male-controlled environment. The very real distance-maintaining effort on their part might have been a reflex of their own gender status and role within the school. I noticed how stridently they acted to guard their classroom spaces from intrusions of one sort or another, possibly because the vast majority of intrusions were by males. Male custodians had free access and routinely sauntered into the classrooms unannounced, mostly while classes were in session. Many times the principal would walk into the classroom, without knocking, to make an announcement, often blithely interrupting the teacher. After putting myself in the teacher's shoes, I began to feel angry: their authority was being undermined; their territory was being challenged. I was concerned with what the students were learning about gender role relationships and expectations. Certainly, such behaviors told them that males had power over females; that males had more authority than females; that male roles carried more (higher) status than female roles. Clearly, the role and status of the female classroom teacher involved a gender expectation of subservience. I never saw a male, whether administrator or custodian, ask permission to enter a classroom and apologize to the teacher for the interruption; yet teachers and other school personnel, whether male or female, always asked permission to see the principal, to intrude on his space. The nonverbal, behavioral lesson was one of male hegemony.

I began to empathize with the expectations accompanying the role of teacher and to understand some of the subtle functional reasons why the gender expectation is for classroom teachers to be female while building administrators are male. Discerning these gender expectations and role relationships, I made it a point not to do anything that by the broadest stretch of imagination could be interpreted as a challenge to the teachers' authority. I assumed their gender expectation would be that I would try to usurp their authority just because I was a man. Hence, I asked permission to enter and leave the classroom, to move around the classroom or talk with students; and I took care not to argue unduly during the many pedagogical discussions we had. My attitude was intentionally respectful rather than merely deferential. I also tried as best I could to dissociate myself from the other males in the school, staying with the female teachers from the time I entered the building until they saw the children to the buses at the end of the day. I wanted to negate the application to me of the teachers' male gender ascriptions.

More sexually oriented gender role questions began to emerge, however. The gender expectation seemed to be that males are sexually aggressive toward females irrespective of place or situation. The female teachers were concerned with maintaining their role as professionals. I indirectly surmised their gender expectation was that males were disrespectful or at least guilty of inappropriate sexual conduct; thus, the female teachers had to be on guard against any sexual conduct that might negate their professional status. They wanted to know if I was married; whether I had any children; why my wife wasn't with me; where I was staying in Deerfield; if I occasionally went home. I felt they wanted to find out if I was "safe"; that is, would I recognize their professional status and act appropriately, or would I act like a man and exhibit sexually inappropriate behavior. I began to understand that part of their initial reserve toward me was because of their gender expectations about my maleness.

To get past this long waiting stage I had to act verbally and nonverbally in a sexually appropriate manner. For example, it would have been inappropriate to maintain long periods of eye contact with these women, to sit close to them during interviews, to peruse their physical forms, to catch their attention as they crossed their legs, or to coyly compliment them on their clothing and hair styles. Instead I talked about lesson plans, pedagogical techniques, and the hardships of being a classroom teacher. I remember feeling a bit frustrated by the need for such posturing, for several of the teachers were attractive and I would have enjoyed flirting with them. But I had to adhere to what I felt would make them feel safe enough for us to move to more relaxed levels of relationship.

I was somewhat mollified when I discovered that these teachers were also prisoners of stereotypic gender expectations (Waller 1932:134–59). They were expected to be sexually modest, if not neutral, discrete, paragons of virtue, proper and sedate in dress and manner—at least in school. Were they as frustrated by their forced adherence to these gender expectations as I was? Although I am vain enough to entertain the idea that more than a few of them might have wanted a sexual relationship with me, they did not dare indicate their desire, and neither did I. The female teachers, the unmarried ones, led dual lives. In school they dressed moderately, yet after school I would see many of them in towns near Deerfield wearing tight jeans and body shirts instead of belted, A-line dresses. Many of them had male friends living outside of Deerfield whom they visited. I came to suspect that any information about sexual behavior in or around the school was a potential prelude to reprimand or dismissal, but only as far as female teachers were concerned. I never saw a female teacher flirt with a male student, but two of the male teachers continually would flirt with female students, and in the lunchroom they would flirt with the female teachers as well—but not vice versa. The gender rules in the school clearly permitted men to behave in a more sexually explicit manner. Understanding these powerful gender expectations made my own temporary adherence to such behavior more palatable.

Finally, I tried to display knowledge and skill that might serve to decrease the inevitable waiting period. My strategy involved continually stressing the fact that I had taught in a public school as well as in a variety of other educational settings; hence, we had a shared knowledge and skill. Indirectly I tried to emphasize that we were teachers first, men and women second; that I was one of them, not an administrator. I felt them taking me more seriously as I displayed more of the qualities stereotypically associated with their profession. I worked hard to get to a level of shared identity with them as teachers, and my various strategies met with success.

Transition

My level of relationship with the female teachers changed when my perceived identity and gender ascriptions began to change. This transition period centered around a specific event and was comparatively short. Over a period of weeks with some teachers, and months with others, I was decreasingly viewed as a threatening male stranger potentially capable of usurping their authority and increasingly seen as a former schoolteacher, a colleague interested in studying classroom behavior. The event I mark as transitional occurred when several teachers asked me to give short talks about anthropology to their classes. Thus, I moved from a stranger isolated in the back of the classroom to temporary acknowledgment as an equal.

This rite of transition involved movement in space. I interpreted the offer to have me speak in the classroom as a sign of shared identity. Remembering the fears these women had of being usurped by men in the classroom, I took it as a compliment that they felt comfortable enough to voluntarily turn over their classrooms to me for one session. I was being asked to do something to validate my claim of being similar to them, to demonstrate my knowledge and skill. I was praised not so much for some specific teaching technique but for possessing a deep knowledge of a particular body of learning. They also commented, with admiration, on my being able to hold the attention of their students. (I suspect that their motives were not entirely gratuitous. During my research in Deerfield I was touted as the *black* anthropologist working in the village. I was held up as a role model for the black students in the school . . . Exhibit A . . ."See, stay in school so you too can become something." I did not think that what I was doing was all that special, or that I have made of my life exactly what I had wanted to make of it, but I let them use me as a role model in exchange for their granting me access to their classrooms so I could carry out my work.)

Incorporation

Those teachers who offered me the gift of their classrooms became more relaxed with me, joked more with me, and laughed more when we were together; and they even began to confide in me. I felt our relationship was becoming especially meaningful when they began to talk about the principal in my presence. They were saying, in effect, that they had made up their minds that I was not put in their classrooms by the administration or by the state to spy on them. More important for my purposes, interviewing went more smoothly with those teachers in whose classrooms I had given the return gift of my knowledge. By seeing me as a teacher, we now were able to talk to one another as colleagues about the classroom processes in which I was most interested. I found myself spending more out-of-class time, mostly in the teachers' lounge, with particular teachers.

The structure of male/female relationships and gender ascriptions in the school, rather than in the minds of the teachers, mitigated against a feeling of substantial incorporation on my part, however. For example, I never felt comfortable spending time alone with female teachers in their classrooms. One teacher very directly told me that students "might talk." While their own gender attitudes toward me had changed somewhat, they remained mindful of the attitudes and expectations of others. I did not feel quite as awkward when sitting with a group of teachers. Further, about half the female teachers were white, and as a black man I was not surprised that my closest informant relationships were with black women. As in the wider society, gender expectations, especially with respect to several of the unmarried white female teachers, monitored relationships by color as well as by sex. Although I never felt that I had been intimately incorporated into the group and setting I had come to research, I did feel that I was able to discern and then devise strategies to partially overcome the prevalent gender ascriptions to the point where they did not inhibit my gathering research information. And that was comfortable and acceptable to me.

The impact of the sex of the stranger is an important factor in field research, a factor not taken into account by van Gennep. The Deerfield case suggests that, especially for men, cross-sex relationships inhibit the process of incorporation. Of course, gender remains an inevitable barrier to access to certain levels of information, and ethnographers must seek to overcome this problem through the use of interpreters and informants of the same sex as the study group. But it is also important to keep in mind that in the cross-sex situation a *complete* state of incorporation is not necessary in order to complete one's research. At Deerfield, my liminal male stranger phase was in most cases significantly shortened by my display of, association with, interest and skill in, and respect for the knowledge ascribed to female teachers. Shared knowledge mitigates the boundaries of gender well enough to permit effective information gathering.

Boat Building, Men, and Rites of Incorporation on Bequia

The island of Bequia (pronounced beck-quay) is nestled in the northern part of the Grenadines, a lush string of thirty-two rather small islands covering the sixty-five kilometers between Saint Vincent to the north and Grenada to the south. The Grenadines lie in the windward archipelago of the Lesser Antilles of the British West Indies. Bequia is a bit over three kilometers wide and eight kilometers long and had a 1980 population of 4,236.

During the midsummer of 1980 I arrived on Bequia to carry out a pilot survey of existing boat-building activities on the island. By word of mouth from sailors and boat builders in the United States I had heard that "the best boats in the Caribbean are built in the Grenadines and the best boats in the Grenadines are built on Bequia." Like most of the northern Grenadines, Bequia's rocky soil impedes primary reliance on agriculture; hence, Bequia's subsistence strategy has long been tied to the sea. I came to the islands to locate the shipwrights who still used traditional methods of boat building; that is, methods with little or no European and North American influences on design and construction techniques.

Stopping

As a stranger I arrived on Bequia at the most inopportune time. Earlier there had been a Marxist revolution on nearby Grenada and a short-lived armed conflict on Bequia itself. At the guesthouse in which I settled, I soon found that it made little initial difference that I introduced myself as a professor from the United States who was interested in learning about traditional boat building, for I was viewed by most of the people I met as a strange black man asking questions.[1] Not surprisingly, about five days passed before people began to volunteer information about shipwrights on the island. As the first week drew to a close, I became nervous: Did I look that much like a revolutionary? I had been stopped in my research until people had made their decisions about my motives for being on Bequia. One morning at breakfast, however, my hostess casually mentioned that there were two men with whom I should speak. She had seemingly decided I was who I said I was, and she was willing to help me proceed with my study. There were many shipwrights on the island, she said, but these two men were older (in their seventies) and were "the best." This week-long stopping phase told me that boatwrights were held in high esteem—at least high enough for them to be either consciously or unconsciously guarded. When I first met with each shipwright I was not surprised that they expected my visit.

Waiting

While on Bequia I divided my time more or less equally between the two shipwrights my hostess recommended, but here I will narrate the process by which my liminal stranger phase was lessened with just one of them. The man to whom I refer, Mr. Atkins, is descended from the Carib Indians aboriginal to these islands. Tall, with a ruddy complexion, and taut even in his seventies, he has been a shipwright in the Grenadines all his life, having learned to build sea vesels from his father. No longer working for himself, for the last several years he has been employed in a small boatyard most recently owned by a young white American male from California.

The waiting phase of my relationship with Mr. Atkins lasted almost two weeks, during which time I visited daily the boatyard where he works. Both directly with words and indirectly with side glances and studied reserve, Mr. Atkins told me that he wanted to know why I had come to see him. He was testing me to see if he could trust and respect me, and to see if I trusted and respected him. Our conversations kept coming back to boats, for it seemed important that he learn how much I knew about boats. I gradually came to feel that he was concerned with what kind of man I was; whether I was to be respected, by his criteria, as a "man."

I reached this conclusion indirectly, because we did not actually talk about what makes some males "men" and others not. I came to see that shipwrights are held in high esteem by other men as well as by women, who would proudly tell me that a relative of theirs used to build boats. (The woman in charge of my guesthouse had an uncle who was a captain on one of the cargo boats running between the islands.) Rather than talking about themselves and their occupations, other men talked to me about the shipwrights they knew. In almost every seafaring culture, as on Bequia, the making and sailing of water craft are confined to males in general and to high-status males in particular (Gladwin 1970; Lewis 1978; Malinowski 1922; Procope 1955; Wilbert 1976). Men use tools to manipulate the elements and bring them under control, something I think men universally tend to admire in each other. Quite consciously, then, I sought to exhibit my passing acquaintance with that knowledge I knew to be traditionally privy to the high-status shipwright on the island. I felt that making a reputation (Wilson 1973) as a man-of-the-sea would foster a more intimate relationship with Mr. Atkins.

To be a high-status male on Bequia means knowing not only about ships, the sea, and sailing but also about "hand and eye." Those not familiar with "hand and eye" probably would not be seen as very masculine by the male shipwright subgroup on the island, just as unemployed men in the United States are often not seen as "real" men. I came to know about "hand and eye" quite by accident, but it proved to be the key to my gaining deeper access to the shipwrights. I take pains here to describe "hand and eye" in some detail to convey what traditionally only a few men on Bequia have come to understand and which has enabled each one to become a master shipwright, a "man" among men.

For the previous ten years or so, Mr. Atkins's work has involved carving a series of curved ribs from cedar limbs to be used as the framework for the boats built in the yard, work which requires the talent of "hand and eye." Termed "timbering," it is the most prestigious task in the yard; and only Mr. Atkins carves the timbers for the boat framework. The other men in the yard told me that if the timbers are not "right," the "form" of the boat as a whole would not be "right." I remember them looking at me as a not-very-significant (male) person for not knowing this. One day while he was working, I bluntly told Mr. Atkins that I knew he was building by "hand and eye," and I recall how he straightened up from his work and just looked at me. I felt his respect; I felt he was really looking at me (as a "man" perhaps) for the first time. The significance, the recognition given by Mr. Atkins, stemmed from a stranger knowing about "hand and eye."

Building by "eye" means that no elaborate plans or drawings are used in the design of a boat. In the United States, for example, the frames of wooden boats are built from a series of drawings. Mr. Atkins is both designer and builder, however, a conceptual feat that separates "men" from the other males. For several months I watched the other shipwright I interviewed build a twenty-five-meter schooner from a rough sketch he had made in the sand. These men had to learn to design and build boats in their own terms rather than in terms of a present plan—not a mean feat. All those who try cannot achieve it, but those who do are held in high esteem. Building by "hand" literally means that no power tools or heavy mechanical equipment are used in the construction of the boat. Fairly large boats can be built by only a few men using an adz or a hatchet, several hand planes, a twist drill, a string plumb, and a two-person saw.

During my waiting period I remember feeling quite like a child trying to get my father's attention. I was a male coming to understand and trying to meet the gender expectations of a higher-ranking male in order to acquire his approval. I knew I was consciously trying to show the shipwrights and others in the boatyard that I too knew something about carpentry, tools, boats, and sailing, that I knew about "hand and eye." I wanted Mr. Atkins to see that, though a stranger, in more vital respects I was much like him, that I loved and respected the knowledge and skills he had and respected. Over the ensuing weeks, then, I sought to convey that I had come to Bequia to know *more* about these things—about how one comes to know just by looking at something as complicated as a boat's hull that it is "right" or "wrong." I felt that I was worthy to know more because of the effort I had made on my own to acquire partial knowledge. I knew I could not proceed otherwise, because the knowledge I sought was too intricately connected with gender expectations. My initial display of knowledge, skills, and interest in boat building thus was instrumental in commanding trust and respect from the shipwrights, and probably for this reason alone I was subtly invited to enter into a more intimate relationship with Mr. Atkins.

Transition

I clearly recall the key event that terminated my liminal stranger phase on Bequia. One morning I went down to the small boatyard at the end of Port Elizabeth, the main village, to watch Mr. Atkins work on "timbering." I had been interviewing him on traditional boat-building techniques. On the beach in front of the yard, tied to a palm tree, were two of the lovely five-meter open-deck boats used by the men of these islands to hunt whales, by boys to deliver goods to yachts in the harbor (much as boys in the United States would use a bicycle), and by males in general as a way to get around the island (I never saw a female sailing one of these craft). The yard also makes these boats, shaped like open pea pods, to sell to tourists. Mr. Atkins had been using them to point out traditional building materials and techniques to me. I made a series of drawings of the craft and spent considerable time admiring them and seeking to understand the intricacies of their "hand and eye" method of construction. They are made, especially the two I saw, like fine furniture: I could find no nails—"water pins," what we call dowels, are used to hold the craft together—and the cedar and spruce pine planks are sealed with varnish and hand-polished to a mirror shine.

That morning Mr. Atkins asked me if I wanted to sail one of them! Actually, the question implied *could* I sail one. I immediately understood the test, as well as the compliment of being invited to make the transition. This was not something that all the males on Bequia are invited to do. I was scared, for these small boats are like nothing I had previously seen or sailed. What if I swamped the boat and failed the test? I knew that if I could not sail the boat I would be seen from then on as one of those hollow men of whom T. S. Eliot spoke, all show and no go. "Men" sail boats as well as build them, and my failure to sail the boat would mark me as someone who knew something about carpentry but who was not a more fully competent "man of the sea."[2] I had to get these high-status men of Bequia to respect me enough to share their deeper levels of knowledge about boat building. The rules I was learning said that this was a "man's" world, and if I failed I would go back to the waiting stage, or I might be stopped altogether. Yet I felt excitement at the thought of sailing a craft I had come to admire, and I knew that Mr. Atkins knew that about me. These shipwrights deeply love the boats they build, and so I knew that Mr. Atkins was giving me a gift, in Mauss's (1967) sense of the term—an invitation to share knowledge and experience and to form a deeper bond.[3] This last thought nurtured confidence.

During my stay on Bequia I never saw one man ask another man anything about boats; instead, men discussed them as equals. Hence, I could not ask anyone how to sail this boat, although I did ask for help in pushing the 275-kilogram craft into the water. Then I headed upwind and immediately almost capsized the boat, for it was comparatively light and the slightest breeze caused it to tip wildly. I wobbled out to Admiralty Bay, certain that I could hear the men in the yard laughing. Whether they were laughing with me or at me, I myself started to laugh, and then set about using my weight to counter the heeling of the boat. As I got the feel of the boat I grew more confident and wanted to show off for the men in the yard (I later learned they had gone back to work and were not even watching me). I began to weave in and out among the large tourist yachts anchored in the water like so many fiberglass spaceships. Easing out the sails, I turned from the wind and let it blow me back to the yard. Seeing me approach, several of the men stopped work to help pull me in. I let down the sails and coasted into the beach. They said I had been out for only about twenty minutes; it had seemed like half a day. Everybody laughed, and I was kidded about the way I had wobbled out to sea. Several men patted me on the back. I was making contact. I felt great. Mr. Atkins did not stop his work but just looked up at me and smiled. I had passed the test. I would take the boat out again at various times, but that first time was a definite transition event. After that, I noticed several important changes in the behavior of Mr. Atkins and the other men toward me.

Entry/Incorporation

Soon Mr. Atkins began to ask me to help him around the yard— not on the boats themselves, but to help him rough out some of the cedar limbs and tree trunks used in making the frames. I carried and fetched things, becoming a kind of apprentice. Mr. Atkins told me these were initial tasks traditionally carried out by boys seeking to learn boat building. He himself had apprenticed this way, and it was nothing to be ashamed of. The other (high-status) men knew that it was something one simply had to do. But more importantly, I was permitted to handle tools such as the adz—not the personal tools owned by each man and carefully wrapped in cloth and taken home at the end of the day, but the more crude yard tools kept in the storage shed. We did not talk about tools, but the gender expectation most definitely was for a "man" to own his own tools and to be able to use them (in most seafaring cultures the possession and handling of tools are primary male activities; see Beck 1973). I felt that I was beginning to be incorporated as well as a male stranger could be. After I had demonstrated my limited knowledge and skill, I was told more about "hand and eye" principles. And in talking to Mr. Atkins about the traditional apprentice system, I was also made aware that a more complete process of incorporation would involve my actually being permitted to work on the boats themselves.

Other significant changes signaled the occurrence of a transition: the men began to share more of their feelings with me. Sitting under the palm trees eating lunch, we would not only talk about boats but also about sex and women. Another gender expectation among these men is that men should be interested in women as well as boats. They asked if I had "found any women yet" and began suggesting the names of women I might call on.[4]

Although the shipwright subgroup is exclusively an association of men, the rites of incorporation into the subgroup involve more than simply being male. While boat building is man's work, the shipwrights on Bequia with whom I spoke do not see all men as equal, and neither do the women. Those males connected with boats and the sea are more respected and are held in higher esteem than those who are not; they are "more male." A "man" must have an almost intuitive understanding of boats and wood. He must unselfishly love boats and love the water; and he must be good with his hands and with tools. Only because of my display of knowledge and skill, as well as the respect I felt for what the shipwrights themselves respected, was I invited to further experience certain activities and knowledge, thereby shortening my liminal stranger phase. Among both males and females my status was enhanced simply by being in the company of the shipwrights. I am certain, for example, that a male stranger coming to the island to research syncretic religious traditions prevalent in the area would be accorded a lower initial status. And in the "old days" on Bequia, when men went out to sea in small boats to hunt large whales, life must have been very difficult for males who were afraid of the water, clumsy with their hands, sickened by the smell of woodpiles, and unnerved by the howl of the wind.

Summary and Recommendations

In this essay I have examined the influence of gender ascription, as specifically applied to ethnographic fieldwork, on the general process of rites de passage, as outlined by van Gennep. My recommendations to fieldworkers should be clear as I summarize and elaborate on the implications of strategies I found useful in negating the influence of sex and gender role expectations in the field.

Of primary importance is the fact that on Bequia, as well as in Deerfield, I found the demonstration and display of appropriate knowledge valued by the host group a particularly effective means of negating the effects of sex- and gender-related impediments to the collection of information. The basic strategy is to heighten a sense of collective identity through an emphasis on shared knowledge. Other researchers might include this strategy in their adaptive arsenal, especially in situations of mismatching between the gender expectations of the stranger and the host group. I found it adaptive in both intra- and intersex situations. The examples presented here strongly suggest that appropriate displays of knowledge and skill effectively reduce the length of time spent in the liminal stranger phase of fieldwork.

More personally, the invitations to display appropriate knowledge and skill enhanced my self-esteem and led people in both field settings to consider me competent and interesting by their own standards. I enjoyed both of my field experiences because I was offered the opportunity to do something as well as to study something. Field research in Deerfield and on Bequia reinforced my personal and professional commitment to participant observation as well as nonparticipant observation as an information-gathering strategy. I liked being invited to participate, by both males and females, in the events and activities I was researching, and I never felt that I compromised my objectivity. My suggestion here is not to "go native," though I personally feel that being invited to do so is a high compliment, but to use as much of oneself as a research instrument as possible. The most remembered experiences of working in other societies and cultures are the times when we participated in some event or activity.

For many of these reasons I think we make both conscious and unconscious choices of the problems and peoples we research. Chagnon (1974:162–97) might not have particularly liked the Yanomamö, but he clearly was drawn to this stereotypically masculine culture for more than professional reasons. And Mead (1950) certainly preferred the gentle Arapesh to the more competitive Mundugumor. Finding a cadre of people in another society and culture who reflect one's own temperament and gender expectations is a buffer against culture shock, and I suspect that Chagnon felt less a stranger among the Yanomamö than he would among Arapesh males. In my case, I liked researching boat building on Bequia because I admire men who do that kind of thing; I have no interest whatsoever in working out gender-related adaptive strategies among the Yanomamö. Am I cheating myself and my profession by not working in settings—the more horrible the better?—where my gender expectations and those of the peoples I study are wildly mismatched? Should anthropologists be titillated by massive culture shock? I have no answers, just questions stimulated by my own research. I am aware of consciously choosing groups and problems I intuitively feel comfortable with, quite apart from professional interest. What I am suggesting here is that this intuitive level of consideration might also include gender ascriptions.

An underlying premise of both van Gennep's and my arguments is that the incorporation of the stranger into the host group is in some ways desirable. The case of Frank Cushing among the male Zuni (Gronewold 1972), however, reminds us that complete incorporation of gender ascriptions results in the elimination of the researcher role—fine for the wayward stranger, perhaps, but not so fine for those who seek information on the Zuni for cross-cultural comparison. To maintain the researcher role, complete incorporation is not the answer. Yet there are strategies we can adopt to negate impediments to the access to and collection of information, such as gender ascriptions, that make it possible to carry out our studies. We can gain access to groups and subgroups without becoming incorporated into them.

All of which, by way of conclusion, begs the question, What is the point of ethnographic research? To my mind there ought to be two goals: the generation of descriptions and (secondary) explanations of societies and their cultures in a form that is supportive of cross-comparisons; and the experiencing of other ways of life for the purpose of self-growth and development. Anthropological publications focus on the first goal and only rarely give sustained consideration to the second. From Herodotus to Montaigne, from Samuel Hearne to Edmund Carpenter, researchers often have been conscious of using the mirror of another society and culture to take a clearer look at themselves.

During the process of field research, both the sex of the stranger as well as the sex and gender ascriptions of the host group affect the character of the pattern by which each moves toward or away from the other. Accompanied by my suggested sex- and gender-based additions, van Gennep's typology remains a useful guide for sequences of experiences one might reasonably expect to encounter during the process of field research.

Notes

Fieldwork on Bequia was funded by grant no. 1-0-101-3284-VC851 from the University Research Council, University of North Carolina at Chapel Hill. Fieldwork in Deerfield was funded by National Institute of Mental Health grant no. MH58496-01. I wrote this article with the support of grant no. 1-0-230-3401-MR044 from the Spencer Foundation.

1. The fact of my being a black male is significant. On Bequia I gathered that the mental picture of a "revolutionary" did not include white males or women. I believe my stopping period would have been shorter if I had fallen into either of these categories.

2. I did not pretend that I had "gone native." The point here is that I was offered an opportunity for a closer degree of participation in the group I came to study. I did not feel as if I were a Bequianian; in fact, I felt as if I were being recognized as a "man of the sea," as it is termed on the island. The identification is emotional and is based on the recognition of shared knowledge with respect to particular experiences. I am reminded of a passage from Powdermaker's (1966:112) account of her stay on the island of New Ireland: ". . . the drums began; I danced. Something happened, I forgot myself and was one with the dancers. Under the full moon and for the brief time of the dance, I ceased to be an anthropologist from a modern society. I danced. When it was over I realized that, for this short period, I had been emotionally part of the rite. Then out came my notebook."

3. Van Gennep (1960:29) mentions offerings and gift giving as acts whereby host groups extend themselves to strangers.

4. Van Gennep (1960:34–35) considers the offering of women to a stranger a prevalent gift inviting further incorporation.

References

Agar, Michael H.
    1980   *The Professional Stranger: An Informal Introduction to Ethnography.* New York: Academic Press.
Beck, Horace
    1973   *Folklore and the Sea.* Middletown, Conn.: Wesleyan University Press.

Bunzel, Ruth L.
   1929 *The Pueblo Potter: A Study of Creative Imagination in Primitive Art.* New York: Columbia University Press.
Chagnon, Napoleon
   1974 *Studying the Yanomamö.* New York: Holt, Rinehart and Winston.
Dreeben, Robert
   1968 *On What Is Learned in School.* Reading, Mass.: Addison-Wesley.
Gladwin, Thomas
   1970 *East Is a Big Bird: Navigation and Logic on Pulwat Atoll.* Cambridge, Mass.: Harvard University Press.
Gronewold, Sylvia
   1972 "Did Frank Cushing Go Native?" In: Solon T. Kimball and James B. Watson (eds.), *Crossing Cultural Boundaries: The Anthropological Experience,* pp. 33–50. New York: Chandler.
Lewis, David
   1978 *The Voyaging Stars: Secrets of the Pacific Island Navigators.* New York: W. W. Norton and Co.
Malinowski, Bronislaw
   1922 *Argonauts of the Western Pacific.* London: Routledge and Kegan Paul.
Mauss, Marcel
   1967 *The Gift: Forms and Functions of Exchange in Archaic Societies.* trans. Ian Cunnison. New York: W. W. Norton and Co.
Mayer, Martin
   1961 *The Schools.* New York: Harper and Brothers.
Mead, Margaret
   1950 *Sex and Temperament in Three Primitive Societies.* New York: Mentor.
Powdermaker, Hortense
   1966 *Stranger and Friend: The Way of an Anthropologist.* New York: W. W. Norton and Co.
Procope, Bruce
   1955 "Launching a Schooner in Carriacou." *Caribbean Quarterly* 4:122–31.
Smith, Michael G.
   1962 *Kinship and Community in Carriacou.* New Haven, Conn.: Yale University Press.
van Gennep, Arnold
   1960 *The Rites of Passage.* trans. Monika B. Vizedom and Gabrielle L. Caffe. Chicago: University of Chicago Press (*Les Rites de Passage.* Paris: E. Nourrey, 1909.)
Wallard, Willard
   1932 *The Sociology of Teaching.* New York: John Wiley and Sons.
Wax, Rosalie H.
   1971 *Doing Fieldwork: Warnings and Advice.* Chicago: University of Chicago Press.

Wilbert, Johannes
  1976   "To Become a Maker of Canoes: An Essay in Warao Acculturation."
          In: Johannes Wilbert (ed.), *Enculturation in Latin America: An An-
          thology*, pp. 303–58. Latin American Studies, vol. 38. Los Angeles:
          University of California Latin America Center.
Wilson, Peter J.
  1973   *Crab Antics: The Social Anthropology of English-speaking Negro
          Societies of the Caribbean*. New Haven, Conn.: Yale University
          Press.

11

Families, Gender, and Methodology in the Sudan

CAROLYN FLUEHR-LOBBAN and RICHARD A. LOBBAN

Our fieldwork in the Sudan began in 1970 while we were doctoral candidates at Northwestern University. From November 1970 until February 1972 we were involved in separate investigations of homicide in the Sudan (Carolyn) and urban social networks (Richard). At that time we were recently married and had no children. Our second field study occurred during a one-month period in 1975, and our third major restudy was undertaken from July 1979 to February 1980. The latter, and a one-month study in 1981, continued Richard's interests begun ten years earlier and sought to replicate the field questionnaire in the same communities, to establish a rigorous diachronic data base. Carolyn's work continued the study of the legal anthropology of the Sudan but was now focused on Islamic, or Shari'a, law. Our most recent fieldwork saw us as seasoned Sudanists, conversant in (colloquial) Arabic, and accompanied by our daughter Josina.

Against this backdrop we are able to offer several perspectives on the role of gender as it influences anthropological methods: the differing views of male versus female researchers; and the rich and problematic dimensions of caring for a child in the field. We also will present some thoughts on anthropological couples engaged in research as individuals and as collaborators. Each of us will speak in turn.

Male Perspectives on Research in the Sudan

As a young graduate student trained in the social sciences at a major center for African studies, I had a great sense of personal confidence as I went off to the field. I had received specialized instruction in computer methods, statistics, and the various intricacies of fieldwork methods, especially as they relate to questions of sampling and valid statistical representation. My study initially proposed to contrast male and female social network configurations, and from the vantage point of Evanston, Illinois, I saw no problem whatsoever in carrying out this research.

Working in the Sudan presented no problem since I had studied maps, knew about the weather extremes, liked the food, and was determined to quickly set about developing some basic fluency in Sudanese colloquial Arabic. After some months I selected two target communities for my urban research and began a period of participant observation with very open-ended questions. Much later, toward the end of my study, I employed a more formal research questionnaire.

Unfortunately, not everything went according to my plan. Even when I had developed sufficient language skill, self-confidence, and rapport with those people who subsequently became my friends, I simply was not able to break through the lines of sexual segregation that are a feature of Sudanese society. As a male researcher I found that it was difficult or impossible or inappropriate to interview females for all sorts of reasons. In the few interviews with women that I was able to conduct with any confidence, I was often confronted with a festive atmosphere, with much twittering and giggling; virtually never would I be in a circumstance where I could interact one-to-one with potential female respondents. Forget all of my training—the rigorous sampling requirements for randomness were not going to happen as long as I, a male fieldworker, wanted to interview women. The importance of sexual segregation was too well established to be transcended by an American graduate student qua anthropologist. Thus, quite early on, I decided that women would not be a major part of my research. The data I have presented in various publications in the decade that followed make no claim about the separate realities of female social networks (Lobban 1975, 1977, 1979). In fact, I am inherently skeptical of most data collected by male fieldworkers in the Islamic world if they claim to describe the outlook, values, or opinions of women.

With my anthropological background I felt very comfortable with the rather passive role of investigator working within the participant observation framework. I could have been more aggressive, more obtrusive, and more persistent if I had really wanted to include female respondents, but I am confident that the harder and further I pushed, the less reliable the data would have been. Not only would I have received highly questionable responses skewed in favor of what the women "thought I was after," but I would have jeopardized my otherwise rewarding and enduring relationships with the males who had become the centerpiece of my research.

The Arab world is not only more conscious of sex lines than the West is, but there is also less ambiguity about age distinction such as we find in our "forever youthful" Western civilization. Young men of less than twenty or so years of age began to disappear from my study as my interests revolved more and more around those men who were within a decade or two of my own age (twenty-five). In my more recent fieldwork (1980) I undertook a very considerable investigation of family histories and genealogical pedigrees, something that older men are much more inclined to be involved with; and, being ten years older myself, I again interacted with a somewhat older age-cohort.

At this point some may argue that my approach was too passive and not sufficiently rigorous to be valid. I am the first to admit my frustration with gathering quantitative data in the field, but at the same time I do have an extremely high degree of confidence that my naturalistic approach easily compensated for what I might have lost in other areas. Also, since I make no claims to describe the women's world, nor that of very young men, I believe my earlier studies were quite sound and, in fact, have been essentially replicated in the study I made in 1980.

Within the age/sex parameters cited here I also exercised control of the study in two other ways. First, I knew the approximate proportion of a number of major lineage or descent groups, and with this as a guide I pursued (when using my structured questionnaire) individuals belonging proportionately to these various groups. Second, my restudy ten years later embraced many of the same individuals who participated in my first study. Thus, in drawing on a very similar universe, I believe I achieved considerable consistency in my results, which are themselves in general harmony with several other studies done in the same communities.

As a male fieldworker, eager to learn and absorb as much as possible and consciously trying to be accepted, I found myself being continually invited to all sorts of events, such as weddings, funerals, sports matches, picnics, automobile rides, casual visiting, and dinner parties. My friends always laughed when I took out my little black book to log the latest invitation which might otherwise be forgotten. Accepted to the extent that I was, I often became more of a participant and less of an observer. I had my own social gatherings at our home (a houseboat on the Nile); I wrote letters of recommendation for applicants to the University of Khartoum and to other places I was affiliated with; I made loans; I was asked for information about birth control; I offered opinions about family affairs; and I took part in many other functions I can't even recall. In truth, I became part of the social networks I had come to study and was mobilized on appropriate occasions. All of this put me on very equal footing with my Sudanese friends, and any guilt about unequal reciprocity vanished.

At times I would plan to meet my friends for some sort of interview, but then tea and cookies would be served around, other neighbors would arrive to chat about the day's events or world affairs, and the afternoon would pass until it was time for evening prayers. Personally, I am not a church-goer, but I was honored by my friends' request to accompany them to the mosque. Although I declined, my absence was understood and respected, coming as I did from a civilization of another "great religious book." I too respected my friends' scrupulous regard for their religious beliefs, and to this day I still feel a sense of ambiguity about those moments when I was asked to go along to the mosque. Their evening prayers have a profound simplicity and attractive devotional style that stress such values as collectivity and personal autonomy, which I share. On many occasions I was asked why I didn't convert to Islam and I never really had a satisfying answer, because I was then and still am attracted to the humility, brotherhood, and decency that are deeply woven into the fabric of Islam.

My friends did not appear hurt by my reaction, and I will always consider it an honor to have had their trust and respect to this degree. I believe that anthropologists ought to give more serious thought to questions of trust and confidence as parameters of the fieldwork experience. I am not referring here to questions of confidentiality and the broader ethics of research, which should be an automatic part of fieldwork. Rather, I am thinking more about long-term commitments to people who have opened their minds, hearts, and homes to the fieldworker out of a basic spirit of decency and cooperation. In reality, these may be human responsibilities above and beyond the requirements of our science, not just wishy-washy liberalism. I am sure that my view of the two Sudanese urban communities I was part of goes far deeper and stretches further than any body of statistics I have collected.

My own age and sex were more important variables in the field than I had ever expected. And as I am now more conscious of this, I believe I have become a better fieldworker.

Female Perspectives on Research in the Sudan

My field experiences in the Sudan were quite different from Richard's. While our fieldwork embodied separate research on autonomous projects, many people expected that as husband and wife we would collaborate. In our case, the complementarity in research as married anthropologists has been primarily social rather than academic.

My own research in the Sudan has been dramatically affected by social institutions of sexual segregation. My initial study in the area of criminal law and homicide brought me into direct contact with one of the dominant male cultural institutions. My reaction, as a young fieldworker, was to withdraw into the archives of Sudanese courts, where I collected data on over four hundred cases of homicide (Fluehr-Lobban 1976). In 1979, as a more experienced fieldworker, I was able to enter and successfully conduct research in one of the more traditional arenas of male culture, the Islamic law and Islamic courts. The discussion here centers on that transformation.

Unlike Richard, I had not structured any aspect of the study of female culture into my original research project. However, faced with the social realities of sexual segregation and with an increasing number of hours being spent with Sudanese women, I realized that my own view of the world of women might be important to record. This became apparent when Richard and I compared notes, after a day of visiting in the two separate domains of a Sudanese home, and found that our experiences were totally different. While the women remained at home, the men went for walks in the gardens; when the men went to the mosque for afternoon prayers, the women either prayed at home or rested after *ghada,* the main meal of the day; at *ghada* the men ate mutton and the women ate pigeon.

As my fluency in Arabic increased, I began to chronicle and probe more deeply into the world of Sudanese women. Indeed, I learned colloquial Arabic mostly in the company of these women; and as a result, my speech patterns are skewed toward the female use of the language. I recall many embarrassing, long periods of silence in the early days of fieldwork as I struggled to learn names for things, idiomatic expressions, anything of the spoken language. An interesting difference between my experience with respect to language and Richard's is that I *had* to use Arabic on most occasions with women, whereas Richard's male friends were often anxious to practice their English and would avoid using Arabic. I would often hear a friend speak to Richard in English and he would respond in Arabic, and so the dialogue would proceed.

As my relationships with women gradually deepened, I began asking questions informally and promoting discussions related to my topic of study, the law, to women's perception and understanding of it, and to their use of the courts. I developed a series of hypothetical situations dealing with female affairs which might touch on aspects of the law—for example, marriage, divorce, inheritance—and used these to promote discussion of the topics in the typical extended family–close neighbors groups of women who would gather in my presence, some as friends, others merely curious. I rarely used a written questionnaire for individual interviews, preferring the richness of the social dynamics and points of view that emerged in group sessions.

What was originally a secondary interest in women led in time to a more serious study of the history of the women's movement in the Sudan and their changing social and political status (Fluehr-Lobban 1977). This deeper investigation into the status of women was promoted by the wide gulf between what I had expected to find among Islamic women, given my Western background and training, and the realities I confronted in the contemporary Sudan. Anticipating docile, passive, constrained, and controlled women, instead I came to know strong, independent, and forceful women, especially among working-class people, something that makes sense only in the context of modern Sudanese history. The Sudan nation was forged in the colonial occupations of the Turks, Egyptians, and British; and Sudanese nationalism grew from resistance during these successive occupations. Women played a role, at times a significant one, in these events. Hence, I am honored to have been given the name of one of these heroines, Mihera bint Abboud, a Shaygīyya woman who led her people in resisting the Turko-Egyptian invading armies in 1821. Many people in the Sudan know me only by this name.

In my second major field research (1979–80), my earlier interests in the law and the status of women developed into a larger study of the Shari'a, the Islamic law that governs the personal and family affairs of Sudanese Muslims. During the first field trip I had visited a number of Islamic courts and had become friends with Sayeda Nagua Kemal Farid, the first woman justice to be appointed to an Islamic court system, as far as we know, in the contemporary Islamic world. On return visits in 1975 and 1979, I raised the possibility of studying the Shari'a and the courts with Justice Nagua and Sheikh Mohammed el Gizouli, then the Grand Kadi of the Sudan, the highest legal authority in Islam. Both were encouraging, and with their help I was able to conduct my research into the realm of Islamic law, a topic barely touched on in social science literature in Africa and the Arab world.

The dynamics of gender in this particular study are worth noting. The Islamic court system, from the lowest levels to the High Court, is male-dominated, as are legal systems in general throughout the world, except in certain notable cases in socialist countries, where a concerted effort to include women has been made. Without a doubt my entry into this world was facilitated, and even engineered, by my friendship with Nagua K. Farid and later by my acquaintance with other female judges in the Sudan judiciary, both in the civil and Shari'a divisions. Whenever I would visit the judiciary or make an initial visit to an Islamic court, it was in the company of or with the assistance of female legal professionals who interceded with male authority figures. Later I could approach these individuals directly, but the initial meeting was arranged and given the proper social stamp of approval by these women. Justice Nagua gave unselfishly of her time, especially to accompany me to courts some distance from Khartoum, in Omdurman and Khartoum North, and our friendship flowered both inside and outside the legal arena, encompassing both of our families. Sheikh Mohammed el Gizouli graciously agreed to take me on as a student, and I would meet with him several times a week to learn the basics of Islamic law and court procedure. His keen sociological awareness and command of English legal vocabulary made this period an extremely fruitful one. Our relationship developed as an outgrowth of my friendship with Nagua, but like so many other professional ties in the Sudan, it became a warm social relationship as well. When we exchanged visits at our homes, we followed the custom of sexual segregation, with Richard visiting the Grand Qadi while I visited with his wife and unmarried children. In a society where the extended family is the norm and the value placed on family life is high, there is no question in my mind that being identified as part of a family, originally with my husband and later with our daughter Josina, was an asset, probably even a vital element in conducting successful field research in the areas we selected.

Let me deal now with the question of being a Western female conducting research in an Islamic setting, for this is indeed a valid consideration. As a woman with a husband and later a young daughter, I was not afforded the status of "honorary male" which many Western female professionals living alone in the Sudan receive. However, as a white female Westerner (the colloquial term is khawajīyya) engaged in research and attached to a family, my status was more ambiguous than Richard's, and as a result I had more social mobility in the system than he did. For example, I could, if I wanted, sit with men alone or with my husband present. Although the option was there, having done so briefly a few times during the first few months of fieldwork, my social discomfort was sufficiently great that I grew to welcome the security and later preferred the informality of the *hareem* (the women's section of the house). Gradually, the more secluded and even "mysterious" world of women was opened to me. As a married woman I was treated to the relaxing pleasure of long sessions where my hands and feet were dyed with henna and various oils and perfumes were applied to my skin. I learned favorite Sudanese recipes and took great pleasure in these aspects of shared womanhood.

As my facility with the language and culture grew, I also grew into the role of professional anthropologist, a major adaptation of which was being a female in the male-dominated public world where I needed to work. Thus, I learned to travel with female friends whenever possible—to the courts, to a government office, and given my high visibility in the society, even to the market or any social gathering when my husband was not able to accompany me. When forced to travel alone, I learned to share taxis with female strangers or to stand with other women while waiting for some means of public transportation. In offices I would seek out female workers as primary vehicles for introducing me to the men I wanted to see, and in general I avoided meeting with men alone until our families had become acquainted. To be accepted, and more importantly respected, in this role meant working with a sense of dignity, honor, and decency when dealing with others. By Western standards my behavior became more restrained, cautious, and controlled, and in the context of the largely Islamic city of Khartoum this was entirely appropriate and thoroughly comfortable for me. My own public dress was modest yet fashionably Western; however, for relaxing at home or with Sudanese friends I would wear a woman's *jellabiyya* (a simply cut gown of the Middle East) and I occasionally dressed in the more formal woman's *tōbe* (a *sari*-like wraparound worn for modesty).

At the university, female professionals, both Sudanese and non-Sudanese, are accepted without explanations, but a female fieldworker in the more traditional society must have a ready speech to explain her presence and her work. The roles of "student at the university" during the first field experience and "professor at the university" were usually sufficient for an introduction. But the next round of questions were often personal: Are you married or not? Do you have children? Why not? It was difficult to explain why I did not have children in 1970–72 and again in 1975, after several years of marriage. Many women were kind enough to intimate that the problem was with my husband and not me. Yet when we had our daughter Josina with us, women and men would freely opine that one child was not enough. Such comments would invariably end in some jesting or a comparison of Sudanese and American life-styles. At no time did I ever perceive a barrier to my conduct of fieldwork in the Sudan. Doors to offices, public institutions like the courts and the university, and Sudanese homes were almost always opened to us.

Perspectives on Families or Couples in the Field

Even though our first fieldwork in the Sudan consisted of individual efforts, we are strong advocates of team approaches to anthropological research. Whatever respective limitations are imposed on a male or a female alone, they may be overcome with a team effort in which areas of research not easily accessible to one member may be accessible to the other.

We did not systematically use a team approach in our own fieldwork, but in ongoing discussions at the dinner table and elsewhere we became familiar with each other's shortcomings and problems. Accordingly, we could ask each other to think about these areas and then spontaneously pursue leads or suggestions as they would emerge. Being self-critical, we could have benefited even more from a joint approach than we did. On a personal level we were viewed as a team by university faculty and colleagues, so we often went out of our way to stress our intellectual autonomy and self-reliance. This may have been our misfortune.

Methodologically, the participant observation stance works best when the research milieu is naturalistic—a joint (husband and wife) approach is perceived in our field area as being more normal. Beyond this, a husband and wife team is not only able to investigate subjects denied to one or the other, but it is less threatening overall. A male fieldworker with a wife in view, or known to be in the vicinity, is not likely to be up to anything other than research. A female anthropologist alone in the field may be a candidate for awkward and unwanted overtures which certainly would be curtailed were she accompanied by her husband, or at least if a husband was known to be around.

Being a couple in the field also led to an easier legitimization of our social status in the context of Sudanese values. An unmarried, young graduate student may be considered less mature and less serious in general, and if work involves research with more senior people, there is a tendency to consider the fieldworker less credible than if he or she has the more "adult" status of "married person." Consequently, our status made it possible to present ourselves more naturalistically, with the result of greater relaxation in field discussions. This was clearly a very positive methodological feature in breaking down social barriers and getting to deeper levels of analysis and understanding.

Children in the Field

Our most recent studies (1979–80) in the Sudan gave us the chance to bring Josina, our firstborn, to the field (Fluehr-Lobban 1981). Our additional roles as father, mother, family people, and so on, resulted in even more research topics emerging naturalistically and in context. We had more varied reasons to interact with the people we met in our research settings since now our daughter could play with their children. Taking a child to the field was certainly a strengthening feature in our analysis, but it was not a decision we made lightly. In many rural areas in Africa, doctors and health facilities are substandard or nonexistent, and for older children there may not be schools or other facilities comparable to those back home. Even in our urban-based situation we experienced some difficulty when Josina twice contracted malaria and also developed a very serious case of bronchial pneumonia. Luckily, medicines and a high-quality pediatrician were located and she received excellent treatment with no lasting, harmful effects. But we know of others who did not fare as well. Even in these circumstances, however, a husband and wife team can be more flexible and accommodating than, say, a single parent who would simply have to suspend work until the child's fever subsided and things returned to their regular state.

With respect to a child's view of fieldwork, we were amazed to see the extent to which our very young daughter was already a culture-bearer and thus could experience culture shock. Josina was with us in the Sudan between her second and third birthdays. In addition to her general fascination with and commentary on the differences between Sudanese and American life, from toilets to food to Islamic prayers, she was also a keen observer of social life. One of her first encounters with what was a scaled-down version of culture shock had to do with the custom of separation of the sexes in homes and on public transport and the like. From the beginning of our intense involvement in Sudanese social life, first living with a family in Omdurman and later with frequent social visiting, Josina protested sexual segregation. She could not understand why her parents had to separate when entering a home, her mother to the *hareem* with the women and children and her father to the more formal *salon* (a public area of the house, used especially by men). She was free to travel

the social distance between the two and made liberal use of the opportunity, finally settling down with her mother and the other children, but she continued to protest for many months into our stay,
pulling at her mother to join her father, and vice versa. Once she
realized the futility of her efforts, she began the game of reporting to
each of us what was going on in the other section of the house, taking obvious delight in her power of mobility. The interesting conclusion is that once she learned the norms, she became a more rigid
enforcer of sexual segregation than the Sudanese, insisting that male
guests in our home sit together and the women sit in a room or section apart. According to custom, men could only embrace men and
women embrace women, and when we violated these more formal
customs, especially in our farewells, Josina never failed to interrupt
us and protest.

Although she found the male children more interesting, tagging
along after them (she does this in the United States as well), she
nevertheless readily identified with aspects of female culture, often
imitating women wearing the traditional outer garment, the tōbe, or
mimicking the exclusively female Dove Dance. She even would
make courageous attempts to imitate her mother and other women
in the loud ululating cries of women which occur at weddings and
on other festive occasions. Despite the bouts with malaria and pneumonia, Josina's presence in the field was an interesting addition to
the entire experience at a time of strong family togetherness.

Sexuality in the Field

Little by little, sexuality in the field is receiving more attention as
we begin to recognize how it affects our roles in field settings. The
topic is an important one for researchers in the Sudan, given the
area's interest in and controversy over tūhūr (female circumcision,
i.e., infibulation and/or clitoridectomy), which is widely practiced
in the northern sections of this Afro-Arab nation. Indeed, there is
such intensity in the current debate among circles of feminists and
various medical practitioners that it would be difficult to avoid this
issue. It is quite clear that tūhūr of any sort, whether "light" or
"Pharaonic," carries a serious risk of infection or disability, especially given the physical conditions under which it is practiced. It is
also clear that the psychosexual perspectives of Sudanese women,
and men, are traumatized by tūhūr. Even if one were to accept the
importance of chastity, one could easily suggest far less drastic
means and use social sanctions to achieve the same result.

With this said, it should also be clear that the ultimate eradication

of female circumcision practices will not be easy, as the British discovered with their legislation; as the Western feminists are discovering with their sometimes hostile reception in the Sudan; and as
reform-minded Sudanese are finding out for themselves. Such pressures may help, but internal and structural contradictions within the
communities of Sudanese men and women will finally be responsible for bringing this form of genital mutilation to an end.

Despite the practice of *tūhūr*, the sexual life of Sudanese men and
women is otherwise quite robust and healthy, with a remarkable degree of openness, given present circumstances. This is probably especially true in discussions between women about sex. Women
speak of rather elaborate and explicit instructions for the use of oint-
ments, perfumes, and incense, and they discuss which positions and
techniques during intercourse might result in the greatest pleasure
for men. At the same time, extramarital sexuality is frowned on and
occurs only very rarely. Until the recent movement to Islamize the
national laws and values, a common male sexual outlet was on a
particular street in the capital city frequented by prostitutes, themselves rarely from the northern Sudan.

With these few notes about Sudanese sexuality as a context, one
can expect that there are certain clear advantages to being married
while undertaking Sudanese anthropological fieldwork. The sex-
related alternatives available to unmarried fieldworkers present a
rather high risk of violating Sudanese cultural values; and once
these traditional values have been offended, it may be quite difficult,
or impossible, to correct such a bad impression. Even those unmarried Western researchers whose sexual partners are other Europeans
or non-Sudanese run these risks, particularly in the case of small-
scale communities in the northern Sudan. In the larger towns and
cities, and perhaps in the southern regions, there is somewhat
greater flexibility permitted. In short, it does seem that with regard
to sexual conduct, a married pair of fieldworkers falls within traditional societal norms more fully and thus presents a more conventional image to Sudanese friends, informants, and associates. Even
if a fieldworker is not legally married, the appearance of a permanent association with a "spouse" is probably an asset, making one
less marginal and less threatening to the system of Sudanese ethics.

On occasion, either one of us was approached for information
about birth control techniques and technology, since it was known
that we were married and that it would be reasonable to ask us about
such things. This helped to build more trust between our Sudanese
friends and us, always an advantage in fieldwork. Despite sexual
segregation in Sudanese society, there is a frankness, even a clinical

interest, in things sexual (as discussed so effectively by Sudanese novelist Tayib Salih in *Season of Migration to the North*). With little or no legitimate access to this side of Sudanese values, one might incorrectly conclude that marked sexual segregation coupled with tūhūr means sexual austerity, which is certainly not the case.

It should be stressed that our comments are made in reference to the communities in the northern Sudan where we have worked; we would not generalize about other regions of the nation. From this perspective, we would say that only very discrete extramarital affairs are tolerated and that it would be difficult to imagine a sexual liason between a European or Western man and a northern Sudanese woman. By contrast, instances of unmarried or unattached Western women entering into sexual relationships with both northern and southern Sudanese men are much more common and frequently have resulted in marriage, especially among those in university and professional life, where there are probably more opportunities for such interaction. This clear double standard must also be taken into consideration by fieldworkers in the Sudan.

Parting Thoughts

We have tried here to capture some of the important features relating to gender that have affected and influenced the conduct of our field research in the Sudan over a ten-year period. The reader should be aware that it is impossible to summarize in so few words the experiences and emotions of a lengthy association with a particular people and culture; what is written here is merely a distillate of those rich years in the field.

Gender variables we became aware of in the field have sensitized us to similar forms of gender-related behavior in the West. Through living in a culture that separates males and females physically, we have become more aware of sexual segregation in our own culture—for example, at parties involving married people especially, there are likely to be two social subgatherings, one male and the other female. Sudanese men aspire to be strong and will fight to protect their own dignity and family honor. At the same time they have an equally strong desire to be poets and lovers of the written and spoken word. Sudanese women beautify themselves in an alluring and feminine fashion, but will make strong stands for their rights within the family or in the larger society. Stereotypes fall away and ultimately we are left with the richness and beauty of human diversity, including gender.

We might be somewhat unique as a research team since both of us are professional anthropologists, and this has had some effect on our relationship. While there was and still is a degree of competition between two closely matched, professional equals (our Ph.D.s were awarded in the same year from the same university, and we were tenured, promoted, and awarded sabbaticals in the same years from the same academic institution), we have managed to keep this a healthy competition that encourages rather than inhibits productive work. Moreover, the field settings we have chosen most often enhanced a feeling of closeness between us and within our family. Our "home" in the field was a respite, a place to share observations from the day's work and a mini-outpost of American culture for our daughter. We have visited families as a family, spent every afternoon during the culturally prescribed rest period together, and frequently strolled together through the market at night. We have rarely been able to match this much togetherness in our life in the United States, where our need for each other is not so dramatic. The openness and generosity so typical of Sudanese culture no doubt helped to make these times in our lives not only among the happiest but also among the closest.

References

Fluehr-Lobban, Carolyn
   1976   "An Analysis of Homicide in the Afro-Arab Sudan." *Journal of African Law* 20:20–38.
   1977   "Agitation for Change in the Sudan." In: Alice Schlegel (ed.), *Sexual Stratification*, pp. 127–43. New York: Columbia University Press.
   1981   "Josina's Observations of Sudanese Culture." *Human Organization* 40(3):277–79.
Lobban, Richard
   1975   "Alienation, Urbanization, and Social Networks in the Urban Sudan." *Journal of Modern African Studies* 12(2):491–500.
   1977   "The Dialectics of Migration and Social Association in the Urban Sudan." *International Journal of Sociology* (special issue on "Studies of African Urbanization") 7(2):99–120.
   1979   "Class, Endogamy, and Urbanization in Three Towns of the Sudan." *African Studies Review* 22(3):99–114.

12

Gender-related Issues in Carrying Out Rapid Team Fieldwork in the Cameroon

TONY LARRY WHITEHEAD and JUDITH BROWN

This paper reports the gender-related experiences of two anthropologists involved in field research that had to be quickly completed in order to respond to the needs of a public health program in the Cameroon. To meet this request a team fieldwork approach to ethnography was adopted, with concomitant gender-related and non-gender-related advantages and disadvantages. In keeping with the theme of this volume, only gender-related issues will be discussed here.

Background

In 1977 the Department of Health Education at the University of North Carolina at Chapel Hill was awarded a four-year contract by the United States Agency for International Development (USAID) to provide technical assistance to the Ministry of Health of the Cameroon in the development of its Practical Training in Health Education Project (PTHE). One of the missions of PTHE was to train itinerant health agents who would identify influential villagers and work with them to organize village health committees. These committees would identify the health needs of their communities and undertake to meet these needs. Such community development activities would be carried out in two regions of Cameroon, the Mefou Department in the Central South Province and the Kadey Department in the Eastern Province. In March 1980 a mid-project evaluation recommended the need for a social anthropological study in the Kadey because the culture diversity of villages in that area might demonstrate whether or not the idea of a village health committee for certain communities was feasible.

I (Whitehead) was approached in July 1980 and asked to quickly prepare a proposal for approval by the Cameroon Ministry of Health and USAID. The research would have to be completed and a report written by March 1, 1981 (within seven months), so that the report's recommendations could be implemented during the last year of the project (1981–82). I accepted this challenge[1] and proposed the utilization of a holistic anthropological model in the Kadey as a guide for the collection and analysis of data (see Whitehead 1984 for a detailed description). I also proposed a team approach to the collection of data using multiple methods (structured and semistructured analysis of statistical and published data, participant observation, audiotaping of special events, and photography) in two representative villages.

The team was to spend the first two months of the project carrying out prefieldwork activities, including the development of data collection instruments, the selection of study sites, and the hiring of translators. This team would be segmented during the prefield stage, with one subteam in the Cameroon being coordinated by a Cameroonian anthropologist and carrying out the selection of study sites and translators. I would coordinate the second subteam in Chapel Hill,[2] with the task of developing data collection instruments to be sent to the subteam in Cameroon for "cultural appropriateness" modifications. At the end of this prefieldwork phase, I would join the Cameroonian subteam and we would begin the actual fieldwork.

The proposal was completed in August 1980 and approved in October. I was told that there were no qualified Cameroonian anthropologists[3] but that Judith Brown, an American medical anthropologist who had spent eight years in Africa and was presently residing in Cameroon, was available to work on the study. As will be illustrated shortly, this turned out to be an excellent choice, not only because of Judith's many years of experience in Africa and the Cameroon, but because she is a woman. The prefieldwork activities went as planned and on December 31, 1980, I left for Cameroon.

Nine weeks remained before we had to submit a report. Judith and I spent a few days in Yaounde getting acquainted and being oriented to the project and to the Kadey. Then Judith, a few health officials, an English-French translator,[4] a driver, and I left for the Kadey and spent our first week in the capital of Batouri, completing our selection of translators and training them. Since we now had only seven and a half weeks left, we decided to spend two weeks in each site and three weeks back in Yaounde analyzing our data and writing the report.

The Setting

The two villages selected for study were Kibili (a pseudonym) in the savanna area north of Batouri and the twin villages of Kaumbole-Kidoso (pseudonyms) in the tropical forest area south of Batouri.

Although the distinct languages of six different ethnic groups were represented in Kibili, a village of 375 persons, we concentrated our study on the three numerically dominant groups, Fulbe (209 persons), Gbaya (71 persons), and Bororo (74 persons). Fulfulde, the native language of the socioeconomically dominant Fulbe and Bororo, was the local trade language of culturally diverse Kibili and its environs. Kaumbole and Kidoso together only have 191 persons, all Kaka who speak the same language and have similar life-styles. As the need for a team approach is greater in a culturally diverse community than in a culturally homogeneous one, the rest of this account will focus on the heterogeneous community of Kibili.

The Bororo of Kibili include both nomadic herders living in cattle camps some distance from the village and those who do some trading and have taken up semisedentary residence in houses in Kibili. The Fulbe, the politically and economically dominant group in Kibili, specialize in trading, clothing, canned goods, household supplies, and the gold and diamonds mined in the area. The wealthiest of the Fulbe own large numbers of cattle and hire Bororo to care for their herds. These Fulbe are quite heavily involved in cattle trading, buying them from both Fulbe and Bororo owners and then reselling them at regional and national markets. A few Fulbe also have fields of food crops and usually hire Gbaya to do the manual labor. The Gbaya are primarily cultivators, growing tobacco on small (one-tenth-acre) plots as their primary cash crops, and manioc, maize, groundnuts, sesame, okra, and yams for subsistence. They also earn some cash, meat, and material goods by doing manual labor for the Fulbe and the Bororo.

The Gbaya have a long history of subordination to the pastoral Fulani (Burnham 1980), and interethnic tensions were still very strong during our fieldwork. The Gbaya, who had been in Kibili the longest of the three groups, frequently complained about how the choice houses and lands were taken over by the Fulbe/Bororo, how the Bororo cows frequently trampled on and destroyed their crops, and how Fulbe merchants were continually cheating them in trade or in payment for services provided. The Bororo and Fulbe, in turn, saw the Gbaya as unclean and lazy nonbelievers who spent most of their time drinking beer, palm wine, and "African gin" (homemade corn whiskey) and playing their drums late into the night. While Kibili was multiethnic, interethnic tensions had contributed to the establishment of ethnically homogeneous settlements in some of the neighboring villages. Shortly after leaving Kibili, we learned of an interethnic brawl there that resulted in the hospitalization of a number of the Gbaya, including one of their chiefs.

Such cultural diversity and interethnic tension required a team effort that included translators who not only spoke French and Fulfulde but were also members of the three dominant ethnic groups. However, since we could not find any local Bororo who spoke French, we were finally able to convince them to accept Fulbe translators (although there was one Fulbe translator we could not use when interviewing Bororo because he had a low opinion of them and was insulting). We employed two Fulbe and one Gbaya male translators. One Fulbe was used in interactions with Fulbe respondents only, and the other was used primarily with Bororo respondents.

Gender-related Advantages of the Team Approach

Sex Segregation, Female Seclusion, and the Value of a Mixed-Sex Team

The primary subdivision of the team while in the field was by sex: Tony and the males on the team only worked with male respondents; Judith and the female translators only worked with female informants. We decided on this strategy because of the practices of sexual segregation and female seclusion in the community. The Fulbe and Bororo are ardent Muslims, and the men reverently take part in public prayers five times each day. There are special places in the Koranic school for girls, but the few girls who do attend are the children of chiefs and other high-status men. Few Muslim girls attend the normal Francophone schools as they are socialized very early that public display is not permitted. Whenever there is the possibility of being seen by any male other than their husbands or closest consanguineal male relatives, Muslim women are to be veiled (Levy 1965:124).

While the non-Muslim women in Kibili move about in public as freely as the men, the Muslim women are rarely seen outside their compounds. But just as the practice of segregation by sex and female seclusion differ in various parts of the Muslim world, so are there differences between the many Muslim ethnic groups in the Kibili area. We found that the degree of female seclusion was greater among the Fulbe, less so among the semisedentary Bororo, and more so among the nomadic Bororo. The men on our team rarely saw Fulbe women, only a glimpse here and there when we were talking to their husbands within the family compounds. Fulbe compounds are surrounded by high thatch fences or walls and the interior courtyard, houses, and kitchen buildings are completely cut off from public view. Fulbe women remain in their compounds with their co-wives, sisters-in-law, and children. Their wells and latrines are within their walls, and their husbands go out to buy the household food. In fact, Fulbe men pride themselves on providing for their wives, who do not have to work as hard as other women do. The women do the cooking, cleaning, washing, child care, and sometimes embroidery, but they know nothing about their husbands' cattle or business affairs. Some Fulbe women make donuts or bean cakes for sale, but they themselves never go to market; instead, their children (both girls and boys) sell their goods and run errands for them.

Fulbe women have a very limited circle of acquaintances. They interact regularly with less than a dozen residents of their own compound. Sometimes after dusk, two or three women, with permission from the male head of household, go out quietly to visit neighboring women. Fulbe women interact almost exclusively with other Fulbe women and children, although Bororo women may visit them occasionally, and Gbaya women sometimes enter Fulbe compounds to sell farm products. Rarely, if ever, do Fulbe women see Bororo or Gbaya men, and they seldom interact with Fulbe men who are not part of their own compound.

The men on our team also rarely saw semisedentary Bororo women, except when interviewing Bororo men in their camps and on Sundays and Fridays at the market in Kibili and Bembili, respectively, where they would be huddled together and would quickly cover up if they were caught unveiled by a strange man. Because we expected this type of female seclusion, we agreed on a sexual division of labor.

We found that the ethnic homogeneity between translator and respondent was not as important for women as it was for men. This was fortunate because we could find neither Bororo nor Fulbe women in the area who could speak French. We had been told by local government officials that because of female seclusion patterns, probably none of the Muslim women would have been allowed to work for us even if they did have the language facility. So we relied on Gbaya women, who were from a lower ethnic status but had more public freedom to attend school and thus had the greatest ability with the French language. During the pre-data-collection period, Judith had used Fulbe men and Gbaya women as translators to determine whether Gbaya women would be acceptable to the higher-status Bororo and Fulbe women. They visited a small number of Muslim women in their compounds to ask whether they would be more comfortable talking through Fulbe men or Gbaya women about family matters and health problems. The women unhesitatingly suggested Gbaya women, implying that ethnic differences were less important than sex differences. Thus, Judith hired two young, unmarried Gbaya women from nearby villages who had relatives in Kibili. They were fluent in French, Fulfulde, and Gbaya and proved to be equally at ease with women of all three ethnic groups. The interviews with Gbaya and non-Gbaya women seemed equivalent in every way, and we concluded that crossing ethnic lines had made no difference to the women, although crossing sex lines would have made interviewing difficult. We wonder if this would be true cross-culturally in highly sex-segregated societies.

While rules regarding the Fulbe and the semisedentary Bororo seemed rather rigid, we found that the nomadic Bororo women in the bush were allowed greater freedom to move about publicly. After we had been in Kibili for about ten days, the men on our team were invited to ceremonies that were being held by two nomadic Bororo groups in the bush some ten and fifteen kilometers from Kibili. At the first site there was a wedding, at the second a naming ceremony for a seven-day-old baby (a festive occasion to which numerous guests are invited). In Kibili, the men on our team had not interacted with the (semisedentary) Bororo women any more than we had with the Fulbe women. At the two ceremonies in the bush, however, after spending considerable time with the men, we were allowed to interact with the women. In both camps the cottages were in a V pattern, and at the point of the V was a large thatched-roof cottage where guests were received. The men gathered fifty to sixty meters in back (south) and to the right of these frontal cottages; to the left (east) were two or three cottages in which large groups of women and children gathered. In both instances we were not only given permission by the men to go over and interact with as well as take pictures of the women, but we were allowed this privilege *unchaperoned* by husbands or any other Bororo males. At first some of the women were bashful and would not look at us or pose for pictures, but most of them were quite bold and wanted their pictures taken. This boldness and the fact that all of the women eventually wanted pictures taken of the children resulted in our being able to talk to all of them. What was even more surprising to us, after being in Kibili, was that as we drove away, about twenty of the women came to the road a few hundred meters outside the camp to wave good-bye. Moreover, about two kilometers down the road we came across two Bororo women hitchhiking. After ten days in Kibili, we were truly shocked to find Bororo women in a situation where they could be approached by strange men in a vehicle.

Gender Role Adoption, Field Adjustment, and Data Collection

The male researchers' experience with the nomadic Bororo sug-gests that with time they might have been able to collect data from the sedentary Bororo and Fulbe women in Kibili. But we did not have much time and it was doubtful that given a year a man could have collected data from women that were as reliable as the data I (Brown) was able to collect within two weeks with my female trans-lators. I did not experience any problems in approaching and inter-viewing secluded women, and I was allowed to continually be in their company. Such freedom probably never would have been given to a male ethnographer, since local men were not allowed such liberties.

Kibili women are accustomed to male nurses and health care workers dealing with their illnesses, pregnancies, and children, so the male members of our team probably could have eventually inter-viewed them. On the few occasions when I asked permission for a male researcher or translator to enter a compound with me, for ex-ample, no one hesitated to allow them in. Perhaps our men also could have gotten permission to interview secluded women, but we doubt that the interviews would have been unchaperoned. The hus-band would probably accompany a male researcher, either because he saw him as a threat or simply to be helpful. His wife would then be likely to consult with him regarding ages, dates, and family his-tory, as well as on topics of community leadership and related prob-lems, rather than expressing her own knowledge and opinions. If the male researcher, hoping to elicit female ideas, asked for a private interview, he might be misunderstood and suspected of mixed or ulterior motives.

As a woman, I was free to wander into a compound at any time without sending word that I was coming or asking permission of anyone. The women secluded inside their compounds were usually quite pleased that I visited them and took an interest in their lives. And by showing up unannounced I was able to join them in their normal groups of women and children, carrying out their routine activities. If the husband happened to be present, he usually ignored us; if the husband tried to join our group, he usually accepted my request for privacy for "women's talk"—something a male re-searcher could not have asked for. I could come when the head of the household was away, which a male researcher could not; I could blend into the women's normal activities, which a man could not.

While my sex contributed to the ease I felt with the women in the community, I am convinced that what served me best was how I carried out the gender role associated with my sex. To establish rapport with my respondents I consciously adopted certain female patterns similar to those expected of Muslim women in Kibili. I chose to sleep inside a family compound under the protection of a Kibili (Fulbe) head of household, and I always wore appropriate attire (a dress and a head scarf). I interviewed Muslim women only inside their compounds and showed interest in the things only women were involved in, such as childbirth, breastfeeding, cooking, and embroidery. I talked about my own family and showed the local women photographs of my husband and children. I tried to adopt the local women's way of greeting and sitting, particularly in the presence of Kibili men. And I exchanged gifts with women, such as kitchen items and toilet soap.

But while I became involved as a participant in community activity, I was detached enough to remain a social scientist and the leader of a team. I differed from my female hosts in that I ate with the male members of the team and also held long conversations with them, both indoors and outdoors, during which we engaged in lively discussions and exchanged ideas and observations. In addition, I circulated throughout the village during the day and at night, and in doing so behaved differently from the Muslim women but not so differently from the non-Muslim Gbaya women. As this type of behavior was not completely foreign to the community, I was able to maintain my research responsibilities without offending the host population.

Gender-related Problems

Personal Difficulties with Sex Segregation and Health Orientations

I (Whitehead) had a few more problems in Kibili than Judith did. The collection of data was easy enough because I knew the kind of data we wanted and I am an experienced fieldworker and interviewer. However, I did have some difficult personal experiences. When we got to Kibili most of the Gbaya were busy with their tobacco and did not come to greet us. As they later told me, they also were embarrassed to meet us because they did not have gifts to give us, as the Muslims did, and because their living conditions were not as nice. As a result of their absence I spent much of my time tracking them down. I found myself feeling more comfortable with the Gbaya than with the Muslims because they seemed to have fewer restrictive cultural rules and seemed freer with information. It was relaxing to sit with Gbaya men and women (as it would be later with the Kaka), drinking beer and talking. (The Muslims seemed to me to spend most of their time praying. The mosque was next door to my house, and the calls to prayer seemingly occurred more than the traditional five times a day.)

Whereas I was intellectually prepared to observe the practice of female seclusion, I was somewhat uncomfortable when faced with the reality of this Muslim tradition. My discomfort grew as I began to suspect that there might be some relationship between female seclusion and the primary health problems of female subfertility and infant mortality which is so prevalent throughout the Kadey.[5] I remember feeling somewhat dismayed one day as I interviewed a Bororo chief who was discussing those same health problems while the bimonthly well-baby clinic his wives and the other Muslim women were not allowed to attend was being conducted within forty meters of us.[6]

Team Fieldwork and the Problem of Intradependency

On reflection, I now realize that the problems cited above were due in part to my lack of experience in Africa and Cameroon, to my language difficulties, and to the short duration of the fieldwork. In time, as I adjusted to the field setting, my difficulties with sex segregation surely would have subsided and my interactions with the Muslims in Kibili would have improved. Instead, I suffered additional problems because of these deficiences. I became quite dependent on the other six male team members, all of whom were Cameroonians. I was particularly dependent on the translators, not only for language translations but also for the correct gestures and protocols that were expected in social interaction. One or more translators were continually at my side, coaching me on such appropriate behaviors as when to say things for the greatest effect, when to enter a social setting, how to exit, who to buy beer for, who should drink first, and so on. The professional male members of the team also lectured me on many issues, such as preparing speeches and being ready to give them, and referring to each professional member of the team as "Doctor" because the people expected it.

One of the most problematic lectures I received concerned the issue of gift giving. When we arrived in Kibili people gave up their houses so we would be comfortable. They also gave us three meals a day and gifts such as chickens or eggs. Many of these people were poor and only rarely ate these items themselves, and I was very concerned about accepting such gifts. I also wondered how we could reciprocate for the housing and food with which we were provided on a daily basis. The Cameroonians on the team lectured me on my lack of understanding of the principles of African hospitality and asserted that I was being "too American" in my continued concern with reciprocating local hospitality. I was told that if I did not accept the people's gifts they would be highly insulted.

This theme of insulting offerers of gifts became so entrenched in my consciousness that I was quite unnerved one evening when a member of the research team offered me a woman. Ordinarily, such a gift would not have caused me so much consternation because I had experienced similar offers in other settings and I knew that such things happened to other fieldworkers. But in Kibili I found myself in an emotional crisis after declining the offer. I had become so dependent on the other men on the team in terms of their acceptance that I felt I might lose their support because I had turned down the gift, which all of them witnessed. In fact, incorporation into the male group of the study team was more important to me than incorporation into the male group of the field community. The short period of time spent with the study population and the task orientation of the research made incorporation into the local male population emotionally unnecessary. However, my dependence on the translators and the other male members of the team made incorporation into their group, or at least a comfortable alliance with it, quite necessary.

My need for the support of male team members made it difficult to discipline those who were accountable to me. Two of the men, who were from Yaounde, were very active womanizers who felt that whenever men travel they should find themselves local "wives." Hence, they brought in local women to share their quarters. While I was concerned with this behavior, I did not openly object, telling myself that it was probably a cultural pattern I did not understand. I rationalized that the gifts these men gave their "wives" helped ease the women's difficult material circumstances. The underlying reason I did not speak out, however, was that I depended on these men and did not want to create any conflicts that might threaten our relationship.

My reluctance to discipline the men resulted in another disorienting experiencing. When we were given permission by nomadic Bororo men to enter a female compound area, the two womanizers on our team exhibited quite a bit of flirtatious behavior. When some of the women responded positively, my resulting concern was prompted as much by fear as ethics—Bororo men carry long, sharp utility knives, which local legal officials had informed us were frequently used in disputes over women. I was not interested in becoming a field fatality, but I still did not know how to discipline these men.

One of the Cameroonian professionals on our team finally took the matter of discipline into his own hands. His chastisements, however, activated tensions that had been smoldering for some time. The professional was from a higher-status ethnic group in Yaounde and all along the two older men had resented his giving them orders. When he accused them of trying to seduce the local female translators, they hotly denied the charge and accused him of telling a lie as revenge for their not following an order he had given them two days earlier (to bring him a woman from Batouri while they were shopping for our supplies).

Clearly, I should have taken the initiative to discipline the men—I was the supervisor of one of them and the other lived with me. Moreover, as someone from outside of Cameroon politics who apparently was not involved in local sexual matters, I probably would have had more influence on their behavior than the Cameroonian official did. In retrospect, I think I should have shared with them my sentiment that as guests of the community and representatives of the national government we should not get involved in local sexual systems.

Conclusion

The account presented here describes some of the advantages and disadvantages of conducting rapid team fieldwork for applied purposes. The planning of pre-data-collection activities and the intensive team data collection activities while in the field contributed to the accumulation of a large body of information in two weeks that could be used not only by the Cameroonian Ministry of Health but also by other health agencies in culturally diverse African societies. By providing all team members with data collection tasks, we were able to document that for culturally diverse communities like Kibili there may be more feasible social units than the village around which to organize functioning health committees. Kibili's committee had not met in the year prior to our arrival, and in any event this village-wide group was controlled by Muslim men, whereas the Gbaya and female populations appeared to be most in need of health services. In such communities, ethnic or kinship groups, Koranic schools and mosques, and (domestic) compound-based women's groups may be more feasible outlets for developing functional committees. We were able to identify health-related problems specific to the various ethnic groups, thus suggesting that other strategies besides village-level committees might work best for solving the health problems of these populations, including the Gbaya in their scattered single-family residences,[7] the Nomadic Bororo in their temporary settlements, and the secluded women of the Fulbe and the semisedentary Bororo populations.

Not only were the Fulbe and Bororo women excluded from the public decision-making process, but Judith found that they knew nothing about the leadership of the village committee. In matters of their children's health and their own reproductive processes, the women often expressed helplessness and resignation: "What can we do? It is Allah's will." In cases of serious illness they were allowed to go to a hospital, but they knew nothing of preventive health programs in their village. They were truly isolated in their own compounds; Judith and her translators were able to collect this type of data only by joining them in their compounds. Although Judith might have been able to cross sexual lines in the collection of data more easily than the men on our team—Kibili men have had contact with Cameroonian and expatriate women in responsible positions in government—by working only with women she was able to concentrate on the relationship between their social and familial status and their knowledge, attitudes, and opinions regarding community, family, and health matters. Even in this shortened fieldwork period she was able to become acquainted with some three dozen Kibili women. By being able to interact with them in their own compounds, their absence from markets, meetings, and well-baby clinics appeared even more striking.

While rapid team fieldwork can be valuable in terms of the quantity and kinds of data collected, there are certain personal and gender-related problems that can occur, as evidenced by Tony's difficulties. At the root of his problems was a lack of experience in the cultural setting and his need to rely on French as well as Fulfulde translators. As a consequence of his overdependence on the other men on the team, Tony found himself unable to discipline the men he supervised when their behavior did not meet the ethical and professional standards he felt were necessary.

Judith, by contrast, was familiar with the cultural setting (see Brown 1980) and was fluent in French. She knew the advantages of partially adopting local female gender ascriptions while maintaining the flexibility that would allow her to carry out her activities as a social scientist and a team leader. Because of her familiarity with the culture and with sex segregation, she did not react negatively toward the Muslims, as Tony did. Judith's position as team leader made it necessary for her to move around freely and meet with the male members of the team; if she had any reservation about her status, it was whether the Cameroonian men on the team were comfortable with a woman as their leader (there were never any indications that this was a problem).

While Judith's role as both leader of the entire team and leader of the female subteam (she was the only professional in the latter group) was always clear, Tony was always unclear about his status on the male subteam. Not only was he dependent on those subordinate to him, but he was unsure of his position in relation to the male professionals from the Ministry of Health. They had begun the process of correcting his behavior before entering Kibili, and their lectures continued even after the team settled into the community. Although Tony was very grateful for this type of assistance during the initial phases of fieldwork, as Rabinow (1977:46–49) has pointed out there is a certain degree of control that those providing such assistance may exert over the ethnographer during this period. The greater the dependence on others by the fieldworker, the greater their control, and the greater the opportunity for those exerting control to create situations that allow it to continue. The more fieldworkers allow themselves to be controlled by others, the less they are able to remove themselves from behaviors that conflict with their own personal sense of correct ethical or professional behavior. We are convinced that it is easier for the fieldworker to remove himself or herself from such conflicts when interacting individually than when the fieldworker is part of a team he or she is emotionally dependent on. Also, when a fieldworker is in the field setting for some duration (a year or more), he or she has the time to work through the stage of total dependence, reduce the amount of control by others, and feel better about following his or her own sense of professional or ethnical decorum. But one is not allowed such emotional transitions when doing rapid team fieldwork.

There are several important lessons to be learned from the Cameroon team fieldwork experience. First, familiarity with the language and with local customs, including gender ascriptions by team members, is most important to field adjustment and fieldwork success. Second, in the orientation of team members considerable emphasis should be given to local gender ascriptions and to the gender and sexual orientations of team members. Attention should also be given to the proper ethical and professional behavior to be followed by team members.

A number of gender-related issues emerged from our experience in Kibili, and we have formulated these as hypotheses for future testing or debate:

1. The fieldworker's sex is a more salient characteristic in a sex-segregated society than in a non-sex-segregated society. In a sex-

segregated society we have an immediate "in" with our own group; in a non-sex-segregated society we must prove ourselves to everyone. In other words, it may be easier for a fieldworker to be accepted in his/her own group in a sex-segregated society than in a non-sex-segregated society.

2. A female fieldworker is accepted by women more quickly than a male fieldworker is accepted by men. Furthermore, a female fieldworker can cross sex lines sooner and more easily than a male fieldworker can.

3. Local ethnic differences are more important to men than to women, and sex differences are more important to women than to men.

4. When interpreters have to be used and sex lines have to be crossed, the same-sex rule should be followed more closely with regard to interpreter and informant than fieldworker and informant because the fieldworker is outside the local sociocultural system. Any fieldworker, male or female, should use a female interpreter with female informants and a male interpreter with male informants.

Notes

The funding for the research on which this essay is based was provided by USAID/Ministry of Health Project no. 631-009; we are grateful for their support. We would also like to acknowledge the Ministry of Health of the Cameroon and the staff of the Practical Training in Health Education Project.

1. I (Whitehead) considered this a challenge because I had no experience in Cameroon, or in Africa for that matter, and spoke only a little French. Then, again, a few years earlier I had a similar proposal turned down because the data collection period was considered too long, and I had looked forward to an opportunity to demonstrate that anthropological data could be collected within the time constraints necessary for the application of the research findings. Moreover, I strongly believe that anthropologists should be involved in such applied research and that the failures of many public service programs to reach proposed objectives, particularly in socioculturally complex societies, is due in part to the lack of culturally sensitive and holistic data anthropologists are trained to provide.

2. Other members of the Chapel Hill subteam included Mr. Lucas Omondi and Ms. Judi Aubel.

3. Toward the end of my stay in the Cameroon I met Paul Kwi, who was not only an accomplished anthropologist but also recently had completed similar fieldwork in a number of villages in the Eastern Province.

4. Although I knew some conversational French, I felt that I would be of greater value to the team if I had a French-English translator along to help out when I had difficulties.

5. Polygamy is the marital norm in both study communities. In addition, every man we talked to who was polygynous had at least one wife who did not have children. In fact, it was common to find men with more wives than total children, a problem of great concern to men.

6. We talked to the two Bororo chiefs in Kibili about the Muslims allowing their wives to attend these clinics as a means of possibly increasing fertility. They met to discuss it but voted against it because it would mean the public exposure of females.

7. Tobacco must be grown in rich soil near an available water supply. Because such soil and water requirements are usually in the bush away from the village, and because tobacco requires nine months of intensive work and care, many Gbaya spend nine months at single-family units near a water hole growing tobacco.

References

Brown, Judith
    1980   "Cameroonian Customs and Courtesies: A Description for Americans Living in the Southern and Western Province of the United Republic of Cameroon." MS. (for distribution to American expatriots in Cameroon).
Burnham, Philip
    1980   Opportunity and Constraint in a Savanna Society. New York: Academic Press.
Levy, Reuben
    1965   Social Structure of Islam. Cambridge: Cambridge University Press.
Rabinow, Paul
    1977   Reflections on Fieldwork in Morocco. Berkeley: University of California Press.
Whitehead, Tony Larry
    1984   "Sociocultural Dynamics and Food Habits in a Southern Community." In: Mary Douglas (ed.), Food in the Social Order: Studies of Food and Festivities in Three American Communities, pp. 97–142. New York: Russell Sage Foundation.

SECTION III

Self, Gender, and Interpretation

13

Breakdown, Resolution, and Coherence: The Fieldwork Experiences of a Big, Brown, Pretty-talking Man in a West Indian Community

TONY LARRY WHITEHEAD

Rabinow (1977:5) has described fieldwork as a process that contributes to "the comprehension of self by detour of the comprehension of the other"; however, he does not analytically describe the process of this odyssey. Such an analytic framework is found in Agar's (1982) application of Gadamer's (1975) concepts of *breakdown, resolution,* and *coherence.* According to Agar, breakdown occurs when there is a "disjuncture between worlds"—the fieldworker's world and the field community's world. At this point the fieldworker's "expectations are not met; something does not makes sense; one's assumption of perfect coherence, to use Gadamer's phrase, is violated" (1982:783). Breakdown then must be eliminated via resolution if the fieldworker is to achieve coherence. In this essay I will use these concepts to analyze my own experience of comprehension of the self via comprehension of the other while carrying out fieldwork in Jamaica, in a town I shall refer to as Haversham, during 1974 and the summer of 1975.

Although Agar (1982:782–83) refers to the important relationship between the self and the other, his discussion of breakdown, resolution, and coherence focuses primarily on the other. However, since researchers usually go to the field without a full understanding of the self, the process Agar describes may well promote understanding of the self as well as the other, echoing Rabinow. In the analysis that follows I will frequently refer to many "field" situations in my past (e.g., my childhood in rural Virginia; attending college in North Carolina; Peace Corps experiences in Turkey; and graduate training in Pittsburgh), since these experiences helped shape the self that I took to Haversham.

213

The Field Site

Haversham is similar to the wider Jamaican society in that more than 95 percent of its population is of African descent, with a small contingent of peoples of European, East Indian, and Chinese ancestry. Traditionally, the area has been economically dominated by sugar estates and peopled primarily by estate owners, managers, and workers, with a peasant population living in the surrounding hills. During the 1920s a sugar factory was built in the area, and following World War II the town experienced both rapid industrial and population growth as additional factories were opened and large numbers of people moved in to take advantage of new employment opportunities. However, this "development" led to higher rates of unemployment and underemployment: the area's long history of slavery and colonialism had left a heritage of illiteracy and low skill levels such that, even in 1976, many old and new Havershamians were not able to exploit these opportunities.[1] The purpose of my research was to study the effects of this "development without employment" (Brazleton 1968) on men's attitudes toward mating and family, as well as their behavior in these areas.

Breakdown: The Self

A Big, Brown, Pretty-talking Man?

According to Agar (1982:783), breakdown occurs when there is "a lack of a fit between one's encounter with a tradition and the expectations contained in the schemas by which one organizes one's experience." Part of the system of schemata by which one organizes and integrates experience is one's sense of self. Rabinow (1977:118–120) points to an informant who was forced to see himself as being of higher socioeconomic status than he had before because of the ethnographer's (Rabinow's) inquiries and objective categorizing. A parallel transformation in perception of the self occurred for me as a consequence of my fieldwork in Haversham.

I am a black American who grew up in the rural South to impoverished sharecropper parents. Regardless of the upward mobility I experienced, when I went to Jamaica I still perceived of myself as one of the little people[2] (i.e., lower status) because of my experiences as a member of an ethnic minority in the United States. During a field project in Jamaica, as a consultant in 1971, I experienced a sense of identification with Jamaicans as "fellow oppressees" within the Euroamerican political economy.[3] This was part of the self I carried to Jamaica in 1974 when I returned to carry out dissertation fieldwork.

With such a self-image in tow, I was shocked when the people of Haversham began referring to me and treating me as a "big," "brown," "pretty-talking" man. "Big" was not a reference to my weight but to my higher social status as they perceived it, and "brown" referred not only to my skin color but also to my higher social status. I was aware of the West Indian correlation between skin color and social status (see, e.g., Henriquez 1953; Kerr 1963; Lowenthal 1972; Simey 1946), but I was not prepared for the personal experience of *my* lightness of skin color being associated with higher socioeconomic and moral status.

People in Haversham who are dark-skinned are considered brown if they exhibit what is perceived as high economic, social, or moral characteristics. For example, my landlady asked me repeatedly if the social worker who first brought me to the community was browner than she was. Then, after meeting her, she accused me of lying. Although physically the social worker was darker, my landlady judged her to be browner because of her higher education, the large car she drove, and the authority with which she walked and talked. In another instance, a number of townspeople were upset with a young man who quietly had moved owing money to a lot of people. Some of them expressed amazement that a brown man would do such a thing, or they were angry because they had been taken in by his browness.

More embarrassing than bothersome were the references to how "pretty" I talked, a comment on my Standard English speech pattern.[4] Frequently, mothers told me that their children were going to school so they could learn to talk as pretty as I did.

My bigness and pretty talk caused numerous data collection difficulties at the beginning of my fieldwork. Lower-income males[5] did not want to talk to me because "little men who could not talk pretty are not capable of talking to big men." Thus, when I tried to hold casual conversations or formal interviews with a number of low-income men, they avoided looking me in the face and often suggested that I talk to someone else who was considered a bigger man than they. Frequently they answered me with meaningless "yes sirs" and "no sirs."

As a big man I was also expected to be very smart and to have special skills in such activities as fixing cars, playing dominoes, drinking beer and other alcoholic beverages, and making money. Early in my fieldwork I found myself becoming quite annoyed at the prospect of sitting around with men for extended periods of time drinking rum and/or smoking ganja (marijuana), loudly slamming dominoes on a board and arguing. The men dismissed me as having no skills in these pastimes.

My early frustration was also due to the increasing problems I encountered in reclaiming loans I had made and in dealing with so-called auto mechanics and with cars in general. Initially I was asked for loans and made them, feeling that it was a way to develop rapport with the townspeople. But when people failed to repay the loans as promised, I began to think of them as liars and con men, and I resented their various tricks to evade me. Also, I had bought an old car, which attracted people and facilitated data collection, particularly from men, who liked to ride around or just sit in the car. The fact that the car was always in need of repair attracted the men as well, and they often gathered to display their mechanical skills. After two months of car ownership and more than a dozen repairs, I decided to get a newer, more reliable model, for I still saw an advantage to having a car. The repair pattern continued with the second vehicle, however, and I eventually got rid of it, deciding that the aggravation outweighed the advantages.

My growing annoyance was only partially due to both cars' continual state of disrepair. It also upset me to hear the men comment on my lack of mechanical skills, especially when I realized that some of them knew even less about car repairs than I did. In some cases they charged me for work that in fact contributed to the car's problems, yet it did not help matters when I complained to those men who had become close friends and informants that I was being cheated. They empathized, but at the same time they showed pride in the accomplishment of the little men (and women) who had outsmarted a big man. The car repair racket represented to them something they could be proud of, because big people, by opportunity, experience, and *nature*, were supposed to be smarter than little people (Whitehead 1980:44).

Because of the political orientation I had brought to the field (see Whitehead 1980:40–44) and my familiarity with the literature on West Indian political economy, I viewed higher-status brown people as the managers of a society that perpetuated a "persistent poverty," as Beckford (1972) called it, among the majority of West Indians. This orientation contributed to my discomfort in the early part of fieldwork as I observed dark-skinned men frequently deferring to men of lighter skin color or higher status in public gatherings, allowing them to monopolize conversations, agreeing with or repeating their statements, and generally flattering them. And I was being regarded as one of those big people, a status I emphatically did not want.

A Man of Sexual Integrity!

Another part of my sense of self concerned my own sexuality. On entering fieldwork I considered myself to be highly ethical in sexual matters; among other things this meant not getting sexually involved with members of the study community. A number of experiences contributed to my orientation in this regard. While in Turkey as a Peace Corps volunteer, I had what I thought were two harmless dates with a Turkish woman, only to find that my actions were interpreted within the Turkish context as intent to marry. I thus found myself engaged to a woman who did not speak English very well and in any event did not want to move to the United States. Two months prior to the end of my two-year tour of duty, I was still trying to adjust to the reality of never returning to America. But I couldn't go through with the marriage, and because of family and kinship involvement in the upcoming event, I left the country under the pretense of returning in a few days. I still carry the guilt resulting from these actions in Turkey.

The lesson of my Turkish experience was reinforced in a briefing I received prior to doing consultant work in Jamaica in 1971. The person I replaced had gotten into a sexual entanglement that eventually threatened the continuation of my university's contract with the government of Jamaica. Thus, I was told to dress like a (health) professional rather than an anthropologist and stay away from the native women.

An additional factor that contributed to my orientation toward sexual ethics in the field came from my graduate student experiences. Some faculty members had made remarks that I felt indicated they thought I was more interested in sexual conquests than in becoming a professional anthropologist. For example, at the end of my first semester I questioned a final exam grade and the professor responded, as he smoked his pipe and stroked his beard: "Whitehead? It is Whitehead, isn't it? There are two types of students: those who are naturally intelligent and those who work hard. Then, there is the pseudo-student who spends most of his time drinking beer with friends and trying to get a new piece of ass every week. You seem like the third type to me." The next year when I complained to my advisor about a grade I had received from another faculty member, he told me that the professor in question had intimated that I seemed more interested in a particular female classmate than in the course topic.

This latter situation was both disturbing and ironic: the young woman in question had come to me and requested that we do our assignments together, on the grounds that I was doing much better in the class than she was (although her final grade was higher). I was indeed perplexed until a fellow black, an advanced graduate student, helped me understand what was happening. He told me that I smiled too much, dressed too nicely (the antithesis of the public health people's view), and hung around too many of the female students. Having been reared in a female extended household, I had always had a lot of female friends, as well as male friends. Most of my classmates were females, and since I tend toward extroversion, a number of them became my friends. Some of the faculty obviously had misinterpreted my behavior, and their misinterpretations had more of an impact on their behavior than I had realized.

At one time during graduate training I had a girlfriend who insisted that I thought becoming an anthropologist meant losing interest in sex. If she thought I was weird, the Havershamians thought I was really bonkers. They simply couldn't understand why I never followed up on suggestions by local men and women to take a Havershamian woman into my house as a housekeeper-concubine, or why I never tried to sweet-talk and seduce women. It didn't help matters that I was thirty-two years old and had no children, an "unnatural" situation for a man my age, regardless of marital status. This "flaw" in my character was particularly troublesome for some of my male Havershamian friends. They did not want me to be defined as a weak man, so they began to circulate rumors that I had a lot of illegitimate children in various parts of the United States, but that "Americans don't like to talk about such things." When I was out with men, they often sweet-talked women for me, setting up dates and even taking me to some of the women's homes and offering to pay them for their services on my behalf. When I didn't respond in the desired manner, they continued to question my sexuality. Particularly disorienting were the frequent comments that failure to become involved sexually with available women was unnatural for a big man like me.

Breakdown: The Other

Separating the Other from the Self

Another reason for the breakdown of the self I brought to the field was my inability to separate my personal from my professional motivations for doing fieldwork. Professionally, I was interested in conducting research worthy of a doctoral dissertation and in making both theoretical and applied contributions. As a black man and a scholar, I had long been opposed to the plethora of literature on the black family that identified male familial marginality as the underlying reason for the higher prevalence (relative to other New World populations) of common-law union, instability of conjugal unions, out-of-wedlock births, and female-headed households (for a review of this literature see Whitehead 1976:4–13; 1978:817–18). These views were shared by Jamaican doctors and nurses with whom I talked in 1971 in family planning clinics across the country. They claimed that the lower-income Jamaican male is socially irresponsible, interested only in impregnating as many women as he can and spreading *pickni* (children) all over the island without providing for them. Such views didn't describe the majority of lower-income black males I had known while growing up in a lower-income black family. Many of these men had maintained some family ties and occasionally worked two or three jobs trying to support their families. A growing body of literature now suggests that the earlier studies of lower-income black male familial irresponsibility were overstatements of fact (see Allen 1981; Anderson 1978; Billingsley 1968; Hill 1971; Stack 1974; Valentine 1978; Whitehead 1978). Thus, I went to Jamaica to document that the attitudes of health personnel regarding male social irresponsibility in Jamaica also overstated the facts.

Much to my discouragement, my early field experiences seemed to point to the conjugal and familial irresponsibility about which Jamaican health personnel had talked. I spent my evenings with men, and in addition to drinking rum and playing dominoes, they did a lot of sweet-talking, arranging for sexual rendezvous and even visiting the homes of women with whom they had supposedly engaged in sex. Moreover, 180 of the 208 adult males in my household composition survey (conducted shortly after my arrival in Haversham) stated they had had children by more than one mate.[6] Many of the men did not know where their outside children were, while a few referred to them as an indicator of their masculine strength.

I was impressed, however, by the strong work orientation of the lower-income men, despite the level of unemployment and underemployment. An amazing number of men would show up to bid for the few short-term public works jobs that the government infrequently offered, and some of the men held two or three menial jobs to support their households and other "relatives." While carrying out the household survey I continually was asked by local men and women to help them find jobs in the factories, something I found extremely depressing since I knew I was helpless in such matters (Whitehead 1980:43–44).

The pronounced work orientation of some of these men was related to their commitment to provide some support for both inside and outside children. Even men who didn't have a steady income tried to periodically provide breadfruit, oranges, or any other produce they could obtain inexpensively to their outside children. Providing something, even a small amount infrequently, is one way a man continues to have access to his outside children and to their maternal relatives, with whom he may be able to form alliances in economic and political ventures. The importance of maintaining such access can be observed in that some mates acknowledge and foster this access by providing support to their mates' children from earlier unions.

These patterns of work orientation and economic provision for children may be viewed as socially responsible behavior shared by lower-income Haversham males and those of higher income. Additionally, I found that higher-income males demonstrated what might be considered socially irresponsible traits. In fact, some of the negative patterns discussed earlier are more prevalent among higher-income males precisely because of their higher socioeconomic status. When I was with both lower- and higher-income men, some of the evening frequently would be spent drinking and talking about, searching for, or sweet-talking women; however, the women responded more positively to the amorous overtures of the higher-income men. It appeared to me that lower-income men often had to be satisfied with just sweet-talking, without the possibility of a sexual liaison. When I was with them I was never offered a female nor taken to the homes of known prostitutes, and they never tried to convince women to meet me in a secret place or visit me in my home. But such practices were common in my interactions with higher-income men, a reflection, among other things, of the advantages higher income brought to the important game of sexual competition and of the double standard enjoyed by big men. A popular ditty in Haversham at this time was: "If I can afford it and you can't, then my wife is my wife, and your wife is my wife"—meaning that if a man has the money to provide a good home, it is all right for him to play around with other women (including other men's wives); of course, his mate should be satisfied with the good home (and children) he has given her and not consort with other men.

Experiences of this sort early in my fieldwork heightened the already negative feelings I had about higher-status Jamaicans. I not only saw them as managers of the political economy that kept most

Jamaicans poor, but I came to view them as relentless in using their privileged status to directly exploit less privileged females. Indirectly, the mates of these women are also negatively affected, for they don't have the protection against cuckoldry that higher economic status is thought to provide. I also felt discomfort when my conversations with higher-income men always ended in questions such as, "Why are you really in Haversham? Don't you have enough poor people in the United States to study?" As a consequence of these feelings I began to spend more time with lower-income men. Subsequently, when I had to interact with higher-income people to get a comprehensive picture of the community, I found that some of them were hesitant to interact with me. I had become identified with lower-income people and with such undesirables as the Rastafarians.[7] Big men with a reputation for acting like little men were considered weak.

Investigator Perceptions of Contradictory Values

The meaning of the term *responsibility* differs according to who is using it. Human services personnel indict lower-income Jamaican males for not taking responsibility for "spreading children all over the island." In contrast, Haversham men and women saw me as socially irresponsible because I was thirty-two and did not have a mate or children. They reasoned that I was selfish, as I had no one with whom to share my wealth and bigness, no one to "leave things to after I was dead."

From my perspective, Havershamians appeared more and more to hold contradictory views on the issues of social responsibility for fathering children. Men in both higher- and lower-income categories frequently commented that the men who had children all over the island represented a major problem in Jamaican economic development, yet these same men proudly showed me pictures of their children by different women who lived in various parts of the island; sometimes they even took me to visit these children, to show them off. When I sat around in the afternoons with men from both economic groups they talked disparagingly about those who drank so much rum that they couldn't support their families or smoked so much ganja that they were going mad. Yet these same men often gathered in the evening and drank what I thought were excessive amounts of rum while smoking ganja cigars. In our discussions men from both socioeconomic groups talked about how much Jamaican men wanted to work or about how hard they worked at two or three jobs simultaneously. Yet these same men might tell me later about jobs they had quit, or how they were fired because they just didn't feel like going to work sometimes, or how they went to work drunk, or how they decided to go to Montego Bay instead of to work. Men from both groups asserted that the government or prime minister should be like a father: on the one hand providing for their needs, while on the other hand punishing them for misdeeds, such as not working. On other occasions the same men referred to the government as oppressive and to themselves as sufferers who should get rid of the oppressor.

Lack of a Theoretical Paradigm

My observations of both the socially responsible and irresponsible behaviors and attitudes and the contradictory statements on the part of men in both socioeconomic groups would have been far less problematic if I had had a theoretical paradigm to adequately encompass those observations. Some writers have mentioned "normative dualism" in West Indian social structure (see M. G. Smith 1966:xxx for a review of the literature) but have followed the tradition of assigning one set of characteritics to one class and a second set of characteristics to another. For example, Henriquez (1953:161–73) did this with his *eunomia* (socially responsible characteristics) and *disnomia* (socially irresponsible characteristics). Wilson (1973) used the terms *respectability* (socially responsible characteristics) and *reputational* (socially irresponsible characteristics),[8] although he viewed respectability as primarily European in origin and practiced in the West Indies by women, and reputational as West Indian in origin and practiced primarily by men. I was initially attracted to his scheme because the terms were frequently used in Haversham with clear connotations of social responsibility and irresponsibility. But, Wilson's dialectical argument ended with racist and sexist overtones that made it very unattractive.[9] Rodman's (1963, 1971) "value stretch" paradigm appeared to be particularly appealing, with one exception. He argued that lower-class Trinidadians hold the same (socially responsible) values as other classes of Trinidadians, but that they sometimes stretch these values (socially irresponsible) because of economic circumstances. Yet he did not say why the other, higher socioeconomic classes also stretch their values.

Kerr's (1963) "conflict" paradigm looked useful because its national character orientation could allow for application to most, if not all, Jamaicans regardless of class.[10] Eventually, however, I came to view his theory as too clinical and too closely akin to the pathological interpretations of Afro-American social structure once popular in the United States (e.g., Frazier 1939; Kardiner and Ovesey 1951; Myrdal 1954) and the West Indies (e.g., Henriquez 1953:161–

72; McCartney 1970). How could a people, a culture, have survived so long if the dominant characteristic of their social system was pathological? More central to my rejection of Kerr's framework, however, was the realization that even though I saw male attitudes and practices as contradictory, the men I observed did not appear to exhibit the conflict she described. They argued for both reputational and respectability values in the same evening, seemingly without knowing that what they were saying was contradictory. My asking if they saw conflicts or contradictions in their arguments prompted discussions of *social balance*. The people of Haversham were operating within a folk-theoretical paradigm that I had not found in the research literature.

Resolution and Coherence: The Other

My analysis of the shortcomings of the theoretical paradigms that seemed most relevant to what I was observing and experiencing contributed to *breakdown,* but it was also the starting point for the process of resolution. Agar (1982:785) states: "It [a breakdown] violates our expectations and calls into consciousness what the phenomenon is not. There follows a dialectic process of questions and answers by which we alter our tradition and bring into existence an account of what the phenomenon is, given our starting point." The breakdown is the starting point because conscious reflection begins when there is a description and the consciousness focuses on it (1982:781). The ethnographer must make sense of the events to achieve coherence, which is the end point of the process. While my resolution process was fueled by an assessment of the literature, I came to coherence through the fieldwork process.

The resolution process was quite painful for me. Not having a theoretical paradigm to help me interpret what I was observing and experiencing caused such anxieties that I was tempted to leave the field a number of times. I frequently lamented that I couldn't do anything with the data I was collecting, not even write a dissertation. I felt that I could never again study or write about poor black people because no matter what I tried to say, if I were to use existing theoretical paradigms it would be misinterpreted as a depiction of a socially irresponsible and a culturally and morally depraved people. My literature review contributed to my breakdown because it presented a tradition that was different from what my informants were telling and showing me. They were saying that not only is it possible for people in different social categories (class, ethnic, social, or sexual groups) to value contrasting cognitive themes, but that these same contrasting themes can be (and are) shared by most people within the community; that the contrasting traits are part of one cognitive system, with attributes perceived in a sort of linear fashion— respectability at one end and reputation at the other; that however well the majority of these traits are exhibited by the majority of people within the community, certain individual or social categories may exhibit more reputational traits while others exhibit more respectability traits; that just where individuals or social categories fall along this linear paradigm depends on cultural rules and definitions, on situational circumstances; and that contrasting themes may exist within a single category of people without entailing conflict or pathology, with the mediating concept of social balance.

I interpret the concept of social balance as part of a larger cognitive system which also includes the concepts *big, little, respectability,* and *reputation,* as well as *strong, weak, good,* and *wicked.* But in discovering these concepts among the Havershamians, I experienced further breakdown because I thought I was looking at the binary opposites, or discriminative pairs, that were so popular in the structural interpretations I was drawn to at the time. Structuralists see such pairs as part of the "ritual proclivity of the human mind" (Needham 1979:75), because it is through the perception of opposites that the "mind builds up its perception of the world" (MacCormack 1980:2, referring to Lévi-Strauss 1978:22–23). The concepts of big and little are amenable to such analysis because they refer to opposite socioeconomic situations. But the other six concepts cannot be usefully viewed as three sets of discriminative pairs; they cannot be isolated and analyzed as opposites. Rather, these concepts must be looked at in terms of the total system of pairs.

Figure 1 shows respectability and reputational traits as the people of Haversham outlined them for me. Exhibiting strength and goodness is thought to be the way a little man can achieve bigness—the ultimate goal of men (and women) in Haversham. What was problematic for me was that reputational traits are also viewed as sources of strength, which seems illogical. How can a goal be achieved through exhibiting traits that seem contradictory to those traits considered necessary for achieving the goal? Again, I found the answer in the concept of social balance.

The idea of social balance is that weakness results not only from *not* exhibiting characteristics of strength but also from *overexhibiting* such traits. A man is considered weak if he exhibits too many or too few respectability or reputational traits; he must keep these in balance. For example, people consider a man weak if he has no children, but he is also weak if he has so many children that his ability

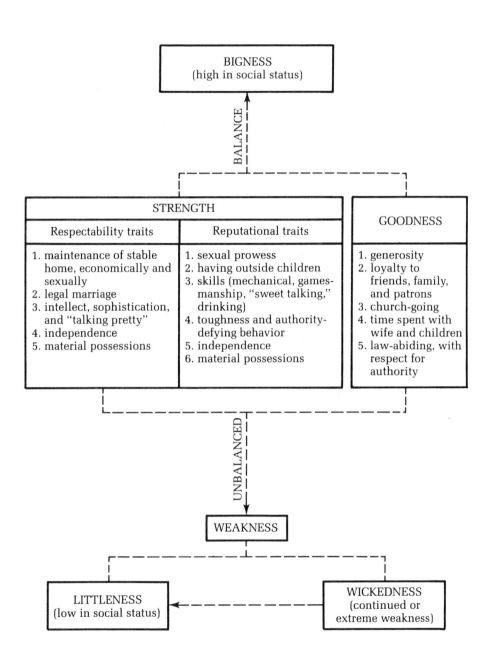

Figure 1. The Cognitive Construct of Masculinity in Haversham

to maintain his home economically is jeopardized. Maintaining a stable home both economically and sexually is a very important indicator of strength (respectability)—a strong man is a good provider and he controls the sexuality of the women in his home. (These traits are related because it is believed that if a man provides well for his women, they have no reason to turn to other men.) But a strong man also exhibits sexual prowess (reputational) by having outside women and outside children, even though they can drain his strength (symbolized by his material possessions, including money, and his semen). A good man is a generous man who provides for his outside women and children, but if he doesn't have enough money for his inside family, then his (inside) home could be "mashed up" and his inside woman will quickly look for outside males to help her. Similarly, when a man gives up semen, the essence of his strength, through sexual contact, he needs time to "build it back up."[11] A man with too many outside women runs the risk of not rebuilding his strength and in his weakened state may not be able to provide for his women (inside and outside) in economic terms or to meet the strong(er) sexual needs of his mate.[12]

To maintain a stable home a good man must spend time there. But a strong man also must spend considerable time with male cronies, to demonstrate the reputational trait of independence from women. While in the company of his male friends, a strong man shows the respectable strength of generosity by buying drinks and being able to drink. Yet he must be careful not to buy so many drinks that he compromises his ability to maintain his home, and not to drink so much that he isn't able to hold a job. While with his male peers a man shows his sexual prowess by sweet-talking women, which is sometimes done more for male approval than for sexual conquest. In fact, it may sufficiently indicate sexual prowess that he does not have to follow through with the sex act, which might only "sap the strength." Sweet-talking differs from talking pretty in that the latter indicates usage of Standard English whereas the former is carried out in the more rhythmic and colorful patois of Havershamians, or in a mixture of patois and Standard English. Using either style of speech in excess is thought to weaken a man, as he is likely to use one type or the other in the wrong situation. A good man is loyal to his patrons, for it is their generosity that aids him in achieving bigness; however, a strong man shows some independence from patrons. A good man is a churchgoer, but to be strong he must also demonstrate some independence from the church. A good man is law-abiding and respects authority, but a strong man must also be tough and occasionally defy authority.

Whereas strength and weakness are opposites in this folk paradigm, the relationship between good and wicked is not totally oppositional. Good traits are respectable traits, but wicked traits are not simply reputational traits. To be considered weak a man must exhibit extreme weakness or be in a continual state of weakness. Men who use power, money, or intellectual skills to embarrass or belittle others, or men who are so independent that their family, friends, and patrons cannot depend on them, are wicked. Their social balance has been destroyed by excessive use of strength. Similarly, the man who repeatedly drinks in excess, or the one who remains in jail because of his tough behavior (and thus can't work and maintain his home), or the one who gambles so much and so often that he has no money, or the one who continually gives all of his money and strength (semen) to outside women and children—these are all wicked men. Drinking too much, or smoking too much ganja, can make one a "mad man," someone who is totally out of balance and is not able to determine the limits of respectability or reputation. The man who has so many children that he can't provide for them or his women, yet continues to have more, is also out of balance and wicked. Havershamians believe that continual wicked behavior leads to homosexuality, the ultimate of wickedness.

Resolution and Coherence: The Self

Resolution and Field Adjustment

As my comprehension of the other began to emerge, so did my comprehension of self, and I was eventually able to develop concrete strategies for field adjustment and a successful research venture. As I experienced Jamaica's systems of stratification and patronage more fully, I became more comfortable with references to me as a big man. Informants explained that I had earned the right to be referred to in that way, and I had to admit that their arguments had credence. I even began to accept and expect being called "brown" as my experiences gave me a better understanding of the Jamaican class-color cognitive construct; indeed, I had grown up among people with a similar construct, though not as extreme, in the southern United States. I also came to realize that people referred to my use of Standard English as "talking pretty," not only to flatter me for patronage reasons (see Whitehead 1984), but also because they wanted to point me out as a role model for their children. Parents viewed education as the key to achieving bigness, and speaking Standard English rather than the local patois was important to them.

I could now interpret differently, within the context of generosity, what I had earlier regarded as the sexual exploitation of lower-status females by higher-status males. Both men and women asserted that poor women need someone to provide for them.[13] One man admitted to me that he didn't have sex with all the women he was reputed to be having liaisons with, as it would drain him of his strength. The sex was available if he wanted it, but the fact that other men knew he had all of these women made it worth "the little something that he gave them every now and then." I explored this idea further with other informants and found them very candid; they even helped me establish a relationship with a woman that was nonsexual. Louisa and I did not live together or have sexual relations, but we were accepted as being very close. In fact, she became a very important informant with regard to female views and was instrumental in locating respondents for my survey of females.

After realizing that sweet-talking was a game that frequently did not entail sexual expectations, I was able to respond to verbal flirtations from females in public places. I also began to understand that when people asked to borrow money and then failed to repay me, they did so with the expectation of generosity and patronage normally associated with big men. By understanding the concept of social balance, I eventually established with men and women that I would loan money or personal items only under certain conditions and that I expected them to be returned after a certain amount of time. Thus, I could be strong (generous) while not permitting the situation to deteriorate to the point that I would appear weak (foolish). The role of generous patron with a sense of balance also made it possible for me to act on my ethical concern that I somehow compensate informants for information.

With my new-found comprehension of social balance, I was now able to tell men that the limits of such balance in my country were different than those in Jamaica. I was able to convince them that men in my country generally cannot drink or smoke as much as the men in their country, which allowed me to gradually taper off drinking and smoking during my interactions with men. When I became sick, I attributed it to the fact that I was out of balance, and some men were so concerned that they insisted I refrain from smoking at all, saying, "The Jamaican man, he is strong, he is used to it."

Thus, my explanation of different senses of balance in Jamaica and the United States was accepted, though it was accompanied by the view that American men are "weaker than Jamaicans." The idea that I was weak in certain areas turned out to be an advantage rather than a disadvantage, however, as it reduced some of the distance between me and those men who saw themselves as too little to talk to a big man. My weaknesses provided a welcome opening for discussions that were difficult to get started otherwise. Little men became more comfortable teasing me; big men became more comfortable chiding me; and I became more comfortable accepting both. But I also learned to establish limits, to establish a balance, so that I wouldn't appear weak and out of balance. I frequently did this by teasing or by taking a turn in the debate at hand, yet I learned not to take my response too far, so as to avoid appearing wicked (e.g., belittling people with my "expansive intellect").[14]

Being chided by big men made me realize that they, too, saw me as a big man and that the big/little dichotomy applied to class differences in Jamaica as well as to intersocietal differences. Jamaica is a small country which has been controlled politically and economically for centuries by powerful external sovereignties, and some Jamaicans seem to apply the big/little concept to their interactions with persons from those controlling countries. Since I appeared to be a very intelligent big man, defeating me in debate helped to close the perceived distance between me and some of the big men in Haversham; when these men pointed out my inherent weaknesses and wickedness as an American, they accomplished the same purpose (see Whitehead 1984 for further discussion of this point). Once I began to accept such castigation, and to establish limits for the sake of balance, I found myself being accepted into the circles of Haversham's big people.

Coherence: True Similarities Between Self and Other

The more I comprehended the concept of balance among Havershamians, the more I began to realize that the concept was probably in operation in other cultures as well,[15] including the one I came from, though it simply is not articulated as well among Americans and may exist only at an unconscious level. In America, as in Haversham, some individuals and groups exhibit more respectability or reputational traits in public than others do. Like Havershamians, Americans seem to differ about where the border between being balanced and unbalanced is situated. The differences in locating that border in both societies arise from cultural and ethnic factors, from situational circumstances, and from personality (that combination of culture, genetics, and individual experiences).

In considering the possibility that the concept of balance exists within the cognitive system of Americans, I realized that it had played a role in my own life experiences. I had been in many social situations in which my behavior was guided by the rules of respectability and reputation, as conceived by the various social groups of which I was a part. As a boy I was rewarded by teachers for being a "good" student (in conduct as well as grades), but my male peers saw me as a goody-goody, as the teacher's pet. To them, I carried such behavior too far and was weak. To gain their acceptance I spent more time with them (exhibiting independence) and developed masculine skills and toughness (reputational behavior)—swimming in snake-infested ponds and running into walls or diving into cow dung to make game-saving catches for my sandlot baseball team.[16]

As a somewhat shy, 109-pound teenager, I was still rewarded for being good in school and going to church (respectable behavior), but I became a big man among my male peers only as a consequence of working with tough tobacco-picking gangs during the summer after my sophomore year.[17] I returned to school the following fall as a 180-pound hulk, to become a three-sports athlete and a ladies' man (reputational). Some of my teachers were shocked at the change in my behavior; to them I had become unbalanced in the direction of reputational traits. One of them even gave me failing grades (my first, ever) during the last semester of my senior year—"for my own good"—because it might force me back to respectability, which would be necessary were I to go on to college.

Male socialization based on reputational traits resulted in my desire to join the Marines and "be a man" after high school, but my mother convinced me to take advantage of an academic scholarship offered by the United Negro College Fund (respectability). I earned relatively good grades in college, went to church, and participated in the gospel choir and the student government (respectability). To be balanced, however, I joined a fraternity that publicly emphasized good grades and community service (respectability) but whose members privately gained status within fraternity circles by having parties, drinking a lot, raising hell, and being successful womanizers. Periodically I carried this reputational behavior too far for the administrators of the small Southern Baptist college I attended, and I found myself on social probation for three semesters of my four years there. I always felt that I wasn't nominated to "Who's Who in American Colleges and Universities" because I was perceived as unbalanced toward reputational traits by the respectable people who made such nominations.

As one of only two blacks in a Peace Corps group of 115 trainees, I was later surprised to learn that the valued reputational characteristics of the white majority were the same ones that had been valued in my past within all-black social settings. Altruistic themes, such as helping people, and personal ones, such as the Peace Corps experience serving as a stepping stone to a professional career, were defined as respectable; but the most popular guys among the trainees were those who drank, raised hell, and were womanizers (reputational). I was enthusiastically invited to be part of this group, as much out of the whites' perception of blacks as totally reputational as out of their attempts to be liberal. I soon learned that my reputational behavior was assigned definite limits by other volunteers, however. For instance, I was given much less scope for womanizing with the female volunteers than the white male volunteers had. Moreover, their perception that I had great reputational strengths occasionally acted as a liability. A couple of fellow trainees often belittled my refusal to dance when they wanted me to, or to drink as much as they did, or to take part in destruction of public property when drunk. After my Havershamian experience, I now know that this belittling represented an attempt to close a perceived reputational distance between us.

These experiences generated in me such trauma and psychosomatic illness that a Peace Corps psychiatrist misdiagnosed me as hating white people and being narcissistic.[18] The man didn't seem to take in the fact that this period was one of significant transition for me. I had just left a life of segregation and active civil rights struggle,[19] and for the first time I was beginning to understand the depth of the racial gap between whites and blacks.[20] I was, in the Peace Corps, in my first integrated situation, surrounded by whites and without familiar symbols (Afro-American) of social support. When I arrived in Portland, Oregon, for Peace Corps training, it was two weeks before I saw another black person (except the other black volunteer, who was not culturally familiar to me since he was twenty years my senior and a retired army officer from the northeastern United States). The first black Oregonian I saw was a cleaning woman; I almost cried for joy. She told me about the pocket of the city where blacks resided, and once I started interacting with these people, my psychological state changed for the better—I became more balanced: I could continue to be black while I learned about being white (i.e., where they would allow me boundaries of respectability and reputation).

I had to deal with the absence of blacks again when I was assigned to Turkey, but my situation was alleviated somewhat since I was adopted by Turkish men (and other Muslim men in Jordan, Syria, and Lebanon) during my travels. These Middle Eastern companions viewed me as another man (similar to other Muslims[21]) who was blocked from showing the strength of Islam by the oppression of America. To the Turks, a strong man is one who protects and controls

his women and children (respectability) and who is skilled at dancing, drinking *raki* (a licorice-flavored fermented drink), and playing
card games, and who has sexual prowess (reputational). My Peace
Corps training had prepared me for the fact that Turkish men draw
a clear line as to how far you can go with their women. But in contrast to my experience with the white American males in training, I
found that the Turks applied the same rules to themselves as to me.
The virgin/prostitute dichotomy guides male sexual behavior. The
good woman remains virginal until marriage; those who don't are
considered prostitutes, who in turn are valued because they allow
men sexual release outside of marriage. In Turkey as in Haversham,
sexual activity outside of marriage is considered an indicator of a
man's strength and is necessary to his health. I was expected to behave as a man of strength, and so the men in my neighborhood took
me out every Friday night. Typically, we spent the first two hours in
tea houses playing cards and backgammon, then we moved on to a
restaurant where the next four hours were spent drinking and eating.
This was followed by two hours in a nightclub, and then the evening
was topped off by visits to an illegal prostitution house or to the legal
karahane.[22] However, I found, as I would later in Haversham, that
these visits were more an arena for displaying male comaraderie
than a place for sexual activity.

When I returned to the United States and graduate school, I found
adjustment difficult, partly because of the normal "reverse culture
shock" that volunteers frequently suffer on reentry. But my difficulties also arose from how some of my professors perceived me—as
lacking the respectable skills of my classmates because I had been
"culturally deprived" and because I seemed to them to be interested
only in drinking, raising hell, and womanizing. People made these
assumptions without first getting to know me, so one could say their
perceptions were based on generalizations about skin color similar
to those later made by the men of Haversham. I would soon come to
find, after finishing my degree and entering the professional academic world, that success in drinking, raising hell, and womanizing
are reputational skills of no little importance to men in academia, as
can be observed during professional conferences. When I was writing my dissertation, the same men who had urged me to take the
ethical position as opposed to sexual involvement with members of
the field community, now belittled my laments about the difficulties
I ran into while maintaining that position in Jamaica. One commented: "I don't understand the problem, everybody gets laid in the
field." I had to learn that contrasting attitudes and practices regarding sexuality also exist among anthropologists.

Conclusion

This was a difficult essay to write for several reasons. I am concerned that my assessment of Haversham males not be interpreted
negatively, for I am writing as much about me and the situations that
have shaped my self as about Havershamians. Haversham males,
both of lower and higher income, are little different from me or the
males in the other settings I have discussed. The only thing they did
that might be judged negatively by some was to allow me to share
their lives, about which I now write. I see their gift as a positive act,
for it helped me to know my self as well as to know them; and it has
given me the ability to better understand others. I would like to think
of this essay as a similar gift to readers who find themselves going
through the processes of breakdown, resolution, and coherence of
self, through comprehension of the other.

Notes

I thank Laurie Price, Anne Salter, Kathy Luchok, Erma Wright, Joseph
Thomas, Lynn Igoe, and Dr. Karen Gentemann for proofreading numerous
drafts of this chapter. I am also grateful to the Provost Development Fund of
the University of Pittsburgh for supporting the research on which this essay
is based. Haversham and all of the proper names used here are pseudonyms.

1. In 1974, professional educators in the area's school system and adult
literacy program gave estimates of adult literacy rates ranging between 66
and 75 percent of adults over eighteen years of age. Factory personnel directors repeatedly told me that the lack of basic literacy skills had led to labor
shortages in their factories, despite the large local population. They pointed
out that lack of reading skills made training more difficult and created dangerous risks not only for the illiterate individual but for other employees as
well (Whitehead 1976:47–49).

2. The phrases "little man" and "little people" were borrowed from Havershamians. I never used them before this fieldwork.

3. The phrase "fellow oppressee of the Euroamerican political economy"
is one borrowed from some Turks who used it to refer to me during my
tenure as a Peace Corps volunteer in Turkey in 1966–67.

4. I was also rather amused by this since I had just left a graduate school
experience in which a well-intentioned professor questioned my choice of
becoming a successful academic because of his interpretation of my deep
Southern accent as an inability to clearly express myself.

5. In making comparative references to higher- and lower-income males,
I have devised a scheme in which men who earned J$15 or less per week
were considered lower-income males, while those who earned J$25 or more
per week were considered higher-income males. In 1974 the value of
U.S.$1.00 fluctuated between J$.88 and J$.91. The reader may think that

there isn't a great difference between an income of J$15 and J$25. However, the upper limit of the men in my higher-income group was J$250 per week. Moreover, most of the participant observation at male gatherings was done with lower-income male peer groups whose members were unemployed or earned less than J$14 per week, and with higher-income male peer groups whose members had regular employment and made between J$40 and J$250 per week. I decided on J$15 as the upper limit for the lower-income men and J$25 as the lower limit for the upper-income men after reviewing results of my household composition survey of 238 randomly selected heads. Of the men in this sample, the greatest concentration of salaries fell within the J$15-and-below category, and the J$25-to-J$35 category. My household composition survey showed that "relative" often included secondary and tertiary as well as primary relatives, informally adopted children, foster children, and people who had become "relatives" because they had mated at one time with true relatives and a child was born from that union (Whitehead 1978a).

6. "Mating" and "mates" are used in this paper as generic categories to include common-law and legal marriages, and common-law and legal spouses, respectively. These terms are used rather than "marriage" and "husband" or "wife" because in Haversham both common-law unions and legal marriages are norms, with common-law unions predominating. Havershamians place more emphasis on coresidence than on legality in referring to a mate as husband or wife.

7. The Rastafarian cult is a messianic movement in which Jamaica is viewed as a hopeless hell and Haile Selassie as the living god who will arrange for expatriated persons of African descent the means to return to Africa (Ethiopia). It is a religion of poor people who smoke the "mighty herb" (marijuana) for spiritual enlightenment. Because of their beliefs, behavioral patterns, dress, and general living conditions, "respectable" Jamaicans consider Rastafarians "low lifes."

8. Actually, Wilson (1973) never really outlined the attributes of reputation and respectability; I was able to pull them out of discussions in various sections of the book. On Providencia, the island Wilson studied, attributes of respectability included church-going, believing in God, legal marriage, maintaining a good home, providing excellent care of the family within the home (pp. 74–75); and having "all the children in her belly" (p. 150). Reputational attributes included self-confidence (p. 74); fathering children, fighting, arguing, and shouting (p. 151); sexual prowess, skills of sweet-talking and sweet-singing, having money and buying gifts for girls (p. 257); being generous to and supportive of friends and family (pp. 123–78); and skills in drinking and gambling (p. 156).

9. By associating respectability traits with Europe, Wilson implied that no other cultures by which West Indians are influenced (African, Asian, Amerindian) could have made such contributions or that they even encompass such traits. But all societies have such attributes because they are necessary to social order and stability. The sexist overtones of Wilson's (1973:224) argument can be found in his recommendation that the reputational characteristics come to dominate or replace those of respectability;

only this, he asserted, will allow West Indian societies to rid themselves of "their colonial yoke." If reputational attributes are associated with men and respectability with women, Wilson in effect recommended that male attributes become dominant over or replace female characteristics.

10. During the 1930s and 1940s the idea that members of a given society shared certain personality characteristics as a consequence of their having been socialized according to the same cultural rules was popular in anthropological theory. Its proponents included, among others, Margaret Mead, Abram Kardiner, and George Devereaux.

11. This is the reason why fifty of the eighty men who were asked, "How often do you have sex?" gave a response of one time per week or less (Whitehead 1976:118).

12. Forty-two of eighty men (52.5 percent) responding to the intensive survey stated that they believed that women enjoy sex more than men. The most frequent reason given for this belief was that men give up their "strength" (their semen and their money) through sex, and the women take it (Whitehead 1976:120).

13. When I made this point in a seminar, a Marxist colleague pointed out that the reason women were in this position was the exploitive system, and she chided me for dismissing this reality so easily. I reiterate my response to her: the statement does not mean that I accept this condition but that people were telling me what their reality was, not what it should be.

14. One of my closest friends and informants, Simeon, was an ardent admirer of Abraham Lincoln, Idi Amin, and Adolf Hitler, because all three came from humble (little) beginnings and became so powerful (big) that leaders of powerful nations were afraid of them. Simeon had a large following of little men like himself because of the brokering role he played for them with big people (see Whitehead 1984 for further discussion of this role). One night I became fed up with listening to Simeon praise Hitler and tell other men who questioned his position to shut up because they were ignorant. I told him that he was ignorant, that he knew very little about the inhuman behavior of Hitler's regime, and I gave him some facts. He was quiet for the rest of the evening, but the next day he let me know that he thought I was wicked because I had used my greater knowledge to belittle him. By this time I understood the concept of balance and was able to point out to him that Hitler was wicked because he used his power to excess. He eventually accepted my position on Hitler but he never did admit that he himself was wicked because he belittled other men with his knowledge. (He did try to berate other little men less, though.) The lesson here is that of remembering that I was big and had to present my position to little men in a way that did not belittle them; only in this way could I avoid appearing wicked.

15. There is a growing body of literature about other cultural areas which mentions many of the traits I have discussed here, particularly literature about the Mediterranean area (e.g., Brandes 1980; Campbell 1964; Cronin 1970; Davis 1969; Gilmore and Gilmore 1979; Pitt-Rivers 1977; Schneider and Schneider 1976). However, Sanday's book *Female Power and Male Dominance* (1981) is the only scholarly work I am aware of in which such

traits are discussed as contrasting notions and the concept of balance is identified as important in the cognitive management of such contrasts. She uses the term in a different context: certain characteristics are associated with males and certain other characteristics are associated with females, with both types existing in both sexes. She further states that, cross-culturally, women have natural ways of signaling womanhood and men do not have equivalent signals of manhood; thus, men must find ways to display their manhood. This role is usually defined as *being what the female is not* (1981:78). But even within such contrasting cognitive constructs of gender, Sanday says that societies generally have constructs that include female attributes in the male sex role plan, and vice versa (1981:94–95). She uses the word *balance* in explaining this phenomenon (1981:161) and quotes from Doris Lessing's book *The Four Gated City* to make her point: "Every attitude, emotion, thought has its opposite held in balance out of sight but there all the time. Push any one of them to an extreme, and . . . over you go to its opposite."

16. Black kids could not swim in the city pool, so we would trek through the woods and sneak onto the forested property of the family who owned the only factory in town. There was a pond where, after we ran out the cottonmouths, we carried out the important ritual of diving into thirty feet of water and scooping up mud as proof of having touched the bottom. Achievements of this sort were very important for status among our summer swimmers. We also played baseball anywhere we could, including in cow pastures. I have never since experienced the thrill of making a game-saving play with a diving catch of a line drive, and then doubling the runner off second base. The fact that I landed in a pile of fresh cow dung was only a small setback, as my friends hoisted me on their shoulders and commented on how the "little guy" had saved the game. I knew I would be the second Willie Mays, until some years later when I was hit in the head by a baseball while upholding my reputation for taking close pitches, and was semiconscious in the hospital for a few days.

17. During the 1950s tobacco companies in Connecticut sent representatives to Virginia, North Carolina, South Carolina, and Georgia to recruit black teenagers to work on their tobacco farms each summer. Boys in my school looked forward to their sixteenth birthday so they could go to Connecticut to work, not only because they could earn more (ninety-one cents per hour) than in the tobacco and peanut fields at home (four dollars a day), but because the Connecticut trip had become a status symbol, a rite of passage into manhood. The boys who had experienced the hard work, the "tobacco rash," and the state-based gang wars in the Connecticut barracks had great stories to tell and truly were regarded as men in my high school. We were all disappointed when in 1960 the Connecticut farmers replaced us with Puerto Ricans who were willing to work for seventy-six cents per hour.

18. This diagnosis of narcissism may be interpreted by some readers as my motivation for writing this essay. However, I believe it is more accurate to think of me as being "reflexive." Reflexiveness differs from narcissism in that not only is one conscious of one's self (narcissism) but one is also conscious of being self-conscious of one's self (Babcock 1980:2).

19. My college years (1961–65) at Shaw University were exciting ones. Desegregation demonstrations were the order of the day and generated a sense of camaraderie among students. The time spent in jail was spiritually moving: those of us inside sang songs and prayed continually, while the remainder of the student body, and students from many nearby white colleges and universities, joined in from outside. When we were finally released and individually cheered before the many media representatives, we indeed felt like heroes.

20. The media was giving a lot of attention to the civil rights movement, and I remember being particularly impressed by a series of articles in *Time* magazine in 1963 about how blacks and whites perceived each other. I began to read more scholarly works about the experience of black people in America and was particularly struck by descriptions of the cruelties of the middle passage, the seasoning period, as well as by other harsh acts characteristic of slavery, and the lynchings and other violence directed toward blacks during and after slavery.

21. Despite the media's presentation of black Americans as generally weak, in Turkey we were expected to be strong because the Turks believed our ancestors had been taken from African areas where Islam was practiced. Male strength is exhibited through athletic skill (including dancing and soldiering). Thus Muhammad Ali, America's Muslim boxer, was demonstrating his strength to the world through his fists; the source of his strength was said to be Allah. I was believed by some Middle Eastern men to be a boxer and a basketball player (another stereotype picked up from the media). After all, didn't my flat nose indicate that it had been broken a number of times from fights or boxing?

22. The term *karahane* in English means "blackhouse." *Karahanes* are prison compounds in urban areas which house women convicted of prostitution.

References

Agar, Michael H.
1982   "Toward an Ethnographic Language." *American Anthropologist* 84:779–95.
Allen, Walter R.
1981   "Moms, Dads and Boys: Race and Sex Differences in the Socialization of Male Children." In: Lawrence E. Gary (ed.), *Black Men*, pp. 99–114. Beverly Hills, Calif.: Sage Publications.
Anderson, Elijah
1978   *A Place on the Corner.* Chicago: University of Chicago Press.
Babcock, Barbara
1980   "Reflexivity: Definitions and Discriminations." *Semiotica* 30(1/2):1–14.
Beckford, George L.
1972   *Persistent Poverty: Underdevelopment in Plantation Economies of the Third World.* New York: Oxford University Press.

Billingsley, Andrew
  1968   *Black Families in White America.* Englewood Cliffs, N.J.: Prentice-Hall.
Brandes, Stanley
  1980   *Metaphors of Masculinity.* Philadelphia: University of Pennsylvania Press.
Brazleton, Robert W.
  1968   "The Caribbean: A Survey of Economic Problems and Policies." In: S. N. Gerber (ed.), *The Family in the Caribbean*, pp. 29–46. Rio Pierdas: University of Puerto Rico.
Campbell, J. R.
  1964   *Honour, Family and Patronage: Study of Institutions and Moral Values in a Greek Mountain Community.* Oxford: Clarendon Press.
Cronin, Constance
  1970   *The Sting of Change: Sicilians in Sicily and Australia.* Chicago: University of Chicago Press.
Davis, Natalie Zemon
  1975   *Society and Culture in Early Modern France.* Stanford, Calif.: Stanford University Press.
Frazier, E. Franklin
  1939   *The Negro Family in the United States.* Chicago: University of Chicago Press.
Gadamer, H. G.
  1975   *Truth and Method.* New York: Continuum.
Gilmore, Margaret M., and David D. Gilmore
  1979   "Machismo: A Psychodynamic Approach." *Journal of Psychological Anthropology* 2(3):281–99.
Henriquez, Fernando
  1953   *Family and Color in Jamaica.* London: Eyre and Spottiswoode.
Hill, Robert
  1971   *The Strengths of Black Families.* New York: Emerson Hall Publishers.
Kardiner, A., and L. Ovesey
  1951   *The Mark of Oppression: A Psychosocial Study of the American Negro.* New York: W. W. Norton and Co.
Kerr, M.
  1963   *Personality and Conflict in Jamaica.* London: Collins.
Lévi-Strauss, Claude
  1978   *Myth and Meaning.* London: Routledge and Kegan Paul.
Lowenthal, David
  1972   *West Indian Societies.* London: Oxford University Press.
MacCormack, Carol P.
  1980   "Nature, Culture and Gender: A Critique." In: C. MacCormack and M. Strathern (eds.), *Nature, Culture and Gender*, pp. 1–14. Cambridge: Cambridge University Press.
McCartney, Timothy
  1970   *Neuroses in the Sun.* The Bahamas: Executive Printers of the Bahamas.

Myrdal, Gunnar
    1954   *An American Dilemma: The Negro Problem and Modern Democracy.* New York: Harper and Brothers.
Needham, Rodney
    1979   *Symbolic Classifications.* Santa Monica, Calif.: Goodyear Publishing Co.
Pitt-Rivers, Julian
    1977   *The Fate of Shechem, or the Politics of Sex: Essays in the Anthropology of the Mediterranean.* Cambridge: Cambridge University Press.
Rabinow, Paul
    1977   *Reflections on Fieldwork in Morocco.* Berkeley: University of California Press.
Rodman, Hyman
    1963   "The Lower-Class Value Search." *Social Forces* 42:205–15.
    1971   *Lower-Class Families: The Culture of Poverty in Negro Trinidad.* New York: Oxford University Press.
Sanday, Peggy
    1981   *Female Power and Male Dominance: On the Origins of Sexual Inequality.* Cambridge: Cambridge University Press.
Schneider, Jane, and Peter Schneider
    1976   *Culture and Political Economy in Western Sicily.* New York: Academic Press.
Simey, Thomas
    1946   *Welfare Planning in the West Indies.* Oxford: Clarendon Press.
Smith, M. G.
    1966   "Introduction." In: Edith Clarke, *My Mother Who Fathered Me,* pp. i–xliv. London: George Allen and Unwin.
Stack, Carol B.
    1974   *All Our Kin.* New York: Harper and Row.
Valentine, Betty Lous
    1978   *Hustling and Other Hard Work.* New York: Free Press.
Whitehead, Tony Larry
    1976   Men, Family and Family Planning: Male Role Perception and Performance in a Jamaican Sugar Town. Unpublished Ph.D. dissertation, University of Pittsburgh.
    1978   "Residence, Kinship and Mating as Survival Strategies: A Jamaican Example." *Journal of Marriage and Family* (Nov.):817–28.
    1980   "Identity, Subjectivity and Cultural Bias in Fieldwork." *The Black Scholar,* 2(7):40–44, 83–87.
    1984   "The Buccra-massa Personality and the Little Man Broker in a Jamaican Sugartown: Implications for Community Health and Education Programs." *Social Science and Medicine* 19(5):561–72.
Wilson, Peter J.
    1973   *Crab Antics: The Social Anthropology of English-speaking Societies of the Caribbean.* New Haven, Conn.: Yale University Press.

14

Changing Self-Image: Studying Menopausal Women in a Newfoundland Fishing Village

DONA DAVIS

From September 1977 to December 1978, I conducted field research in a small, Anglican fishing village, Grey Rock Harbour, located on the southwest coast of Newfoundland (Davis 1983). I was particularly concerned with gathering data on women's experience of menopause and relating it to the interaction of various sociocultural factors that may affect female status and self-image. As my fieldwork progressed, not only did I learn how life in a sex-segregated society affects gender roles, status, and self-image among Newfoundlanders, but the Newfoundland experience and the Newfoundland women taught me a great deal about my own cultural biases.

In this essay I discuss the impact of gender role categories on my fieldwork experience. The first section documents the process by which the informants' and my stereotypes of each other changed to fit the realities of everyday life and the growth of close personal friendships. The second section addresses the effects of the informants' and my conflicting conceptions of appropriate gender role behavior. It describes the intended and unintended consequences of the strategies I employed in my attempt to live my own life according to my own needs and values, at the same time trying to follow local customs. The final, major section deals with my attempt to enter into the private realm of the village women to explore their views on gender, menstruation, and menopause. Through long private conversations about the meaning of gender, female sexuality, body-image, and health, I came to reexamine my own beliefs and middle-class, medicalized biases about menopause, the nature of mind and body, and women's status as social and sexual beings.

Getting There and Settling In

My main concerns just prior to entering the field had little to do with getting sick, suffering from some imagined hardship, or surviving the challenges of fieldwork. Rather, they dealt with "making my entrance" and the nature of the data I hoped to collect. I had read a great deal about the traditional Newfoundlander's fear and distrust of strangers, particularly those strangers from "the mainland." For months prior to my departure I spent many sleepless nights worrying about how I was going to go into a village of strangers, find a place to stay, and explain to the locals why I was there. The major hurdle to be overcome in this respect was not the Newfoundlanders' attitudes toward me but rather my own personal disposition to be shy and unassertive. Furthermore, just thinking about the nature of the data I would be gathering on menopause-related phenomena was enough to make my digestive system run amok. I realized I would be asking questions that would offend my own mother, and I wondered how rural, middle-aged family women would react to very intimate questions from a young, single woman, a stranger.

With regard to the latter fear, I constantly found myself fantasizing scenarios in which I would randomly pick out a strange woman in some public place and start asking her questions I had found on other researchers' menopause interview schedules. The poor woman would only be asked the questions I most feared asking, such as, "Who enjoys sex more, you or your husband?" or "Can you describe your menstrual discharge?" The phantom woman of my imaginings would either look at me in disgust and walk away, or else tersely ask me to leave. These fantasies were my practice for a rejection that was never realized, however, because I suspected that such questions did not belong in a casual survey and in fact would have offended even me. I actually put off asking any intimate questions until I had been in the field for nine months, so in a sense my shyness and unassertiveness were assets. My more aggressive, experienced friends might have been doomed from the outset, as there is little room for aggressive men or women, especially outsiders, in rural Newfoundland communities. Furthermore, a more experienced interviewer may have placed far more confidence in an interview schedule than was warranted.

Dreams and fears aside, I finally found myself ready to leave for the field. Fortified with the good wishes of family and friends, and relieved that my status as a pre-fieldwork graduate student was about to be terminated, I set off for Newfoundland. I gloried in my independence, in my ability to strike out on my own. I felt that this was what anthropology was all about and imagined myself becoming the Margaret Mead of menopause.

Heading directly for St. John's, Newfoundland's largest, most cosmopolitan city, I figured that two weeks at that province's Memorial University would be a good place to begin familiarizing myself with the region. My plan was to use library resources and consult with local anthropologists about choosing a field site. Somehow I imagined I would meet someone at the university who would declare, "Menopause? What a wonderful idea. There's hardly any data on women here. I know just the village for your study. I even know a middle-aged fisherman's wife, menopausal, with children ages five to twenty who would love to have you live with them, and will charge only a very low fee." In reality people were supportive, although some regarded my plans to do an ethnography of menopause as a joke of sorts. The selection of a village was left entirely up to me and was, in fact, not a very difficult task. Because of my strict set of criteria, there were only three villages on the island that were suitable.[1]

I had intended to stay with a family composed of a middle-aged woman, her fisherman husband, and their children, as such an arrangement would maximize my menopause observation opportunities. Instead, I was taken in by a woman who was a very young seventy-eight years old. She had had many boarders before, including schoolteachers and men who had worked on road construction for utility companies or the fish plant. At the time I lived with her she also had a permanent boarder, an elderly retarded man. My plan was to reside with this woman until I could find a permanent residence with a woman who was "more menopausal." However, within a week I was considered more family than boarder, and it became clear that any attempt to find accommodations elsewhere would have been an insult to her hospitality.

Being in the field was a personal triumph for me, one that symbolized my overcoming many elements of the subservient status of calculated ineptitude and insecurity it was easy to fall into as a woman and a graduate student. The sense of accomplishment I felt by getting to the village and settling in was acknowledged by every Grey Rock Harbour woman I met during those first few days: "Well, my dear, just fancy that, coming all that way by yourself and then coming to Grey Rock Harbour, a total stranger. Does your mother know where you be?" Ironically, just as I felt I was finally meeting the challenges of the women's movement and living up to my ideals of the "new woman," I was asked if my mother knew where I was. Clearly I was to live in a society where the evaluations of gender roles and female activities were markedly different from my own. At first I viewed myself as modern and progressive and the village women as traditional. They, in turn, admired me and respected my achievements but in no way were envious of my life-style, particularly my independence. The longer I resided in Grey Rock Harbour, however, and the more I learned about the village women, the more I began to learn about myself from them. In this sense, my fieldwork turned out to be both a lesson in letters (academics) and in life.

First Impressions: The Walking Menopause of Grey Rock Harbour

When I first arrived in the village, I viewed all women as potential informants, or "walking menopauses," and they, in turn, viewed me as "the little girl with the book." For their part, the awkwardness of my initial status as a stranger was enhanced by the fact that I was well-educated, female, almost thirty, unmarried, and a mainlander— there was no preexisting community role in which to place me. And my initial views of local women and how to get along with them were colored by erroneous, middle-class, academic presuppositions.

I had entered this carefully chosen village with essentially three different frames of reference which had been acquired through reading all the material I could find about life in Newfoundland. Life here was described variously, with emphasis placed either on the Marxist theoretical perspective, the ethnic distinctiveness and folksy traditionalism of the island, or the promotion of tourism. The Marxist perspective paints a rather dreary, negative picture of New-foundlanders, portraying them as victims of oppression with a long history of poverty. Other academic perspectives emphasize the historic isolation of the Newfoundland settlements which has resulted in the preservation of many Old Country (English and Irish) traditions and lore and the continued survival of peasant-type communities. The tourist literature is of the cod-fog-log-dog ilk and is aimed at presenting Newfoundland as a colorful and friendly place in which to deposit tourist dollars. I was to find that these economic, historic, and idyllic frames of reference had little relevance to either my study or day-to-day harbor life.

Grey Rock Harbour is a breathtakingly beautiful village. Colorful houses, granite cliffs, moss barrens, and the crisp, cool smell of the sea combine to give the place an exciting, romantic aura. The fishermen's distinctive form of dress, the women's plumpness and uniformity of hairstyle, and generally poor dental health were the local characteristics that made an initial impression on me. However, I was profoundly disappointed during my first few days there, for I had expected the village to be much more traditional than it appeared.

Newfoundland villages are called "outports," a term that connotes being traditional, or away from the mainstream. This overemphasis on the traditional aspects of village life can obscure the fact that although Newfoundlanders remain a distinct ethnic group, their life-style resembles, for the most part, that of contemporary rural Canadians. Soon after Newfoundland's confederation with Canada in 1949, the traditional peasant-type villages, based on a subsistence economy, became linked to each other and to the mainland through improved transportation and communications networks. Grey Rock Harbour's isolation was eliminated with the construction of a dirt road to the village in the early 1960s, followed by electricity, telephones, television, and all the conveniences of modern society.

The people of Grey Rock Harbour did not meet my stereotype of the poor and oppressed: nearly one-fourth of the families had cars; their homes were small but comfortable; and men, women, and especially children dressed in the latest fashions from the Simpson-Sears catalog. It did not look as though I would share much "suffering poverty with the poor." Perhaps, I reasoned, this would not be such a great adventure after all. My anthropological ego was hurt. I wanted to prove my hypotheses and develop my theories around the differences between my own and my hosts' cultures, but it became clear that this decision was a bit premature. Initial impressions of both the hosts and me reflected the prejudices of our respective social environments. My stranger status was enhanced because they saw me as an outsider, someone very different from them. (Later, however, locals came to see me as one of them.) I was at first overwhelmed and disappointed by the women's similarity to me and only through time did I begin to see them as very different from me.

Immediately after moving in I began to accompany my landlady in her extensive realm of social activities, all exclusively for women. Before the week was out I attended a Dart League play night of the Anglican church, prepared fish for and attended a church supper and dance; went to a church fair for children, a card party, and a wedding shower; played two nights of bingo; and went with my landlady on visits to her doctor and to numerous relatives.

During the first couple of days in the village I developed an acute desire to see into the future and often wondered who and what I would know in the coming weeks and months. I looked at groups of women and tried to guess if they were pre-, peri-, or postmenopausal. I hung desperately on every word that was said to me, especially if the words were spoken by middle-aged women. I memorized what they said and what I overheard, to be typed up as my fieldnotes as soon as I got home. Once again I fantasized about interviewing: I would randomly select a woman playing darts, skinning fish, or walking to the post office and conduct my imaginary interview. And just as in my prefield fantasies, I was again rebuffed, but this time it was not an isolated incident—one offended woman could put me in jeopardy with the entire community.

Initially, women in groups were silent and ignored me, and out of a sense of insecurity I clung to my landlady. It was difficult to tell if the women were hostile, indifferent, or merely shy. Fortunately, most group meetings involved some kind of activity where conversation was not necessary. During one-to-one visits, however, conversation was lively, humorous, and interesting. I was overwhelmed by the task ahead of me and desperately hoped the charm would last.

First Impressions: The Little Girl with the Book

It is difficult to describe people's initial opinions of me. The novelty of my arrival was of intense community interest and led to much gossip, as the only legitimate role for a single, strange woman was that of schoolteacher. Much later I was informed that many villagers thought I was a Jehovah's Witness who had come to this Anglican community seeking converts. It was rumored that I had conned the old lady with some story about being a student so that she would accept me as a boarder. However, after I talked with the minister and he introduced me in church, the rumor was dispelled.

While the first round of rumors characterized me as dangerous or threatening, the second round portrayed me as quite harmless. After several days it was said that I was handicapped—deaf as a doornail. There were several reasons for such a rumor to circulate. At first, it was difficult for me to understand the local accent, and the men in particular did not address me directly. Additionally, most people misinterpreted my frequent use of "uh huh" whenever someone finished a sentence or communicated an idea. To me it meant, "Yes, I understand"; to the locals it meant, "Repeat it." Newfoundlanders also were not familiar with my name, Dona, although Madonna is a commonly used female name. When someone would say "Madonna," I did not associate that name with me; in fact, I thought they were swearing and ignored them. This second rumor reflected the fact that I was becoming accepted in the community.

As the initial rumors of my religious and handicapped status died down, my landlady began to receive constant telephone calls about me. I even overheard her describing what I ate. Eating everything I was served seemed to be very important; it proved that I was not picky or uppity. Helping out by washing dishes and making my own bed was also important, as were the reasons why I was in Grey Rock Harbour and what I was going to be doing. And, of course, there was endless concern about my parents and my family background. Actually, my landlady should have been the ethnographer, for she remembered everything I said and passed it on to her curious callers. Over and over again I heard her say, "She's just like having one of you over to tea."

All in all, people tended to view me in terms of statuses they attributed to me, including my female status, my unmarried status, my mainlander/outsider status, and my status as a highly educated person in a profession unknown to them. The latter, which was so important to me, meant little to the locals. I had worried about how I would introduce myself to people in the field and how I would explain my presence and my topic areas, especially menstruation and menopause. I wanted to be honest, but it seemed very trite and unprofessional to go into a community and say, "Hi, I'm Dona Davis and I've come here to study you." That is precisely what I did, however, and to my amazement it appeared to be a sufficiently detailed explanation. People were more concerned about me than about why I was there. A locally well-known female writer had written a short story about one of the village women, and people saw me as being there for a similar purpose.

My more elaborate response to questions like, "Well, my dear, where do you come from and what brought you to Grey Rock Harbour?" included the fact that I was a student working on a doctoral degree in anthropology and that I wished to learn from them all that I could not learn from books. I told them the book (dissertation) I would write about my experiences in Newfoundland would enable me to continue my professional career. Since the villagers had no social category for professional anthropologists or, for that matter, professional women, they evaluated and responded to me much as they would to any woman in the community. And if I didn't fit in completely with local female role and behavior patterns, I was excused—after all, I was an outsider.

In spite of my growing positive opinion of myself and my sense of professional importance, the women with whom I interacted daily had little interest in my book but were extremely keen on finding out how I got to be almost thirty and had remained single. By referring to me as the "little girl with the book" the locals saw me as some kind of glorified schoolgirl. I was "little" because I was not an adult; all adult women were married and had children. The epithet characterized their initial reaction toward me and defined me as unintimidating, acceptable, likable, and in a way pathetic (being without a spouse). I had wanted very much to be accepted and was pleased with peoples' reactions. The biggest compliment they could pay me was, "She's just like one of us." I was juggling two frames of reference about women, theirs and mine, and as I saw it, the more I appeared to be like them, the more successful I would be at achieving my own goals.

Second Impressions: The Women of Grey Rock Harbour

It was not long before "my walking menopauses" became real people, and I began to realize that they were as unsure of me as I was of them. While I feared offending them by the nature of my inquiries, they feared humiliating themselves through their lack of education—many said to me, "You must find us some ignorant," or "some stunned." Through time, as we came to know each other better, many of the defensive postures began to drop. Despite my initial frustration with the quietness of the women, once assured that I was not there to write a book that would mock them or portray them as "backward," and that I had a great deal of admiration and respect for them, the women talked to me at great length about their lives.

Their life histories were fascinating. Many women spoke eloquently, delightfully including humorous tales in their recollections. Unlike me and my more academic friends who were revelling in our own glorified and intellectualized independence, many of these village women had had independence and responsibility forced on them very early in life.[2] As I collected more and more histories from women who were middle-aged or older, I began to realize how much change they had experienced. The present-day woman, in her late thirties or older, had successfully bridged two eras, locally referred to as "before the road" and "after the road." The era before the road was charcterized by hard work, prolonged periods of fisherman/husband absence, overcrowded multifamily dwellings, malnutrition, high fertility, poor health, and a cashless economy. The change symbolized by the road, which in the early 1960s made the village accessible by land, was in a sense twofold: it marked both the onset of modernization and the elimination of acute poverty. Women now living in comfortable houses with washing machines and 28-inch color television sets took great delight in describing how, before the road, they had had to knit their children's sweaters from cords picked out of flour sacks and how all they had to put in a child's Christmas stocking was a slice of apple and a simple homemade toy.

The women freely admitted that there were good and bad aspects of both eras. Some felt the change came too fast, but most of them readily embraced the new era. Not only did they feel they were now better off than in the past, but life before the road had become a metaphor for folk heroism. Those women who grew up and started their families, delivering babies at home, before the 1960s, were accorded a very special respect for their stoic endurance and resourcefulness in raising a family under the adverse conditions of a harsh climate and acute poverty.

My interest in these women's lives was taken as a compliment. Many times I felt I was hearing a well-rehearsed narrative which had been told time and time again to children and grandchildren for entertainment. My questions helped the women to elaborate on their stories and, of course, their telling the stories to me was an excuse to relate the "new story" again to children, grandchildren, and telephone callers for the next two days. My university-sponsored interest in their life histories reinforced their heroine status and was a source of great pride. Each woman eagerly anticipated my visit, and the visit itself tended to enhance the status of each new informant.

The more I learned from the women in Grey Rock Harbour, the more I became enchanted by them. I developed a deep respect for their ability to adapt to change, for their life accomplishments, and for their common sense and earthy humor. As I gradually fit into the village society, I felt less able to evaluate their status in academic terms. I was becoming more of a humanist than a scientist. Like my informants, I felt I had led two different lives: one in the sheltered ivory towers of academia, where everything made sense "on paper," and the other in a more real world, where one learned by experience. Analysis of women's lives in terms of ideas and theories such as social conflict, subsistence strategies, power and dominance, or public and private spheres of activity seemed to have little relevance in understanding the situation of the local women, their view of the world, or their self-perceptions. Within the context of the outport itself, and its meaningful cultural realm, the women of Grey Rock Harbour had a high, secure, unchanging status. While the literature is replete with theories that encompass the negative aspects of women's status, there are few models that deal with the more positive aspects. Since I had just spent several years of my life intensively rebelling against traditional female roles, I was very surprised to learn that women who derived pleasure and satisfaction from a more narrowly restricted housewife/mother role did not meet the caricature I had long held of such women as powerless, apathetic, alienated, and dull. In fact, their lives were far from dull.

My initial impression of the village women as being too modern was replaced by an appreciation of how they had united two eras. They communicated to me a sense of dignity, integrity, and pride in being female. Unlike me, who had been driven by self-doubt and a feeling of inferior or secondary status to achieve more and more,

these women readily embraced the female roles of their society—
roles that were enhanced by strong positive values on female activities, strong female support groups, an active social life, and a deep
sense of pride in their community, past and present. At first I
thought, "They are just like me. Have I come all this way to do a
study that could have been done much closer to home?" However,
as I learned more about the women of Grey Rock Harbour, this impression faded and I became keenly aware of the uniqueness of their
life histories and subculture.

Second Impressions: She's Just like One of Us

Ironically, the women who initially saw me as a stranger in time
came to see me more and more as one of them. People liked me; I
was considered a good sport, happy-go-lucky, fun to have around,
and from a good family. Women were almost awed by my education
and thought I "talked real good." However, there were inconsisten-
cies in their perceptions of my status. As they began to view me as
one of them, they also began to rationalize those qualities that made
me just like them. I was very well educated, but contrary to their
stereotype of the well-educated I was very friendly and did not "put
on airs" or act as if I were superior to them. I was a mainlander, in
general a negative characteristic, but I was from a small town in New
England, which, if one has to be a mainlander, is better than being
from mainland Canada or a big American city. The locals probably
also saw me as spoiled, pampered, a bit naive, and relatively un-
tested by the realities of life.

Women were especially concerned with why I was not married.
People considered me young, but I was very old to still be single.
Being almost thirty and unmarried would usually point to some flaw
in a woman's character, but I was considered attractive, likable, and
a hard-enough worker. I could cook and knit and I kept myself clean.
At times people probably suspected some deep, dark secret in my
past (like sterility) as they tried to come up with some explanation
of why I had never married. However, to make me more acceptable
to them, they simply rationalized that I was probably too picky and
had just not met the right man. Over and over during the first two
weeks in the community I was told, "Who knows, perhaps you will
meet one of us Newfies and stay here." Month after month I was
asked what I thought of the village and, if I had any choice, would I
like to live in Grey Rock Harbour the rest of my life. Women felt
complimented to be so much admired by me and saw themselves as
role models for me. They felt they could "set me right" and get me
"settled down" like a proper woman.

There were two events that really shocked all of the women—my slide show and my menopause interview (to be discussed later). After about eight months of fieldwork, I offered to show slides of my travels. I had taken numerous pictures of local women, which they were constantly asking to see. I planned to show them pictures of women from my previous travels and then fit the slides of them into the finale, and in this way give them some indication of the nature of "women's studies." The church league sponsored my show and the turnout was huge, mainly because each of the women wanted to see herself on the screen. I showed slides I had taken in southern Europe, the Middle East, Africa, and South America, explaining various aspects of women's lives in each pictorial setting. When I was finished and the lights were turned on, instead of the amused enthusiasm I had expected, their faces registered shock. No one asked questions and they all quietly filed out of the church hall. I was very upset and felt that I had somehow offended them. It was weeks before anyone asked me another question about my travels, and eventually I showed my slides to several other groups. But I had not anticipated this initial response. When I finally asked a good friend what had happened, she told me they were all surprised to see that I had done things and gone places they had never dreamed of. This did not fit with their impression of me as a little girl, and it made them feel insular, backward, and embarrassed about all the advice they had given me. They had come to define me socially as "one of us" and my slide show emphasized my status as an outsider and stranger; I would probably leave Grey Rock Harbour just as I had left other places.

In time, the slides and the adventures they depicted became lively topics of conversation during my afternoon visits. However, from that time on I was considered a bit more grown-up, although I was still not given adult status. All in all, their impressions of me remained more constant than mine did of them, in part because they viewed me from a personal perspective and I was trying to include them in an entire social milieu. They responded to me as a likable person who had come to share their lives for a while. I saw my relationship with them as a surprisingly pleasant opportunity to further my academic career.

Impression Management

To collect reliable data on menopause and the more intimate aspects of women's lives, it was important that my potential informants find me likable, trustworthy, and nonthreatening. I was asking them to give me information that was seldom communicated, even between close friends or relatives. My behavior in both the public and private spheres could influence how women responded to my inquiries. Since I had a very high profile in the community, all of my activities became topics of gossip. The Newfoundlanders are very tolerant of one's sexual behavior and tend to judge it in its total context, so it was up to me to present my behavior in the correct context. Only gradually did I come to understand this. Initially, I was very concerned about my sexual conduct and how local men would respond to my unmarried status. Thus, I rigidly adhered to the ideal norms of the society. However, in attempting to meet my own emotional needs while following local customs as I perceived them, I discovered that the boundaries of acceptable behavior were flexible.

I had no problems concerning my conduct with women in the public sphere. Their activities were focused around particular social events, such as cards, darts, and preparing for church suppers or dances. Public female behavior was quite structured, and the major reason for most public activities was to have fun. Except for bingo, which bored me, I became reasonably proficient at activities such as darts and the local forms of dancing. I took my share of responsibility, calling numbers at bingo, serving at weddings, and helping to clean the church hall; I was very friendly to everyone and was considered a good sport.

At public activities that involved socializing with both men and women, such as at the church dances, I was also considered a good sport. I danced with anyone who asked me, although there was an unspoken rule not to dance too often with any one woman's husband. If a man had too much to drink and started to bother me, it was up to one of my male "relatives" to ward him off. I drank the men's drink, beer, rather than the women's drink, lemon gin, and the men often tried to get me drunk, but I always stopped after a few beers. Getting drunk was not appropriate behavior for a female.

For the sake of my reputation, particularly among the older women, I did not go unescorted to the local club's dances, where there was a live band and heavy drinking every Saturday night, often accompanied by fights over women. At the club, men did not regard me in the same platonic manner they did at the church dances. I did not want local men to think that I thought I was too good for them, nor did I want to cause any problems between married or unmarried couples, so I simply attended very few club functions. In retrospect, this was a wise decision.

Most of my time was spent with women, and I rarely found myself in the company of men when there were no women present. I have very little knowledge about how men responded to me or how they felt about me. They did a lot of gossiping and sexual joking about local women, but aside from teasing the retarded man who was a fellow boarder about his "new girlfriend," I do not know what they said about me. However, there was one indication that local men perceived me in terms of my sexuality. After a long winter of New-foundland cooking, I had gained about twenty pounds, so when the snow melted I decided to start jogging. Locals thought this was very funny. Initially I thought they reacted this way either because by their standards I was not overweight or because they saw it as a use-less waste of energy. After a couple of days, however, I noticed sev-eral men at my jogging site. Some of them started running behind me, staying almost out of view. Soon my female friends began to tease me about my jogging and my jogging companions. According to local notions of biology, all adults have sexual urges, a form of energy which, if not released through sexual activity, can make one hyperactive, sick, or crazy. In the men's view I was jogging out of unrequited lust. Their joke on me was seeing who could keep up with me and match my sexual energy; my joke on them was to let them jog up close to me and then sprint ahead, leave them huffing and puffing far behind. It was quite a community joke for some time, but the black fly season eventually put an end to the competition.

In the realm of private behavior (my activities in people's home) there was also little problem with being accepted. I met privately with men only in the company of their wives, usually at meals or children's birthday parties. On such occasions we talked casually about fishing, moose hunting, or local gossip. Sometimes after a fam-ily dinner, when the women congregated in the kitchen to talk, I stayed with the men; no one seemed to mind.

After several months in the village the elderly widow who first took me in became ill and I moved into the home of a husband, wife, and baby. The husband was my age, but, despite the fact that we lived in the same house, I seldom saw him except at mealtime. He worked part of the year on transport barges on the Great Lakes; and when he was home, he was up and gone before I was and either retired early or went out to the club at night. When family spats occurred I either left the house or pretended that nothing was hap-pening, as any other villager in similar circumstances would do, al-though I secretly sided with the wife. So far as I could tell, my presence created no problems; I was accepted in their home just as a long-lost relative would have been.

My relations with men in both the public and private spheres were fairly well circumscribed by rules of appropriate behavior. Problems did not arise, because the rules were easy to follow and because I seldom found myself alone with males. The locals were acutely interested in my love life, and there was an initial rush at matchmaking. Any man who was both my age and single usually had some readily noticeable flaw, such as a tendency to drink too much, slight retardation, or strange running sores all over his body, and when I mentioned this I was told, "Well, my dear, your days to be picky are long gone."

When I arrived in Grey Rock Harbour I was not the only stranger to set up temporary residence. A new village-wide water system was being installed and the supervising engineer was male, my age, and single. He lived in an old trailer six miles out of town. Local matchmakers arranged a meeting and we became close friends. After a few weeks in the village I was delighted to find someone with a background similar to mine, and I often went to his trailer for privacy and some peace and quiet in which to work. All sorts of speculation about our relationship circulated throughout the village. My friends found it amazing that two strangers should meet in a fashion reminiscent of the Harlequin Romances the more studious women liked to read. To them it was a dream come true, a miraculous "last chance" for two picky people.

This situation, more than any other, caused an acute dilemma—satisfying my private needs and anticipating a negative public reaction to my behavior. I good-humoredly accepted a great deal of sexual joking but was uncomfortable about my status as a potential role model for younger children. With my community-wide reputation in mind, I made a point of returning to my boardinghouse fairly early in the evening after an out-of-town visit. One night, however, there was a severe snowstorm and I was not able to get back to the village. The roads had not been plowed and the snow was over the hood of my car. Since there was no telephone in the trailer, I could not call my host and explain what had happened. I was afraid that rumors would circulate and ruin my good image. Yet when I returned to the village the next morning and sheepishly walked into the house, I got a hardy slap on the back from the mother of my landlady. She winked at me and said, "Why, you ole Newfie, you're no better than the rest of us." Throughout the next week I was publicly and privately teased about my "honeymoon."

Villagers have a very matter-of-fact attitude toward real and ideal behavior. Ideally, women should wait until after marriage to have sexual relations; in reality, most of the young women become sexually active soon after menarche. Sex is viewed as a natural and healthy activity; people are meant to be paired. My activities were the topic of gossip and teasing, but I was not judged as immoral and negative sanctions were not brought against me. The sympathy, understanding, and common sense of the women endeared them to me. If anything negative was said about me in this respect, I never heard it. "Having a boyfriend" or being "paired off" seemed to make people a bit friendlier and more at ease around me. Clearly, my sexuality caused no problem in the community—I was simply breaking a rule everyone else broke. The real sin would have been in trying to hide my activities or to deny them. That would have been viewed as pretending to be better than the village women and would have gravely damaged my good image.

My relations in the public spheres of men and women and in the private sphere of men were important for building my image in the community as a whole. However, the outcome of my research depended specifically on my private relationships with women. I began to find myself repeatedly visiting five special women, developing close personal ties with them and their families. These women became my "mothers and sisters in the field." In spite of the differences in age, education, background, worldview, and life-style, we had stimulating and meaningful discussions about our pasts, the present, and our futures. During these long conversations we talked about shared commonalities, such as our respective families, home life, the trials of growing up, and my experiences in Grey Rock Harbour. I told them very little about my career or about the academic ideas or theories I was there to explore. In other words, I managed the impression of myself around my similarities with village women and glossed over our differences.

I had laid the groundwork well. People liked and respected me; they readily welcomed me into their homes and felt comfortable talking with me. I felt that it was now time to start intensively collecting data on the details of women's experience of menopause.

The Menopause Scene

"You May Think This Is a Really Dumb Thing to Ask but. . . ."

The central focus of my research on female sexuality in the Newfoundland setting concerned the relationship between women's status and their experience of menopause. Gathering information that would lead me to conclude that for the most part women's status was high throughout their lifetimes was a fairly easy, straightforward endeavor. However, collection of explicit data on women's experience of menopause was anxiety-provoking for both me and my informants. I had established myself in the village, observed the women in their personal and public realms, overcome my initial biases, and gotten them to accept and like me. I had been careful to appear neither too naive nor too currupt. I took an active interest in village events but was careful not to become a gossip. Women came to depend on me in their reciprocity networks. I had worked and played with them for nine months, and now I was ready to start asking them direct personal questions about sexuality at middle age. Or was I?

Actually, I had already learned a great deal about women's experience of menopause. I was constantly in the company of middle-aged women, and conversations frequently turned to menopause, menstruation, sex, and childbirth. To the best of my ability I would mentally note the conversation and record it in fieldnotes as soon as I got home. After several months my menopause file was quite thick. I may have unconsciously trained my informants to talk about "The Change," as they called it; in any event I am sure that when the topic came up, my rapt attention and interest were positive reinforcement for menopause-related discussion. However, because menopause talk often meant hours at the typewriter for me, there were times when I wished that they would just change the subject and converse about something less relevant to my research.

Women freely talked about menopause but mostly in a general, nonpersonal way. I never heard a woman volunteer any information on how it affected her relationship with her husband, for these women did not talk to anyone about the intimate aspects of their married lives. As I came to understand local customs about how to approach such delicate matters of conversation, I realized that my positivist's barrage of interview questions was clearly inappropriate for a stranger–older woman situation. Women knew that I was interested in health at middle age, but they were unaware of my specific interests because I delayed my menopause interviews until the last three months of fieldwork. Clearly, my shyness and indecision were the biggest assets I took to the field. If I had depended on direct questioning, and if I had started formal interviews early in fieldwork, I probably would have earned the reputation of an obnoxious busybody, or I even might have been run out of town. More importantly, however, I would have ended up merely measuring how closely villagers came to my own medicalized, intellectualized, middle-class notions of menopause.

When I prepared my research proposal I felt that I had developed a very "enlightened" view of menopause. I hypothesized a social causation theory, stating that if the status of women was high and unchanging, the women would report fewer symptoms and have more positive attitudes toward menopause. I wanted to study menopause with an emphasis on the normalcy of the process. After a year in Newfoundland, I came to realize that such "enlightened" views also reflected a middle-class, feminist, medical bias based on the gender role stereotypes of my own cultural background.

In the field I designed a structured interview, to be administered orally, which was divided into three sections: general background, women's status and self-esteem, and women's health, with an emphasis on female complaints—menopause-relevant questions. I compiled a list of every woman in the community between the ages of thirty-five and sixty-five and chose the women I knew best to interview first. These initial interviews were quite traumatic. The women were shocked that I would ask such questions. One woman told me that they had all come to see me as one of them but that this showed me to be a stranger after all: "We just forgot about all your schooling, what do you think of us now?" What I really wanted to know was what she thought of me. Another long-time confidant told me that she was glad I had saved the interviews for last: "If you started with all this mess, you would not have lasted two weeks. Who else are you going to do this to?" I had really offended my best friends, and I was devastated. Then and there I promised myself that I would never do another sex study as long as I lived.

I still felt it was necessary to collect data that I could use for comparisons with other menopause studies, so I dropped a few of the more personal questions and set out again. If an informant became uncomfortable during the interview, I asked the questions in a general discussion format. Ironically, those women with whom I was less familiar were not so surprised or offended by my questions, but neither were they as truthful in their answers. I attempted to conduct interviews in one section of town at a time, so that all the women in that section would be prepared for my visit sometime in the near future. I would call a woman in the morning to ask if I could "come over with my questions" that same afternoon. Attempting to schedule appointments any further ahead of time was futile. Some women were hesitant; some were often busy and had to be called several times. Yet not one woman refused to be interviewed when refusal would have been very easy. I think they felt sorry for me, having to ask so many embarrassing and "peculiar" questions, but they were also delighted to have me over to see their houses, to chat with them, and to have some tea. This was the big payoff for successful impression management.

After the first couple of interviews, word about the delicate nature of my questions began to circulate through the female networks. A typical response to my telephoned request for an interview would be, "Why, my dear, a poor old woman like me doesn't know anything about those things, but you're welcome to come over anyway." Husbands were often requested to be absent when I came for an interview. I believe that the women were shy and hesitant because of what they felt was their lack of education, rather than because of the personal nature of my questions. Many women viewed the questionnaire as some sort of test—a way of measuring some ability, such as how smart or how educated they were, which they could not clearly discern. Indeed, it was difficult for many to respond to interview questions, especially those that were not open-ended (the ability to do so appears to be conditioned by years of schooling). I reassured each interviewee that these questions were about Grey Rock Harbour and her, and on those subjects she was the expert and I was the student. Before each interview I sat down and chatted about things I had learned from them, explained what I was going to ask and why, and assured the informant of confidentiality. I told how many interviews I had already completed and generally got the woman relaxed and the conversation flowing. The first part of the questionnaire was received as relatively innocuous. It was instrumental in getting the woman comfortable with the interview situation and stimulated her to respond freely on the basis of her own experiences, setting the tone for the questions that followed.

It was impossible to do more than one interview a day. Afternoons were best since women were busy with housework in the mornings and curious children and husbands were present at night. The major problem during the day was "The Story." I would go to a woman's house at 1:00 and begin the interview at 1:30. At 2:30 many informants would become restless and suggest turning on "The Story," two televised soap operas watched habitually by most women, which tended to interrupt the interview for one-half to one hour. An afternoon tea was usually served (women baked special treats just for me) when the interview was finished. The shortest interviews lasted one and a half hours, while those with more loquacious women lasted up to five hours. In several cases informants reported that they had never said these things to another living soul. Often I was asked to explain, either during or after an interview, such things as what the drugs they were taking did, what was removed in a hysterectomy, what "in blunt terms" was "cut off" in a vasectomy, and what "sexuals" (homosexuals) actually do. It took three and a half months (May to August) to collect thirty-eight interviews; I would have liked more, but I ran out of time.

If the administration of questionnaires in Grey Rock Harbour taught me one thing about the experience of menopause, it was that in that particular cultural setting, dependence on questionnaire data was an inferior way of attempting to understand the way in which status may affect the experience of menopause. Through this very painful process of interviewing I came to realize that to "get the question right," the women were awkwardly trying to anticipate what kind of answers I expected. Not only were my interviews reaffirming my stranger status and upsetting my informants, they were interfering with the communication of relevant information. Clearly, Grey Rock Harbour middle-aged women did not ascribe much importance to menopause or the symptoms that may accompany it.

My admiration for the village women was enhanced as I began to realize that their views on menopause were very different from my own and those of many of the specialists in the area of menopause studies. The women did not explain menopausal phenomena by what they had read in books; neither did they accord it any special status as a life stage. Local notions of nerves and blood were drawn on to explain various facets of health and how they may vary throughout the life cycle. From the perspective of a middle-aged woman experiencing psychogenic bodily changes, these folk notions made more sense than the medical or social science analyses that abound in the academic literature.

Three key factors characterized Grey Rock Harbour women's reactions to menopause: (1) bodily, personality, and sociocultural processes are not compartmentalized; (2) menopause is a normal process; and (3) the major symptoms of menopause are not unique to mid-life or the cessation of menses. Menopause-related experiences are explained in terms of their more general emic concepts of nerves and blood. Menopause is commonly called "The Change," although that term also applies to menarche, menstruation, or any problem with the menstrual cycle. The vague nature of reference to specific menstrual events reflects the fact that such bodily processes are considered private matters unfit for polite conversation; that puberty, menstruation, and menopause are not sharply differentiated from each other since age grading between females lacks importance; and that all these processes are explained by the more general concepts of nerves and blood. The impropriety of direct questions about menopause was circumvented by inquiries such as, "What happens to your nerves at The Change?"

All villagers recognized common features of nerve and blood states. For example, nerves may be tight, unstrung, or strong, while blood affects health in terms of its volume, viscosity, and quality. However, nerves and blood are hardly formally defined diagnostic categories, and much to my frustration they were neither well-defined nor used consistently among the locals. For example, one informant would describe dark menstrual blood as healthy and light menstrual blood as a sign of ill health, while another informant would state just the opposite. Similarly, having bad nerves referred to a wide range of behavior, including a simple fear of height and/or uncontrollable crying spells. The fact that there were disagreements over specific aspects of the nature of nerves and blood merely reflects the individualization of experience and explanations that are characteristic of small communities. This lack of agreement did not hamper use of the terms, however; people referred to their daily health in terms of nerves and blood and were not concerned with the consistency of the concepts but rather that they could explain a wide range of basically normal, bodily and mental states using one convenient conceptual framework. Although these terms do not appear to eliminate negative symptoms or mediate discomfort, their use provides a vocabulary with which a woman may discuss her experiences of the depression, agitation, irrational behavior, change in menstrual patterns, and/or flashes many women experience at mid-life.

The concepts of nerves and blood cannot be understood apart from their social ramifications. Cultural configurations are such that the middle-aged Grey Rock Harbour woman can actually use her case of nerves for status enhancement. These women do not experience guilt, confusion, or self-depreciation at middle age. Due to several factors, including their high position in the society, the stability of their status and role throughout the adult life cycle, and the value of high esteem accorded female activities by all segments of the society, these women can depend on certain cultural beliefs to buttress their social position and self-esteem through the menopausal years, which otherwise may be plagued with emotional and physical problems. The relevant factors here are the cultural rewards for the "stoic female" and the idealization of women who grew up and had their families "before the road."

A "good woman" is one who has worked hard all her life and has stoically endured or surmounted all the trials of "the old days when we were all poor." These women are regarded as folk heroines and glorified for successfully raising a family in the face of overwhelming odds. Nerves have a finite quality; one can use them up with excessive suffering or hardship early in life. Thus, it is believed that the more a woman has suffered during her lifetime, the more difficult "The Change" will be for her.

Stoicism does not imply silent endurance. If stoicism is to be applauded, it must be voiced. Nerves, in general and during "The Change," are a popular topic of conversation. Women freely talk about their complaints over the telephone, while visiting, and at organizational meetings. Although most complaints are voiced to peers, women feel free to relate them to husbands, neighbors, and relatives, with no loss of face to themselves. Difficulty at menopause is not believed to be a sign of moral inferiority. It is generally considered that women who complain at menopause do so for real cause. "The Change" is seen as a test of fortitude and endurance, providing odds against which a woman should continue to act like her natural self and "take it as it comes."

The socially acceptable open avenues of conversation between middle-aged women reaffirm the normalcy of menopause as an experience common to all women, define and explain symptoms and the appropriate responses to those symptoms, and provide social support for the woman who is "not quite herself." Thus the experience of menopause allows for reaffirmation of social networks while at the same time legitimating one's menopausal complaints and enhancing one's status in the eyes of significant others. My reading and research before leaving for the field had not prepared me for what I found in this regard. In light of my observations, then, my study changed from a positivistic to a particularistic mode of analysis. It was obvious that these women knew a great deal more about women's experience of menopause than I did.

The Change Reconsidered

In summary, by listening rather than by asking questions, I found that Newfoundland women do not distinguish between biological, psychological, and social realms of experience. The folk notions of nerves and blood act in the conceptual integration of these realms throughout adult life. The women have a folk system to explain what happens to their minds and bodies at menopause and a female support system for those who experience difficulty. Their experience of what I, but not necessarily they, would call menopause-related phenomena cannot be understood apart from their extensive social networks, open communication channels, and a varied range of meaningful activities.

Personal factors are important in all phases of the fieldwork process. If the Newfoundlanders had not liked me I would have gotten very little information from them. If I had not been quiet, shy, and very sensitive about offending them, I may not have come to see how different my own views about women in general and menopause in particular were from theirs. I thought I was enlightened and nonethnocentric in matters concerning menopause; I thought I could expose sexist and medicalized views about menopause. Actually, I expected to expose that which was patently obvious—an overdependence on medical models. What I ended up exposing were the deeply ingrained prejudices I had brought to the field with me, including medicalized, sexist, and class-biased presuppositions.

The major objective of my research proposal and subsequent fieldwork was to show that a medical model of menopause was misleading, mainly because it treated a normal life-cycle event as an illness or as an incipient illness. I wanted to prove these models wrong and expected to do so by finding a society where women did not have problems with, or negative attitudes toward, menopause. To me a normal menopause meant menopause without symptom complaints or negative social connotations. I wanted to study folk notions or menopause with a biased methodology. I was going to show how menopause was really normal, using the same formal research instruments others had used to show that menopause should be equated with being sick. It takes a great deal of audacity to plan a cross-cultural study on women's experience of menopause with a methodology that reflects the gender biases of the enthographer's culture. With my middle-class, academic background, I was guilty of a colonialism of ideas. As an academic, an analyst, and a scientist, I felt that my ideas were superior and set out to test them with the village women as guinea pigs. My overreaction to what I considered to be medicalized sexism prevented me from seeing what any Newfoundland woman, relying on experience and common sense, would realize: "The Change" is a biological, psychological, and social phenomenon, and health and ill health are not necessarily mutually exclusive opposites. Menopause, like other times in life, may be accompanied by problems. However, the problems are nothing out of the ordinary, nothing with which most women cannot cope. I had invested approximately four years of my life in the intensive study of menopause only to conclude, in agreement with Grey Rock Harbour women, "It ain't no big thing." It was the Newfoundland women themselves who supplied me with the words and concepts, such as nerves and blood, I needed to more adequately explain women's experience of menopause.

My biases were also sexist to the extent that I stereotyped the traditional female roles of mother and wife as simple and unsophisticated, chosen only by women because they lacked other opportunities or because they were afraid or incompetent to try anything else. I had entered the field believing that the best representatives of womanhood were those women most like myself, achievers in the public sphere. In Grey Rock Harbour I discovered that the stoic endurance, quiet dignity, strong female networks, and lively social life that characterize local women are also valuable female achievements. There is no way to escape the fact that we are the products of our own personalities, our own life histories, our own cultures. Beliefs and behaviors underlying gender are among those we accept almost automatically. Further studies will surely be enhanced by a better understanding of gender in cross-cultural perspective.

Notes

1. I sought a community that: (1) was large enough to include one hundred women between the ages of thirty-five and sixty-five; (2) was somewhat isolated, with access only by sea until recently; (3) was homogeneous, with clear boundaries, a simple occupational structure, one community-wide nonfundamentalist Protestant religion, and lacking any marked social stratification; (4) had a viable inshore fishery, and where fishing was the mainstay of the community and unemployment was low; (5) lacked roles for women other than housewife/mother and fishery-related roles; (6) had low levels of out-migration and equal representatives of all age-grades in the population structure; and (7) had not been previously studied.

2. Some of these women had been forced to leave their homes at a young age because their parents lacked the resources needed to feed and clothe them; others left their homes and communities, lured away from crowded households, with hopes of obtaining meager wages and a degree of freedom from parental domination. Some married at an early age, but most sought opportunities to be "serving girls," working as servants in homes where an older girl was needed to help with the housework and to care for younger children. In their view, leaving the village to "go serving" with an Italian family in North Sydney, Nova Scotia, was as dramatic a change in life-style as living in an African village would have been to me.

Reference

Davis, Dona L.
　　1983　*Blood and Nerves: An Ethnographic Focus on Menopause*. St. John's: Memorial University of Newfoundland Institute of Social and Economic Research.

15

On Trying to Be an Amazon

JEAN JACKSON

When I think of how naïve I was about the significance of being a woman doing fieldwork in the Central Northwest Amazon, I wince. In one of my letters home I said something like, "I am like a man from Mars here; I suppose I should say *woman* except that I am so foreign to the Bará they probably don't see much difference." Of course, I didn't really believe that, even in the beginning, and I now realize that it was actually wishful thinking more than simple naïveté. In the bad old days before the women's movement, female graduate students were led to believe that despite our gender-related deficiencies, if we were made of the "Right Stuff" we could overcome those deficiencies and get at the truth. It was never questioned, of course, that being female constituted a deficiency; in fact, we all pretended that our sex didn't really matter. We also never questioned that the truth was to be obtained from shamans, judges, politicians, and so on, all of whom happened to be men. Since I never saw these assumptions for what they were—assumptions—I never questioned them. I simply knew that I had to neuter myself intellectually and overcome my handicap in order to be able to talk to the right informants and to know what to do with the data once these men consented to talk to me.

As my letters home revealed, I was in fact very concerned about the consequences of being rather unchangeably female, afraid that it mattered so much that I would always be ineligible for membership in the club of fieldworkers who were made of the "Right Stuff." In my heart of hearts I knew that no amount of traveling to the far reaches of the Amazon, or anywhere else, would make any real difference.

As a result of my fieldwork experience, growing up more, and the women's movement, I did come to see these assumptions as just that—and incorrect ones besides—but for the most part I did so only after I had returned home. I realized that one of the reasons I had wanted to go so far away was in hopes that being female in such a place wouldn't make the difference I feared it would. Going to the

Amazon, in other words, would make me an Amazon—a strange, strong, mythical creature, undeniably female but worthy of respect, independent of men, and rather masculine in some important ways. A cartoon sent to me by my friend Jerry Moles at Stanford, depicting how people there were coming to think of me as a result of my letters home, shows that my subconscious hopes about neutering myself were not totally idiosyncratic (see Figure 1). Various drawings portray me as a bone-in-the-nose native, queen of a jungle tribe, a jungle trader, and, yes, a muscle-bound Amazon. All but one image were either ambiguous as to gender or downright masculine. The only unmistakably female one (that of the white goddess or queen) shows a person of authority and high status, qualities I seldom felt I had. I believe that such positive female images were also a part of my motivation for going to such a remote area, but they lay beneath the surface.

It is common knowledge that when you do fieldwork you find out about the culture you're studying, your own culture, and yourself. You—your eyes, your ears—are the yardstick, the microscope, the data-acquiring instrument. And who you are is in part a result of the categories to which you belong: marginal native though you may think of yourself, you are still a participating member of your own culture and you carry those perceptions and understandings with you. Furthermore, the people you study expect certain behaviors from you and relate to you in particular ways because of their understanding of who you are. Glimpses into yourself, and inklings of how they see you, cannot help but make you a better fieldworker, although you cannot learn how to become self-reflexive by reading a fieldwork manual. Such glimpses occur in two ways: directly, as a result of the daily experiences of fieldwork, and indirectly, when you begin to really understand why you chose where to go and what to do in the first place. This essay, then, is about how my membership in the American category *female* influenced my choice of a research topic and, conversely, how doing fieldwork allowed me to better comprehend my own culture and my position in it, in particular my being a woman.

I realized after returning from the field that I had wanted to go to the Amazon and work in a small-scale society because in this setting I could put my womanly attributes to advantage. All of this is difficult to articulate even now; certainly, I would have been able to verbalize little at the time. No one else talked this way, and the idea of admitting how important my gender might be was too threatening. But it is clear that I wanted to get away from my own culture, get to

Figure 1. Fieldwork fantasies.

a place where my defect would not be so noticeable and, if possible, turn it to my advantage. I am thinking here of what Margaret Mead and Ruth Benedict represented—qualitative, humanistic, even intuitive approaches based on long-term, warm, face-to-face interaction. My choice also had to do with my being accepted easily, because as a woman I would be comparatively nonthreatening. And since all the world's women are in some important respects seen as basically the same, I would be more easily integrated into the society I chose to study because I would seem less foreign and incomprehensible.

For the most part this naïveté and romanticism were rudely exposed to me for what they were very early on. For one thing, my hope to be welcomed because I was "just" a woman contradicted my hope that my gender would not matter as much as it seemed to in my own society. For another, I had to deal with the conflict between the intuitive, osmosis model of field research and the standards of objectivity and rigor I had acquired during my training at Stanford University. In addition, despite the pleasant fantasy of easy acceptance as just another woman, my real self-image was in fact one of speaking softly, yes, but also carrying the big stick of (relative) wealth, power, and authority, which in fact was mainly a potential prop for my sagging self-esteem during times of feeling like an idiot, a child, or an exploited and misunderstood nice guy. That I had recourse to that image was important, however.

I now see that one reason I chose to go to the Amazon was that my vision of myself there was in some ways a more positive one than I had experienced in my own culture (this is also nicely illustrated in the cartoon). In other words, I could have my cake and eat it too. I would be accepted, maybe even incorporated, into the kinship and family networks of the settlement I lived in, in ways I felt I had not been in my own culture. And I could succeed at this endeavor without losing my femininity—an area of great anxiety for me and many other women at that time. The feminine mystique was very much a part of our operating instructions, and yet there we were in graduate school, trying to make it in a man's world. We told ourselves that discrimination against women didn't exist in the modern world, and yet it is very clear that one reason I wanted to go into this particular heart of darkness was to prove that I was as good as the rest. Fieldwork thus would concomitantly be easy because I was a woman and so difficult that I would pass the test and demonstrate that my being female shouldn't deny me first-class citizenship in my own society.

Both assumptions—that I would be able to "pass" as some sort of creature from an alien planet whose gender did not matter very much, and that I would be able to overcome my deficiencies as a woman and get data from the only people worth getting it from, the men—were found to be totally fallacious after a short stay in Tukanoan society. Being the main dimensions of social differentiation in small-scale societies, age and sex classifications are of paramount importance and visibility. Futhermore, Tukanoan society is highly sex-segregated and, one might say, virulently patrilineal and patrilocal (when women move at marriage, for example, they change language as well as residence and daily companions).

I had to deal with the fact that my being a woman obviously mattered; and since there were very few other statuses and categories to belong to, in some senses it mattered more than in American society. In fact, I spent most of my time with women—those second-class citizens from whom no decent data would be forthcoming. To this day I am appalled at the degree to which I unquestioningly accepted the proposition that women, including me, were inferior creatures. One of the lessons of fieldwork was the actual experiencing of—as opposed to reading about—a culture where women did not feel as inferior in the ways I (although largely unconsciously) did. I realized this about Tukanoan women at the same time I was comprehending that in many respects Tukanoan society was a male-dominated one, where both men and women overtly expressed sexual antagonism.

I carried out fieldwork in the Vaupés territory of Colombia and Brazil, also known as the Central Northwest Amazon. The people inhabiting this remote area, known as Tukanoans, are basically egalitarian horticulturalists who also hunt, fish, and gather. I studied their very complex marriage system, one involving over sixteen exogamous patrilineal descent units, each affiliated with a different language. This was not my original research topic, however, and what I explore in this essay are some of the factors that led me to choose this topic after realizing my original proposal was impossible to carry out.[1] These factors are related to the opinions and feelings I had about marriage, the roles of husband and wife in present-day American society, and in general the role of women in Western culture. I was at the time unaware of the effects of these concerns on my decision. To some degree sorting it all out is still going on.

One feature of the Tukanoan marriage system that fascinated me almost from the beginning was that men found it difficult to get married—it was seen as an accomplishment for them in a way not true for women. Of course I had read about such situations in the cross-cultural record prior to going to the field, but experiencing it first-hand made a strong impression on me. Although in our culture we

have all manner of rather sappy platitudes about how difficult it is
for a young man to win the hand of a pure-hearted girl, in actuality
it is the women who are taught to worry about making a "good"
marriage. This is not to deny that most men see getting and staying
happily married as an important and oftentimes demanding and difficult task. Nevertheless, the assumption in our culture is that all
women would get married if they could and all men could if they
would, but the reverse is true in Tukanoan society. Fifty years ago in
traditional American society we would have wondered of a father
with five daughters, "How will he get them all married?"; such a
concern in Tukanoan society would be expressed for a man with five
sons.

I began to delve into the marriage system, in particular examining
the social structural and emotional implications it held for its male
and female participants—its costs and benefits, if you will. I believe
I was successful in comprehending much of the way the system
works: its structure, and the psychological consequences that lead
to marriage being a difficult decision for a woman to make. Most
Tukanoan women marry, but it is nonetheless true that contracting a
given marriage is a real achievement for a man and his kinsmen.[2] I
think that one reason this system fascinated me was that it resonated
with many of my ideas about American marriage patterns. While
very real benefits are to be gained by a woman marrying "well"—
financial, social, emotional, and so forth (just watch any soap op-
era)—I had always felt that American women also gave up a lot, or
at least ran the risk of doing so, when they married. I had found no
confirmation of this either in my general education or anthropological training. When I returned from the field, I recognized many of
my puzzled feelings—and their validation, in fact—in Jessie Bernard's *The Future of Marriage* (1972). But in the field many of my
doubts about how we idealize marriage versus how it really is in
American society found their initial expression as a result of seeing
the Tukanoan system in action.

While growing up in American society in the 1950s and 1960s, I
had sensed that the received wisdom about marriage and the position of women in general was not the whole story. I sensed that
women relinquished a lot in all the conventional forms of male-
female interaction. I have since learned of books and articles available at that time dealing with such issues (e.g., Hershberger 1948;
Hacker 1951; Komarovsky 1946). But for me and for many women
such questions were never even formulated. Taking marriage as an
example, that women might choose whether or not to marry, and
make this choice on the basis of perceived costs and benefits to mar-

rying or staying single, was never posed as a possibility. All women would get married if they possibly could, and to remain unmarried was the worst kind of failure. There was no choice permitted in people's evaluations, you simply had not "caught a man." It was while contemplating the choices I saw Tukanoan women making that I came to see that this and similar questions about women's choices and women's roles could be asked.

Tukanoan women fall in love, and far fewer of them never marry than is the case for our own society, yet getting (and staying) married was seen as more difficult for a man. I think that to some extent getting and staying successfully married is difficult in both societies. Equally true, there are advantages and disadvantages to getting married in both societies. What really makes the difference is that this is acknowledged in Tukanoan society, just as the opposition between the sexes is openly acknowledged in ways unheard of in American society—despite the fact that the battle between the sexes finds expression in daily and extraordinary events here as well as in the Vaupés. Part of the differences lies in the fact that, to quote Murphy and Murphy (1974:110) on the Mundurucú, "the battle of the sexes is not carried on by individual gladiators, as in our society, but by armies" (see also the 1975 film Mehinacu, based on fieldwork by Thomas Gregor). Such overt hostility between the sexes can signal the real on-the-ground power women have rather than how lowly they are; one result of such pronounced sex segregation is the female solidarity and political clout that it can give rise to, in real contrast to our own society (see Sanday 1974). For me, such expressions, in particular the symbolic and ritual ones, were important because some of the contradictions I had been vaguely aware of in my own culture were very emphatically and honestly (in my opinion) communicating to Tukanoan people the way matters really stood. This is not to deny that all sorts of contradictions exist on many levels in Tukanoan society, some of which are not explicitly stated in ritual, myth, or daily discourse. But they are different from the contradictions I live being a member of my society. I believe that crossing this cultural boundary led me to see the ones in my society more clearly, and I hope it has allowed me to see some of the ones Tukanoans live by virtue of having a perspective different from theirs.

At the risk of sounding horribly Rousseauistic, I have come to the conclusion that, in part because of the honesty with which the sexual lines of divergence and at times battle are drawn, Tukanoan women have in some profound senses a less spoiled and conflicted sex identity than I or any number of intellectual women friends of mine have. In a sense this has to do with Tukanoan women's life choices being less ambiguous—although perhaps no less painful—than ours. Tukanoan women have some say-so about what marriages they will make, and this is reflected in the social construction of marital reality. But I don't want to imply that their lives are never filled with tragedy because of the consequences of the decisions they have made as women. However, they can make decisions and live out their lives without the constant concern that by choosing one set of options they are denying an extremely important aspect of their identity. I, and many other women, have often felt conflicted about choosing to be the person I wanted to be, in particular an ambitious, academically successful and respected scholar, because it seemed that I could not also be feminine. Being smart, or powerful, desexualized me, or so I often felt. Tukanoan society is far from my idea of paradise, in particular with respect to the relative position of the sexes, and yet this makes my conviction that Tukanoan women have less of a conflicted sense of gender identity than I or others like me stand out all the more. We all know what I'm talking about when I speak of contradictions (e.g., Komarovsky 1946; Horner 1970; Broverman et al. 1970), so I won't belabor the point. But let me note that when I said I was looking for a place where being a female would not matter so much, in a sense I found it. Even though for Tukanoan women being female is the identity feature of the most significance, and even though Tukanoan society is clearly male-dominated, if one is female and a Tukanoan, one is not frustrated and invalidated in many of the ways American women were before various gender role contradictions were brought to everyone's attention as a result of the women's movement.

My fantasy of having an easier time in fieldwork because I was a woman, and therefore more empathetic and intuitive (or at least seen as such) and less threatening, was true to some extent. Although I had not expected to spend most of my time in all-female groups, despite my prejudices and feelings that I was "wasting my time" (Hugh-Jones 1979: xiv expresses similar fears), I enjoyed being with them, just as I had enjoyed being with women during previous fieldwork projects in Mexico and Guatemala.

I enjoyed being with the men, too. Because it was such a sex-segregated society and I needed access to the male world, I did not try to become as completely a Tukanoan woman as I could have. Expectably, this produced a certain amount of conflict, because at times I was purposely breaking the rules, rules I was just beginning to understand and Tukanoans were just beginning to expect me to follow. I would smoke cigars, chew coca, and join the men's circle in the front of the longhouse at night, chafing at feeling doubly an outsider. I remember the mixed feelings when, for the first time on a canoe trip, I was fed after my boatmen. I was both elated and irritated: I was being seen more and more in Tukanoan terms and less as a white, but I was, of course, being seen as a Tukanoan *woman*. My femaleness had superceded my status as an affluent and high-status outsider. Although more of an insider, I was being assigned to my proper place on the inside—second place. Understandable, then, was my ambivalence, since I had liked the deference and respect shown me by being served first. I wanted the best of both worlds (see Siskind 1973:19) and was irked when I couldn't have it. I knew that, finally, it was childish and silly to want to retain status symbols from white Colombian culture. The last thing I wanted was to increase the rapidity with which Tukanoans were being forced to forsake their own values for those of the national society. They were not even really *my* values; I only needed such reassurances when I felt insecure. Because I was an outsider, all the claims I had to high status seemed to come from the foreign, rather than the indigenous, value system. I would feel myself wanting to pull rank and then be exasperated for having such shameful impulses.

It is true that oftentimes in fieldwork one overreacts as a consequence of the feelings of helplessness and disorientation endemic to experiences of total immersion in a strange culture. Other anthropologists have sensitively and revealingly written about such feelings (e.g., Briggs 1970; Maybury-Lewis 1965; Rabinow 1977). I often felt as though I belonged in all the worst categories—female, deaf and mute, ignorant, juvenile, physically weak. Since I had neither husband nor children, I was not only "just" a woman but barely even that. It is undeniable that being female restricted me in some very important ways. But equally important, I think, is the need I felt to shore up my self-esteem when I felt belittled or foolish, and this often had to do with my own self-deprecation and sense of inadequacy because I was "just" a woman. I wanted to be seen as a Tukanoan woman rather than a foreigner, but not completely a woman, because I still felt a need to prove I was as good as the men—not surprising since that was what I had been trying to do for years in my own culture. A no-win situation, and one that made for additional difficulties from time to time. I now see that it was the times when I felt invalidated as a person because of being a woman that made me the most uptight and defensive.

One example of this involves a canoe trip when my head boatman tried to be macho and take the canoe upriver through a rapids under power rather than drag the unloaded canoe along the shore in the proper, safe manner. The canoe capsized and much of the cargo was lost. I was justifiably furious, but I now also realize that I felt I was to blame . . . that if I had been a man such a thing would not have occurred. I was, in fact, not responsible: the rules of river travel in the Vaupés are quite explicit on such points. But I felt apologetic for being a woman (just as I often felt for being white) and thought the boatman wouldn't have been so foolhardy if I had had the authority and superior judgment of a man. I am not denying that the boatman probably did have problems dealing with the fact that I was both a woman and white, because the two categories do contradict each other in any number of respects. But my point is that I guaranteed additional problems by getting hooked by my own assumptions about having no authority and only illegitimate power. It was impossible, I thought, for a woman to really run things, and so I was to blame for the accident.

My anxiety and insecurity doubtless showed in some ways and in fact increased the tension and potential misunderstanding in some of the interactions I had during my stay—a good example of a self-fulfilling prophecy. And while I cannot imagine what a Tukanoan woman would do in such situations (she would never find herself in them in the first place), I do believe that some of the binds I felt over my gender role are not felt by Tukanoan women. This is, again, not to say that Tukanoan women aren't caught in other binds produced by the built-in contradictions in sex role prescriptions in their own society. I am aware of the tendency to romanticize the fieldwork experience and to become nostalgic about the integrity of life among one's "own" natives. I do feel, however, that many of the antagonisms and built-in oppositions that exist between Tukanoan men and women are more clearly stated, both in ritual and myth and in everyday life, than they were in my own culture when I was growing up. The surfacing and communicating of these hostilities and structured oppositions, many of them very deep (see Dinnerstein 1976; Chodorow 1978), although causing a great deal of pain, confusion, and anger, including backlash, has been beneficial and far less hypocritical than the previous situation.

I returned home better equipped to understand how varied the forms of female subordination can be, and I have, since then, tried to apply those lessons to my personal life as well as to my intellectual endeavors. Being forced to consider how my being female and what that meant to me influenced the research—my presentation of self, choice of research project, and data gathering—led me to think about male dominance and female subordination perhaps far more clearly than I would have otherwise. Forced to revise my definitions of sexual politics to understand the Tukanoan case, I was led to think through the problems I had had with my own cultural gender identity. The sexual subordination characterizing the Central Northwest Amazon is so different from Western varieties that from my perspective Tukanoan society appeared to be sexually egalitarian in several important respects. With Tukanoan women and men illustrating these different forms of gender power, I could better understand why I had felt defective as a female graduate student, as a single woman, and as a woman in my own culture. This, in turn, allowed me to comprehend sex roles and related issues, among Tukanoans and in general, in a more sophisticated and objective fashion, even though the route to that objectivity involved much subjectivity and introspection.

Notes

1. These are not the only important considerations leading to a change in research, however; others are discussed in Jackson (1976, 1983).

2. For an analysis of the "costs and benefits ratio" of marriage for men and women, see Jackson (1983: chap. 10).

References

Bernard, Jessie
   1972   The Future of Marriage. New York: Bantam.
Briggs, Jean
   1970   Never in Anger: Portrait of an Eskimo Family. Cambridge, Mass.: Harvard University Press.
Broverman, Inge K., Donald M. Broverman, Frank E. Clarkson, Paul S. Rosenkrantz, and Susan R. Vogel
   1970   "Sex-role Stereotypes and Clinical Judgements of Mental Health." Journal of Consulting and Clinical Psychology 34(1):1–7.
Chodorow, Nancy
   1978   The Reproduction of Mothering: Psychoanalysis and the Sociology of Gender. Berkeley: University of California Press.
Dinnerstein, Dorothy
   1976   The Mermaid and the Minotaur: Sexual Arrangements and Human Malaise. New York: Harper and Row.
Gregor, Thomas
   1975   Mehinacu. London: Granada Television.
Hacker, Helen Mayer
   1951   "Women as a Minority Group." Social Forces 30(Oct. 30):60–69.
Hershberger, Ruth
   1948   Adam's Rib. New York: Pellegrini and Cudahy.

Horner, Matina
    1970   "The Motive to Avoid Success and Changing Aspirations of College Women." In: *Women on Campus*, pp. 12–23. Proceedings of a symposium sponsored by the Center for the Continuing Education of Women. Ann Arbor, Mich.

Hugh-Jones, Christine
    1979   *From the Milk River: Spatial and Temporal Processes in Northwest Amazonia.* Cambridge: Cambridge University Press.

Jackson, Jean E.
    1976   "Vaupés Marriage: A Network System in the Northwest Amazon." In: C. Smith (ed.), *Regional Analysis, Vol. 2: Social Systems*, pp. 65–93. New York: Academic Press.
    1983   *The Fish People: Linguistic Exogamy and Tukanoan Identity in Northwest Amazonia.* Cambridge: Cambridge University Press.

Komarovsky, Mirra
    1946   "Cultural Contradictions and Sex Roles." *American Journal of Sociology* 52(3):184–89.

Maybury-Lewis, David H. P.
    1965   *The Savage and the Innocent.* Boston: Beacon Press.

Murphy, Yolanda, and Robert F. Murphy
    1974   *Women of the Forest.* New York: Columbia University Press.

Rabinow, Paul
    1977   *Reflections on Fieldwork in Morocco.* Berkeley: University of California Press.

Sanday, Peggy R.
    1974   "Female Status in the Public Domain." In: Michelle Z. Rosaldo and Louise Lamphere (eds.), *Women, Culture and Society*, pp. 189–206. Stanford, Calif.: Stanford University Press.

Siskind, Janet
    1973   *To Hunt in the Morning.* New York: Oxford University Press.

16

Gender Bias and Sex Bias: Removing Our Cultural Blinders in the Field

ELIZABETH FAITHORN

For twenty months in the early 1970s I lived among the Kafe of the Eastern Highlands of Papua New Guinea, studying Kafe gender definitions, the female life cycle and the overall patterning and tenor of male-female relations. In the course of this research I found myself, of necessity, closely examining my own sense of identity as a female, my beliefs about femininity and masculinity, and my own intersexual relationships. The depth of this self-examination directly related to the quality of the fieldwork, for as my self-perceptions became clearer and more conscious, my ability to enter Kafe female life empathetically and "from the inside" greatly increased. My research among the Kafe resulted in a perspective on Highlands women and their relations with men that was rather different than that being presented by most other Papua New Guinea ethnographers at the time. I believe this difference was at least in part attributable to the effects of a prevailing androcentric perspective that had been carried into the field setting by male and female ethnographers socialized and educated in Western culture and society.

Try as hard as we might, it is still not possible to go into another culture completely free of the one into which we were first socialized, and this can have a profound and often unrecognized effect on the results of our research. Where we look for information, who we talk to about what, how we interpret what we see and hear, even what we think of to question, can all be influenced by our own cultural conditioning. Whether our research focus happens to be on matters of gender and sex role or not, our own concepts of femininity and masculinity and learned role behaviors as women and men do impinge on our fieldwork.

In this essay I discuss two sorts of cultural bias relevant to a general focus on gender identities and field research, of which I became aware in the course of preparing for and carrying out my research among the Kafe. One I call *gender bias*, and the other, *sex bias*. In this context, gender refers to cultural definitions of masculine and feminine, whereas sex refers to the transcultural biological division of the human species into male and female subclasses (see Oakley 1972). These terms are obviously connected, in that in any given culture males are socialized to exhibit masculine gender attributes, and females, feminine ones. However, what is considered as masculine in one culture may be defined as feminine in another, as in Mead's (1935) classic study of gender roles in three different Oceanic cultures. Thus, in using these terms I refer to the assumptions that we fieldworkers carry with us from our own culture, both about gender role definitions and about the relative importance of the sex-class distinction, when we do our research work in another culture.

Gender bias comes from our deep-rooted learned beliefs about femininity and masculinity, about what being a woman or a man means, and interpreting ourselves and others as if those beliefs were in fact true and applicable cross-culturally. Coming out of Western society, male and female fieldworkers both have shared until quite recently a predominantly "male" perspective in studying other cultures. Women have not been adequately represented in the ethnographic literature; and, when they do appear, they have almost exclusively been portrayed in their roles as wife and mother. Even female fieldworkers have frequently looked to women as informants only on issues of family, child-rearing, and domestic activites, whereas they go to men to discuss politics, economics, ritual life, and warfare—issues associated with masculine gender in the West and often considered more significant than feminine domains in the analysis of human society. Gender bias has also led to an assumption that men and women are not particularly interested in or informed about the activities and beliefs associated with their opposite gender's domain, let alone major participants in those activities. Thus the feminine perspective of the man's world, or the masculine view of the woman's, has also been generally omitted from the record.

One curious side effect of this gender bias is that female ethnographers often find themselves being perceived as having a masculine gender in the field, or even being thought of as a man or some curious kind of neutral category of person. I had this experience myself, initially, and have talked with other anthropologists about the issue. It is not very difficult for a female fieldworker to live within a culture that perceives her as a "woman acting like a man," assuming the host culture will tolerate such behavior. It is difficult, however, to have others actually wonder what sex a woman in the field is, and to be asked for proof of sexual identity, as I was.

In the past decade there has been growing recognition of the effects of gender bias in field research, and attempts have been made to balance the traditional male perspective with research focused on women in more depth and detail. We now have good ethnographic accounts of women's lives in many parts of the world and a growing body of theory dealing with such issues as female status cross-culturally, public-private domain distinctions in relation to male and female identities and roles, and symbolic analyses of masculinity and femininity (see Friedl 1975; Hammond and Jablow 1976; MacCormack and Strathern 1980; Martin and Voorhies 1975; Reiter 1975; Rosaldo and Lamphere 1974). Nevertheless, on a deeper level gender bias remains problematic, for it cannot be eliminated simply by doing more research on women or expanding our notions of possible feminine and masculine roles in the past or in the future. The very concepts with which we work in analyzing society and culture also must be reexamined for gender bias. For example, it has been suggested by many anthropologists that from a cross-cultural perspective women have lower status than men. But what does status actually mean? How do we decide what variables are important in measuring status? Are we certain that the variables we choose are free from gender bias? (For an important contribution to this issue see Sanday 1974.) Another such example is the realm of politics. Again, from a cross-cultural perspective politics has been considered by most anthropologists to be a male domain, with women generally participating informally or indirectly. However, traditional definitions of and implicit assumptions about politics are also coming under the scrutiny of those who have researched folk models of politics in other cultures and are concerned about eliminating gender bias in this area (e.g., Collier 1974; Rogers 1975). The point here is that the ways we perceive and define fundamental aspects of culture and society—the etic categories—can in fact reflect gender bias without our recognizing this.

The second bias I wish to discuss is what I call the sex bias. This, too, is an assumption that lies deeply rooted within our own culture about the overriding importance of the division of the sexes in the analysis and understanding of human behavior. The very emphasis that we put on the division of the social world by sex, even acknowledging the great diversity of gender definition within this, still keeps us looking at women and at men, rather than at people, at human beings. We say that anthropology is the study of human behavior, but in practice it is largely the study of male and female behavior, and men have been studied more thoroughly than women. We are now attempting to fill in the gaps by studying women and focusing on the dynamics, symbolic and literal, between the two. This is without question important and necessary work. Nevertheless, the emphasis that has been put on this broad sexual dichotomy by Western researchers obscures a lot of the detail and richness of cultural belief systems and daily social interaction not based primarily on a recognition of sex and gender. Goodale (1980), for example, refers to this problem in her discussion of Kaulong gender. She points out that for the Kaulong, the important social distinction is between married person and unmarried person (of either sex), not between male and female.

Anthropologists generally agree that there has been a sexual division of labor in all known human societies. This does not mean that people in all cultures spend most of their time being aware of and relating to one another as women and men first and foremost, though this is generally true for adults in Western society. Yet frequently, in reading the ethnographic record, this is the impression we come away with.

A sex bias is difficult to rectify, for it requires that we fieldworkers must acknowledge ourselves as whole persons instead of primarily as women or as men, and we must be able to think in terms of unity as comfortably and easily as we now think in terms of dichotomies and polarities. Until this happens we cannot help but go into the field with a view of reality based predominantly on the distinction between male and female, literally and symbolically, and then impose that reality to some degree on those other cultures we choose to study.

I would now like to discuss these two biases, the gender bias and the sex bias, in the context of my own field research. I became aware of them in the process of preparing for and doing work among the Kafe and have reflected on them for several years since my return from Papua New Guinea.

In the spring of 1970 I took my Ph.D. qualifying exams at the University of Pennsylvania and together with my husband, a fellow graduate student in anthropology, began to make definite plans for fieldwork. We had agreed to do our respective dissertation research projects in the Highlands of Papua New Guinea, and my husband had already received approval of his grant application from the National Science Foundation. I wrote up my own grant proposal after the exams, it was also approved, and we left for the field in April 1971.

I was interested in the quality of female life, the social identities and roles available to women throughout a life cycle, and the nature of the relationships between men and women in cultures other than my own. I had decided to focus on this general area of research for my dissertation work by doing a study of female life among a Highlands group. There were both personal and professional reasons for this choice. At that point in my life, as I was juggling the roles of new wife and budding professional, I felt a great deal of confusion and ambivalence about my various goals and expectations. The roles available to women, especially vis-à-vis men, in my own culture felt limiting and frustrating. I both relished and feared the challenge of living in a social environment unlike my own familiar one, even though Papua New Guinea societies were allegedly even more "male-dominated" than American society. I hoped that my focus on women's lives and their relations with men in another culture might help to clarify some of my own thoughts and feelings about being female within my own cultural environment.

While reading the available ethnographic literature on the Papua New Guinea Highlands in writing my dissertation proposal, I noticed that there was frequent comment on the distinctive nature of the relations between Highlands men and women. Some ethnographers described the quality of intersexual relations as hostile and antagonistic, while others characterized them as complementary. Nevertheless, there was general agreement that women and men occupied quite different domains of daily and ritual life, that women had little or no power or authority in political, economic, or social affairs outside the household, and that the people themselves viewed women as inferior and subordinate to men. Even so, as I read the literature closely, I noticed many references to female participation in what were considered traditional male spheres. It was also evident that men and women developed a wide variety of interpersonal relationships and that women did not necessarily regard themselves, nor did men regard them, as weak and powerless, even though in some contexts they did perceive themselves as different from men in important ways.

Following the tradition of ethnographic fieldwork, most anthropologists working in the Highlands area collected the major portion of their data on sex roles and gender from men, supplemented by their own observations. Women were not frequently consulted about their perceptions and understandings of cultural belief and activity. I hoped to avoid the biases and imbalances that came from working primarily with male informants by associating closely and communicating directly with Kafe women as well as men.

From my preliminary research at the university I had formed a set of expectations about what I would find in the Highlands. These appeared to be societies in which women were separated from the rest of their group when they menstruated or gave birth, were betrothed to men chosen by others and sent away at very early ages, sometimes against their own desires, to marry and live with unfamiliar groups of people, and were physically abused when they transgressed social rules. They spent long hours in the gardens producing food for others, were excluded from important formal rituals and life-crisis ceremonies, and were considered inferior beings, dangerous and contaminating. However, when I arrived among the Kafe I met women who were proud and articulate, who did not express conflict or anxiety about their lot as a "subordinate" group, who went about their work with a determination of purpose to which I was unaccustomed among the women of my own subculture. They joked, bantered, sang and danced, fought, laughed and cried, and sat with a piece of work in their hands conversing with others about the affairs of the world around them.

At first, much to my surprise and in spite of my best intentions, I discovered that it was more comfortable for me to relate to the Kafe men than to the women. The men were more likely to speak Pidgin English, which I used for verbal communication before learning Kafe, and I experienced them as more enthusiastic about our presence in the village. They gave me mats to sit on to protect my clothing from the dirt, investigated my belongings and stroked my long hair, and asked questions about America and my family and friends. The men most often brought me special foods from the gardens— white potatoes, cabbages, green onions, and tomatoes, all grown as cash crops for the European market. They told me what my name was to be, what village I came from, who my Kafe "relatives" were. They also organized the building of our house, were dismayed when I refused to have a houseboy or a kerosene refrigerator, and gave me coffee trees to harvest and land to plant my first gardens.

The women mostly sat back during that early time. They laughed kindly but not helpfully at my first fumbling attempts to learn their language and to try my hand at weaving the net bags they made with such skill and proficiency. They seemed to regard me with distrust and skepticism, not believing that I could handle a digging stick, plant seeds, and make something grow; split and beat until flat the bamboo for the walls of our house; or wash clothes on rocks in a cold mountain stream. When I asked them questions they often laughed and avoided answering, or refused my offers of help, teasing me when I couldn't easily grasp what was going on.

A young woman sat down with me one day and in all seriousness seemed as if she were trying to help me learn the language. I was very grateful and practiced the long phrase she taught me until my pronunciation satisfied her. Then she told me to speak my newly learned sentence to a group of women sitting nearby. They burst into peals of laughter and thrust an infant into my lap. It turned out that I had been taught to say, "Give me your baby so that I may nurse it." Women do occasionally nurse another's baby, but only if the relationship is very close or the mother is ill. I was embarrassed and felt betrayed and manipulated. Soon after, as I was sitting with a group of women who were pestering me about whether I truly was a woman and whether I had female breasts, one of them finally insisted that I lift my blouse for them all to see the positive proof of my female sex. I felt I had no choice but to comply, and again I felt humiliated and coerced into behaving in ways uncomfortable for me.

I did respect these women, however. They were strong and self-sufficient, certainly not self-deprecating, but they also threatened me tremendously. I felt self-conscious and very guarded around them in a way that I did not feel around Kafe men. For the first few months I was physically unwell and extremely frustrated and worried about my work. I felt that I should somehow clearly identify and ally myself with these Kafe women, given what I intended to study, but I was also reluctant to seek them out as much as I felt I should, not knowing quite how to deal with the ambivalence I felt toward them.

This ambivalence really puzzled me. In many respects my fieldwork situation was ideal. I was there with a man who very much wanted to be there himself, as an anthropologist doing his own research and as my husband sharing the field experience. We usually work well together as anthropologists, participating in and observing an event or a happening in the field from two different perspectives and then comparing notes, filling in the gaps, and ending with more information than we might obtain if we were alone. We also felt we had a solution to the potential problem of data limitation resulting from sex and gender issues: we could collect information for one another if informants were more comfortable with my husband as a man or with me as a woman in discussing certain topics.

The Kafe had, of their own volition, set us up in a situation ideal for learning the culture from the inside out—they adopted us immediately. From our second night in the field we had Kafe names, relatives, and a whole genealogical history. My husband was Vihafa, a man of Homaya village where we lived, son of Yuo and Bobore'no, a prominent household in one of the three major houselines of the village. I was Ayalunta, from Bafo village down the valley, with my own set of parents and other kin. Following the Kafe tradition I had married a man of a clan not my own and moved to his father's village to live in patrilocal fashion. I had several Bafo sisters who had also

married Homaya men, and they were particularly helpful in socializing me into the village. The ties between Homaya and Bafo were
close. Their lands were also adjacent geographically, so I was given
gardening rights to land from my own consanguineal relatives, as
well as to land belonging to my husband's lineage, as is the typical
practice.

From the very beginning we entered into this fictitious reality with
our Kafe neighbors, where we all addressed each other and attempted to interact together as if these kinship ties were true. At the
same time, of course, all of us also acknowledged and dealt with the
reality of two outsiders, white Westerners, living in an indigenous
Highlands village—the first time for us and for the Kafe with whom
we settled. The trick for me, and I am sure for everyone else as well,
was to somehow find a comfortable balance between these two realities and the different identities inherent in each of the two contexts.
There were continual opportunities to discover that balance.

Early one day, for example, my husband and I attended a large
village gathering where food was cooked jointly by several households in a large earth oven. This kind of communal feasting occurred
frequently, at least a couple of times a week throughout our entire
stay, and was catalyzed by a variety of circumstances, from visiting
relatives to life-cycle events (first menstruations, marriages, funerary
distributions) to the harvesting of a particularly productive garden
or the killing of a pig that had intruded into a neighbor's fields. They
were a time when informal public discussion could take place, when
stories and gossip were passed on, minor conflicts resolved, and
when people providing food and other resources could enhance
their personal prestige through acts of hospitality and generosity.

This was one of the first such events we attended. When, after the
meal, it began to rain, people gathered inside the large house of the
host and hostess. My husband went in and I started to follow, but
our host politely and firmly escorted me to a second door and told
me to enter his house that way. I did so, and this precipitated a lively
discussion about Kafe houseplans and the social rules regarding the
use of doors and physical space within the house—usually large,
round, one-room bamboo-and-thatch structures. It was explained
that my husband could enter the house by either door, but I, as his
wife, had to use the door that led to the half of the house occupied
by our hostess. Ethnographically this was an extremely valuable discussion for my research. However, I found myself inwardly feeling
resentment that women were restricted in that fashion; I was more
comfortable being Lisa than Ayalunta at that moment, for Lisa was
not part of the reality that limited women in this particular way.

Another memory is of a day when a group of Homaya villagers, including me and my husband, walked down the valley three or four miles to a market that was supposedly going on in another settlement. One woman had a large stack of firewood that she was carrying to deliver down the road, and she gave some to me, showing me how to carry the wood and the net bag I had with me in correct Kafe female fashion. Everyone enjoyed the spectacle and was very complimentary about how well I managed to juggle the load. After a while a man offered to take the wood from me. In this case, however, I really enjoyed playing the role of Ayalunta, acting as the Kafe women do, and knew that his offer came from recognizing me in my other role as Lisa. I refused the offer, gaining even more approval from the group.

This sort of thing happened many times as we learned to interact with the Homaya villagers in their reality. I realized that I was manipulating my roles so that I could be Ayalunta when it felt advantageous or comfortable and not Ayalunta when it didn't; but I also knew that the other Kafe women didn't have the same choice. I believe that the ambivalence I felt toward them initially stemmed largely from not wanting to be perceived as "one of them" continuously and thus losing my flexibility in having the best of both worlds. It wasn't until I had begun to know both men and women as individuals and formed friendships with some, felt less compatible with others, that I also began to feel more comfortable with the women in general, seeking them out because I wanted to be with them. With the passage of time and some sense of knowing me better, they also began to open up more, sharing their world and specifically including me in their activities.

That first day we arrived in Homaya, people were still clearing their belongings out of a small house in which we were to live until our own house was built. I remember one woman clearly amid all the excitement of that day and the scores of people hovering about, pointing, jostling, investigating us and our possessions. She was busily removing the last of her things from the house, a small, lean, rather wrinkled woman with a hard and determined expression on her face and an abrasive voice. I found her quite intimidating, so tough and aloof, and I thought to myself that she was certainly not among my potential new friends in the village. In her presence I felt acutely and painfully aware of myself as an intruder, and the role of scientist and researcher with which I had identified seemed self-righteous and uncaring.

I knew that part of the generous hospitality we were receiving was because in some way we represented for some of the Kafe a potential pathway to understanding and participating in a different world. The Western industrialized world, interfacing with the traditional Highlands cultures for only fifty years, had been introduced to the Kafe through the often arrogant and paternalistic attitudes of foreign planters and entrepreneurs, government personnel, and missionaries. Along with the denigration of indigenous cultures and belief systems came a world of material wealth and power, of mobility and adventure. My husband and I were a part of that world, and the people around us, as well as genuinely welcoming us into their lives, also attempted to befriend and impress and gain favor.

The woman who had left such an impression on me that first day turned out to be my given mother-in-law, and she eventually became one of my closest real friends in Homaya. We began to know each other when she arrived one morning to attempt a Kafe cure for my lingering ill health during the first few months of fieldwork. She offered her help, and shortly thereafter, as she prepared a new garden, I offered mine. Gradually we formed a relationship based not only on our fictive kinship ties but also on mutual respect and affection. She taught me a tremendous amount about the Kafe world and the roles of women in that world, through conversation but more so by allowing and encouraging me to accompany her as she went about her life. When I left nearly two years later, we cried together and I was truly saddened at leaving her. She was one of the few people who evoked such an emotional response from me, though there are many other Kafe for whom I feel deep affection. Perhaps it was because I believed so strongly when I first saw her that a bridge of understanding and communication between us would never be possible. Being around her strength and vitality and her sense of herself as a person gave me a sense of myself that had not been there before but has remained as her gift to me.

I see now that my initial response to these people came in part from my own ethnocentric attitudes about males and females. I related more easily to the men at first because they seemed to behave in ways more familiar to me. Many of them were protective, flattering, treating me somewhat like another man, somewhat like a child, and somewhat like a curious creature. The women, however, were not familiar. They did not seek the attention I received, they were not particularly interested in my life or background, they did not attempt to form alliances with or against me. They maintained and enhanced their own self-respect and self-worth without relying primarily on men for approval. They eventually taught me a great deal about interdependence (in contrast to dependence/independence) and about developing a self-identity as a person (see Faithorn 1977).

I would not say that the Kafe themselves consider their primary identity as that of person, although it is recognized and definitely comes into play in certain social contexts. For the Kafe the primary social idiom is kinship. The first thing to be aware of, in most social contexts, for both Kafe men and women is, "How am I related to this person or these people?" This almost always determines appropriate behavior, obligations, and expectations and is more complex than it first appears. People are frequently related in more than one way, with both ties through father and mother being reckoned, and they may also chose to recognize a consanguineal relationship in one set of circumstances and an affinal one in another. Kinship ties are continually being manipulated to maximize the individual's access to natural and human-produced resources. The important thing about Kafe kinship, with regard to a discussion of gender and fieldwork, is that kinship considerations in almost all circumstances far outweigh gender and sex considerations.

I had initially, from my own experience and from discussions described earlier, assumed that women always entered a Kafe house through the door leading to the wife's area, while men could enter through that door or the one leading to an area reserved exclusively for male use. However, when I visited my Bafo relatives, who were my own consanguines, I was informed that I could enter any Bafo house through either door because I was a daughter and a sister in this village. On returning to Homaya I observed adult daughters and sisters of Homaya walking through both doors to enter village houses. In discussion on these points I was then told that women who are consanguineally related to the man of the house may enter however they wish, and further, they are not restricted to certain areas in the house; but women in the wife category—meaning wives, possible wives, or female relatives—are restricted in their use of door and house. This distinction not only operated with respect to houses but also to a variety of other social contexts. As a result I had to watch my behavior very carefully in Homaya as an inmarrying woman, whereas when I went to Bafo I felt comparatively free and easy.

This situation became more complicated, however, when I one day watched a Homaya woman in the wife category blithely go through the "male" door of her husband's age-mate's house without causing any comment at all. When I questioned the man in whose house this had occurred, he explained that although this woman was married to a Homaya man she was actually his "small mother" through an intricate pattern of kinship ties. In view of this, she was free to use his house without restrictions and could herself choose which role she wanted to honor in her interactions with him.

Another case in point has to do with the concept of pollution among the Kafe. I have written on this elsewhere (Faithorn 1975), discussing Kafe beliefs about contexts in which individuals may be of danger to themselves or others through exposure to contaminating substances (such as menstrual blood, the blood lost in childbirth, semen) and pointing out that males as well as females are potential polluters. I was quite surpirsed when I stumbled on the belief that men can pollute, for it had not occurred to me to ask that question directly. Based on everything I had read and heard about Highlands cultures, I had assumed that pollution was only associated with female sexuality and was expressed among the Kafe, as elsewhere, in terms of women potentially threatening the health and vitality of men.

One very rainy day I went to visit at the house of a female acquaintance in Homaya. She and her husband and several other villagers were sitting around the fire. After I gave them some food I had brought as a gift, in the net bag that I, like most Kafe, carried everywhere, I put my bag on the ground with the intention of sitting on it, as the dirt floor was damp and cold. Before I could sit down, however, the bag was snatched out from under me with great exclamation by those in the group. They told me that if I had sat on the bag I could no longer use it to carry food for my husband or for any of the other Homaya residents. I asked them if I would have to throw the bag away in that case and was told that I could give it to my brother or my parents or any of my other consanguineal relatives, as it would pose no danger to them. In the same manner, if my brother sat on his bag he could pass it on to me but could not use it to carry food to his wife or other affines. The discussion went on from there and was the key to my understanding that from the Kafe perspective, substances rather than people are dangerous in certain contexts. The substances emanate from people's bodies and may endanger others, male and female, if not properly controlled.

During those twenty months with the Kafe I began to recognize how unconsciously I made assumptions about behavior on the basis of sex distinctions and how easily that could lead to a misunderstanding of the true social dynamics operating among these people. As this sex bias became more and more obvious, I had to do some serious thinking about fieldwork and objectivity, and I despaired of actually perceiving the Kafe truly as they perceive themselves. At the same time I became really excited about the possibility of eliminating the sex bias within myself and learning a new primary identity, that of person rather than woman. Needless to say, such an identity shift does not occur easily or quickly. It seems to be more a process of peeling off one layer of cultural conditioning after an-

other, and it has led me, inwardly and outwardly, to some very unexpected places. I have no doubt that many other unrecognized
cultural biases remain that obscure accurate perception of cross-
cultural reality, but I do believe that this sex bias is one that can and
should be consciously acknowledged and hopefully eliminated by
people doing research in other cultures.

Fieldwork is a time when one truly has the opportunity and the
responsibility to become self-aware. Participant observers are constantly confronted with their own limiting belief systems and learn
how to perceive reality in other ways, possibly incorporating some
of these new ways into an expanding version of their own. It can be
a training ground through intense experience for living in any environment with detachment, compassion, and a sense of interconnect-
edness with others. Yet it is difficult; there is a resistance and a
constant pull toward separateness. Aspects of one's identity must be
shed as various cultural biases are given up. To give up the sex bias,
however, does not mean giving up male and female identities but
rather seeing those identities as contextual. In some contexts it is
appropriate to identify with that aspect of the self primarily, in other
contexts some other aspect or combination of aspects is appropriate.

The gender bias and the sex bias in cross-cultural research have
both come out of a larger social context; that is, prevailing Western
cultural attitudes and values. The gender bias collectively began to
be recognized in the 1970s. It is now time for us also to recognize
the sex bias, and within our own society to learn how to perceive
and interact with one another more easily as people.

References

Collier, Jane Fishburne
  1974 "Women in Politics." In: Michelle Zimbalist Rosaldo and Louise
        Lamphere (eds.), *Women, Culture and Society*, pp. 89–96. Stan-
        ford, Calif.: Stanford University Press.
Faithorn, Elizabeth
  1975 "The Concept of Pollution among the Kafe of the New Guinea
        Highlands." In: Rayna Reiter (ed.), *Toward an Anthropology of
        Women*, pp. 127–40. New York: Monthly Review Press.
  1977 "Women as Persons: Aspects of Female Life and Male-Female Re-
        lations among the Kafe." In: Paula Brown Glick and Georgeda
        Buchbinder (eds.), *Sex Roles in the New Guinea Highlands*, pp.
        86–95. Cambridge, Mass.: Harvard University Press.
Friedl, Ernestine
  1975 *Women and Men: An Anthropologist's View.* New York: Holt, Rine-
        hart and Winston.

Goodale, Jane
   1980   "Gender, Sexuality and Marriage: A Kaulong Model of Nature and Culture." In: Carol MacCormack and Marilyn Strathern (eds.), *Nature, Culture and Gender*, pp. 119–42. Cambridge: Cambridge University Press.

Hammond, Dorothy, and Alta Jablow
   1976   *Women in Cultures of the World*. Menlo Park, Calif.: Cummings Publishing Co.

MacCormack, Carol, and Marilyn Strathern (eds.)
   1980   *Nature, Culture and Gender*. Cambridge: Cambridge University Press.

Martin, M. Kay, and Barbara Voorhies
   1975   *Female of the Species*. New York: Columbia University Press.

Mead, Margaret
   1935   *Sex and Temperament in Three Primitive Societies*. New York: William Morrow.

Oakley, Ann
   1972   *Sex, Gender and Society*. New York: Harper and Row.

Reiter, Rayna (ed.)
   1975   *Toward an Anthropology of Women*. New York: Monthly Review Press.

Rogers, Susan Carol
   1975   "Female Forms of Power and the Myth of Male Dominance: A Model of Female/Male Interaction in Peasant Society." In: *Sex Roles in Cross-Cultural Perspective*. Special issue of *American Ethnologist* 2: 727–56.

Rosaldo, Michelle Zimbalist, and Louise Lamphere (eds.)
   1974   *Women, Culture and Society*. Stanford, Calif.: Stanford University Press.

Sanday, Peggy R.
   1974   "Female Status in the Public Domain." In: Michelle Zimbalist Rosaldo and Louise Lamphere (eds.) *Women, Culture and Society*, pp. 189–206. Stanford, Calif.: Stanford University Press.

Summary: Sex and the Fieldwork Experience

TONY LARRY WHITEHEAD and LAURIE PRICE

In the introductory essay, the editors identify several views from earlier works which argue that certain differences in fieldwork experiences are sex-specific: (1) Female fieldworkers undergo greater
pressure to conform to local gender ascriptions than do male fieldworkers. (2) Female fieldworkers are allowed greater freedom in
crossing local sex and gender boundaries than are male fieldworkers. (3) Female fieldworkers are under greater pressure to have sexual relations than are male fieldworkers. (4) Female fieldworkers are
more sensitive to the field situation than male fieldworkers, and are
therefore more likely to attempt to understand the systemic relationship between the fieldwork process and the fieldworker's sense of
self. (5) Sharing the field site with a spouse, children, or colleague
can be prohibitive to the fieldwork process and to the type of introspection necessary for the growth of self and objectivity.

The editors also state that these views are debatable, in part because they have been formulated primarily on the basis of the experiences of female fieldworkers. Valid consideration of these issues
obviously requires comment from writers of both sexes. A fuller discussion of possible associations between the sex of the fieldworker
and the fieldworker's experiences is also desirable because of the
potential contribution to more effective training of cross-cultural
fieldworkers. Although contributors to this volume do not specifically address the five issues cited, in this concluding essay we will
present our interpretation of how their discussions relate to these
views in order to facilitate further thinking and possible debate on
the influence of sex and gender on cross-cultural fieldwork. We have
corresponded with some of the contributors to clarify and confirm
certain interpretations, and their comments are included in the following discussion.

Issues 1 and 2

The reason we decided to discuss these two issues as one is because they are contradictory. Contributors of both sexes state or im-

ply that they were under pressure to conform to local gender ascriptions and felt a lack of freedom in crossing local sex and gender boundaries (see, e.g., Giovannini and Krieger, among the female contributors, and Angrosino, Whitehead, and Lobban, among the male contributors). The adoption of gender-related restrictions or gender-related freedoms, as depicted in all of the accounts, seems to have resulted from voluntary decisions by fieldworkers based on their perceptions of host community expectations. In time, fieldworkers often find, as did Giovannini and Krieger, that absolute conformity to local gender ascriptions is not expected—that as outsiders, fieldworkers are often accorded more behavioral freedom than community members.

Conformity to local gender ascriptions may be a strategy followed by the fieldworker to gain both acceptance in the field community and a fuller appreciation of the sociocultural dynamics of the field culture. This strategy is implied by Turnbull and by Fluehr-Lobban and Lobban and is explicitly framed in personal correspondence from these authors. For example, Lobban states:

> The industrious active style of work demanded by a successful career in anthropology while state-side had to be suspended and replaced by a more passive, more adaptable style in the field. I wanted to be guided in the field, not be a leader or innovator; such were the realities of my experience with the anthropological method of participant observation. When in the field one becomes a "student" in the fullest sense of the word, passive, humble, insecure, and at the same time, receptive to learning new values, ideas and the outlook of a different culture.

The advantages of conformity to gender ascriptions as a fieldwork strategy are variable, depending on the characteristics of the field culture. While Turnbull and Fluehr-Lobban and Lobban found it useful to conform to gender role expectations of the host populations, both Giovannini and Krieger found such conformity to be a net disadvantage. The latter often seems to be the case with fieldwork in societies that are highly sex-segregated—by adopting local gender ascriptions a fieldworker cuts himself or herself off from interactions with one-half of the host population. The drawbacks of such conformity can be partially mitigated by a mixed-gender team approach to fieldwork; thus, Lobban's positive attitude toward gender role conformity may be partially attributable to the fact that his wife was doing fieldwork concurrently and provided him with information about female activities. But Oboler, who had similar data collection assistance from her spouse, argues that even with such support the wholehearted adoption of local gender roles that entail sexual segregation for a fieldworker acts as a barrier to comprehensive understanding of local social relationships. Whereas conforming to local ascriptions may on occasion increase the informant's ease of interaction with the fieldworker, on other occasions it may act as a barrier to learning about deviations from and dissatisfactions with prevailing social norms. Deviations and dissatisfactions occur frequently in societies undergoing change but may go undetected by fieldworkers who ascribe uncritically to gender roles that often reflect only the study community's "front self" (Goffman 1959). If Davis had subscribed totally to the Newfoundlanders' front self, which presented a norm of premarital sexual chastity, she might never have gotten to know the back self, which regards premarital sex as normal. Krieger makes a similar point regarding norm transgressions in Egypt.

Whitehead's essay suggests that some societies also allow members more room for deviation from traditional norms than might be readily perceived by the fieldworker. The notion of "balance" in reference to masculine behavior in Haversham (Jamaica) implies that a man may exhibit contrasting behavioral traits as long as he knows the limits for each kind of behavior. The overexpression of one kind of behavior is associated with the underexpression of another kind, and a man exhibiting such imbalance is considered weak. The notion of balance means that fieldworkers in Jamaica can carry behavioral conformity to a particular set of traits too far, and thus damage their standing in the community.

Krieger suggests that similar dynamics were at work in her Egyptian field community. While there were certain norms for correct gender behavior, following them with excessive zeal was worse than not recognizing them at all. Scaglion extends the discussion to his fieldwork among the Abelam:

> Males of importance are expected to be "generous" and "flexible" [that is, to agree to things and let minor slights pass], but at the same time be decisive and forceful to maintain status. This apparent paradox is maintained by careful balance: too much of either behavior is bad (as is too little). I tended to be somewhat on the "passive" side at first so as not to offend anyone, but gradually increased "forcefulness" as time went on. By American standards, Abelam are rather passive anyway, as am I, so again, not much behavior modification was necessary for me personally.

Davis wrote us about a similar experience in her Newfoundland fieldwork with regard to her having a boyfriend there. Outwardly, premarital chastity was presented as the norm, and she felt that as a role model for other single women in the community she should show exemplary behavior. Thus, she tried to avoid any behavior that might suggest she had a sexual relationship with a man living nearby. However, after a snowstorm forced her to spend the night at her friend's trailer, she discovered that premarital sex was, in actuality, considered the norm. She eventually learned that women accepted the fact that their daughters, like themselves, "can't fight their natural urges." Davis also found that she was more acceptable for "discretely giving in than holding out (or pretending to)." Once people believed she had a boyfriend, they regarded her as "just like the rest of us."

Lobban discerned no such contrasting themes among the men in his Islamic Sudanese field community. He says that the sharp clarity of male role expectations, which included such values as pride, dignity, reserve, austerity, simplicity, humility, and sharing, was comfortable for him because they were values he had long appreciated personally. Fluehr-Lobban wrote us that even though she was allowed greater gender role freedom than local women in terms of her professional associations with men, she still felt the need to conform to many rather rigid aspects of Sudanese female behavior, such as:

1. Lowering my eyes when being introduced to a strange male;
2. Female use of the language (less formal expression, higher pitch to the voice), and appropriate female hand gesturing to accompany speech;
3. In public, waiting to be introduced before introducing myself; generally hesitating, indecisive behavior which is not ordinarily my style;
4. Staying within the security of the female group and relating to males through the females attached to them as relatives, friends, and employees.

It was through such behavioral patterns that Fluehr-Lobban says she began to "see, understand and therefore investigate more deeply the solidarity of women in groups in Afro-Islamic Society." Her comments suggest that varying mixtures of conformity and freedom are ideal in different locales. In her particular fieldwork site, Fluehr-Lobban had the freedom to interact with males but was under pressure to conform to local male-female interaction norms while doing so.

In our opinion, the most appropriate conclusion to reach on this issue is that the degree of pressure to conform to local gender ascriptions is influenced by the sex of the fieldworker in some locales. But while pressure may be greater on males in some field cultures, it is greater on females in others. More importantly, we emphasize that factors other than sex also affect gender role freedom, such as the length of time the fieldworker stays in a setting, the field methods used, and a host of personal and personality characteristics of the fieldworker, including age, marital status, and gender orientation. Gonzalez expresses this same view: "What is possible, acceptable or proper in any given case depends upon a careful balancing of the nature of the anthropological goals, the willingness of our hosts to reveal their thoughts, their actions, and their culture to outsiders, our skills in overcoming their hesitations and finally our own needs and limitations which in turn are influenced by our age, gender, ethnicity, and individual psychological makeup." Scaglion reiterates this point when he states that adoption of a particular gender strategy in the field depends on the specific field setting, the fieldworker's personality, and the particular research being conducted. He found that conformity to Abelam gender role expectations presented him with few problems of field adjustment and data collection. And he adds that if his own gender orientation had been considerably different from that of the Abelam men, it probably would have been misinterpreted; but if the field setting had been different, he might have adopted a different field strategy to match.

Contributors to this volume demonstrate consensus that there is a complex set of factors affecting behavioral patterns adopted by fieldworkers. Personal correspondence indicates that most feel this issue is better conceptualized not in terms of conformity versus freedom of male or female fieldworkers, but rather in terms of the ability of fieldworkers to follow the community's lead about what is most appropriate and effective given fieldwork goals in the community. In achieving the most successful adaptation, one's sex is not as important as one's *gender role flexibility*. Comments to this effect address the following concerns: (1) flexibility in adapting to a variety of different gender role behaviors (Fluehr-Lobban, Gonzalez, Angrosino); (2) flexibility in adopting a somewhat neutral professional stranger role when necessary (Jackson, Fluehr-Lobban, Faithorn); (3) flexibility modeled after local patterns of manipulating roles and impressions (Krieger, Davis); and (4) flexibility in creating new roles (Jackson).

Fluehr-Lobban uses the same analogy as does Turnbull when she argues that "flexibility is the key and frequently the anthropologist can be aptly compared to an actor adopting different roles for specific situations." She notes that a fieldworker frequently may be called on to interact competently with a government minister and a peasant farmer within the same few hours. Although Turnbull and Lobban testify to the importance of conforming to local gender ascriptions in fieldwork, there is flexibility built into even their approach. Both suggest that sexual role changes *planned* by the fieldworker are self-defeating if pressed too far because such planning indicates that the fieldworker is attempting to be the mover rather than being moved by the host culture in its natural ebb and flow. On balance, they too advocate flexibility in fieldworker responses to the lead of the host community.

Issue 3

The essays in this volume do not warrant the conclusion that female fieldworkers are under more pressure than male fieldworkers to engage in sexual relations; neither do they warrant the opposite conclusion. It is interesting that only one female contributor (Conaway) discusses such issues, while a number of male contributors give these issues a prominent place in their papers. As addressed by male contributors, issues of sexuality in fieldwork include: (1) being considered lesser men by members of the field community because of celibate status (Angrosino, Whitehead); (2) how to handle the situation of being offered women in the field (Angrosino, Whitehead, Turnbull); and (3) how to be nonthreatening sexually (Angrosino, Johnson, Scaglion). The imbalance in treating sexuality issues in this volume does not necessarily mean that these difficulties are more prevalent for male than for female fieldworkers, however. None of the contributors was asked specifically to focus on this topic, and cultural mores may make it more difficult for female contributors to address these issues in a personal way.[1]

It is striking, and also intriguing, that little attention has been given to sexuality issues in most reflections on fieldwork. We assume that others who have done cross-cultural fieldwork are aware of numerous cases in which fieldworkers suffered personal or professional problems as a result of either overt sexually related experiences or misinterpretation of certain behaviors as sexually related.[2] Yet such experiences are very rarely shared professionally with individuals preparing for their first fieldwork experience. In anthropology, at least, this lack of public discussion of field sexuality seems to proceed from a taboo.[3] In reality there is a double taboo at work—sanctions against discussing sexuality publicly, particularly for women, and the sanctions mentioned in the introductory essay against public acknowledgment of factors that might undermine "objectivity" in fieldwork.

Issue 4

Rohrlich-Leavitt, Sykes, and Weatherford (1973) borrow Du Bois's (1939) concept of "double consciousness" to support their position that women are more in touch with the gender self during the field-work process. Where Du Bois notes that blacks in the United States had to develop a double consciousness—of a black and white world—Rohrlich-Leavitt and her collaborators argue that Western females have developed a similar kind of double consciousness as a result of also occupying traditionally subordinate status, and that this double consciousness is expanded during fieldwork (1973: 567). Cesara (1982) strongly supports this position. Some readers may conclude that more female contributors to this volume exhibit this type of sensitivity because they focus less on issues of sexuality and more on broad issues of gender self, such as: (1) the contribution of the field experience to the realization that aspects of the prefield gender self led to the selection of the study culture (Jackson); (2) understanding one's own prefield gender biases regarding the field culture (Jackson, Faithorn, Davis); (3) understanding how not only self but also one's gender and professional socialization result in gender biases and misconceptions about the topic to be studied (Davis); (4) the realization that the genderless fieldworker is no more possible than the depersonalized fieldwork (Davis, Conaway); (5) the struggle to merge the field self with the home self (Gonzalez); and (6) insights that broaden one's ability to interpret male-female relationships and marriage in one's home culture (Jackson).

The male contributors who address sexuality by no means focus *only* on such issues. Their essays also speak to broader issues of gender self. For example, Johnson's reflection concerning male-female relationships in a Midwestern school system shows his active concern about being nonthreatening, both sexually and in broader gender/political terms, as perceived by the female teachers in his field community. Scaglion, who went to New Guinea intending to study conflict resolution, is now publishing papers on reproduction and gender relationships, a change that was stimulated by his reflection on the way social segregation affected his data collection procedures and his personal interactions with Abelam men and women. Turnbull came to better comprehend gender among the Mbuti through reflections on his personal experience of being carried through several age categories in which gender expectations differed. Whitehead's comprehension of the concept of social balance emerged as a consequence of continual reflection on the anguish he suffered due to his observations of and experiences with Jamaican males in a wide variety of contexts.

We are not suggesting that either male or female fieldworkers are on the whole more sensitive to gender issues in the field. Rather, our major aim is to point out that many other factors besides sex influence sensitivity to the field culture. Other crucial factors include fieldworker personality, training, prefield biases of various types, gender role orientation, and other ideological orientations.

Cesara (1982) argues that female fieldworkers have greater gender role flexibility and field sensitivity than their male counterparts, and that they are therefore less subject to bias than male fieldworkers. She supports this view by referring to the fieldwork experience she and her husband shared. Specifically, she says that her husband tended to interact only with host culture males while she "balanced her time between both sexes." She asserts that her husband consequently saw the universe of the field culture only through the bias of two kinds of men—the men of the field culture and American men. She, on the other hand, saw the host culture universe through the eyes of both field culture males and females, as well as through her own—"a woman of culturally mixed upbringing and culturally mixed gender" (1982:15).

Cesara suggests that since much of the anthropological literature has been written by men, or by women with a "male" orientation, this literature is filled with male bias. Her argument is one that was put forth earlier by Mead (1970), who suggested that both male and female anthropologists have in the past tended to view female activities as relatively insignificant in the larger cultural picture. Thus, male fieldworkers often regarded the crossing of local gender boundaries as unimportant even if opportunities were offered to do so by the field community. Scheper-Hughes (1983) echoes this point when she argues that an androcentric bias pervades anthropological fieldwork research and has led to preference for male over female informants, disproportionately greater attention to "male domains," and misperception of female values and activities, even by female fieldworkers.

The exposé by feminist anthropologists of male bias in cross-cultural fieldwork should be considered an advance in the discipline of anthropology in its quest to achieve greater levels of objectivity. However, Scheper-Hughes (1983) also cites a point made by Susan Carol Rogers during a 1982 AAA symposium discussion on "Confronting Problems of Bias in Feminist Fieldwork": that feminism itself can be another source of bias. Essays in this volume by Faithorn and Jackson address the problem of male bias and the bias they discovered in their own feminist orientations. These authors, as well as Davis, support the notion that gender-related field bias is not sex-specific: females as well as males may carry such biases.

We want to reiterate here our position that many types of bias influence fieldwork perspectives—some based on gender, others on characteristics such as ethnicity, age, class, and political ideology. Biases form part of the fieldworker's sense of self, which has been shaped by the communities in which she or he has interacted in significant ways. Recognition, acceptance, and working through these biases are critically important processes for everyone who wants to do successful and valid fieldwork.

Issue 5

When Whitehead was a Peace Corps volunteer, he envied married volunteers because he viewed them as enjoying the advantages of a mate who could provide emotional and sexual support during difficult periods of adjustment to a foreign culture. However, in subsequent discussions with Peace Corps personnel, he often heard the opinion that Peace Corps experiences led to the breakup of many marriages. In not a few cases, personality differences and varying abilities to cope with the demands of fieldwork created great tension between couples; in addition, these couples were forced to cooperate more closely and spend more time together than couples normally do in the United States. Physically and culturally unfamiliar and often arduous conditions added to the strain on the relationships.

Anthropologists have cited both the advantages and disadvantages of being accompanied in the field, particularly by a spouse and/or children. These fall into three general categories: (1) support in responding to physical difficulties; (2) emotional support; and (3) enrichment of the research experience. Golde (1970:778) argues that the advantages of doing fieldwork alone are few; she suggests that research is enriched and that the individual fieldworker's psychological health is enhanced by sharing the field site with another person undergoing parallel experiences. Fluehr-Lobban and Lobban, who pursued different research interests in the Sudan, found that the participation of each spouse in his/her own local sex group proved very valuable to the other's research. They were able to gain a more complete picture of the sexually segregated community in which they worked by communicating with each other in the evenings about their daily experiences. They also commented that working together as a team contributed to their psychological well-being, because they could share experiences on an emotional as well as an intellectual level. Although Oboler suffered some early difficulties in her fieldwork due to the host culture's reaction to the presence of her husband, as time went on she found that the relationship with her husband was strengthened by their shared experience. This happened in part because her husband took an active role in the data collection process, but also because he underwent a process of (gender) self-discovery facilitated by experiencing cultural differences in how the Nandi of Kenya viewed him as a man.

Those who argue against being accompanied in the field cite the extra responsibility. Fieldworkers in such situations must monitor their family's health and safety as well as their own, and the field situation may be particularly hazardous for young children because of adverse health conditions and the absence of adequate medical care.[4] Anthropologists are in consensus that the fieldwork process, especially the early stages, generates much emotional stress and anxiety, and the obligation to give emotional support to others may be a serious additional burden (Firth 1972:15). This seems to be particularly true for anthropologists who are accompanied to the field by nonanthropologist spouses. Often, that spouse may not have the same commitment, interest, or "objective" orientation in the field setting as the trained anthropologist.

This particular issue was the focus of a debate in the letters to the editor section of the *Anthropology Newsletter* (vol. 18) from March to November 1977. Morris Simon, writing from Singapore, outlined in a humorous way some of the problems he encountered as a professional but nonanthropologist spouse of an anthropologist. He referred to the hardship of sacrificing his own professional activities to accompany his wife on her visits to undesirable locations. His involvement in these field forays seemed necessary because when he did not get involved, members of the field community inquired about why he was not there to protect her and why he gave her permission to make such trips alone. Simon described the discomfort of such visits due to his distaste for some of the cultural practices in the field culture, such as betel nut chewing, which his wife gladly participated in.

In separate letters, Janice Hogle and Carol C. Mukapadhyay roundly criticized Simon, noting especially that female nonanthropologist spouses have traditionally accompanied their anthropologist husbands to the field without much attention to their special problems. In response to Hogle, Veronica Friel-Simon argued that her husband's letter had been misinterpreted and in fact reflected a sense of humor that was one of the ways he provided her with valuable emotional support during stressful periods of fieldwork. Hattula Moholy-Magy and Mary Ellen Conaway both pointed out that the dialogue generated by Simon's letter represented valuable exploration of an important fieldwork issue that had been receiving little attention. Conaway called for further work to explore the topic and began to conceptualize this volume in response to her own request.

Powdermaker (1966) has stated that although there are emotional advantages to having others accompany you to the field, being alone gives greater intensity to the field experience. It "frequently provides more intimate data because the fieldworker is thrown upon the natives for companionship . . . whereas a family or team may make relationships with the natives more difficult. One member may be quickly accepted and the other disliked. It is usually easier for people to relate to one stranger than to several" (1966:114). Cesara (1982:21) expresses a similar view in suggesting that fieldwork is an important period of mental growth and change, and that one needs to be alone during these periods. She feels that female and male experiences in fieldwork will be and should be distinctly different due to different gender socialization in Western culture and its effects on how men and women react to fieldwork phenomena (1982:15–23). For this reason she argues that women should not be accompanied to the field by a man, particularly a husband: "There are simply times in the lives of men and women when marriage is inappropriate. It suffocates the flow of creative thought and personal growth, something that is understood by every living and dead creative mind" (1982:21). She states that Western male fieldworkers are more prone to sex bias than their female counterparts because males are more likely to restrict their observations in the host culture to male activities, while females are more likely to observe both male and female activities. And because of this tendency toward sex bias on the part of males, and the tendency of Western males to be dominating and possessive in their marriage relationships, Cesara feels that the presence of a husband can negatively influence the female anthropologist's interactions with and interpretations of the field culture.

Davis suggested to us that a young single female fieldworker can achieve access to information that she could not get otherwise because of the tendency of people in many cultures to want to adopt young single females. Because of her age and marital status, she frequently received advice that turned out to be very important data regarding gender-related values and beliefs. The Newfoundland women she worked among saw themselves as "examples of womanhood par excellence—a role made for me to emulate. If I had been married or had had a co-worker, I probably would not have been adopted by so many women."

Others argue that youth and single status can result in more limited access to older members of the host population and to members of the opposite sex, particularly in societies that are highly segregated by age and sex. A number of the contributors to this volume, either in their essays or through personal correspondence, suggest that in most societies being married or having children is considered the natural state for adults. Thus, the unmarried fieldworker may be considered a child, making it difficult for that individual to gain access to various social actors. According to Scaglion, being a single adult among the Abelam was less advantageous than it was for Davis in Newfoundland. In Abelam society men are usually not taken very seriously until they are in their early thirties, married and with children, and have begun to amass wealth. Although he was married and had one child, his wife and baby did not accompany him to the field, and as a result the polygamous Abelam viewed him as single. His single status, coupled with his relative youth, made it difficult to collect certain kinds of data concerning "serious" male behavior such as yam-growing activities.

The presence of children in the field may give a married couple legitimacy, and the anxieties that often accrue from questions about not having children are thereby avoided. Oboler found her status in the host community improved after she became pregnant and moved from "probably infertile" to "childbearing" woman. In some cultural contexts, even single men of a certain age might be questioned about not having children, as Whitehead was in Jamaica.

Those contributors who have taken children to the field wrote us regarding the various problems such a decision entails, including: numerous health and safety matters (Fluehr-Lobban and Lobban); disruptions in fieldwork due to worry about the child and/or guilt about negative events that may arise (Oboler); anxiety about finding caretakers for the child while the parents are doing fieldwork (Gonzalez, Oboler); concern about schooling arrangements (Oboler); and coming to terms with the effects that culture shock may have on youngsters (Fluehr-Lobban).

Anthropologists have developed strategies to minimize the incidence of such problems, such as thorough medical preparation (vaccinations and first-aid kits), careful selection of field sites (as close to medical facilities as possible), and, finally, much careful thought about whether or not to even take children to the field. On balance, anthropologists who have taken children to the field and have written about it report that the experience was a rewarding one, both emotionally and in terms of research (e.g., Frisbie 1975; Gladwin 1960). The provision of emotional support was not unidirectional (fieldworker to family members); they also received valuable emotional support from family members during the course of fieldwork. Much as spouses can enrich research and other fieldwork processes by gathering information from their own local sex group, children often make valuable contributions in describing the attitudes and behavior of their peers in the host community (Powdermaker 1966:114). Gonzalez and Fluehr-Lobban and Lobban report in this volume that children can provide another important perspective on the field culture if parents are attentive to the field experiences of their children. The case of Fluehr-Lobban and Lobban's three-year-old daughter is particularly interesting. At first she questioned the sex-segregated roles her parents conformed to socially in the Sudan, but eventually she became enculturated to view such segregation as culturally appropriate behavior, a process her parents keenly noted (Fluehr-Lobban 1981).

Conclusion

As the essays in this volume indicate, many factors affect the experiences a fieldworker has in an unfamiliar cultural setting and the strategies he or she adopts for successful fieldwork. We conclude that the sex of the fieldworker is only one among many different factors, and probably not the most significant one at that. Analyses of fieldwork processes as they affect and are affected by the fieldworker's self will be more productive if we take a broader view of the dynamics involved; it is not just "male versus female."

Factors that influence fieldwork success form two complexes: those internal to the fieldworker and those external to the fieldworker. Internal factors include both physical traits—age, race, physical capabilities, appearance, sex, and others—and psychological ones—temperament, political and other ideological orientations, gender orientations, sexual orientations, and orientations regarding field adjustment. External factors include type of field culture, geophysical nature of the field site, specific personality types within the field setting, field methods used, and length of time spent in the field community.

This volume was compiled not as a how-to book regarding self, sex, and gender in cross-cultural fieldwork, but rather as a casebook of experiences to be shared with our readers. We hope these essays encourage further exploration and dialogue centered around the issues identified, as well as other issues related to self, gender, and fieldwork. We hope also that this dialogue will include nonanthropologists who are experiencing or using the results of cross-cultural fieldwork. Such dialogue should prove beneficial not only to the quality of fieldwork but to the growth of fieldworkers as social beings engaged in continual and creative human interaction. We feel, and we judge that the majority of contributors to this volume would agree, that to successfully handle the complexity of internal and external factors affecting fieldwork, fieldworkers must first utilize all of their senses to facilitate better understanding of the field culture, the field experience, and the self; and second, they must develop the kind of flexibility that allows them to go where the field community leads.

Notes

1. After almost twenty years of contact with cross-cultural volunteers and former volunteers, Whitehead is intrigued to note that males tend to regard male sexual contacts with or interest in host country females as something to be taken for granted and to joke about; but female counterparts in the field who are rumored to have had such contact are referred to disparagingly as "groupies." He has been fascinated during the same period to notice similar orientations on the part of male anthropologists. When discussing this book with male colleagues, they frequently treated the topic lightly, for instance with jokes such as, "Why do a book to document that you can get laid anywhere?" The in-house anthropology reviewer (a male) of one of the commercial publishing houses to which this manuscript was sent turned the joke into a criticism of the manuscript without having read any of the essays. Had he read them, he would have realized that none of them discusses sexual activity or desire while in the field. While Whitehead's observations here do not constitute a representative sample of cross-cultural volunteer workers or anthropologists, they do suggest that male writers (e.g., Malinowski 1967; Osgood 1953; Rabinow 1977) feel freer to address sexual desire and behavior in fieldwork than do female writers. We know of only one book in which a female fieldworker writes about having sex with a local man, and her work appears under a pseudonym (Cesara 1982:55–56). Women might justifiably feel that it would be professionally catastrophic to be referred to as a "field groupie."

2. In Whitehead's two decades of working with individuals involved in cross-cultural fieldwork, he has a plethora of such stories: misinterpretation of local dating patterns which result in unwanted engagements, pregnancies, and/or marriages; sexual extortion and/or rapes (or attempts) by host country informants, colleagues, or supervisors; and fieldwork and/or lives jeopardized by real or perceived liaisons with already married or betrothed locals. There are also many stories about incidents that do not involve actual sexual behavior but focus instead on certain actions of the fieldworker that the field coummunity *interprets* to signify sexual motivation or invitation: the female worker who had to leave a Muslim country because her dress (elbow-length sleeves) was perceived to be a bad influence on local women; the fieldworker who jeopardized her health project because her skirts were

perceived to be too short and she was said to sometimes sit with her underwear exposed; fieldworkers who swim nude in public pools or in rivers where local men and women are fishing and washing clothes; and the young male fieldworker in a Middle East country who was almost lynched by theretofore friendly locals because he did not know that you do not kiss a person of the opposite sex on both cheeks unless he or she is a close consanguineal relative.

3. The taboo-breaking quality of public reports on sex-related field problems within the discipline was best captured by another colleague from whom a paper for this volume was solicited. He drew an analogy between the discipline of anthropology and a culture with stringent taboos: to discuss sex-related difficulties in cross-cultural fieldwork is one of those taboos. When it was explained that the book was to be about gender-related difficulties and not about sex, he asked, "But how can you talk about gender and not about sex?" We agree, and we hope that these brief comments will encourage others to question this taboo and work toward constructive communication about issues of sexual behavior in fieldwork.

4. Lobban mentions that during fieldwork in the Sudan, research was periodically suspended by such problems as intestinal disorders, pneumonia, scorpion bites, traffic accidents, and bouts with malaria. During a coup d'etat, he and his family literally ducked flying bullets and had to store water in their bathtub and confront other physical hardships.

References

Cesara, Manda
  1982 Reflections of a Woman Anthropologist: No Hiding Place. New York: Academic Press.
Du Bois, W. E. B.
  1939 Black Folk: Then and Now. New York: Holt.
Firth, Rosemary
  1972 "From Wife to Anthropologist." In: S. T. Kimball and J. B. Watson (eds.), Crossing Cultural Boundaries, pp. 10–32. San Francisco: Chandler.
Fluehr-Lobban, Carolyn
  1981 "Josina's Observation of Sudanese Culture." Human Organization 40(3):277–79.
Frisbie, Charlotte
  1975 "Field Work as a Single Parent: To Be or Not to Be Accompanied by a Child." In: T. R. Frisbie (ed.), Collected Papers in Honor of Florence Hawley Ellis, pp. 98–119. Norman, Okla.: Hopper.
Gladwin, Thomas
  1960 "Petrus Maila, Chief of Moen." In: J. Casagrande (ed.), Company of Man, pp. 41–62. New York: Harper.
Goffman, Erving
  1959 The Presentation of Self in Everyday Life. New York: Doubleday.

Golde, Peggy
    1970 "Odyssey of Encounter." In: Peggy Golde (ed.), *Women in the Field*, pp. 67–96. Chicago: Aldine.

Malinowski, B.
    1967 *A Diary in the Strict Sense of the Term*. London: Routledge and Kegan Paul.

Mead, Margaret
    1970 "Field Work in the Pacific Islands, 1925–1967." In: Peggy Golde (ed.), *Women in the Field*, pp. 292–331. Chicago: Aldine.

Osgood, Cornelius
    1953 *Winter*. New York: W. W. Norton and Co.

Powdermaker, Hortense
    1966 *Stranger and Friend: The Way of an Anthropologist*. New York: W. W. Norton and Co.

Rabinow, Paul
    1977 *Reflections on Fieldwork in Morocco*. Berkeley: University of California Press.

Rohrlich-Leavitt, Ruby, B. Sykes, and E. Weatherford
    1973 "Aboriginal Women: Male and Female Anthropological Perspectives." In: R. Rohrlich-Leavitt (ed.), *Women Cross-Culturally: Change and Challenge*, pp. 567–80. The Hague: Mouton.

Scheper-Hughes, Nancy
    1983 "Introduction: The Problem of Bias in Androcentric and Feminist Anthropology." *Women's Studies* 10(2):109–16.

Notes on Contributors

Michael H. Agar, professor of anthropology at the University of Maryland at College Park, received his Ph.D. in anthropology from the University of California at Berkeley. He has done fieldwork in South India, Austria, and the urban United States. His current research interests are in the area of ethnographic theory and method with a view toward application. He has published numerous works in the area, including *The Professional Stranger* (1980) and most recently *Speaking of Ethnography* (1985).

Michael V. Angrosino received his Ph.D. in anthropology from the University of North Carolina at Chapel Hill and is currently associate professor of anthropology at the University of South Florida. His research interests and publications in medical anthropology focus on mental health, mental retardation, aging, and alcoholism. He has done extensive fieldwork among East Indians of the Caribbean, and in 1974 coauthored (with Julia Crane) *Anthropology Field Projects: A Student Handbook.*

Judith Brown received her Ph.D. in social anthropology from Harvard University. She has lived in Africa a total of eight years, doing fieldwork in Liberia, Tunisia, Zaire, and Cameroon, where she has participated in numerous applied anthropology projects. Her research and publications involve health, nutrition, and family planning. She is at present living in Zaire, where she works as a private consultant.

Mary Ellen Conaway is museum administrator for the city of Tempe, Arizona, and is also affiliated with the museum studies program at Arizona State University. She received her Ph.D. in anthropology and certificate of Latin American Studies from the University of Pittsburgh. Her field experience includes work among urban American Indians in Wisconsin and the Guahibo of Amazonian Venezuela. Her research interests center on migration, material culture, and museums.

Dona Davis received her Ph.D. in anthropology from the University of North Carolina at Chapel Hill and is associate professor of anthropology at the University of South Dakota. Her field research in Newfoundland focused on women's status and their experience of menopause, and she has published several articles and a book about menopause based on that fieldwork. Recently, she has been involved in co-editing (with Jane Nadel) *Women in Fishing Economies* and in research concerning ethnicity and aging in rural South Dakota communities.

Elizabeth Faithorn is director of the master's program in cultural anthropology at the California Institute of Integral Studies, in San Francisco, and a private consultant in research anthropology and organization development. She is particularly interested in the study of organizational culture, and intercultural communication.

Carolyn Fluehr-Lobban is associate professor of anthropology at Rhode Island College. She received her Ph.D. in anthropology from Northwestern University and has conducted extensive research in the Sudan in 1970–72, 1975, and 1979–80, along with husband and fellow anthropologist Richard Lobban. She has been a Mellon Fellow of the University of Pennsylvania (1981–82) and a fellow of the American Research Center in Egypt (1982–83). Her publications include *Islamic Law* and *Society in the Sudan*, as well as others on the subject of legal anthropology and the status of women.

Maureen Giovannini is assistant professor of anthropology at Boston University. She received her Ph.D. in anthropology from Syracuse University and has conducted fieldwork in the urban northeastern United States and in Sicily. Her research interests and publications include work in medical and applied anthropology as well as work in gender roles and symbolic anthropology.

Nancie L. Gonzalez is professor of anthropology at the University of Maryland at College Park and since 1980 has also been affiliated with the university's family and community development department. She received her Ph.D. in anthropology from the University of Michigan and served as the National Science Foundation program director for anthropology from 1975 to 1977. She has done extensive fieldwork among the Garifuna in both Guatemala and the United States and has published numerous books and articles on her work, including *Black Caribbean Household Structure* (1969).

Jean Jackson is associate professor of anthropology at the Massachusetts Institute of Technology, where she teaches courses on such subjects as sex roles, language and culture, and ethnographic research. She received her Ph.D. from Stanford University and has done fieldwork in Mexico, Guatemala, and among tropical forest Indians in Colombia. She recently published *The Fish-People: Linguistic Exogamy and Tukanoan Identity in the Northwest Amazon* (1983).

Norris Brock Johnson is associate professor of anthropology at the University of North Carolina at Chapel Hill. He received his Ph.D. in anthropology from the University of Michigan at Ann Arbor and also holds degrees in literature from Michigan State University. His publications have focused on the material culture and spatial aspects of socialization and on rites of passage. His current research interests are comparative art and the anthropological study of literature. He has carried out ethnographic research in the midwestern United States, the West Indies, France, and in Japan while on a Fulbright lectureship. He has recently published *West Haven: Classroom, Culture and Society in a Rural Elementary School* (1985).

Laurie Krieger received her Ph.D. in anthropology from the University of North Carolina at Chapel Hill. Her research interests include applied, medical, and population anthropology, gender roles, and symbolic anthropology. She has conducted fieldwork on menstruation, gender roles, and contraceptive acceptability and has also worked among adolescents in the southeastern United States.

Richard A. Lobban, Jr., received his Ph.D. in anthropology from Northwestern University and is professor of anthropology at Rhode Island College, where he also directs the African and Afro-American Studies Program. He recently returned from a two-year post as senior research associate and head of the Urban Development Unit at the Social Research Center, American University, Cairo. His publications and research interests chiefly concern Afro-Arab studies, urbanization, and social organization. A founder of the Sudan Studies Association, he has spent five years living in the Nile Valley with his wife, Carolyn Fluehr-Lobban.

Regina Smith Oboler received her Ph.D. in anthropology from Temple University and currently teaches anthropology and sociology at Kutztown University, in Pennsylvania. Her scholarly interests include gender, social organization, economic anthropology, socioeconomic change, and the relationship between history and anthropology. She has done research in urban and small-town settings in the United States, as well as in rural western Kenya. In addition to her recent book *Women, Power, and Economic Change: The Nandi of Kenya* (1985), she has published several articles based on her fieldwork.

Laurie Price received a Ph.D. in anthropology and an M.P.H. in epidemiology from the University of North Carolina at Chapel Hill and has carried out fieldwork on U.S. social movements in the highlands of Ecuador. Her research and publications concern natural discourse, cognition, and gender roles in coping with illness. She is at present a postdoctoral fellow in social ecology at the University of California at Irvine.

Richard Scaglion received a B.S. in mathematics from Lafayette College and a Ph.D. in anthropology from the University of Pittsburgh, where he is currently an associate professor of anthropology. He is also a research associate with the Carnegie Museum of Natural History. He is best known for his work with the Abelam tribe of New Guinea, as well as for his legal research with the Law Reform Commission of Papua New Guinea.

Colin M. Turnbull recently retired from his position as professor of anthropology at George Washington University in Washington, D.C., and as research associate at the American Museum of Natural History in New York City. He received his Ph.D. in social anthropology from Oxford University and has done fieldwork in India, Asia, the Pacific, and Africa. He has published several books concerning his work among the Mbuti Pygmies of Zaire and among other groups in Africa. His current interests center on the cooperation of anthropology and other disciplines in dealing with contemporary issues.

Rosalie H. Wax is professor emerita of anthropology at Washington University in St. Louis. She received her Ph.D. from the University of Chicago. Her fieldwork experience has been extensive and includes work with Japanese-

Americans and American Indians. Her publications include the classic *Doing Fieldwork: Warnings and Advice* (1971).

Tony Larry Whitehead is associate professor of social anthropology in the health education department at the University of North Carolina at Chapel Hill. He received his M.S. in public health and Ph.D. in anthropology at the University of Pittsburgh. He spent two years as a Peace Corps volunteer in Turkey and has conducted anthropological fieldwork in Jamaica, Cameroon, and the American South. His research interests include family organization, culture and food, male roles in family planning, community organization, and risk factors in hypertension.

Index